OXFORD SURVEYS ON EUKARYOTIC GENES

Volume 1 : 1984

OXFORD SURVEYS
ON
EUKARYOTIC GENES

EDITED BY

NORMAN MACLEAN

VOLUME 1

1984

OXFORD UNIVERSITY PRESS

Oxford University Press, Walton Street, Oxford OX2 6DP

London   Glasgow   New York   Toronto
Delhi   Bombay   Calcutta   Madras   Karachi
Kuala Lumpur   Singapore   Hong Kong   Tokyo
Nairobi   Dar es Salaam   Cape Town
Melbourne   Auckland
and associated companies in

Beirut   Berlin   Ibadan   Mexico City   Nicosia

OXFORD is a trade mark of Oxford University Press

ISSN 0265-0738
ISBN 0 19 854157 0

Filmset by Eta Services (Typesetters) Ltd, Beccles, Suffolk
Printed in Great Britain at the University Press, Oxford

Contents

Contributors

Douglas O. Clary: Department of Biology, University of Utah, Salt Lake City, Utah 84112, USA

Nicholas J. Cowan: Department of Biochemistry, New York University Medical Center, 550 First Avenue, New York, N.Y. 10016, USA

Eric A. Fyrberg: Department of Biology, The Johns Hopkins University, Baltimore, MD 21218, USA

B. Groner: Ludwig Institute for Cancer Research, Inselspital, CH-3010 Bern, Switzerland

A. Guiochon-Mantel: Groupe de Recherches sur la Biochimie, Endocrinienne et la Reproduction (INSERM U.135), Faculté de Médecine de Bicêtre, Université Paris-Sud, 94270 Le Kremlin-Bicêtre, France

W. H. Günzburg, Institute of Genetics, Kernforschungszentrum, D-7500 Karlsruhe, Federal Republic of Germany

Alan Hall: Institute of Cancer Research, Royal Cancer Hospital, Chester Beatty Laboratories, 237 Fulham Road, London SW3 6JB, UK

N. E. Hynes: Ludwig Institute for Cancer Research, Inselspital, CH-3010 Bern, Switzerland

Paul A. M. Michels: Division of Molecular Biology, The Netherlands Cancer Institute, Plesmanlaan 121, 1066 CX Amsterdam, The Netherlands (Present address: International Institute of Cellular and Molecular Pathology, Avenue Hippocrate 75, B-1200 Brussels, Belgium)

E. Milgrom: Groupe de Recherches sur la Biochimie, Endocrinienne et la Reproduction (INSERM U.135), Faculté de Médecine de Bicêtre, Université Paris-Sud, 94270 Le Kremlin-Bicêtre, France

H. Ponta: Institute of Genetics, Kernforschungszentrum, D-7500 Karlsruhe, Federal Republic of Germany

Cary Queen: Laboratory of Biochemistry, National Cancer Institute, Bethesda, Maryland 20205, USA

B. Salmons: Institute of Genetics Kernforschungszentrum, D-7500 Karlsruhe, Federal Republic of Germany

J. F. Savouret: Groupe de Recherches sur la Biochimie, Endocrinienne et la Reproduction (INSERM U.135), Faculté de Médecine de Bicêtre, Université Paris-Sud, 94270 Le Kremlin-Bicêtre, France

David R. Wolstenholme: Department of Biology, University of Utah, Salt Lake City, Utah 84112, USA

Introduction

Just as the increase in knowledge of atomic structure and the behaviour of subatomic particles produced major changes in the physical sciences during the past half century, so the present rapid advance in understanding of genetic fine structure is precipitating great changes in our view of biology and biochemistry. For those who are privileged to be active in genetic research at the present time, this progress in resolving details of gene structure and function is a matter of great excitement and stimulation. It would have seemed incredible 25 years ago, when I was an undergraduate student, that small plastic tubes containing copies of specific cloned eukaryotic genes should be daily flown across the Atlantic between European and American laboratories.

The explosion of information in molecular genetics has both fueled a surge of new journals and encouraged the production of jumbo editions of some existing ones. The wave of papers on molecular genetics, crammed as they are with a wealth of hard data, has posed problems for conventional bindings and forced hard-pressed editors and publishers to redefine their manuscript acceptance conditions in new and more restrictive terms. The current literature has adapted itself to this amazing proliferation of new information in a number of different ways. As well as initiating new journals and larger versions of some existing ones, the genetics boom has spilled over into many journals previously unconcerned with this aspect of biological science. Taken together, all of these changes in the range of publications involved has made "keeping up with the literature" increasingly difficult even for the cognoscenti and simply impossible for those on the fringes of the subject.

It is against this background that we are launching this new annual review journal. It seems to those of us involved in its preparation and production that there is a real need for authoritative and relatively concise accounts which will detail present knowledge about specific gene sequences. What we are attempting is an annual volume covering some ten different sequences or gene families, each sequence or family having been fairly thoroughly investigated in the preceding year or so. In this way we hope to make a valuable contribution to the advance of molecular genetics both for the strongly involved researcher and also for those on the periphery with an interest and desire to keep abreast of important developments in this area. The volumes should constitute a regularly expanding source of reliable and lucidly presented information in step with the developments in molecular genetics which will surely accrue over the next few decades.

Norman Maclean

1 The *Drosophila* mitochondrial genome
DOUGLAS O. CLARY AND
DAVID R. WOLSTENHOLME

Introduction

The mitochondrial genome of multicellular animals consists of a single circular molecule which has been highly conserved in size during evolution
(approximately 16 kb; Altman and Katz 1976). Greatest attention has been
given to the mitochondrial DNA (mtDNA) of mammalian species in regard
to structure, expression and replication. Complete nucleotide sequences have
been determined for mtDNA molecules of human (Anderson, Bankier, Barrell, de Bruijn, Coulson, Drouin, Eperon, Nierlich, Roe, Sanger, Schreier,
Smith, Staden and Young 1981), mouse (Bibb, Van Etten, Wright, Walberg
and Clayton 1981) and cow (Anderson, de Bruijn, Coulson, Eperon, Sanger
and Young 1982) and partial sequences of other mammalian mtDNA molecules have been obtained (Pepe, Holtrop, Gadaleta, Kroon, Cantatore,
Gallerani, De Benetto, Quagliariello, Sbisa and Saccone 1983; Grosskopf
and Feldmann 1981; Taira, Yoshida, Kobayashi, Yaginuma and Koike 1983;
Brown and Simpson 1982). From these and other data concerning the structure
and processing of RNA molecules of mammalian mitochondria (Battey and
Clayton 1978; Cantatore and Attardi 1980; Montoya, Ojala and Attardi 1981;
Ojala, Merkel, Gelfand and Attardi 1980; Ojala, Montoya and Attardi 1981)
it has been determined that each mammalian mtDNA molecule contains the
genes for the RNA components of the mitochondrion's polypeptide synthesizing system (two rRNAs and 22 tRNAs) and for five known polypeptides
(cytochrome b, cytochrome *c* oxidase (CO) subunits I, II and III, and ATPase
subunit 6). Eight additional open reading frames occur which have been
designated URFs (unidentified open reading frames), and there is considerable
evidence that these too encode polypeptides. Polyadenylated messenger RNAs
(mRNAs) have been identified which correspond to each of the URF genes,
(Battey and Clayton 1978; Montoya, Ojala and Attardi 1981; Ojala, Montoya
and Attardi 1981; van Etten, Michael, Bibb, Brennicke and Clayton 1982) and
distinct polypeptide products of URF1, URF3 and URFA6L have recently
been isolated (Chomyn, Mariottini, Gonzalez-Cadavid, Attardi, Strong,
Trovato, Riley and Doolittle 1983; Mariottini, Chomyn and Attardi 1983).
  In different mammalian mtDNAs gene order is the same and in all cases
there are very few, if any, nucleotides separating adjacent encoding regions.
The templates for all of the genes except those for URF6 and eight tRNAs
are contained in one (H) strand of the molecule. In all but four cases tRNA
genes punctuate genes for rRNAs and polypeptides and appear to play a role
as processing sites for multicistronic transcripts with lengths as great as that

of the whole molecule (Ojala, Montoya and Attardi 1981), which are initiated in or close to the replication origin-containing region (Montoya, Christianson, Levens, Rabinowitz and Attardi 1982; Montoya, Gaines and Attardi 1983; Chang and Clayton 1984). Some modifications of the standard genetic code are found in mammalian mtDNAs, and it has been argued that the 22 tRNAs specified by mammalian mtDNA are sufficient to permit translation of all of the polypeptides encoded by mtDNA (Barrell, Anderson, Bankier, de Bruijn, Chen, Coulson, Drouin, Eperon, Nierlich, Roe, Sanger, Schreier, Smith, Staden and Young 1980; Anderson *et al.* 1981; Bibb *et al.* 1981).

The origin of replication of mammalian mtDNA lies within a region of approximately 1 kb delimited by the tRNA^{pro} and tRNA^{phe} genes. This region, from which transcripts are absent or rare, varies considerably in nucleotide sequence and in length between, and to a lesser extent, within species (Greenberg, Newbold and Sugino 1983).

The only other vertebrate mtDNA for which substantial structural information has been obtained is that of the amphibian *Xenopus laevis*. The relative locations of the rRNA genes, tRNA genes, replication origin and a number of polyadenylated RNAs have been mapped (Ramirez and Dawid 1978; Ohi, Ramirez, Upholt and Dawid 1978; Rastl and Dawid 1978), and recently nucleotide sequences of some segments of the molecule have been determined (Wong, Ma, Wilson and Roe 1983). From the information available, gene content and arrangement appear to be the same as that in mammalian mtDNAs.

Among invertebrates only *Drosophila* mtDNAs have been studied extensively. A unique feature of these molecules is the occurrence of a region exceptionally rich in adenine and thymine (Polan, Friedman, Gall and Gehring 1973; Bultmann and Laird 1973; Peacock, Brutlag, Goldring, Appels, Hinton and Lindsley 1974; Fauron and Wolstenholme 1976) which contains the replication origin (Goddard and Wolstenholme 1978, 1980). This region is approximately 1 kb in size in most *Drosophila* species. However, in different members of the *D. melanogaster* species group, the A + T-rich region varies from 1 kb to 5 kb (Fauron and Wolstenholme 1976). As in the replication origin-containing regions of mammalian mtDNAs, extensive sequence divergence has occurred in these A + T-rich regions both within as well as between species (Fauron and Wolstenholme, 1980*a* and *b*) and they do not appear to be transcribed (Battey, Rubenstein and Clayton 1979; Merten and Pardue 1981). Recently we have completed the nucleotide sequence of the mtDNA molecule of *D. yakuba* (Clary, Goddard, Martin, Fauron and Wolstenholme 1982; Clary, Wahleithner and Wolstenholme 1983, 1984; Clary and Wolstenholme 1983*a*, 1983*b*, 1984 and unpublished). Also, approximately 30 per cent of the nucleotide sequence of *D. melanogaster* mtDNA (Clary *et al.* 1982; Clary, Wahleithner and Wolstenholme 1983; de Bruijn 1983) and 10 per cent of the nucleotide sequence of *D. virilis* mtDNA have been obtained (Clary *et al.* 1982; Clary and Wolstenholme, unpublished).

We present here the nucleotide sequence of *D. yakuba* mtDNA together with a discussion of our findings regarding the structure, content and arrangement of the genes within this molecule and unique modifications of the *Drosophila* mitochondrial genetic code. We also summarize what we have learned from comparisons of the *D. yakuba* mtDNA molecule with the mtDNA molecules of mammals and with the partial sequences of other *Drosophila* mtDNAs.

Materials and methods

Stocks of *Drosophila yakuba* (2371.6, Ivory Coast), and *D. virilis* (2375.8, Chile) used in these studies were originally obtained from the species stock collection of the Genetics Foundation, University of Texas at Austin. The stock of *D. melanogaster*, (Oregon R-Utah) was obtained in 1972 from Dr E. W. Hanley at the University of Utah.

MtDNA was obtained by caesium chloride-ethidium bromide centrifugation of SDS-lysates of ovaries dissected by hand from yeast-fed *D. yakuba* and *D. virilis*, and from SDS-lysates of mitochondrial fractions obtained from embryos of *D. melanogaster*, as described in Wolstenholme and Fauron (1976).

The major restriction sites of *D. yakuba* mtDNA used in sequencing experiments are shown in Fig. 1.2. *Eco*RI and *Hin*dIII fragments of *D. yakuba* mtDNA were cloned into pBR325 and pBR322 respectively, using as host *Escherichia coli*, K12, HB101. These cloned fragments, or subfragments produced by further restriction enzyme digestion were recloned into M13mp2, M13mp8 or M13mp9. The *Hin*dIII-D fragment of *D. melanogaster* mtDNA was cloned from a *Hin*dIII digest of the mtDNA directly into M13mp8. Using the replicative forms of M13 DNA molecules containing various restriction fragments of *D. yakuba* mtDNA, partial deletions of the mtDNA fragments were generated using DNaseI digestion (Hong 1982). Viral DNAs containing suitable deletions of the original mtDNA restriction fragments were selected by size using agarose gel electrophoresis.

Experimental details regarding restriction enzyme digestions, electrophoresis, cloning of *D. yakuba* mtDNAs into pBR322, pBR325 and M13 DNA, and purification of single-stranded and double-stranded M13 DNAs are given or referred to in Clary *et al.* 1982 and Clary and Wolstenholme 1983a.

All DNA sequences were obtained from M13-cloned fragments by the extension-dideoxyribonucleotide termination procedure (Sanger, Nicklen and Coulson 1977) using $[\alpha^{32}P]$ dATP (600–800 Ci/mM; New England Nuclear) (Clary *et al.* 1982).

Sequences were stored and assembled using the computer method of Staden (1982) in a Digital Equipment Computer 20/60. Transfer RNA genes were identified within sequences from their ability to fold into the characteristic cloverleaf structure of tRNAs and from the trinucleotide in the anticodon position in these structures, either by eye or using the TRNA program of Staden (1980). Nucleotide sequences were analyzed by the SEQ program (Brutlag, Clayton, Frieland and Kedes 1982). Polypeptide and presumptive polypeptide genes were identified by comparing predicted amino acid sequences with corresponding amino acid sequences of previously identified genes of mouse mtDNA (Bibb *et al.* 1981) using the TYPIN and SEARCH programs (Jue, Woodbury and Doolittle 1980; Doolittle 1981). Mouse mtDNA was chosen for comparisons because its average G + C content of 36.7 per cent (Bibb *et al.* 1981) is the closest to that of the *Drosophila* mtDNA molecule (23.3 per cent outside the replication origin-containing region) of the mammalian mtDNA molecules which have been sequenced.

Clones of various *Eco*RI and *Hind*III restriction fragments of *D. yakuba* mtDNA (see Fig. 1.2) and complete restriction site documentation of the molecule derived from the nucleotide sequence are available upon request.

Results and discussion

GENE CONTENT AND ORGANIZATION

The sequence of the 16019 nucleotides of the entire mtDNA molecule of *D. yakuba* is shown in Fig. 1.1. The sequence contains 13 open reading frames which have been shown to correspond to the 13 polypeptide genes of mouse mtDNA (Table 1.1). These are the genes for the five identified polypeptides,

Table 1.1

Comparisons of polypeptide genes of D. yakuba *and mouse.*

Gene	Number of Amino acids		Percentage Nucleotide sequence homology[a,b]	Percentage Amino acid sequence homology[b]
	D. yakuba	mouse	*D. yakuba*/mouse	*D. yakuba*/mouse
Cyt b	378	381	65	67
COI	512	514	72	75
COII	228	227	64	57
COIII	262	261	67	65
ATPase6	224	226	49	36
URF1	324	315	52	46
URF2	341	345	47	35
URF3	117	114	52	42
URF4L	96	97	34	40
URF4	446	459	51	42
URF5	573	607	42	33
URF6	174	172	38	17
URFA6L	53	67	59	26

[a] These values do not include nucleotides concerned with termination.
[b] These values include all deduced insertion/deletions. The mouse data are taken from Bibb *et al.* (1981).

SEGMENT I

A+T rich region   tRNA^{ile} ➤
AAAAAAAGATGAGTTTTTTATTATTAATGAATTGCCTGATAAAAAGCGGTTACCTTGATAGGGTAAATTATGCAGT   50

TTTCTGCATTCATTGACTGATTTATATATTATTTAAAAAGAAGGTTTTATATTTAATAGAATTAAACTATTTCTA   125

                    ◄ tRNA^{gln} tRNA^{f-met} ➤
AAAGTATCAAAAACTTTTGTGCATCATACACCAAAATATATTTATTATAAAAAGATAAGCTAATTAAGCTACTGG   200

                                    URF2 ➤
                                 I F Y N S S K I L F T
GTTCATACCCCATTTATAAAGGTTATAATCCTTTTCTTTTTAATTTTTTATAATTCATCAAAAATTTTATTTACC   275

  T I M I I G T L I T V T S N S W L G A W M G L E I
ACAATTATAATTATTGGAACATTAATTACAGTTACATCTAATTCTTGGTTAGGAGCTTGAATAGGTTTAGAAATT   350

  N L L S F I P L L s D N N N L M S T E A S L K Y F
AATTTGTTATCTTTTATCCCCCTATTAAGAGATAATAATAATTTAATATCTACAGAAGCTTCTTTAAAATATTTT   425

  L T Q A L A S T V L L F S S I L L M L A N N L N N
TTAACCCAAGCTTTGGCATCAACTGTTTTATTATTTTCTTCAATTTTACTTATATTGGCAAATAATTTAAATAAT   500

  E I N E S F T S M I I M S A L L L K s G A A P F H
GAAATTAATGAATCTTTTACATCAATAATTATTATATCGGCCTTATTATTAAAAAGAGGAGCCGCTCCTTTTCAT   575

  F W F P N M M E G L T W M N A L M L M T W Q K I A
TTTTGATTTCCTAATATAATAGAAGGATTAACATGAATAAATGCTTTGATATTAATAACTTGACAAAAAATTGCT   650

  P L M L I S Y L N I K N L L L I S V I L S V I I G
CCATTAATATTAATTTCTTATTTAAATATTAAAAATTTATTATTAATTAGTGTAATTTTATCAGTTATTATTGGA   725

  A I G G L N Q T S L R K L M A F S S I N H L G W M
GCAATTGGAGGTTTAAACCAAACTTCACTCCGAAAATTAATAGCATTTTCTTCTATTAATCATTTAGGATGAATA   800

  L s s L M I s E s I W L I Y F I F Y S F L S F V L
TTAAGATCTTTAATGATTAGAGAATCAATTTGATTAATTTATTTTATTTTTTATTCATTCTTATCTTTTGTATTA   875

  T F M F N I F K L F H L N Q L F S W F V s K I L
ACATTTATATTTAATATTTTTAAATTATTTCATTTAAATCAATTATTTTCTTCATTTGTAAACAGAAAAATTTTA   950

  K F S L F M N F L S L G G L P P F L G F L P K W L
AAATTTTCATTATTTATAAATTTTTTTATCTTTAGGTGGATTACCTCCATTTTTAGGATTTTTACCAAAATGATTA   1025

  V I Q Q L T M C N Q Y F L L T L M M M S T L I T L
GTAATTCAACAATTAACAATATGTAATCAATATTTTTTATTAACATTAATAATAATATCAACTTTAATTACATTA   1100

  F F Y L R I C Y S A F M L N Y F E N N W I M E M N
TTTTTTTATTTACGAATTTGTTACTCAGCTTTTATATTAAATTATTTCGAAAATAACTGAATCATGGAAATAAAT   1175

  M N S N N T N L Y L I M T F F S I F G L F L I S L
ATAAATAGTAATAATACTAATTTATATTTAATTATAACTTTTTTTTTCAATTTTCGGATTATTTTTAATTCTTTA   1250

  F F F M L * tRNA^{trp} ➤
TTTTTTTTTATACTTTAAGGCTTTAAGTTAACTAAACTAATAGCCTTCAAAGCTGTAAATAAAGGGTATTCCTTT   1325

                                            ◄ tRNA^{cys}
AAGTCTTAGTAAAAATTTACTCCTTCAAAATTGCAGTTTGATATCATTATTGACTATAAGACCTAGATTTAATTT   1400

                                                       COI ➤
                                    ◄ tRNA^{tyr} (M) S
ATTGATTAAGAAGAATAATTCTTATAAATAGATTTACAATCTATCGCCTAAACTTCAGCCACTTAATCCATAATC   1475

  R Q W L F S T N H K D I G T L Y F I F G A W A G M
GCGACAATGGTTATTTTCTACAAATCATAAAGATATTGGAACTTTATATTTCATTTTTGGAGCTTGAGCCGGAAT   1550

  V G T S L s I L I R A E L G H P G A L I G D D Q I
AGTAGGAACATCTTTAAGAATTTTAATTCGAGCAGAATTAGGTCATCCAGGAGCATTAATTGGAGATGATCAAAT   1625

  Y N V I V T A H A F I M I F F M V M P I M I G G F
TTATAATGTAATTGTTACTGCACATGCTTTTATTATAATTTTTTTTATAGTAATACCTATTATAATTGGGGGGTT   1700

  G N W L V P L M L G A P D M A F P R M N N M s F W
TGGAAATTGATTAGTGCCCTTTAATATTAGGAGCTCCTGACATAGCATTCCCACGAATAAATAATATAAGATTTTG   1775

6 Douglas O. Clary and David R. Wolstenholme

```
      L  L  P  P  A  L  S  L  L  L  V  s  s  M  V  E  N  G  A  G  T  G  W  T  V
ATTACTACCTCCTGCTCTTTCTTTATTATTAGTAAGAAGAATAGTTGAAAACGGAGCTGGTACAGGTTGAACTGT   1850

      Y  P  P  L  S  S  G  I  A  H  G  G  A  S  V  D  L  A  I  F  S  L  H  L  A
TTACCCTCCTTTATCTTCAGGTATCGCTCATGGTGGAGCTTCTGTAGATTTAGCTATTTTTTCTCTTCATTTAGC   1925

      G  I  S  S  I  L  G  A  V  N  F  I  T  T  V  I  N  M  R  S  T  G  I  T  L
TGGAATTTCTTCAATTTTAGGAGCTGTAAATTTTATTACGACTGTAATTAATATACGATCAACTGGAATTACATT   2000

      D  R  M  P  L  F  V  W  S  V  V  I  T  A  L  L  L  L  L  S  L  P  V  L  A
AGACCGAATACCTTTATTTGTATGATCAGTAGTTATTACTGCTTTATTACTTTTACTATCTTTACCAGTTCTTGC   2075

      G  A  I  T  M  L  L  T  D  R  N  L  N  T  S  F  F  D  P  A  G  G  G  D  P
CGGAGCTATTACTATATTATTAACAGACCGAAATTTAAATACTTCTTTTTTTGATCCAGCTGGAGGAGGAGATCC   2150

      I  L  Y  Q  H  L  F  W  F  F  G  H  P  E  V  Y  I  L  I  L  P  G  F  G  M
TATTTTGTACCAACATTTATTTTGATTTTTTGGTCACCCTGAAGTTTATATTTTAATTTTACCGGGATTTGGAAT   2225

      I  S  H  I  I  s  Q  E  S  G  K  K  E  T  F  G  S  L  G  M  I  Y  A  M  L
AATTTCTCATATTATTAGACAAGAATCTGGTAAAAAGGAAACTTTCGGTTCTTTAGGAATAATCTATGCTATACT   2300

      A  I  G  L  L  G  F  I  V  W  A  H  H  M  F  T  V  G  M  D  V  D  T  R  A
TGCTATTGGATTATTAGGATTTATTGTTTGAGCTCATCATATATTTACAGTTGGAATAGACGTTGATACACGAGC   2375

      Y  F  T  S  A  T  M  I  I  A  V  P  T  G  I  K  I  F  s  W  L  A  T  L  H
TTATTTTACTTCTGCTACTATAATTATTGCGGTTCCTACAGGAATTAAAATTTTTAGATGATTAGCTACTTTACA   2450

      G  T  Q  L  S  Y  S  P  A  I  L  W  A  L  G  F  V  F  L  F  T  V  G  G  L
TGGAACTCAACTTTCTTATTCTCCAGCTATTTTATGAGCTTTAGGATTTGTTTTTTTATTCACAGTAGGAGGATT   2525

      T  G  V  V  L  A  N  S  S  V  D  I  I  L  H  D  T  Y  Y  V  V  A  H  F  H
AACAGGAGTTGTATTAGCTAATTCATCAGTTGATATTATTTTACATGATACTTATTATGTAGTAGCTCATTTCCA   2600

      Y  V  L  S  M  G  A  V  F  A  I  M  A  G  F  I  H  W  Y  P  L  F  T  G  L
CTACGTTTTATCAATAGGAGCTGTATTTGCTATTATAGCAGGTTTTATTCACTGATACCCATTATTTACTGGATT   2675

      T  L  N  N  K  W  L  K  S  Q  F  I  I  M  F  I  G  V  N  L  T  F  F  P  Q
GACATTAAATAATAAATGGTTAAAAAGTCAATTTATTATTATGTTTATTGGAGTAAATTTAACATTTTTTCCCCCA   2750

      H  F  L  G  L  A  G  M  P  R  R  Y  S  D  Y  P  D  A  Y  T  T  W  N  V  V
ACATTTTTTAGGATTAGCAGGAATACCTCGACGTTATTCAGATTACCCTGATGCTTACACTACATGAAATGTTGT   2825

      S  T  I  G  S  T  I  S  L  L  G  I  L  F  F  F  Y  I  I  W  E  S  L  V  S
GTCTACTATTGGGTCAACTATTTCATTATTAGGAATTTTTATTTTTTTTCTATATTATTTGAGAAAGTTTAGTGTC   2900

      Q  R  Q  V  I  Y  P  I  Q  L  N  S  S  I  E  W  Y  Q  N  T  P  P  A  E  H
TCAACGACAAGTAATTTATCCAATTCAATTAAATTCATCTATTGAATGATATCAAAATACACCCCCAGCTGAACA   2975

      s  Y  S  E  L  P  L  L  T  N  ***      tRNA leu →
                                                  UUR
TAGATATTCTGAATTACCACTTTTAACAAATTAATT|TCTAATATGGCAGATTAGTGCAATGGATTTAAGCTCCAT   3050

                                 COII →
                 M  S  T  W  A  N  L  G  L  Q  D  s  A  S
ATATAAAGTATTTTACTTTTATTAGAA|AATAAATGTCTACATGAGCTAATTTAGGTTTACAAGATAGAGCTTCTC   3125

      P  L  M  E  Q  L  I  F  F  H  D  H  A  L  L  I  L  V  M  I  T  V  L  V  G
CTTTAATGGAACAATTAATTTTTTTTTCATGATCATGCATTATTAATTTTAGTAATAATTACAGTATTAGTAGGAT   3200

      Y  L  M  F  M  L  F  F  N  N  Y  V  N  R  F  L  L  H  G  Q  L  I  E  M  I
ATTTAATGTTTATATTATTTTTTAATAATTATGTAAATCGATTTCTTTTACATGGACAACTTATTGAAATAATTT   3275

      W  T  I  L  P  A  I  I  L  L  F  I  A  L  P  S  L  R  L  L  Y  L  L  D  E
GAACTATTCTCCCAGCTATTATTTTATTATTTATTGCTTCTTCCTTCATTACGATTACTTTATTTATTAGATGAAA   3350

      I  N  E  P  S  V  T  L  K  S  I  G  H  Q  W  Y  W  S  Y  E  Y  S  D  F  N
TTAATGAACCATCAGTAACTTTAAAAAGTATTGGTCATCAATGATACTGAAGTTATGAATATTCAGATTTTAATA   3425

      N  I  E  F  D  S  Y  M  I  P  T  N  E  L  A  I  D  G  F  R  L  L  D  V  D
ATATTGAATTTGATTCATATATAATTCCTACAAATGAATTAGCAATTGATGGATTTCGATTATTAGACGTTGATA   3500

      N  R  V  I  L  P  M  N  S  Q  I  R  I  L  V  T  A  A  D  V  I  H  S  W  T
ATCGAGTAATTTTACCAATAAATTCACAAATTCGAATTTTAGTAACAGCCGCAGATGTAATTCATTCTTGAACAG   3575

      V  P  A  L  G  V  K  V  D  G  T  P  G  R  L  N  Q  T  N  F  F  I  N  R  P
TCCCAGCTTTAGGAGTAAAGGTTGACGGAACTCCTGGACGATTAAATCAAACTAATTTTTTTTATTAACCGACCAG   3650
```

```
G  L  F  Y  G  Q  C  S  E  I  C  G  A  N  H  S  F  M  P  I  V  I  E  S  V
GGTTATTTTATGGTCAATGTTCAGAAATTTGCGGGGCTAATCATAGTTTTATGCCAATTGTAATTGAAAGTGTTC    3725

P  V  N  N  F  I  K  W  I  S  s  N  N  S  *  tRNA^lys ➤
CTGTAAATAATTTTATTAAATGAATTTCTAGAAATAATTCTT|CATTAGATGACTGAAAGCAAGTACTGGTCTCTT    3800

                                              tRNA^asp ➤
AAACCATTTTATAGTAAATTAGCACTTACTTCTAATGA|TAAT|AAAAAATTAGTTAAATTATATAACATTAGTATG    3875

             URFA6L ➤
             I  P  Q  M  A  P  I  s  W  L  L  L  F
TCAAACTAAAATTATTAAATTATTAATATTTTTTA|ATTCCACAAATAGCACCAATTAGATGATTATTACTATTTA    3950

I  V  F  S  I  T  F  I  L  F  C  S  I  N  Y  Y  S  Y  M  P  T  S  P  K  S
TTGTTTTTTCTATTACATTTATTTTATTTTGTTCTATTAATTATTATTCATATATACCAACTTCACCTAAATCTA    4025

                              ATPase6 ➤
                              M  M  T  N  L  F  S  V  F  D  P  S
N  E  L  K  N  I  N  L  N  S  M  N  W  K  W ***
ATGAATTAAAAAATATTAAATTTAAATTCTATAAACTGAAAATGATAACAAATTTATTTTCTGTATTTGACCCTTC    4100

A  I  F  N  L  S  L  N  W  L  s  T  F  L  G  L  L  M  I  P  S  I  Y  W  L
AGCAATTTTTAATTTATCATTAAATTGATTAAGAACATTTTTAGGACTTTTAATAATTCCTTCAATTTATTGATT    4175

M  P  S  R  Y  N  I  F  W  N  S  I  L  L  T  L  H  K  E  F  K  T  L  L  G
AATACCTTCTCGTTATAATATTTTTTGAAATTCAATTTTATTAACACTTCATAAAGAATTTAAAACTTTATTAGG    4250

P  S  G  H  N  G  S  T  F  I  F  I  S  L  F  S  L  I  L  F  N  N  F  M  G
ACCTTCAGGTCATAATGGATCTACTTTTTATTTTTATTTCTTTATTTTCATTAATTTTATTTAATAATTTTATAGG    4325

L  F  P  Y  I  F  T  s  T  S  H  L  T  L  T  L  S  L  A  L  P  L  W  L
TTTATTTCCTTATATTTTTACAAGAACAAGTCATTTAACTTTAACTTTATCTTTAGCTCTTCCTTTATGATTATG    4400

F  M  L  Y  G  W  I  N  H  T  Q  H  M  F  A  H  L  V  P  Q  G  T  P  A  I
TTTTATATTATATGGTTGAATTAATCATACACAACATATATTTGCTCACTTAGTACCTCAAGGTACACCTGCAAT    4475

L  M  P  I  M  V  C  I  E  T  I  s  N  I  I  R  P  G  I  L  A  V  R  L  T
TTTAATACCTTTTATAGTATGTATTGAAACTATTAGAAATATTATTCGACCGGGAACTTTAGCTGTTCGATTAAC    4550

A  N  M  I  A  G  H  L  L  L  T  L  L  G  N  T  G  P  S  M  S  Y  L  L  V
AGCTAATATAATTGCTGGACATCTTCTATTAACCTTATTGGGAAATACAGGACCTTCTATATCTTACTTACTACT    4625

T  F  L  L  V  A  Q  I  A  L  L  V  L  E  S  A  V  T  M  I  Q  S  Y  V  F
AACATTTTTATTAGTAGCCCAAATTGCTTTATTAGTTTTAGAATCAGCTGTAACTATAATTCAATCCTATGTATT    4700

                                                COIII ➤
A  V  L  s  T  L  Y  S  s  E  V  N **  M  S  T  H  S  N  H  P  F  H  L  V
TGCTGTTTTAAGAACTTTATACTCTAGAGAAGTAAATTAATGTCTACACACTCAAATCACCCTTTTCATTTAGTT    4775

D  Y  S  P  W  P  L  T  G  A  I  G  A  M  T  T  V  S  G  M  V  K  W  F  H
GATTATAGCCCATGACCTTTAACAGGTGCTATTGGAGCTATAACAACTGTATCAGGTATAGTAAAATGATTTCAT    4850

Q  Y  D  I  S  L  F  L  L  G  N  I  I  T  I  L  T  V  Y  Q  W  W  R  D  V
CAATATGATATTTCATTATTTTTATTAGGTAATATTATTACTATTTTAACAGTTTATCAATGATGACGAGATGTT    4925

S  R  E  G  T  Y  Q  G  L  H  T  Y  A  V  T  I  G  L  R  W  G  M  I  L  F
TCACGAGAAGGAACTTACCAAGGATTACATACTTACGCAGTAACTATTGGTTTACGATGAGGAATAATTTTATTT    5000

I  L  S  E  V  L  F  F  V  s  F  F  W  A  F  F  H  s  S  L  S  P  A  I  E
ATTTTATCAGAAGTTTTATTTTTTGTTAGATTTTTTTGAGCATTTTTTCATAGAAGTTTATCTCCAGCAATTGAA    5075

L  G  A  S  W  P  P  M  G  I  I  S  F  N  P  F  Q  I  P  L  L  N  T  A  I
TTAGGAGCTTCATGACCTCCTATGGGAATTATTTCATTTAATCCATTTCAAATTCCTTTATTAAATACAGCTATT    5150

L  L  A  S  G  V  T  V  T  W  A  H  H  s  L  M  E  s  N  H  S  Q  T  T  Q
CTTTTAGCTTCAGGAGTTACAGTAACTTGAGCTCATCATAGATTAATAGAAAGAAATCATTCACAAACTACTCAA    5225

G  L  F  F  T  V  L  L  G  I  Y  F  T  I  L  Q  A  Y  E  Y  I  E  A  P  F
GGATTATTTTTTACAGTTTTACTTGGGATTTATTTCACAATTTTACAAGCTTATGAATATATTGAAGCTCCATTT    5300

T  I  A  D  S  V  Y  G  S  T  F  Y  M  A  T  G  F  H  G  V  H  V  L  I  G
ACTATTGCTGATTCAGTTTATGGTTCAACTTTTTATATGGCCACTGGATTCCATGGAGTTCATGTTCTAATTGGA    5375

T  T  F  L  L  V  C  L  L  R  H  L  N  N  H  F  S  K  N  H  H  F  G  F  E
ACAACTTTCTTATTAGTATGTTTATTACGTCATTTAAATAATCATTTTTCAAAAAATCATCATTTTGGATTTGAA    5450
```

```
       A  A  A  W  Y  W  H  F  V  D  V  V  W  L  F  L  Y  I  T  I  Y  W  W  G  G
     GCAGCTGCATGATACTGACATTTTGTTGATGTAGTTTGATTATTTTTATATATCACAATTTACTGATGAGGAGGG          5525

     ***                                  tRNA^gly
     TAACCTTTTATTATTAATTACATATCTATATAGTATAAAAGTATATTTGACTTCCAATCATAAGGTCTATTAATA          5600

                        URF3
                        I  F  S  I  I  I  I  A  S  V  I  L  L  I  T  T  V  V  M  F  L
     AATAGTATAGATAATTTTTTCTATTATTATTATTGCTTCAGTAATCTTATTAATCACAACTGTTGTTATATTTTT          5675

        A  S  I  L  S  K  K  A  L  I  D  R  E  K  s  S  P  F  E  C  G  F  D  P  K
     AGCTTCAATTTTATCAAAAAAAGCTTTAATTGATCGAGAAAAAAGATCACCTTTTGAATGTGGATTTGACCCTAA          5750

        S  S  S  R  L  P  F  S  L  R  F  F  L  I  T  I  I  F  L  I  F  D  V  E  I
     ATCTTCTTCTCGATTACCATTTTCATTACGATTTTTTTTAATCACTATTATCTTTTTAATTTTTGATGTAGAAAT          5825

        A  L  I  L  P  M  I  I  I  L  K  Y  S  N  I  M  I  W  T  I  T  S  I  I  F
     TGCTTTAATTCTTCCTATAATTATTATTTTAAAATATTCTAATATTATAATTTGAACAATTACTTCGATTATTTT          5900

        I  L  I  L  L  I  G  L  Y  H  E  W  N  Q  G  M  L  N  W  S  N  ***
     TATTTTAATTTTATTAATTGGGCTATACCATGAATGAAATCAAGGTATATTAAATTGATCAAATTAATAAATATT          5975

           tRNA^ala
     TAAAGGGTTGTAGTTAATTATAACATTTGATTTGCATTCAAAAAGTATTGAATATTCAATCTACCTTATATATAT          6050

                             tRNA^arg
     ATATATATATATATATAATTGAATATGAAGCGATTAATTGCAGTTAGTTTCGACCTAACCTTAGGTATTATATAC          6125

              tRNA^asn
     CCTTATTTTTTAATTGAAGCCAAAAAGAGGCGTATCACTGTTAATGATATAATTGAGTATAAACTCCAATTAAGG          6200

     tRNA^ser                                                              tRNA^glu
          AGY
     AAGTATGGTCGATCAAGTAAAAGCTGCTAACTTTTTTTCTTTTAATGGTTAAATTCCATTTATACTTCTATTTATAT       6275

     AGTTTAAAATAAAACCTTACATTTTCATTGTAATAATAAAATAATTTATTTTTATAAATTACTATAATTAATTCA          6350

                                                              ◄―tRNA^phe
     CTATATTCAAAGATTAATTAATCTCCATAACATCTTCAGTGTCATACTCTAAATATAAGCTATTTGAATATAAAA         6425
                                                                      *  L
                                                                     ◄―URF5
```

SEGMENT II

```
                 ◄―tRNA^ile  A+T rich region
     CAAGGTAACCCTTTTTATCAGGCAATTCATTAATAATAAAAAACTCATCTTTTTTTTTTTTTTTTTTTTATTATTT       15976

     ACTATTTTTTTTTTAAAAGATTACAATTTTTAAAAATTAATTGATTTATATTAGATAACACATTTTAGGAATTCA         15901

     TAAAATATTTTTATAAAAATTATTAAAATAATTTTATTTTTCTATATAGATATATATGTAATATAAATCTTCAAC         15826

     TATATATAAATATATAAATATATAATAATTAATTAAATTATTATATTATTTATATAAATCCAAGAATGTTATATA         15751

     AATATTTGAATATAGATTTTTTTTTTACAAATTATGTTACCATTTTTGGATTGTGAAATTTTTTATTTAAATTGTT        15676

     AACTATATTATAATATATTAAACATTTATATATATATAGATTATCTATTAATTTAGAACTTAGTATACAAAAATT        15601

     TTTTTTTTAAAAAAAAAAAAAGAATAGGTTTTTTATTATTTTATAAATAATTATTAATTAGAAAAATTTATTTAA        15526

     TTAATATAATTTTAAAATTAATATTTTAAAAATTATTATAATTTATTAATTAATTTATAAAATTTTTTAATTTAT        15451

     TTAATTAACAAATATTGTTTTATAATTTTTATTTATAAATAATTATTTTGTTTAATAAATATAGTAAATTTTATT        15376

     AATTTTAATTTTTATTATTTTAATGTATAAAAAAAATAATTTTATTTGTATAAATATTAAAAAAATAAATATGTAA       15301
```

```
ATAAGGTATTTAATTTAAGAAATTATTATATTTTATTATAGGGGAATAAGTTATCAGATTTAGTGATTAAAAATA  15226

ATTATTTAAATAGTTTATTATAAGTTACAAATTTTATTATTTTTTTAAAAATTTTACTAATTTTAATTATTAATT  15151

ATTTATGATAAAAAATAATTTGAATTTTATTTAATATACTAATATATATATATATATAAATTAAATTATTTTT  15076

GTTTATAAAGTTTTTATTTATTAATTATTATTTAAATTATCTATTATTTTTTATTTTATTTATTTTATAAAAA  15001

                                               s-rRNA➤
TTATTTTGATAAATTTTATTAAATTTATATTATAAATAAATTTTTTTATTGTATATTTTTAAAGTTTTATTTTGG  14926
                                             ▲         ▲

CTTAAAAATTTGTTATTAGTTTGATTTATATGTAAATTTTTGTGTGAATTTATATTTATTTAAAAAATAAATATA  14851

TTATAAATTATTTATTCGCAGTAATTAATATTATTAATTAAAGAAATTTAGAAATAGCAATATTAAAAAGTATTG  14776

ACCAAATTGGTGCCAGCAGTCGCGGTTATACCAATAATACAAATAAATTTTTTTAGTATGAATTAAATTGATTTA  14701

TTTAAAAATAAAATTAAATATATTAAGTGAAATTTTATATTTAAATTATTTTATAAAATAATAATTGAAGTTAAA  14626

AAATTTTAATAAAAAACTAGGATTAGATACCCTATTATTTAAAATGTAAATAAATTGCTAAAGTAGTAATAGTTA  14551

TGTTCTTGAAACTTAAAAAATTTGGCGGTATTTTAGTCTATCCAGAGGAACCTGTTTTGTAATCGATAATCCACG  14476

ATGGACCTTACTTAAATTTGTAATCAGTTTATATACCGTCGTTATCAGAATATTTTATAAGAATAATAATATTCA  14401

ATAATTTTAATAAAAATTTATATCAGATCAAGGTGTAGCTTATATTTAAGTAATAATGGGTTACAATAAATTTAT  14326

TTAAACGGATAAAATTATGAAAAAATTTTTGAAGGTGGATTTGGTAGTAAAATTATAAAGATTAATAATTTGATT  14251

TTAGCTCTAAAATATGTACACATCCCCCCTCCCTCTTATTATTAAGGTAAGATAAGTCGTAACATAGTAGATGTA  14176

                     tRNA^val ➤
CTGGAAAGTCTATGTAGAATGA̲C̲A̲A̲T̲T̲T̲A̲A̲A̲G̲C̲T̲T̲A̲T̲T̲A̲A̲G̲T̲A̲A̲A̲G̲C̲A̲T̲T̲T̲C̲A̲T̲T̲T̲A̲C̲A̲T̲T̲C̲A̲A̲A̲A̲C̲A̲T̲T̲T̲T̲T̲G̲T  14101
               l-rRNA ➤
G̲C̲A̲A̲A̲T̲C̲A̲A̲T̲A̲T̲A̲A̲A̲T̲T̲G̲ATTATATTTTATTTATTAATTTTAATTATTTTATATAAAAATATTAGAAATAACTAT  14026

AAATTTAAAAGTTTTAGTATTGTTTAAAGAAAAAATAATTTTAATAATACTATATTACTATTCTAAAACAAAATT  13951

GAAATAATTTGAAAAAATTTTATTTTAAAAGAAAATTTAATTTATTGTACCTTGTGTATCAGCGTTTATTAAATA  13876

AAAAATAAATATTTATTTTTCTCGATTTTAAAAGAGTTAATATAATATTTAAGTTAATGTGACAAAATTATTTAT  13801

AATATTATATTAGAAATGAAATGTTATTCGTTTTTAAAGGTATCTAGTTTTTTAAGAAATAAATTTAATTTAGAA  13726

ATTATAAATTTATTTAATTATTTATTTAATTAAATAATTTATAATTTTAATATTTTATGGGATAAGCTATAAAAT  13651

AAATTTTTAAAAATAATAAATAAATTTAATAAATATATGCTTAGAATTAGCAATTATTAAAAAATGTGTTATAAT  13576

TTATTTTATAAATTAAATTATTTATTAAATTTTAATTATTTATTAAAATATTAATTTTAATATTTAAAATTAAGT  13501

AATAATGATAGAATTAGTATATAATATTGTTAAAATAAATTTTTATGAAAAGTTTAAATAAAGAATTCGGCAAAA  13426

ATAATGTTCGCCTGTTTAACAAAAACATGTCTTTTTGAATTATATATAAAGTCTAACCTGCCCACTGAAAATTTT  13351
```

```
AAATGGCCGCAGTATTTTGACTGTGCAAAGGTAGCATAATCATTAGTCTTTTAATTGAAGGCTGGAATGAATGGT  13276

TGGACGAAATATTAACTGTTTCATTTAAATTTAAAATAGAATTTTATTTTTTAGTCAAAAAGCTAAAATTAATTT  13201

AAAAGACGAGAAGACCCTATAAATCTTTATATTTTATTTATTTTAATTATAAAGATTAATTTAATTTTAATAAAT  13126

TAAAATATTTTATTGGGGTGATATTAAAATTTAAAAAACTTTTAATTTTAAAAAACATTAATTTATGAATAATTG  13051

ATCCATTAATAATGATTAAAAAAATTAAGTTACTTTAGGGATAACAGCGTAATTTTTTTGGAGAGTTCATATCGAT  12976

AAAAAAGATTGCGACCTCGATGTTGGATTAAGATATAATTTTGGGTGTAGCCGTTCAAATTTTAAGTCTGTTCGA  12901

CTTTTAAATTCTTACATGATCTGAGTTCAAACCGGTGTAAGCCAGGTTGGTTTCTATCTTTAAAAAATTATAATA  12826

TTTTAGTACGAAAGGACCAAATATTAAAATAATTATATTTTTATATAAGAATATTATTAATATATAATAA[ACTAT  12751
```

```
                                                                    URF1 ▶
    leu ▶                                                           M  E
tRNA CUN
TTTGGCAGATTAGTGCAATAAATTTAGAATTTATATATGTAATTTTTATTACAAATAGTA]CTTGTTTTATATAGA  12676
 F  I  L  S  L  I  G  S  L  L  L  I  I  C  V  L  V  S  V  A  F  L  T  L  L
ATTTATTTTATCATTAATTGGAAGTTTATTATTAATTATTTGTGTATTAGTAAGTGTAGCTTTTTTAACTTTATT  12601
 E  R  K  V  L  G  Y  I  Q  I  R  K  G  P  N  K  V  G  L  M  G  I  P  Q  P
AGAACGTAAAGTTTTAGGGTATATTCAAATTCGTAAAGGACCTAATAAAGTTGGTTTAATAGGAATTCCTCAACC  12526
 F  C  D  A  I  K  L  F  T  K  E  Q  T  Y  P  L  L  S  N  Y  L  s  Y  Y  I
TTTTTGTGATGCAATTAAATTATTTACAAAAGAACAAACTTATCCATTATTATCAAATTATTTAAGATATTATAT  12451
 S  P  I  F  S  L  F  L  S  L  F  V  W  M  C  M  P  F  F  V  K  L  Y  S  F
TTCTCCTATTTTTTCTTTATTTTTATCTTTATTTGTTTGAATATGTATACCTTTTTTTTGTTAAATTATACTCTTT  12376
 N  L  G  G  L  F  F  L  C  C  T  s  L  G  V  Y  T  V  M  V  A  G  W  S  S
TAATTTAGGTGGATTATTTTTTTTTATGTTGTACAAGATTAGGAGTTTATACAGTTATAGTAGCTGGCTGATCTTC  12301
 N  S  N  Y  A  L  L  G  G  L  R  A  V  A  Q  T  I  S  Y  E  V  s  L  A  L
TAATTCTAATTATGCTTTATTAGGGGGTTTACGAGCTGTGGCTCAAACTATTTCTTATGAAGTTAGATTAGCTTT  12226
 I  M  L  S  F  I  F  L  I  G  S  Y  N  M  I  Y  F  F  Y  Y  Q  I  Y  M  W
AATTATATTATCATTTATTTTTTTAATTGGGAGTTATAATATAATTTATTTTTTTTTATTACCAAATTTATATATG  12151
 F  L  I  I  L  F  P  M  S  L  V  W  L  T  I  S  L  A  E  T  N  R  T  P  F
ATTTTTAATTATTTTATTTCCTATAAGTTTAGTTTGATTAACAATTTCATTAGCTGAAACTAATCGAACTCCTTT  12076
 D  F  A  E  G  E  S  E  L  V  S  G  F  N  V  E  Y  s  s  G  G  F  A  L  I
TGATTTTGCTGAAGGTGAATCAGAATTAGTTTCAGGATTTAATGTAGAATATAGAGAGGTGGTTTTGCTTTAAT  12001
 F  M  A  E  Y  A  s  I  L  F  M  s  M  L  F  C  V  I  F  L  G  C  D  V  F
TTTTTATGCAGAAATATGCTAGAATTTTATTTATAAGAATATTGTTTTGTGTAATTTTTTTAGGTTGTGATGTATT  11926
 N  L  L  F  Y  V  K  L  T  F  I  S  F  V  F  I  W  A  R  G  T  L  P  R  F
TAATTTATTATTTTATGTAAAATTAACTTTTATTTCATTTGTATTTATTTGAGCTCGAGGTACATTACCTCGGTT  11851
 R  Y  D  K  L  M  Y  L  A  W  K  C  F  L  S  F  S  L  N  Y  L  L  F  F  I
TCGTTATGATAAATTAATATATTTAGCTTGAAAATGTTTTTTATCATTTTCTTTAAATTATTTATTATTTTTTAT  11776
 G  F  K  I  L  L  F  S  F  L  L  W  I  F  F  S  K  K  L  M  E  N ***
TGGGTTTAAAATTTTATTATTTTCTTTTTTATTGTGAATTTTTTTTTAGTAAA[AAGTTAATAGAAAATTAAATTCT  11701
```

```
                              ◀── tRNA ser UCN
[ATCTTATGTTTTCAAAACATACGCTTGTTCAAGCTCATTAACT]AATTAATTAATTTAATAAAATTATCTCATCATT  11626
                                             *** N  L  L  N  D  W  W  K
TTGTAACTAGTGGGTTAATTAAATAATATAAAAAAATAAATAATAGTTAAAATTTGTCCAATTAATACATAAGGTT  11551
 T  V  L  P  N  I  L  Y  Y  L  F  Y  I  I  T  L  I  Q  G  I  L  V  Y  P  E
CTTCAACTGGTCGAGCTCCAATTCATGTTAATAAAATTACTGTAACTAATATAGATCAAAATAAAATTTGGTTAA  11476
 E  V  P  R  A  G  I  W  T  L  L  I  V  T  V  L  M  S  W  F  L  I  Q  N  I
```

```
TTGGATAAAATTGGATTCCTCGGAATTTTCTTAAATTATAAAAAGGTAAAATTATTAAAATTGCAATTGATAAAA  11401
 P  Y  F  Q  I  G  R  F  K  s  L  N  Y  F  P  L  I  M  L  I  A  I  S  L  V

CTAATGCAATAACTCCTCCTAATTTATTAGGAATTGAACGAAGAATTGCGTAAGCAAATAAAAAATATCATTCTG  11326
 L  A  I  V  G  G  L  K  N  P  I  S  R  L  I  A  Y  A  F  L  F  Y  W  E  P

GTTGAATGTGAGCTGGTGTTACTAAAGGATTAGCAGGAATAAAGTTATCTGGGTCTCCCAATAAATTTGGTCTAA  11251
 Q  I  H  A  P  T  V  L  P  N  A  P  I  F  N  D  P  D  G  L  L  N  P  s  I

TTAAAACTAATGAAATTAGAATAAAAATTATTACAATAAATCCTACAATATCCTTAAATGTGAAGTATGGGTGAA  11176
 L  V  L  S  I  L  I  F  I  M  V  I  F  G  V  I  D  K  F  T  F  Y  P  H  F

AAGGAATTTTATCAATATTAGAATTTAAACCAATAGGGTTATTAGATCCTGTTTGATGTAAAAGTAGATGAA  11101
 P  I  K  D  I  N  S  N  L  G  I  P  N  N  S  G  T  Q  H  L  F  L  L  H  I

TTATAGTTATAGCAAGAACAATAAAAGGTAAAATAAAATGAAATGTGAAAAATCGAGTTAAAGTAGCATTATCTA  11026
 M  T  M  A  L  V  I  F  P  L  I  F  H  F  T  F  F  R  T  L  T  A  N  D  V

CAGCAAATCCTCCTCATAATCATTGTACTAAGTCTATACCTAAATAAGGGATAGCTGACAATAAATTAGTAATTA  10951
 A  F  G  G  W  L  W  Q  V  L  D  M  G  L  Y  P  I  A  S  L  L  N  T  I  V

CAGTTGCTCCTCAAAATGATATTTGTCCTCAAGGTAAAACATAACCTATAAAAGCTGTTCCTATTACTAAAAATA  10876
 T  A  G  W  F  S  M  Q  G  W  P  L  V  Y  G  M  F  A  T  G  M  V  L  F  L

AAATAATTACTCCTACTAATCAAGTTGGTGTAAATAAATATGATCCGTAATAAATTCCTCGACCAATATGTAAGT  10801
 I  I  V  G  V  L  W  T  P  T  F  L  Y  S  G  Y  Y  I  G  R  G  I  H  L  Y

AAATACAAATAAAAAAAAATGATGCACCGTTAGCGTGTAAAGTTCGTAATAATCAACCATAATTTACATCTCGGC  10726
 I  C  I  F  F  F  S  A  G  N  A  H  L  T  R  L  L  W  G  Y  N  V  D  R  C

AAATATGATTAACACTATAAAAAGCTAAGTTAACATCTGCTGTGTAGTGTATAGCTAAAAATAATCCAGTTAAAA  10651
 I  H  N  V  S  Y  F  A  L  N  V  D  A  T  Y  H  M  A  L  F  L  G  T  L  I

TTTGAATAATACATAATCCAAGTAATGATCCAAAATTTCATCATCTTGAAATATTAATTGGAGCTGGTAAAT  10576
 Q  I  I  L  C  L  G  L  L  S  G  F  N  W  s  S  I  N  I  P  A  P  L  D

CAACTAAAGCATTATTAGCAATTTTAAATAAAGGGTGGGAATTCGTAAAGGTTTATGCATTAATTAAGATATTA  10501
 V  L  A  N  N  A  I  K  F  L  P  H  S  N  R  L  P  K  H  M  ***  S  M  M
                                                    ◄───── Cyt b

TTCGGATAGGACCTTTAAATAGTTTAGTAATTTTTACTACAACAATTAAAGTAATTAATAAATAATTTATTAATA  10426
 R  I  P  G  K  F  L  K  T  I  K  V  V  V  I  L  T  I  L  L  Y  N  M  L  L

AAATTGTTACAAAATTTGTTGGAAAATTATATAATTTATTTAAAGATAAAGAATTTTCTGTAAAATAAGAATTTA  10351
 I  T  V  F  N  T  P  F  N  Y  L  K  N  L  S  L  S  N  E  T  F  Y  S  N  M

TTTCAATAATAGATTGTATTTCGTTATTTATTAAAAATAAAGTAATAGAAGTTTTATCAAGAATTATTGATAAAA  10276
 E  I  I  S  Q  M  E  N  N  M  L  F  L  T  I  S  T  K  D  L  I  M  S  L  I

TAAATATAAAAAATAAAATAAATATGGAAAATAAAGTTAATTTAATTGATAAATTAAATATTTCATTAGAAGCTA  10201
 F  M  F  F  L  I  F  M  S  F  L  T  L  K  I  S  L  N  F  M  E  N  S  A  L

ATGATGTAACATAAATAAATAAAACAAGTATTCCTCCTAAAAAAATTAAAAATAAAATGTATGAGTATCAAAAC  10126
 S  T  V  Y  I  F  L  V  L  M  G  G  L  F  I  L  F  L  I  Y  S  Y  W  F  S

TTTTAGTTATTAATCCTGAAAGTAAACATACAAAAATTGTTTGAATTAATAAAGTTAATCCTAAAGCTAATGGT  10051
 K  T  M  L  G  S  L  L  C  V  F  I  T  Q  I  L  L  T  L  G  L  A  L  P  H

GAATTATATTAAAAAAAAATAATAGATGTAGTAATAATTAATGAATATAATATTAATTGAATAATTTCAAGAGGTA  9976
 I  M  N  F  F  I  I  S  T  T  I  I  L  S  Y  L  M  L  Q  I  I
                                                      ◄──── URF6

tRNA^pro ──►
GTTTATTTATAAAATATTAATTTTGGGGATTAATGAAAAAGAAATTTCTTTTCTCTTGAAGTTTTAAAAGAAATA  9901

                                         URF4L ──►
                        ◄──── tRNA^thr  M  I  M  I  L  Y  W  S
ATCTTATTTTTGATTTACAAGACCAATGTTTTTATTAAACTATTAAAACTAATGATTATAATTTTATATTGAAGT  9826

 L  P  M  I  L  F  I  L  G  L  F  C  F  V  S  N  R  K  H  L  L  S  M  L  L
TTACCTATAATTTTATTTATTTTAGGTTTATTTTGTTTTGTTTCTAATCGAAAACATTTACTTTCAATACTTTTA  9751

 S  L  E  F  I  V  L  M  L  F  F  M  L  F  I  Y  L  N  M  L  N  Y  E  N  Y
AGTTTAGAATTTATTGTTTTTAATATTATTTTTTTATATTTATTTATTTATTTAAATATACTAAATTATGAAAATTAT  9676
```

```
   F  s  M  M  F  L  T  F  s  V  C  E  G  A  L  G  L  S  I  L  V  S  M  I  R
   TTTAGAATAATATTTTTAACATTTAGAGTATGTGAAGGAGCTTTAGGTTTATCAATTTTGGTTTCTATAATTCGT   9601
                                            URF4
   T  H  G  N  D  Y  F  Q  S  F  s  I  M ** M  L  K  I  I  L  F  L  L  F  L
   ACTCATGGTAATGATTATTTTCAATCTTTTAGAATTATATAATGTTAAAAATTATTTTATTTTTATTATTTTTAA   9526

   T  P  V  C  F  I  N  N  M  Y  W  M  V  Q  I  M  L  F  F  I  s  F  I  F  L
   CTCCTGTTTGTTTATTAATAATATATATTGAATGGTACAAATTATACTATTTTTTATTAGATTTATTTTTTTAT   9451

   L  M  N  N  F  M  N  Y  W  S  E  I  S  Y  F  L  G  C  D  M  L  S  Y  G  L
   TAATAAATAATTTTATAAATTATTGATCAGAAATTTCTTATTTTTTAGGATGTGATATATTATCTTATGGTTTGG   9376

   V  L  L  S  L  W  I  C  S  L  M  L  L  A  s  E  s  I  N  K  Y  N  N  Y  K
   TTTTGCTTAGTTTATGAATTTGTTCATTGATATTATTAGCTAGAGAAAGAATTAATAAATATAATAATTACAAAA   9301

   N  L  F  L  L  N  I  V  I  L  L  L  L  L  V  L  T  F  S  s  M  s  L  F  M
   ATTTATTTTTATTAAATATTGTTATTTTGTTATTATTATTGGTTTTAACTTTTCTAGAATAAGATTATTTATAT   9226

   F  Y  L  F  F  E  s  s  L  I  P  T  L  F  L  I  L  G  W  G  Y  Q  P  E  R
   TTTATTTATTTTTGAAAGAAGATTAATTCCTACATTATTTTTAATTTTAGGATGAGGTTATCAACCGGAACGAT   9151

   L  Q  A  G  V  Y  L  L  F  Y  T  L  V  S  L  P  M  L  I  G  I  F  Y  V
   TGCAAGCTGGTGTTTATTTATTATTTTATACTTTATTAGTTTCTTTACCTATATTAATTGGAATTTTTTATGTAA   9076

   M  N  K  T  G  S  M  N  F  Y  L  M  N  N  F  M  F  N  Y  D  L  L  Y  F  C
   TAAATAAAACTGGGTCAATAAATTTTTATTTAATAAATAATTTTATGTTTAATTATGATTTATTATATTTTTGTT   9001

   L  L  C  A  F  L  V  K  M  P  M  F  L  V  H  L  W  L  P  K  A  H  V  E  A
   TATTATGTGCTTTTTTTAGTGAAAATACCAATATTTTTAGTACATTTATGATTACCTAAAGCTCATGTTGAAGCTC   8926

   P  V  S  G  S  M  I  L  A  G  I  M  L  K  L  G  G  Y  G  L  L  R  V  I  N
   CTGTATCTGGTTCTATAATTTTAGCTGGTATTATATTAAAATTAGGAGGTTATGTGTTTATTACGAGTAATTAATT   8851

   F  L  Q  L  M  N  L  K  Y  s  F  V  W  i  s  i  s  L  V  G  G  V  L  M  s
   TTTTACAATTAATAAATTTAAAATATAGATTTGTTTGAATTAGAATTAGATTAGTAGGAGGTGTGTTAATAAGAT   8776

   L  V  C  L  R  Q  T  D  L  K  A  L  I  A  Y  S  S  V  A  H  M  G  I  V  L
   TAGTATGTTTACGACAAACTGATTTAAAGGCTTTAATTGCATATTCATCAGTTGCTCATATAGGAATTGTTTTAG   8701

   A  G  L  L  T  M  T  Y  W  G  L  C  G  S  Y  T  L  M  I  A  H  G  L  C  S
   CTGGTTTATTAACAATAACTTATTGAGGATTATGTGGATCTTATACATTAATAATTGCTCATGGTTTATGTTCTT   8626

   S  G  L  F  C  L  A  N  V  S  Y  E  R  L  G  s  R  s  M  L  I  N  K  G  L
   CTGGTTTATTTTGTTTAGCAAATGTTTCTTATGAACGATTAGGAAGACGAAGAATATTAATTAATAAGGGGTTAT   8551

   L  N  F  M  P  A  M  T  L  W  W  F  L  L  s  S  A  N  M  A  A  P  P  T  L
   TAAATTTTATACCTGCTATAAACTTTATGATGATTTTTATTAAGATCAGCTAATAATAGCAGCTCCTCCAACGTTAA   8476

   N  L  L  G  E  I  S  L  L  N  s  i  V  S  W  S  W  I  S  M  I  M  L  S  F
   ATTTATTAGGAGAAATTTCTTTTATTAAATAGAATTGTTTCTTGGTCATGAATTTCAATAATTATATTATCTTTTT   8401

   L  S  F  F  s  A  A  Y  T  L  Y  L  Y  S  F  S  Q  H  G  K  L  F  S  G  V
   TATCTTTCTTTTAGAGCAGCCTATACTTTATATTTATATTCTTTTAGTCAACATGGTAAATTATTTTCTGGGGTAT   8326

   Y  S  F  s  s  G  K  I  R  E  Y  L  L  M  L  L  H  W  L  P  L  N  L  L  I
   ATTCATTTAGAAGAGGTAAAATTCGGGAATATTTATTAATATTATTACATTGATTACCTTTAAATTTATTAATTT   8251

   L  K  s  E  S  C  I  L  W  L *  tRNA his
   TAAAAAGAGAATCATGTATTTTATGATTATATTTAAATAGTTTAAAAAAAAATACTAATTTGTGGTGTTAGTGATA   8176
                                          URF5
                                          I  C  s  i  s  F  I  N  L  I  S  I  S
   TGAAGTTATTCATTTTAGATCGTGAAATATTTATCAATTTGTAGAATTAGATTTATTAATTTAATTTCTATTAGT   8101

   L  T  C  F  L  L  S  L  Y  Y  L  L  N  N  M  V  Y  F  I  E  W  E  V  V  S
   TTAACATGTTTTTTTATTAAGTTTATATTATTTATTAAATAATATAGTTTATTTTATTGAATGAGAAGTAGTATCT   8026

   L  N  S  M  s  i  V  M  T  F  L  F  D  W  M  S  L  L  F  M  S  F  V  L  M
   TTAAATTCTATAAGAATTGTGATAACTTTTTTATTTGATTGAATAAGTTTATTATTTATATCTTTTGTTCTTATA   7951

   I  A  S  L  V  I  F  Y  s  K  E  Y  M  E  S  D  E  N  I  N  R  F  I  M  L
   ATTGCTTCTTTAGTAATTTTTTATAGAAAAGAATATATAGAAAGTGATGAAAATATTAATCGGTTTATTATATTA   7876

   V  L  M  F  V  L  S  M  M  L  L  I  I  s  P  N  L  V  s  I  L  L  G  W  D
   GTATTAATATTTGTTTTGTCAATAATATTATTAATTATCAGACCAAATTTAGTGAGAATTCTATTAGGGTGAGAT   7801
```

```
    G  L  G  L  V  S  Y  C  L  V  I  Y  F  Q  N  I  K  S  Y  N  A  G  M  L  T
GGATTAGGACTTGTTTCTTATTGTTTAGTAATTTATTTTCAAAATATCAAATCTTACAATGCTGGAATATTAACT        7726

    A  L  S  N  R  I  G  D  V  A  L  L  L  A  I  A  W  M  L  N  Y  G  s  W  N
GCATTATCTAATCGAATTGGAGATGTGAGCTCTTCTTCTTGCTATTGCTTGAATATTAAATTATGGTAGATGAAAT        7651

    Y  I  F  Y  L  E  V  M  Q  N  E  F  S  M  L  M  I  G  S  L  V  M  L  A  A
TATATTTTTTTATTTAGAAGTTATACAAAATGAATTTTCAATATTAATAATTGGTAGTTTAGTTTATATTAGCTGCT        7576

    M  T  K  s  A  Q  I  P  F  S  S  W  L  P  A  A  M  A  A  P  T  P  V  S  A
ATAACTAAAAGAGCTCAAATTCCTTTTTCTTCTTGATTACCAGCTGCTATAGCTGCCCCTACTCCTGTCTCTGCT        7501

    L  V  H  S  S  T  L  V  T  A  G  V  Y  L  L  I  R  F  N  I  V  L  S  T  S
TTAGTCCATTCTTCTACTTTAGTAACAGCAGGAGTTTATTTATTAATTCGATTTAATATTGTTTTAAGTACTTCT        7426

    W  L  G  Q  L  L  L  L  L  S  G  L  T  M  F  M  A  G  L  G  A  N  F  E  F
TGATTAGGACAATTATTGTTGTTATTATCAGGTTTAACTATATTTATAGCAGGACTGGGGGCTAATTTTGAGTTT        7351

    D  L  K  K  I  I  A  L  S  T  L  S  Q  L  G  L  M  M  s  I  L  S  M  G  F
GATTTAAAGAAAATTATTGCGTTGTCAACTCTTAGTCAATTAGGATTAATAATAAGAATTTTATCTATGGGATTT        7276

    Y  K  L  A  M  F  H  L  L  T  H  A  L  F  K  A  L  L  F  M  C  A  G  A  I
TATAAAATTAGCTATATTTCATTTATTAACTCATGCTTTATTTAAAGCTTTATTATTTATATGTGCAGGAGCTATT        7201

    I  H  N  M  N  N  S  Q  D  I  R  L  M  G  G  L  s  I  H  M  P  L  T  S  A
ATTCATAATATAAATAATTCTCAAGATATTCGGTTAATAGGAGGGTTGAGAATTCATATACCTTTAACTTCAGCT        7126

    C  F  N  V  S  N  L  A  L  C  G  M  P  F  L  A  G  F  Y  S  K  D  M  I  L
TGTTTTAATGTTTCTAATTTGGCTTTATGTGGAATACCATTTTTAGCTGGATTTTATTCTAAGGATATAATTTTA        7051

    E  I  V  s  I  s  N  I  N  M  F  S  F  F  L  Y  F  F  S  T  G  L  T  V  S
GAAATTGTTAGAATTAGAAATATTAATATATTTTCATTTTTTTTATACTTTTTTTCCACAGGTTTAACAGTAAGT        6976

    Y  S  F  R  L  V  Y  Y  S  M  T  G  D  L  N  C  G  S  L  N  M  L  N  D  E
TATTCTTTTCGGTTAGTATATTATTCAATAACTGGAGATTTAAATTGTGGAAGTTTAAATATATTAAATGATGAA        6901

    S  W  V  M  L  R  C  M  L  C  L  L  I  M  s  I  I  G  G  s  M  L  N  W  L
AGTTGAGTAATACTTCGGGGGTATACTAGGCTTATTATTTATAAGAATTATTGGAGGTAGAATGTTAAATTGGTTA        6826

    I  F  P  F  P  Y  M  I  C  L  P  G  Y  L  K  M  L  T  L  F  V  C  I  V  G
ATTTTTCCTTTTCCTTATATAATTTGTTTACCTGGGTATTTAAAAATATTAACATTATTTGTTTGTATTGTTGGG        6751

    G  L  F  G  Y  L  I  S  I  s  N  L  Y  S  L  N  K  S  L  L  N  Y  N  L  T
GGTTTATTTGGGTATCTAATTTCTATCACAAAATTTATATTCTTTGAATAAATCTCTATTAAATTATAATTTAACA        6676

    L  F  L  G  S  M  W  F  M  P  Y  I  s  T  Y  G  M  I  F  Y  P  L  N  Y  C
TTATTTTTACCTTCAATATGATTTATACCTTATATTAGAACTTATGGAATAATTTTTTATCCTTTAAATTATGGT        6601

    Q  L  V  V  K  S  F  D  Q  G  W  S  E  Y  F  G  G  Q  H  L  Y  Y  K  L  S
CAATTAGTTGTAAAAAGTTTTGATCAAGGTTGGTCAGAATATTTTGGGGGTCAACATTTATATTACAAGTTATCA        6526

    N  Y  S  K  T  L  F  L  M  H  N  N  S  L  K  I  Y  L  M  L  F  V  F  W  I
AATTATTCTAAAACTTTATTTCTGATACATAATAATAGTTTAAAAATTTATTTAATATTATTTGTATTTTGAATT        6451

    M  I  L  F  S  F  L  L  F  L  *   tRNA^phe
ATAATTTTATTTAGTTTTTTATTATTTTTATATTCAAATAG
```

Fig. 1.1. The entire nucleotide sequence of the *D. yakuba* mtDNA molecule. The sequence is presented in two segments so as to optimize the proportion of the molecule which can be shown as the sense strand of the various rRNA and polypeptide genes. The two segments comprise the left (segment I) and right (segment II) portions of the molecule (Fig. 1.2a) delimited by the junction of the tRNA^ile gene and the A + T-rich region, and the junction of the tRNA^phe and URF5 genes. The numbering shown begins with the first nucleotide of the tRNA^ile gene and proceeds through that gene, continuously around the entire molecule, and terminates with the last nucleotide (♯16019) of the A + T-rich region which lies adjacent to the tRNA^ile gene. Transfer RNA genes are boxed and the anticodon of each is underlined. The nucleotide sequence shown for each gene is the sense (or codon) strand of genes which are accompanied by an arrow pointing to the right and the antisense (or template) strand of genes which are accompanied by an arrow pointing to the left. The predicted amino acid sequences (one letter code) are shown above the nucleotide sequences presented as sense strands of polypeptide genes, and below nucleotide sequences presented as antisense strands. The location of the 5′ end of the small rRNA gene derived from considerations of sequence homology and potential secondary structure similarity to mouse mtDNA is indicated by the large arrowhead. The small arrowhead indicates the position at which there is an abrupt change in sequence homology to the corresponding segment of *D. virilis* mtDNA (see text). Asterisks indicate partial or complete termination codons. In the amino acid sequences, a lower case letter s indicates the tentative assignment of serine to an AGA codon. The (M) at the beginning of the COI sequence indicates uncertainty regarding translation initiation of this gene (see text).

cytochrome b, cytochrome *c* oxidase (CO) subunits I, II and III, ATPase subunit 6 (ATPase6) and the eight presumptive polypeptide genes which have been designated URF (unidentified reading frame) 1, 2, 3, 4L, 4, 5, 6 and A6L. The *D. yakuba* sequence contains two rRNA genes identified by nucleotide sequence homologies to the rRNA genes of mouse and other mammalian mtDNAs, and to bacterial and eukaryotic nuclear-coded rRNAs. Also, there are 22 tRNA genes located either singly or in clusters of two to six between the polypeptide and rRNA genes.

Between the tRNA^{ile} gene and the small rRNA gene occurs a sequence of

Fig. 1.2a. Gene arrangement in the *D. yakuba* mtDNA molecule. The locations of the A + T-rich region, the origin of replication (O), and the direction of replication (R) relative to *Eco*RI and *Hin*dIII restriction sites (inner circles) were determined by electron microscope studies (Fauron and Wolstenholme 1976; 1980; Goddard and Wolstenholme 1980). Identification and arrangement of the various genes resulted from nucleotide sequence studies (Clary *et al.* 1982; Clary, Wahleithner and Wolstenholme 1983, 1984; Clary and Wolstenholme 1983*a,b*, 1984 and unpublished). Each tRNA gene (hatched area) is identified by the one letter amino acid code, and individual serine and leucine tRNA genes are identified by the codon family (in parentheses) which their transcription products recognize. Arrows within and outside the molecule indicate the direction of transcription of each gene. The wavy line indicates the uncertain location of the 5′ terminus of the large rRNA gene. The numbers of apparently noncoding nucleotides which occur between the different genes are shown at the gene boundaries on the inner side of the gene map. Negative numbers indicate overlapping nucleotides of adjacent genes. An asterisk indicates an incomplete termination codon (T or TA). The location of all *Eco*RI, *Hin*dIII, *Cla*I, *Bgl*II and *Xho*I restriction sites, which were used to obtain the clones of segments of the *D. yakuba* mtDNA molecule from which nucleotide sequences were obtained are shown on the inner map. The letters within the three concentric circles identify the fragments of the restriction enzymes indicated. The two arrows labeled I and II, lying between the restriction map and the gene map identify the two segments of the sequence shown in Fig. 1.1.

Fig. 1.2b. Gene map of the circular mammalian mtDNA molecule (derived from that given for mouse (Bibb *et al.* 1981)). The solid arcs inside the molecule identify polypeptide gene-containing segments which are rearranged relative to *Drosophila* mtDNA. The arrow marked T indicates a translocation. The small circular arrows (I) indicate inversions. Rearrangements of tRNA genes between mtDNA molecules of *Drosophila* and mouse are not shown. O_H and O_L indicate the origin of heavy and light strand synthesis. Other details are as in Fig. 1.2a.

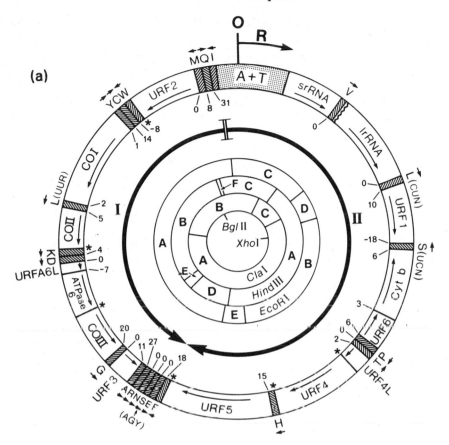

(a)

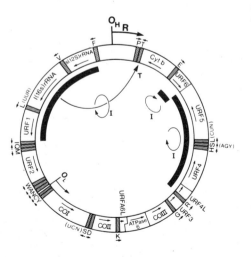

(b)

1077 nucleotides that is 92.8 per cent A + T and lacks open reading frames greater than 123 nucleotides. This region constitutes the major portion of the A + T-rich region of *D. yakuba* mtDNA previously identified from electron microscope studies (Fauron and Wolstenholme 1976, 1980a) and shown to contain the replication origin (Goddard and Wolstenholme 1980). While it is known that the replication origin is between 250 to 450 nucleotides from the left end of the A + T-rich region, its location has not been precisely defined (Goddard and Wolstenholme 1980; Wolstenholme, Goddard and Fauron 1983).

The relative arrangement and direction of transcription of genes in the *D. yakuba* mtDNA molecule are shown in Fig. 1.2a. Overall, the proportions of the two complementary strands of the molecule which serve as templates for transcription of genes are approximately equal. All genes in that half of the molecule to the right of the A + T-rich region, except for cytochrome b, URF6, $tRNA^{ser}_{UCN}$ and $tRNA^{thr}$, are transcribed in the same direction as that in which replication proceeds around the molecule. All the genes in the other half of the molecule, with the exception of three tRNA genes (gln, cys and tyr), are transcribed in the other direction.

Mammalian mtDNAs differ from *D. yakuba* mtDNA in regard to the relative arrangement of a number of genes and the general pattern of gene transcription (Fig. 1.2b). In mammalian mtDNA, the rRNA genes, all of the polypeptide genes except URF6, and 14 tRNA genes are transcribed in the same direction, which is opposite to the direction of replication (Anderson *et al.* 1981, 1982; Bibb *et al.* 1981). The difference in gene arrangement between the *D. yakuba* and mammalian mtDNA molecules (Fig. 1.2b) seems to have resulted from a minimum of three translocations involving the rRNA genes and polypeptide genes and a minimum of ten translocations of tRNA genes. It is interesting to note that the arrangement relative to each other of the five known polypeptide genes (cytochrome b, COI, COII, COIII and ATPase 6) is almost identical in the *D. yakuba* and mammalian mtDNA molecules and that in both cases they are all transcribed in the same direction.

A difference in gene arrangement between sea urchin and mammalian mtDNAs has recently been reported (Roberts, Grula, Posakony, Hudspeth, Davidson and Britten 1983). In sea urchin mtDNA, the COI gene is adjacent to the 16S rRNA gene, and the 16S rRNA gene is apparently separated from the 12S rRNA gene by about 3 kb.

POLYPEPTIDE CODING GENES

Differences in size occur between all of the corresponding polypeptide genes of *D. yakuba* and mouse. However, in 11 cases the difference in length is less than 3 per cent (Table 1.1). There is an overall 6 per cent difference in size between the *D. yakuba* and mouse URF5 genes due mainly to differences at the 5′ end of the genes; of the first 65 codons of the mouse URF5 gene a total of 32 are absent from the *D. yakuba* URF5 gene which includes a block of the first 26 codons. The *D. yakuba* URFA6L gene lacks the equivalent of a region containing 12 codons at the 3′ end of the mouse URFA6L gene which overlaps the 5′ end region of the ATPase 6 gene. The overall difference in size between the URFA6L genes of mouse and *D. yakuba* is 20 per cent.

INITIATION CODONS

It has been argued that in mammalian mtDNAs the first ATN codon in an open reading frame serves as the translation initiation codon (Anderson *et al.* 1981; Montoya, Ojala and Attardi 1981; Bibb *et al.* 1981). In *D. yakuba* mtDNA the cytochrome b, COII, COIII, ATPase6, URF4L and URF4 genes have an ATG codon at the beginning of the reading frame (Table 1.2), which immediately follows the preceding tRNA gene, or is separated from it by no more than five nucleotides. An ATT codon occurs at the beginning of the reading frame of the URF2, URF3 and URFA6L genes, in each case immediately adjacent to the preceding tRNA gene. An inframe ATT also occurs near the beginning of the reading frames of the URF5 and URF6 genes, but separated from the preceding tRNA genes by 15 and 6 nucleotides, respectively. The first ATN codon in the reading frame of the

Table 1.2

Comparisons of initiation codons and termination nucleotides and codons in the corresponding 13 polypeptide genes of D. yakuba, *mouse, human and bovine mtDNAs.*

Gene	Initiation Codon				Termination Codon			
	D. yakuba	Mouse	Human	Cow	*D. yakuba*	Mouse	Human	Cow
Cytochrome b	ATG	ATG	ATG	ATG	TAA	T	T	AGA
COI	ATAA	ATG	ATG	ATG	TAA	TAA	AGA	TAA
COII	ATG	ATG	ATG	ATG	T	TAA	TAG	TAA
COIII	ATG	ATG	ATG	ATG	TAA	T	T	T
ATPase 6	ATG	ATG	ATG	ATG	TA	TA	TA	TA
URF1	ATA	ATT	ATA	ATG	TAA	T	TA	TA
URF2	ATT	ATA	ATT	ATA	T	T	T	T
URF3	ATT	ATC	ATA	ATA	TAA	TAA	T	TA
URF4L	ATG	ATG	ATG	ATG	TA	TAA	TAA	TAA
URF4	ATG	ATG	ATG	ATG	T	T	T	T
URF5	ATT	ATC	ATA	ATA	T	TAA	TAA	TAA
URF6	ATT	ATG	ATG	ATG	TAA	TAA	AGG	TAA
URFA6L	ATT	ATG	ATG	ATG	TAA	TAA	TAG	TAA

Data for mouse, human and cow are from Bibb *et al.* 1981; Anderson *et al.* 1981; Anderson *et al.* 1982, respectively.

URF1 gene is ATA which is separated from the preceding tRNA gene by ten nucleotides. The view that ATA and ATT are initiation codons in *D. yakuba* mtDNA is supported by the finding that the URF1, URF3, URF6 and URFA6L genes totally lack ATG codons. Also, the first ATG codon in both the URF2 and URF5 genes occurs near the centre of each gene.

In *D. yakuba* mtDNA, as in mammalian mtDNA, only one gene for a tRNA which is expected to recognize methionine-specifying codons (AUG and AUA) has been located, and in mammals there is evidence that both mt-tRNA^{met} and mt-tRNA^{f-met} are specified by that gene (van Etten *et al.* 1982). The *D. yakuba* mt-tRNA^{f-met} gene (Fig. 1.3) contains two features which are highly conserved among all known initiator tRNAs: the CAT anticodon and three consecutive G-C nucleotide pairs at the base of the anticodon stem. However, the nucleotide 5′ to the CAT anticodon is a T in the *D. yakuba* mt-tRNA^{f-met} gene, rather than a C which is found in this position in mammalian mt-tRNA^{f-met} genes. It has been suggested that in mammalian mitochondria the CAU anticodon of the tRNA^{f-met} can recognize all four AUN codons as specifying methionine when they occur as initiator codons (Anderson *et al.* 1981; Bibb *et al.* 1981). However, as none of the polypeptides encoded by URF genes of metazoan mtDNAs have been directly sequenced, it is not known whether an initiator AUU codon specifies isoleucine or methionine.

The COI genes of both *D. yakuba* and *D. melanogaster* mtDNAs lack an ATN initiation codon and it has been reasoned that the quadruplet ATAA may serve this function (de Bruijn 1983; Clary and Wolstenholme 1983*b*). Important to this argument is the finding that the nucleotide located 5′ to the CAT anticodon of the *D. yakuba* tRNA^{f-met} gene is a T, rather than a C. This U residue in the corresponding tRNA is expected to pair with the fourth nucleotide of the AUAA sequence to increase the efficiency of codon-anticodon interaction and at the same time be functional in allowing the tRNA^{f-met} to read the entire AUAA sequence as a codon, and thus permit continuation of reading in the correct frame (Clary and Wolstenholme 1983*b*).

The translation initiation codon of the bacteriophage MS2 A-protein gene (Fiers, Contreras, Duernick, Haegmean, Merreganet, MinJou, Raeymakers, Volckaert, Ysebaert, Van de Kerckhove, Nolf and Van Montagu 1975) and of some *Escherichia coli* genes (Gay and Walker 1981) is GUG. A GTG codon occurs as the first inframe triplet of the open reading frame interpreted as the URF5 gene in *D. yakuba* mtDNA (Fig. 1.1) and also of the open reading frame interpreted as the URF1 gene in mouse mtDNA (Bibb *et al.* 1981). As in both of these cases the first ATN codon is separated by an unusually large number of nucleotides (15 for *D. yakuba* URF5, and nine for mouse URF1) from the preceding tRNA gene, it seems worth considering the possibility that in metazoan mtDNA, GUG may occasionally serve as an initiation codon.

TERMINATION CODONS

The only termination codon found in *D. yakuba* mtDNA is TAA, although TAG is the termination codon of the *D. melanogaster* COIII gene (Clary, Wahleithner and Wolstenholme 1983). Among mammalian mtDNAs TAA alone is found in mouse, while some bovine and human genes end in TAG or AGA, and AGG appears to be the termination codon of the human URF6 gene (Table 1.2). Four of the *D. yakuba* polypeptide genes end with a T which always directly precedes the 5′ terminal nucleotide of a tRNA gene. Two other genes, ATPase6 and URF4L, end with TA which in each case is immediately adjacent to the ATG codon of the following polypeptide gene, COIII and URF4L, respectively. Terminal T and TA nucleotides are also found in mammalian mitochondrial genes. It has been argued that the initial transcription products of mammalian mtDNAs are multicistronic RNA molecules, and that following precise cleavage to yield individual gene transcripts, those of genes ending in U or UA acquire a complete termination codon by polyadenylation (Anderson *et al.* 1981; Ojala, Montoya and Attardi 1981). It seems plausible that such a mechanism also operates in *Drosophila* mtDNA as both polyadenylated mRNAs and mRNAs which could contain multiple gene transcripts have been reported for *D. melanogaster* and *D. virilis* (Battey, Rubenstein and Clayton 1979; Merten and Pardue 1981).

It has been proposed that the secondary structure of the tRNAs which separate polypeptide genes (and rRNA genes) is the recognition signal which facilitates precise cleavage between gene transcripts (Ojala *et al.* 1980; Ojala, Montoya and Attardi 1981). In mammalian mtDNAs the ATPase6 gene ends in a TA which is followed by the ATG codon of the COIII gene, a situation identical to that described above for the junction of the ATPase6 and COIII genes, and the URF4L and URF4 genes of *D. yakuba* mtDNA. From studies with HeLa cells there is evidence for precise cleavage between the terminal UA of the ATPase6 transcript and the AUG initiation codon of the COIII transcript, but the regulatory signal by which this is facilitated is unknown (Anderson *et al.* 1981; Ojala, Montoya and Attardi 1981).

The only genes which have the same terminal nucleotide(s) in *D. yakuba*, mouse, human and bovine mtDNAs are URF2 and URF4 (a T in each case) and ATPase6 (a TA) (Table 1.2).

RIBOSOMAL RNA GENES

Using hybridization and electron microscopy, Klukas and Dawid (1976) demonstrated that the small rRNA gene of *D. melanogaster* mtDNA overlaps the A + T-rich region by about 200 nucleotides, that the large rRNA gene is separated from the small rRNA gene by about 160 nucleotides and that both genes are transcribed in the direction away from the A + T-rich region. Based on these findings, a similar arrangement of the rRNA genes and the A + T-rich region was deduced from heteroduplex data for a number of *Drosophila* species (Fauron and Wolstenholme 1980*a*), and it was determined that replication of all the *Drosophila* mtDNA molecules examined proceeds around the molecule in the same direction as rRNA transcription (Goddard and Wolstenholme 1978, 1980).

Sequencing of *D. yakuba* mtDNA confirmed the relative location of the A + T-rich region and the rRNA genes, and revealed that the tRNA^{val} gene separates the two rRNA genes (Figs 1.1 and 1.2; Clary *et al.* 1982) and that the tRNA$^{leu}_{CUN}$ gene separates the large rRNA gene from the URF1 gene. However, we have been unable to detect a tRNA gene between the small rRNA gene and the replication origin-containing region, where the tRNA^{phe} gene is located in mammalian mtDNA.

The small and large rRNA genes were identified by sequence homology of specific regions to approximately corresponding regions of mouse rRNA genes and *E. coli* rRNAs (Clary *et al.* 1982). Comparisons to sequence of the 3' end of the small mt-rRNA of mosquito (and of mouse and other mammals) indicate that the 3' nucleotide of the *D. yakuba* small mt-rRNA gene is adjacent to the 5' end of the tRNA^{val} gene (Clary *et al.* 1982). From considerations of sequence homology and similarities in secondary structure potential to the 5' end region of the mouse small mt-rRNA gene (Zwieb, Glotz and Brimacombe 1981), we have tentatively assigned nucleotide 14942 (Fig. 1.1) as the 5' terminus of the *D. yakuba* small rRNA gene (Clary and Wolstenholme, unpublished). A further indication that the 5' end of the small mt-rRNA gene is close to nucleotide 14942 was obtained from a comparison of the nucleotide sequence of this region of the mtDNA molecules of *D. yakuba* and *D. virilis*. Between nucleotides 14949 and 14950 there is an abrupt change in homology: the 50 nucleotides downstream from this point in the two sequences are 90 per cent homologous, while the 50 nucleotides upstream are only 40 per cent homologous.

An *Eco*RI site is located within the large mt-rRNA gene, 644–649 nucleotides downstream from the tRNA^{val} gene. The sequence of 677 nucleotides between this *Eco*RI site and the tRNA$^{leu}_{CUN}$ gene is highly homologous (68 per cent in each of two regions of >250 nucleotides) to the corresponding region of the mouse large mt-rRNA gene. Also, it seems likely from secondary structure considerations that the nucleotide which is adjacent to the 5' end of the tRNA$^{leu}_{CUN}$ gene is the 3' terminus of the large mt-rRNA gene (Clary, Wahleithner and Wolstenholme 1984). The 643 nucleotides which lie between the tRNA^{val} gene and the *Eco*RI site are only 9.5 per cent G + C, and we have been unable to detect within this region convincing sequence homologies or secondary structure similarities to the mouse large mt-rRNA gene which would allow us to identify the 5' end of the *D. yakuba* large mt-rRNA gene. However, the approximate size of the large mt-rRNA gene of *D. melanogaster* (1500 nucleotides) given by Klukas and Dawid (1976) is consistent with the interpretation that the entire sequence (1326 nucleotides) between tRNA^{val} and tRNA$^{leu}_{CUN}$ is the large rRNA gene. It appears from the above considerations that the maximum sizes estimated for the small mt-rRNA (796 nucleotides) and large mt-rRNA (1326 nucleotides) genes of *D. yakuba* are the smallest so far recorded for any metazoan mtDNA.

TRANSFER RNA GENES

All but one (tRNA$^{ser}_{AGY}$) of the 22 tRNA genes (and the tRNAs predicted from them) have a similar general structure which resembles that of their mammalian counterparts. Five of these genes (ile, lys, asp, ser(AGY) and asn) are between 84 per cent and 93 per cent homologous to corresponding tRNAs from mosquito (*Aedes albopictus*) (HsuChen, Cleaves and Dubin 1983a, 1983b, Dubin, HsuChen, Cleaves and Timko 1984). As has been found for all metazoan mt-tRNA genes, the trinucleotide sequence CCA, which occurs at the 3′ terminus of prokaryotic and eukaryotic nuclear-coded tRNA genes is absent from the *D. yakuba* mt-tRNA genes. The *D. yakuba* mt-tRNA genes vary in size from 63 nucleotides (tRNA^{cys}) to 72 nucleotides (tRNA^{val}) (Fig. 1.3). The sizes of the amino-acyl stem (seven nucleotide pairs), the anticodon stem (five nucleotide pairs) and the anticodon loop (seven nucleotides) are strictly conserved. Within the dihydrouridine arm, the stem varies from three to four nucleotide pairs and the loop from three to eight nucleotides. The so-called variable (or extra) loop is always four or five nucleotides and the TψC arm contains a stem of four or five nucleotide pairs and a loop of three to eight nucleotides.

The *D. yakuba* mt-tRNA genes differ among themselves in regard to the presence or absence of various nucleotides which are conserved in prokaryotic and eukaryotic nuclear-coded tRNAs (Gauss and Sprinzl 1983a, 1983b). Only the conserved T$_{33}$ and Pu$_{37}$ nucleotides which lie immediately 5′ and 3′ respectively, to the anticodons are found in all the *D. yakuba* mt-tRNA genes. The conserved Pu$_{26}$ is found in all but the *D. yakuba* tRNA^{glu} gene (where it is a C). Also the conserved nucleotide pair, Py$_{11}$-Pu$_{24}$ occurs in all *D. yakuba* mt-tRNA genes except tRNA^{f-met} and tRNA^{trp} where in each case a G-C pair is found in this position.

Tertiary bonding occurs between many of the conserved nucleotides of prokaryotic and eukaryotic nuclear-coded tRNAs, particularly those in the dihydrouridine and TψC arms (Kim 1979). The lack of conservation in the corresponding regions of the tRNAs predicted from *D. yakuba* mt-tRNA genes suggests that tertiary bonding is different and possibly not as strong as in prokaryotic and eukaryotic nuclear-coded tRNAs. Also, those nucleotides which are conserved in the dihydrouridine and TψC arms of prokaryotic and eukaryotic nuclear-coded tRNA genes appear to be important as recognition sites in the control of transcription of individual tRNA genes

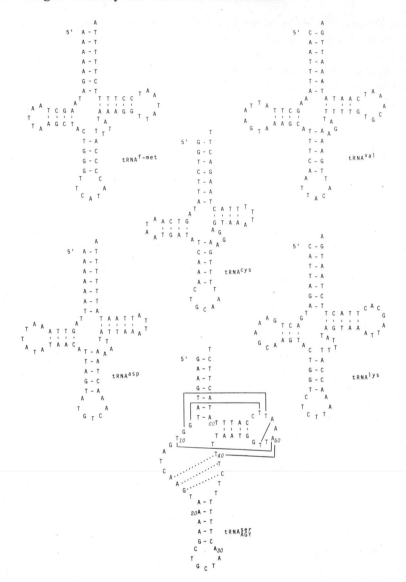

Fig. 1.3. Six tRNA genes of *D. yakuba* mtDNA shown in the presumed secondary structure of the corresponding tRNAs. In the diagram of the tRNA$_{AGY}^{ser}$ gene are indicated possible secondary interactions between nucleotides in the dihydrouridine replacement loop and the variable loop (dotted lines), and other tertiary interactions (solid lines) which have been proposed for tRNA$_{AGY}^{ser}$ from bovine and other mammalian mitochondria (de Bruijn and Klug 1983). The numbering system is specific for the tRNA$_{AGY}^{ser}$ gene.

(Rajput, Duncan, DeMille, Miller and Spiegelman 1982). Although little is known concerning the control of transcription of *D. yakuba* mtDNA, it appears that in mammalian mtDNA, transcripts of individual tRNAs (in which the size and nucleotide content of the dihydrouridine arm and TψC arms are also variable) are cleaved from primary multicistronic transcripts that initiate in or close to the replication origin-containing region of the molecule (Montoya *et al.* 1982; Montoya, Gaines and Attardi 1983; Chang and Clayton 1984). Thus in mammalian mtDNA at least, the lack of conservation of nucleotides in the dihydrouridine and TψC arms of the tRNA genes can be correlated with the absence of primary transcripts of individual tRNA genes.

Homology of the 22 *D. yakuba* mt-tRNA genes and their mammalian counterparts range from 32 per cent (tRNA^{arg}) to 70 per cent (tRNA^{asp} and tRNA^{thr}). The mean G + C content of the *D. yakuba* tRNA genes (24.3 per cent) is similar to the mean G + C content of the 13 polypeptide genes (23.3 per cent). However, two tRNA genes (asp and glu) are only 8.8 per cent G + C. In both of these tRNA genes, the amino-acyl and TψC stems comprise only A-T nucleotide pairs. Other tRNA genes (gln, gly, leu(CUN), pro and his) also contain one or more stems lacking G-C pairs.

The tRNA$^{ser}_{AGY}$ gene (Fig. 1.3) of *D. yakuba* mtDNA is unusual in that the dihydrouridine arm is replaced by an 11 nucleotide loop, within which secondary structure formation seems unlikely. Also, the variable loop (six nucleotides) and the TψC loop (nine nucleotides) are larger than in any other *D. yakuba* tRNA gene. Strong support for our interpretation of this sequence was provided by isolation of a tRNA from mosquito tissue culture cells which is 91 per cent homologous to the *D. yakuba* tRNA$^{ser}_{AGY}$ gene sequence and can be folded into a similar structure (Dubin *et al.* 1984). A tRNA$^{ser}_{AGY}$ gene in which a five nucleotide loop replaces the dihydrouridine arm has been found in the mtDNAs of different mammals (de Bruijn and Klug 1983), and the corresponding tRNA from bovine and human mitochondria has been identified (Arcari and Brownlee 1980; de Bruijn, Schreier, Eperon, Barrell, Chen, Armstrong, Wong and Roe 1980). Recently, from information concerning tertiary structure obtained through chemical probing experiments, de Bruijn and Klug (1983) have described a structural model for the bovine tRNA$^{ser}_{AGY}$. Interactions similar to many of those proposed between nucleotides of the bovine tRNA$^{ser}_{AGY}$ could also occur in the tRNA predicted from the *D. yakuba* tRNA$^{ser}_{AGY}$gene (Fig. 1.3; Clary and Wolstenholme 1984).

CODON USAGE AND THE GENETIC CODE

Data from thermal melting and buoyant density studies revealed that the regions of the *Drosophila* mtDNA molecules outside the A + T-rich region were also unusually low in G + C (Polan *et al.* 1973; Bultmann and Laird

1973; Peacock *et al.* 1974; Fauron and Wolstenholme 1976; Wolstenholme, Fauron and Goddard 1980). From the nucleotide sequence of *D. yakuba* mtDNA it has been determined that the polypeptide genes have an average G + C content of 23.3 per cent. The genes of the five known polypeptides have G + C contents (range 24.2 per cent (ATPase 6) to 30.1 per cent (COI)) which are higher than the G + C contents of the URF genes (range 15.2 per cent (URF6) to 22.3 per cent (URF5)).

Codon usage among the 13 polypeptide genes of *D. yakuba* mtDNA is summarized in Table 1.3. It is particularly striking that 93.8 per cent of all codons end in A or T. The range of codons ending in A or T for the known polypeptide genes is 91.6 per cent (COI) to 95.5 per cent (ATPase 6) and for the URF genes, 92.7 per cent (URF5) to 98.1 per cent (URFA6L). However, among these 13 genes only the codons CAG, CGC, AGG and TAG are not found, and TAG is utilized as the termination codon of the *D. melanogaster* COIII gene (Clary, Wahleithner and Wolstenholme 1983).

The triplets AGA and AGG which specify arginine in the standard genetic code are used only as rare termination codons in human and bovine mtDNA (see above) and are not used at all in mouse mtDNA. Also, a gene for a tRNA which might be expected to recognize these codons has not been located in mammalian mtDNA. In contrast, internal AGA codons (but not AGG codons) are present in all *D. yakuba* mitochondrial genes except URF6. However, none of the total of 73 AGA codons found in the genes of *D. yakuba* mtDNA correspond in position to arginine-specifying codons (CGN) in the equivalent genes of mouse mtDNA. Also, none of the AGA codons of *D. yakuba* cytochrome b, COI, COII, COIII and ATPase6 genes correspond to arginine-specifying codons (AGA) in the equivalent genes of yeast. As direct amino acid sequence determinations have not been made of any of the proteins coded by *D. yakuba* mtDNA, it has not been possible to definitively determine the amino acid specified by AGA in the *Drosophila* mitochondrial genetic code. However, from the following considerations it seems most likely that AGA specifies serine.

While the 73 AGA codons found in *D. yakuba* mtDNA correspond in position to codons specifying 14 different amino acids in the equivalent mouse genes, AGA codons correspond to more than twice as many serine-specifying codons (a total of 23) than to codons specifying any other amino acid (ten for alanine). Also, of the seven AGA codons found in the *D. yakuba* COI gene, which has a higher homology to the mouse COI gene (Table 1.1) than has been found for any other *D. yakuba*-mouse mito-chondrial gene comparison, five correspond in position to serine-specifying codons in the mouse COI gene (Fig. 1.4). Also, five of these seven *D. yakuba* AGA codons correspond in position to serine-specifying codons in the yeast COI gene (Fig. 1.4). Similar arguments have been made by de Bruijn (1983) from comparisons of the corresponding nucleotide sequences of four complete and two partial polypeptide genes of *D. melanogaster* and human mtDNAs.

Table 1.3

Codon usage in the 13 polypeptide genes of D. yakuba *mtDNA*

Phe	TTT	313	Ser	TCT	120	Tyr	TAT	142	Cys	TGT	40
	TTC	17		TCC	4		TAC	28		TGC	2
Leu	TTA	542		TCA	102	TER	TAA	7	Trp	TGA	96
	TTG	25		TCG	3		TAG	0		TGG	6
Leu	CTT	36	Pro	CCT	79	His	CAT	65	Arg	CGT	8
	CTC	2		CCC	3		CAC	12		CGC	0
	CTA	19		CCA	45	Gln	CAA	70		CGA	45
	CTG	2		CCG	3		CAG	0		CGG	6
Ile	ATT	345	Thr	ACT	97	Asn	AAT	193	Ser	AGT	34
	ATC	15		ACC	3		AAC	13		AGC	1
Met	ATA	195		ACA	85	Lys	AAA	76	(Ser)	AGA	73
	ATG	18		ACG	2		AAG	9		AGG	0
Val	GTT	90	Ala	GCT	125	Asp	GAT	54	Gly	GGT	67
	GTC	3		GCC	9		GAC	10		GGC	2
	GTA	93		GCA	37	Glu	GAA	82		GGA	129
	GTG	8		GCG	2		GAG	1		GGG	22

The total number of codons in the 13 *D. yakuba* polypeptide genes is 3735, which includes seven TAA codons. AGA is shown as serine (see text). AGG has not been found in *Drosophila* mtDNA (Clary, Wahleithner and Wolstenholme 1984). TAG has been interpreted as the termination codon of the *D. melanogaster* COIII gene (Clary, Wahleithner and Wolstenholme 1983). TGA and ATA are assumed to specify tryptophan and methionine, respectively (see text).

Further, strong evidence in support of the interpretation that AGA specifies serine in the *D. yakuba* mitochondrial genetic code was obtained from considerations of frequencies of nucleotide substitutions between AGA and AGT codons of the URF2, COI, COII, COIII, ATPase6 and URFA6L genes of *D. yakuba* and *D. melanogaster* mtDNAs (Wolstenholme and Clary, unpublished, see below). The frequency of substitution in the third position of these codons (A↔T; 21.2 per cent) was close to the mean frequency (20.6 per cent) of substitutions which did not result in an amino acid replacement (that is, were silent) among all codons ending in A or T in the six genes. If in *Drosophila* mtDNA AGA codes for a different amino acid than AGT (which is expected to code serine as in all other known genetic codes) then a frequency of third position A↔T substitutions between AGA and AGT codons of approximately 0.5 per cent (the mean frequency of third position substitutions which result in an amino acid replacement) would have been expected.

All 13 *D. yakuba* mitochondrial genes contain internal TGA codons. Of the total of 96 TGA codons found, 70 correspond in position to tryptophan-specifying codons (TGA or TGG) in mouse mitochondrial genes, indicating that in *D. yakuba* mtDNA, as in mammalian and fungal mtDNAs (Fox

```
Cytochrome c Oxidase subunit I

mouse      MFINR..... .........L L.......... .A.S...... ..Q....L.. ..........  60
D. yakuba (M)-SRQWLFST NHKDIGTLYF IFGAWAGMVG TSLsILIRAE LGHPGALIGD DQIYNVIVTA
yeast      M-VQR..Y.. .A...AV... MLAIFS..A. .AMSLI..L. .AA..SQYLH GNSQLFL.VG
                                             ▲

...V...... ..M....... ......I... .......... S......SFL ...ASS...A ..........  130
HAFIMIFFMV MPIMIGGFGN WLVPLMLGAP DMAFPRMNNM sFWLLPPALS LLLVssMVEN GAGTGWTVYP
..VL...CL. ..AL...... Y.L..II..T .T....I..I A..V..MG.V C.VTSTL..S ..........
                                            ▲

..AGNPV.A. .....T.... ....V...... .I.....I.. .KPPAM.QYQ T.......L. ..V....... 200
PLSSGIAHGG ASVDLAIFSL HLAGISSILG AVNFITTVIN MRSTGITLDR MPLFVWSVVI TALLLLLSLP
....IQ..S. P.......A. ..TS...L.. .I...V.TL. ..TN.M.MHK L......IF. ..F.......

...AG..... .......T.. .......... .......... .......... ..I...VVTY Y.....P..Y 270
VLAGAITMLL TDRNLNTSFF DPAGGGDPIL YQHLFWFFGH PEVYILILPG FGMISHIIsQ ESGKKETFGS
..SAG..... L...F..... EV........ .E........ .......I.. ..I...VVST Y.-..PV..E
                                                                  ▲

M..VW..MS. .F........ ......L... ...C...... ...I...V.V .S.......G NIKW...M.. 340
LGMIYAMLAI GLLGFIVWAH HMFTVGMDVD TRAYFTSATM IIAVPTGIKI FsWLATLHGT QLSYSPAILW
IS.V...AS. .....L..S. ..YI..L.A. .......... ...I...... .S....IY.G SIRLATPM.Y
                                                       ▲

....I..... .....I..S. ..L..V.... .......... .......... ...V..F... S.F..DDT.A 410
ALGFVFLFTV GGLTGVVLAN SSVDIILHDT YYVVAHFHYV LSMGAVFAIM AGFIHWYPLF TGLTLNNKWL
.IA.L....M ......A... A.L.VAF... ....G..Y.. .....I.SLF ..YYY.S.QI L..NY.E.LA

.AH.A...V. ..M....... ...S...... .......... .T..SM..F. ..TAV.IMIF M...AFA.K. 480
KSQFIIMFIG VNLTFFPQHF LGLAGMPRRY SDYPDAYTTW NVVSTIGSTI SLLGILFFFY IIWESLVSQR
QI..WLI... A.VI...M.. ..IN.....I P.....FAG. .Y.AS...F. AT.SLFL.I. .LYDQ..NNK

E.MSVSYAST NL..LHGC.. PY.TFE.PTY VKVK*
QVIYPIQLNS SIEWYQNTPP AEHsYSELPL LTN-*
S...AKAPS. ...PLLTS.. .V.SFNT-.A VQS-*
                      ▲
```

Fig. 1.4. Comparisons of the amino acid sequences of cytochrome c oxidase sub-unit I (COI) predicted from the nucleotide sequence of the COI gene of *D. yakuba* with the corresponding amino acid sequences of mouse (Bibb *et al.* 1981) and yeast (Bonitz *et al.* 1980*b*). A dot indicates an amino acid which is conserved relative to *D. yakuba*. A dash indicates an amino acid which is absent. Termination codons are indicated by an asterisk. Wide vertical solid arrows indicate *D. yakuba* amino acids specified by AGA which are shown as a lower case s to represent the tentative assignment of serine (see text). The (M) at the beginning of the COI *D. yakuba* sequence indicates uncertainty regarding translation initiation.

1979; Barrell, Bankier and Drouin 1979; Heckman, Sarnoff, Alzner-De Weerd, Yin and RajBhandry 1980; Barrell *et al.* 1980; Bonitz, Berlani, Coruzzi, Li, Macino, Nobrega, Nobrega, Thalenfeld and Tzagoloff 1980*a*), TGA specifies tryptophan.

From considerations of the frequency of third position substitution between ATG and ATA codons in corresponding *D. yakuba* and *D. melanogaster* genes (similar to those discussed above for AGT and AGA codons) it appears that in the *Drosophila* mitochondrial genetic code, as in the mammalian mitochondrial genetic code (Barrell *et al.* 1980; Bibb *et al.* 1981), ATA specifies methionine rather than isoleucine (Wolstenholme and Clary, unpublished).

A gene expected to code for a tRNA with an anticodon (TCT) which would specifically recognize the codon AGA has not been found in *D. yakuba* mtDNA. As all available evidence indicates that AGA specifies serine, it seems reasonable to assume that the 5′ GCU anticodon (of tRNA$^{ser}_{AGY}$) which is expected to recognize AGU and AGC codons also recognizes AGA codons. This would necessitate either selective two-out-of-three nucleotide pair recognition (Lagerkvist 1981) or effective pairing of the G in the wobble position of the anticodon with C, U and A. Other cases of unusual base pairing of the nucleotides in the wobble position of the anti-codons have been indicated for mtDNAs. Codon recognition of the CAU anticodon of tRNA^{f-met} has been discussed above. Also, in *Drosophila* mtDNA while genes contain both AAA and AAG codons, only a tRNA^{lys} gene with a CTT anticodon (Fig. 1.3) has been located (Clary and Wolsten-holme 1983*a*; de Bruijn 1983). A similar tRNA^{lys} has been isolated from mosquito mitochondria (HsuChen, Cleaves and Dubin 1983*b*).

A scheme has been proposed by Barrell *et al.* (1980), which would require only the 22 tRNAs encoded by mammalian mtDNA for translation of all mtDNA encoded polypeptides. A similar scheme has been proposed for fungal mitochondria (Heckman *et al.* 1980; Bonitz *et al.* 1980*a*). When all four codons in a box of the genetic code specify the same amino acid (four codon families) these codons are recognized by the same tRNA which always has a U in the wobble position. When only two codons in a box specify one amino acid (two codon families) and the other two specify a different amino acid, then each two codon family is recognized by a separate tRNA. For two codon families ending in a purine the corresponding tRNA has a U in the wobble position while for those ending in a pyrimidine, the corresponding tRNA has a G in the wobble position. Our data are consistent with the view that a similar mechanism of translation, which incorporates the unusual modifications involved in some codon/anticodon interactions discussed above, is operative in *D. yakuba* mitochondria.

INTERGENIC NUCLEOTIDES

The *D. yakuba* mtDNA molecule, like the mammalian mtDNA molecule, is a remarkably compact structure. There is no evidence suggesting that introns occur within rRNA and polypeptide genes in *D. yakuba* mtDNA and, except for the replication origin-containing region, apparently noncoding nucleo-tides between genes are either absent or occur in small numbers (1–31). Nevertheless, the total number of noncoding nucleotides (183) is considera-bly greater than in the mtDNAs of mouse (64), human (87) and cow (57) (Bibb *et al.* 1981; Anderson *et al.* 1981, 1982).

Replication of mtDNA molecules of vertebrates and *Drosophila* is uni-directional around the molecule from a specific site referred to as the re-plication origin (Fig. 1.2a and 1.2b), and is an unusually asymmetrical process (Clayton, 1982; Wolstenholme, Goddard and Fauron 1983). In mtDNAs of cultured mammalian cells replication begins with synthesis of one strand (H strand) from a location (O_H, Fig. 1.2b) between the tRNA^{pro} and tRNA^{phe} genes and proceeds for two-thirds of the genome length before synthesis on the second strand (L strand) commences. Initiation of L strand synthesis in all mouse L cell and most human KB cell mtDNA molecules occurs within a specific sequence of 32 (mouse) or 31 (human) nucleotides which can fold into a hairpin loop with a perfect 12 base pair stem, and is located between the tRNA^{asn} and tRNA^{cys} genes (Clayton 1982). This 31-32 nucleotide sequence (which is included in the number given above for intergenic nucleotides of mammalian mtDNAs) is highly conserved in other mammalian and amphibian mtDNAs (Anderson *et al.* 1982; Taira *et al.* 1983; Wong *et al.* 1983). However, such a sequence is not found in the corresponding region of *D. melanogaster* or *D. yakuba* mtDNA (de Bruijn 1983; Clary and Wolstenholme 1983b), or in any other intergenic region of the *D. yakuba* mtDNA molecule (Fig. 1.1). This sequence difference relative to mammalian mtDNAs is consistent with the results of our electron microscope studies on replicative forms of *Drosophila* mtDNA molecules (Goddard and Wolstenholme 1978, 1980). While evidence for a highly preferred site of initiation of second strand synthesis in *D. melanogaster* mtDNA molecules was obtained (Goddard and Wolstenholme 1978), from considerations of various mapping data (Fauron and Wolstenholme 1980a; Clary *et al.* 1982; Wolstenholme, Goddard and Fauron 1983) it appears that this site lies close to the boundary of the tRNA^{ile} gene and the A + T-rich region of this molecule, rather than between the COI and URF2 genes.

NUCLEOTIDE SEQUENCE COMPARISONS BETWEEN *D. YAKUBA* AND *D. MELANOGASTER*

A segment of the *D. melanogaster* mtDNA molecule containing the complete genes for COI, COII, COIII, ATPase6 and URFA6L, most of the URF2 gene and seven tRNA genes has been sequenced (de Bruijn 1983; Clary, Wahleithner and Wolstenholme 1983). Gene content and gene order within this sequence is the same as that found in *D. yakuba* mtDNA. Also, the lengths of the five complete polypeptide genes are identical in the two species. We have analyzed nucleotide substitutions between the polypeptide and tRNA genes in the *D. yakuba* and *D. melanogaster* mtDNAs (Wolstenholme and Clary, unpublished). The overall frequency of substitutions between the polypeptide genes is 7.2 per cent, almost twice that found between the tRNA genes (3.9 per cent). This is in agreement with observations made on mtDNAs from closely related primates (Brown *et al.* 1982). Substitutions which do not result in an amino acid replacement (silent substitutions) account for 86 per cent of the 336 substitutions found between the *D. yakuba* and *D. melanogaster* polypeptide genes. This value is higher than the average of 78 per cent found by Brown *et al.* (1982) for the frequency of silent substitutions between polypeptide genes of human, chimpanzee and gorilla mtDNAs which had an overall average sequence divergence of 9.9 per cent though lower than the value of 94 per cent found for silent substitutions between the COII genes of two rat species which had diverged by 7.9 per cent of their nucleotides (Brown and Simpson 1982). Ninety-two per cent and 89 per cent respectively, of all substitutions between primate and between rat sequences were transitions, and a disproportionately high number of these were C↔T substitutions in the sense strand. In contrast, the nucleotide substitutions found between the polypeptide genes of the *D. yakuba* and *D. melanogaster* mtDNAs comprised approximately equal frequencies of transitions (49 per cent) and transversions (51 per cent). Third position transitions were twice as frequent among codons of two codon families than among codons of four codon families, due mainly to a difference in C↔T substitutions. As all transitions are silent, this finding suggests that in *Drosophila* mtDNAs the products of transitional mutation are not free from selective pressures. Further, in the third position of codons of four codon families, transversions were 4.6 times more frequent than transitions (the expected ratio of transversions to transitions is 2:1) and were almost exclusively A↔T substitutions. A higher frequency of A↔T substitutions might be expected in the *Drosophila* genes than in mammalian genes, due to the high proportion (94 per cent) of codons ending in A or T in the *Drosophila* mtDNAs. However, the observed frequency of A↔T substitutions between *D. yakuba* and *D. melanogaster* polypeptide genes is significantly greater than the expected value calculated from the ratios of third position nucleotides in codons of these genes. This observation is consistent with the view that in the two *Drosophila* mtDNAs there is continuous selection against G and C nucleotides in the third position of codons. We have no explanation as to why a mtDNA would become A + T-rich during long term evolution (the ancestral lines which led to present day insects and mammals are thought to have diverged about 600 million years ago (Clary *et al.* 1982)). However, it seems plausible from our data that at least since divergence of the lines which led to *D. yakuba* and *D. melanogaster* there has been selection to maintain a high A + T nucleotide composition, possibly as a response to the optimum requirements of various replication- and/or transcription-related enzymes in mitochondria.

Summary

The mitochondrial genome of *Drosophila yakuba* is a circular DNA molecule of 16019 nucleotide pairs. The sequence contains the genes for two rRNA molecules, 22 tRNA molecules, five known polypeptides (cytochrome b, cytochrome *c* oxidase subunits I, II, III and ATPase subunit 6) and eight unidentified polypeptides (URF1, 2, 3, 4L, 4, 5, 6 and A6L). Between the tRNA^{ile} and small rRNA genes there occurs a sequence of 1077 nucleotides that is 92.8 per cent A + T and lacks reading frames greater than 123 nucleotides. Replication of the molecule originates in this A + T-rich region and proceeds toward the small rRNA gene. Non-coding nucleotides between genes are either absent or occur in low numbers (1 to 31). A sequence equivalent in size and secondary structure potential to the sequence associated with the initiation of second strand synthesis in mammalian mtDNA is missing in *Drosophila* mtDNA. While the genes found in *D. yakuba* and mammalian mtDNAs are the same, the relative arrangement of many of these genes differs considerably in the two molecules. The proportions of the two strands of the *D. yakuba* molecule which serve as template for transcription of genes are approximately equal. This contrasts with the situation in mammalian mtDNAs where all genes except those for URF6 and eight tRNAs are transcribed from one strand. The dihydrouridine and TψC loops of *D. yakuba* mt-tRNA genes are highly variable in size, and among these genes there is a general deficiency of nucleotides which are highly conserved in prokaryotic and eukaryotic nuclear-coded tRNAs. The *D. yakuba* tRNA$^{ser}_{AGY}$ gene is unusual in that an eleven nucleotide loop replaces the dihydrouridine arm. *D. yakuba* mitochondrial polypeptide genes utilize 59 sense codons. However, 93.8 per cent of all codons used end in A or T. Unique variations occur in the *Drosophila* mitochondrial genetic code. AGA appears to specify serine rather than arginine as in the standard code, or termination as in the mammalian mitochondrial code. The *Drosophila* COI gene lacks a standard translation initiation codon, and may utilize a four nucleotide codon ATAA for that purpose. As in other metazoan mitochondria, TGA and ATA specify tryptophan and methionine, respectively. As a tRNA with an anticodon (TCT) specific for AGA codons does not appear to be encoded in *D. yakuba* mtDNA, it seems likely that the GCU anticodon of the *D. yakuba* tRNA which recognizes AGY (serine) codons can also recognize AGA. Of 336 nucleotide substitutions found between six corresponding polypeptide genes of *D. yakuba* and *D. melanogaster* mtDNAs, 86 per cent were silent, and transitions and transversions were equally frequent. Analysis of frequencies of silent substitutions in the third position of codons suggests that there is continuous selection against fixation of such substitutions which are G or C.

Acknowledgements

We thank Raymond F. Gesteland, John R. Roth and John F. Atkins for discussions during the course of this work, and Felix Machuca for excellent technical assistance. This work was supported by National Institutes of Health Grants GM 18375 and RR 07092.

References

Altman, P. L. and Katz, D. D. (1976). In: Biological Handbooks I. Cell Biology. (ed.) pp. 217–219. Federation of American Societies for Experimental Biology, Bethesda, Maryland.

Anderson, S., Bankier, A. T., Barrell, B. G., de Bruijn, M. H. L., Coulson, A. R., Drouin, J., Eperon, I. C., Nierlich, D. P., Roe, B. A., Sanger, F., Schreier, P. H., Smith, A. J. H., Staden, R., and Young, I. G. (1981). Sequence and organization of the human mitochondrial genome. *Nature* **290**, 457–465.

—— de Bruijn, M. H. L., Coulson, A. R., Eperon, I. C., Sanger, F., and Young, I. G. (1982). The complete sequence of bovine mitochondrial DNA: conserved features of the mammalian mitochondrial genome. *J. Mol. Biol.* **156**, 683–717.

Arcari, P. and Brownlee, G. G. (1980). The nucleotide sequence of a small (3S) seryl-tRNA (anticodon GCU) from beef heart mitochondria. *Nucleic Acids Res.* **8**, 5207–5212.

Barrell, B. G., Anderson, S., Bankier, A. T., de Bruijn, M. H. L., Chen, E., Coulson, A. R., Drouin, J., Eperon, I. C., Nierlich, D. P., Roe, B. A., Sanger, F., Schreier, P. H., Smith, A. J. H., Staden R., and Young, I. G. (1980). Different pattern of codon recognition by mammalian mitochondrial tRNAs. *Proc. Natl. Acad. Sci. U.S.A.* **77**, 3164–3166.

Barrell, B. G., Bankier, A. T., and Drouin, J. (1979). A different genetic code in human mitochondria. *Nature* **282**, 189–194.

Battey, J. and Clayton, D. A. (1978). The transcription map of mouse mitochondrial DNA. *Cell* **14**, 143–156.

—— Rubenstein, J. L. R., and Clayton, D. A. (1979). Transcription patterns of *Drosophila melanogaster* mitochondrial DNA. In: *ICN-UCLA Symposia on Molecular and Cellular Biology*, Vol. XV, Extrachromosal DNA (cd. D. J. Cummings, I. B. Dawid, P. Borst, S. M. Weissman, and C. F. Fox) pp. 427–442. Academic Press, New York.

Bibb, M. J., Van Etten, R. A., Wright, C. T., Walberg, M. W., and Clayton, D. A. (1981). Sequence and gene organization of mouse mitochondrial DNA. *Cell* **26**, 167–180.

Bonitz, S. G., Berlani, R., Coruzzi, G., Li, M., Macino, G., Nobrega, F. G., Nobrega, M. P., Thalenfeld, B. E., and Tzagoloff, A. (1980*a*) Codon recognition rules in yeast mitochondria. *Proc. Natl. Acad. Sci. U.S.A.* **77**, 3167–3170.

Bonitz, S. G., Coruzzi, G., Thalenfeld, B. E., Tzagoloff, A., and Macino, G. (1980*b*). Assembly of the mitochondrial membrane system. Structure and nucleotide sequence of the gene coding for the subunit 1 of yeast cytochrome oxidase. *J. Biol. Chem.* **255**, 11927–11941.

Brown, G. G. and Simpson, M. V. (1982). Novel features of animal mtDNA evolution as shown by sequences of two rat cytochrome oxidase subunit II genes. *Proc. Natl. Acad. Sci. U.S.A.* **79**, 3246–3250.

Brown, W. M., Prager, E. M., Wang, A., and Wilson, A. C. (1982). Mitochondrial DNA sequences in Primates: tempo and mode of evolution. *J. Mol. Evol.* **18**, 225–239.

Brutlag, D. L., Clayton, J., Frieland, P., and Kedes, L. H. (1982). SEQ: a nucleotide sequence analysis and recombination system. *Nucleic Acids Res.* **10**, 279–304.

Bultmann, H. and Laird, C. D. (1973). Mitochondrial DNA from *Drosophila melanogaster*. *Biochim. Biophys. Acta* **299**, 196–209.

Cantatore P. and Attardi, G. (1980). Mapping of nascent light and heavy strand transcripts on the physical map of HeLa cell mitochondrial DNA. *Nucleic Acids Res.* **8**, 2605–2625.

Chang, D. D. and Clayton, D. A. (1984). Precise identification of mitochondrial

32   Douglas O. Clary and David R. Wolstenholme

promoters for transcription of each strand of human mitochondrial DNA. *Cell* **36**, 635–643.

Chomyn, A., Mariottini, P., Gonzalez-Cadavid, N., Attardi, G., Strong, D. D., Trovato, D., Riley, M., and Doolittle, R. (1983). Identification of the polypeptides encoded in the ATPase 6 gene and in the unassigned reading frames 1 and 3 of human mtDNA. *Proc. Natl. Acad. Sci. U.S.A.* **80**, 5535–5539.

Clary, D. O., Goddard, J. M., Martin, S. C., Fauron, C. M.-R., and Wolstenholme, D. R. (1982). *Drosophila* mitochondrial DNA: a novel gene order. *Nucleic Acids Res.* **10**, 6619–6637.

—— Wahleithner, J. A., and Wolstenholme, D. R. (1983). Transfer RNA genes in *Drosophila* mitochondrial DNA: related 5′ flanking sequences and comparisons to mammalian mitochondrial tRNA genes. *Nucleic Acids Res.* **11**, 2411–2425.

—— Wahleithner, J. A., and Wolstenholme, D. R. (1984). Sequence and arrangement of the genes for cytochrome b, URF1, URF4L, URF4, URF5, URF6 and five tRNAs in *Drosophila* mitochondrial DNA. *Nucleic Acids Res.* **12**, 3747–3762.

—— and Wolstenholme, D. R. (1983a). Nucleotide sequence of a segment of *Drosophila* mitochondrial DNA that contains the genes for cytochrome c oxidase subunits II and III and ATPase subunit 6. *Nucleic Acids Res.* **11**, 4211–4227.

—— and Wolstenholme, D. R. (1983b). Genes for cytochrome c oxidase subunit I, URF2 and three tRNAs in *Drosophila* mitochondrial DNA. *Nucleic Acids Res.* **11**, 6859–6872.

—— and Wolstenholme, D. R. (1984). A cluster of six tRNA genes in *Drosophila* mitochondrial DNA that includes a gene for an unusual tRNA$_{AGY}^{ser}$. *Nucleic Acids Res.* **12**, 2367–2379.

Clayton, D. A. (1982). Replication of animal mitochondrial DNA. *Cell* **28**, 693–705.

de Bruijn, M. H. L. (1983). *Drosophila melanogaster* mitochondrial DNA, a novel organization and genetic code. *Nature* **304**, 234–241.

—— and Klug, A. (1983). A model for the tertiary structure of mammalian mitochondrial transfer RNAs lacking the entire dihydrouridine loop and stem. *EMBO Journal* **2**, 1309–1321.

—— Schreier, P. H., Eperon, I. C., Barrell, B. G., Chen, E. Y., Armstrong, P. W., Wong, J. F. H., and Roe, B. A. (1980). A mammalian mitochondrial serine transfer RNA lacking the 'dihydrouridine' loop and stem. *Nucleic Acids Res.* **8**, 5213–5222.

Doolittle, R. F. (1981). Similar amino acid sequences: chance or common ancestry. *Science* **214**, 149–159.

Dubin, D. T., HsuChen, C. C., Cleaves, G. R., and Timko, K. D. (1984). Sequence and structure of a serine transfer RNA with GCU anticodon from mosquito mitochondria. *J. Mol. Biol.* **176**, 251–260.

Fauron, C. M.-R. and Wolstenholme, D. R. (1976). Structural heterogeneity of mitochondrial DNA molecules within the genus *Drosophila*. *Proc. Natl. Acad. Sci. U.S.A.* **73**, 3623–3627.

—— and Wolstenholme, D. R. (1980a). Extensive diversity among *Drosophila* species with respect to nucleotide sequences within the adenine + thymine-rich region of mitochondrial DNA molecules. *Nucleic Acids Res.* **8**, 2439–2452.

—— and Wolstenholme, D. R. (1980b). Intraspecific diversity of nucleotide sequences within the adenine + thymine-rich regions of mitochondrial DNA molecules of *Drosophila mauritiana*, *Drosophila melanogaster* and *Drosophila simulans*. *Nucleic Acids Res.* **8**, 5391–5409.

Fiers, W., Contreras, R., Deurinck, F., Haegmean, G., Merregaert, J., Min Jou, W., Raeymakers, A., Volckaert, G., Ysebaert, M., Van de Kerckhove, J., Nolf, F., and Van Montagu, M. (1975). A protein gene of bacteriophage MS2. *Nature* **256**, 273–278.

Fox, T. D. (1979). Five TGA 'stop' codons occur within the translated sequence of the yeast mitochondrial gene for cytochrome *c* oxidase subunit II. *Proc. Natl. Acad. Sci. U.S.A.* **76**, 6534–6538.

Gauss, D. H. and Sprinzl, M. (1983*a*). Compilation of tRNA sequences. *Nucleic Acids Res.* **11**, r1–r53.

—— and Sprinzl, M. (1983*b*). Compilation of sequences of tRNA genes. *Nucleic Acids Res.* **11**, r55–r173.

Gay, N. J. and Walker, J. E. (1981). The atp operon: nucleotide sequence of the promoter and the genes for the membrane proteins and the subunit of *Escherichia coli* ATP-synthase. *Nucleic Acids Res.* **9**, 3919–3926.

Goddard, J. M. and Wolstenholme, D. R. (1978). Origin and direction of replication in mitochondrial DNA molecules from *Drosophila melanogaster*. *Proc. Natl. Acad. Sci. U.S.A.* **75**, 3886–3890.

—— and Wolstenholme, D. R. (1980). Origin and direction of replication in mitochondrial DNA molecules from the genus *Drosophila*. *Nucleic Acids Res.* **8**, 741–757.

Greenberg, B. D., Newbold, J. E., and Sugino, A. (1983). Intraspecific nucleotide sequence variability surrounding the origin of replication in human mitochondrial DNA. *Gene* **21**, 33–49.

Grosskopf, R. and Feldmann, H. (1981). Analysis of a DNA segment from rat liver mitochondria containing the genes for cytochrome oxidase subunits I, II and III, ATPase6 and several tRNA genes. *Current Genetics* **4**, 151–158.

Heckman, J. E., Sarnoff, J., Alzer-DeWeerd, B., Yin, S., and RajBhandary, U. L. (1980). Novel features in the genetic code and codon reading patterns in *Neurospora crassa* mitochondria based on sequences of six mitochondrial tRNAs. *Proc. Natl. Acad. Sci. U.S.A.* **77**, 3159–3163.

Hong, G. F. (1982). A systematic DNA sequencing strategy. *J. Mol. Biol.* **158**, 539–549.

HsuChen, C. C., Cleaves, G. R., and Dubin, D. T. (1983*a*). Sequences of three transfer RNAs from mosquito mitochondria. *Plasmid* **10**, 55–65.

—— Cleaves, G. R., and Dubin, D. T. (1983*b*). A major lysine tRNA with a CUU anticodon in insect mitochondria. *Nucleic Acids Res.* **11**, 8659–8662.

Jue, R. A., Woodbury, N. W., and Doolittle, R. F. (1980). Sequence homologies among *E. coli* ribosomal proteins: evidence for evolutionarily related groupings and internal duplications. *J. Mol. Evol.* **15**, 129–148.

Kim, S-H. (1979). Crystal structure of yeast tRNA^Phe and general structural features of other tRNAs. In: *Transfer RNA: structure properties and recognition* (ed. P. R. Schimmel, D. Soll, and J. N. Abelson) pp. 83–100. Cold Spring Harbor Laboratory. Cold Spring Harbor, New York.

Klukas, C. K. and Dawid, I. B. (1976). Characterization and mappping of mitochondrial ribosomal RNA and mitochondrial DNA in *Drosophila melanogaster*. *Cell* **9**, 615–625.

Lagerkvist, U. (1981). Unorthodox codon reading and the evolution of the genetic code. *Cell* **23**, 305–306.

Mariottini, P., Chomyn, A., and Attardi, G. (1983). Antibodies against synthetic peptides reveal that the unidentified reading frame A6L, overlapping the ATPase 6 gene is expressed in human mitochondria. *Cell* **32**, 1269–1277.

Merten, S. H. and Pardue, M. L. (1981). Mitochondrial DNA in *Drosophila*. An analysis of genome organization and transcription in *Drosophila melanogaster* and *Drosophila virilis*. *J. Mol. Biol.* **153**, 1–23.

Montoya, J., Christianson, T., Levens, D., Rabinowitz, M., and Attardi, G. (1982). Identification of initiation sites for heavy-strand and light-strand transcription in human mitochondrial DNA. *Proc. Natl. Acad. Sci. U.S.A.* **79**, 7195–7199.

—— Gaines, G. L., and Attardi, G. (1983). The pattern of transcription of the

34   Douglas O. Clary and David R. Wolstenholme

human mitochondrial rRNA genes reveals two overlapping transcription units. *Cell* **34**, 151–159.

—— Ojala, D., and Attardi, G. (1981). Distinctive features of the 5' terminal sequences of the human mitochondrial mRNAs. *Nature* **290**, 465–470.

Ohi, S., Ramirez, J. L., Upholt, W. B., and Dawid, I. B. (1978). Mapping of mitochondrial 4S RNA genes in *Xenopus laevis* by electron microscopy. *J. Mol. Biol.* **121**, 299–310.

Ojala, D., Merkel, C., Gelfand, R., and Attardi, G. (1980). The tRNA genes punctuate the reading of genetic information in human mitochondrial DNA. *Cell* **22**, 393–403.

—— Montoya, J., and Attardi, G. (1981). tRNA punctuation model of RNA processing in human mitochondria. *Nature* **290**, 470–474.

Peacock, W. J., Brutlag, D., Goldring, E., Appels, R., Hinton, C. W., and Lindsley, D. L. (1974). The organization of highly repeated DNA sequences in *Drosophila melanogaster* chromosomes. *Cold Spring Harbor Symposia on Quant. Biol.* **38**, 405–416.

Pepe, G., Holtrop, M., Gadaleta, G., Kroon, A. M., Cantatore, P., Gallerani R., De Benedetto, C., Quagliariello, C., Sbisa, E., and Saccone, C. (1983). Non random patterns of nucleotide substitutions and codon strategy in the mammalian mitochondrial genes coding for identified and unidentified reading frames. *Biochem. Internat.* **6**, 553–563.

Polan, M. L., Friedman, S., Gall, J. G., and Gehring, W. (1973). Isolation and characterization of mitochondrial DNA from *Drosophila melanogaster*. *J. Cell Biol.* **56**, 580–589.

Rajput, B., Duncan, L., DeMille, D., Miller, R. C., Jr., and Spiegelman, G. (1982). Transcription of cloned transfer RNA genes from *Drosophila melanogaster* in a homologous cell free extract. *Nucleic Acids Res.* **10**, 6541–6550.

Ramirez, J. L. and Dawid, I. B. (1978). Mapping of mitochondrial DNA in *Xenopus laevis* and *X. borealis*: the positions of ribosomal genes and D-loops. *J. Mol. Biol.* **119**, 133–146.

Rastl, E. and Dawid, I. B. (1978). Expression of the mitochondrial genome in *Xenopus laevis*: a map of transcripts. *Cell* **18**, 501–510.

Roberts, J. W., Grula, J. W., Posakony, J. W., Hudspeth, R., Davidson, E. H., and Britten, R. J. (1983). Comparisons of sea urchin and human mtDNA: evolutionary rearrangement. *Proc. Natl. Acad. Sci. U.S.A.* **80**, 4614–4618.

Sanger, F., Nicklen, S., and Coulson, A. R. (1977). DNA sequencing with chain-terminating inhibitors. *Proc. Natl. Acad. Sci. U.S.A.* **74**, 5463–5467.

Staden, R. (1980). A computer program to search for tRNA genes. *Nucleic Acids Res.* **8**, 817–825.

—— (1982). Automation of the computer handling of gel reading data produced by the shotgun method of DNA sequencing. *Nucleic Acids Res.* **10**, 4731–4751.

Taira, M., Yoshida, E., Kobayashi, M., Yaginuma, K., and Koike, K. (1983). Tumor-associated mutations of rat mitochondrial transfer RNA genes. *Nucleic Acids Res.* **11**, 1635–1643.

van Etten, R. A., Michael, N. L., Bibb, M. J., Brennicke, A., and Clayton, D. A. (1982). Expression of the mouse mitochondrial DNA genome. In: *Mitochondrial genes* (ed. P. Slonimski, P. Borst, and G. Attardi) pp. 73–88 Cold Spring Harbor Laboratory, Cold Spring Harbor, New York.

Wolstenholme, D. R. and Fauron, C. M.-R. (1976). A partial map of the circular mitochondrial genome of *Drosophila melanogaster*: Location of *Eco*RI sensitive sites and the adenine-thymine rich region. *J. Cell Biol.* **71**, 434–448.

—— Fauron, C. M.-R., and Goddard, J. M. (1980). The adenine + thymine-rich region of *Drosophila* mitochondrial DNA molecules. In: *The organization and expression of the mitochondrial genome. Developments in Genetics* (ed. C. Saccone

and A. M. Kroon) Vol. 2, pp. 241–250. Elsevier/North Holland Biomedical Press, Amsterdam.
—— Goddard, J. M., and Fauron, C. M.-R. (1983). Replication of *Drosophila* mitochondrial DNA. In: *Developments in Molecular Virology* Vol. 2. *Molecular events in the replication of viral and cellular genomes* (ed. Y. Becker) Vol. 2, pp. 131–148. Martinus Nijhoff B. V. The Hague.
Wong, J. F. H., Ma, D. P., Wilson, R. K., and Roe, B. A. (1983). DNA sequence of the *Xenopus laevis* mitochondrial heavy and light strand replication origins and flanking tRNA genes. *Nucleic Acids Res.* **11**, 4977–4995.
Zweib, C., Glotz, C., and Brimacombe, R. (1981). Secondary structure comparisons between small subunit ribosomal RNA molecules from six different species. *Nucleic Acids Res.* **9**, 3621–3640.

2 Tubulin genes and the diversity of microtubule function

NICHOLAS J. COWAN

Introduction

With the exception of anucleate red blood cells, microtubules are a feature of all eukaryotic cells, and are present as long filamentous structures of about 24 nm in diameter. The major subunit proteins of microtubules are α- and β-tubulins, each with a molecular weight of around 55 000 daltons. These proteins, in association with others (the so-called microtubule associated proteins) form complex assemblies that are central to eukaryotic cell function; the mitotic spindle, centrioles, cilia, flagella, and elements of the cytoskeleton. Thus, microtubules are involved in aspects of cellular growth, division, motility and shape. In spite of this diversity of function, both structural and biochemical evidence point to a strict evolutionary conservation among tubulin proteins. For example, comparison of limited N-terminal sequence data on α-and β-tubulins from sea urchin and chicken shows considerable homology; in α- tubulin, there are no differences within the first 25 residues (Luduena and Woodward 1973). In addition, antibodies raised against tubulins from one species cross-react with tubulin from others (Osborne and Weber 1977), implying the existence of common antigenic determinants. Finally, cloned cDNA probes encoding chicken α- and β-tubulins are able to cross-hybridize, even at high stringency, with genomic DNAs from a variety of other eukaryotic species (Cleveland, Lopata, Cowan, McDonald, Rutter and Kirschner 1980).

Because of the multiplicity of microtubule function, it is perhaps not surprising that the structure of α- and β-tubulin has been evolutionarily conserved. However, the mechanisms underlying the involvement of microtubules in so many different (and apparently unrelated) cellular processes are wholly unknown. Two general models may be considered to explain the functional diversity of microtubules. (1) A number of different α- and β-tubulin genes can be transcribed, each yielding a similar but distinct polypeptide. Small differences in the polypeptide sequence could then constitute signals for functional specificity, and result in the assembly of unique kinds of microtubule that are destined for a specific cellular role. (2) Microtubules are assembled from tubulins translated from a pool of mRNAs, a consequence of the transcription of one or more α- and β-tubulin genes. Functional specificity could then be conferred on the assembled (or assembling) structure via post-translational modification and/or interaction of one or more tubulins with cellular factors that are independent of tubulin genes themselves. Investigating the validity of these general models requires an examination of tubulin proteins and, additionally, a knowledge of tubulin gene structure and the factors that regulate tubulin gene expression. Structural analysis of tubulin genes from several species also allows evolutionary comparisons to be made, and adds to a general understanding of the organization and expression of multigene families. This review describes our current knowledge of tubulin gene sequences, and includes a discussion of their evolutionary implications and the factors that influence their expression.

Number and complexity of tubulin genes

HETEROGENEITY OF TUBULIN PROTEINS

The literature is replete with reports describing heterogeneity or 'microheterogeneity' in α- and β-tubulin proteins. With few exceptions, these publications describe multiple bands or spots following resolution on one- or two-dimensional gel systems. However, such heterogeneity could be a consequence either of the expression of several genes each yielding a slightly different protein, or of the post-translational modification of one or more gene products, or both. Because experiments that focus on protein microheterogeneity cannot by their nature distinguish between these alternatives, no conclusions can be usefully drawn from them about the complexity of the tubulin multigene families, and no attempt is made to review them here. Sequence heterogeneity at the amino acid level, on the other hand, does provide definitive evidence of the transcription of multiple tubulin genes, even though only limited inferences about genetic structure and organization can be made from amino acid sequence data. The complete amino acid sequence of α- and β-tubulin from porcine brain microtubules has revealed that internal sequence heterogeneity does indeed exist (Ponstingl, Little, Krauhs and Kempf 1981; Krauhs, Little, Kempf, Hofer-Warbinek, Ade and Ponstingl 1981) (Figs 2.1 and 2.2). The two chains, when optimally aligned, are 41 per cent homologous, indicative of divergence from a common ancestral gene. Both chains are devoid of disulphide bridges. In the case of α-tubulin, at least six positions (around amino acid 270) can each be occupied by one of two amino acids. Assignment of these alternative sites to specific peptides allowed Ponstingl et al. (1981) to conclude that four distinct α-tubulin genes are expressed in porcine brain. Analysis of β-tubulin from the same source also revealed internal microheterogeneity, which points to the expression of at least two different β-tubulin genes.

TUBULIN-SPECIFIC cDNA PROBES

Because the purification of tubulin protein depends on the *in vitro* polymerization of microtubules, the product obtained from cells or tissue express-

```
                           10            20            30            40            50
human (kα1)   M R E C I S I H V G Q A G V Q I G N A C W E L Y C L E H G I Q P D G Q M P S D K T I G G G D D S F N
human (bα1)
pig
rat (λαT14)
chicken (pT1)


                           60            70            80            90           100
human (kα1)   T F F S E T G A G K H V P R A V F V D L E P T V I D E V R T G T Y R E L F H P E Q L I T G K E D A A
human (bα1)
pig                                                                  Q
rat (λαT14)
chicken (pT1)


                          110           120           130           140           150
human (kα1)   N N Y A R G H Y T I G K E I I D L V L D R I R K L A D Q C T G L Q G F L V F H S F G G G T G S G F T
human (bα1)
pig                                                                  S
rat (λαT14)
chicken (pT1)                                                        S


                          160           170           180           190           200
human (kα1)   S L L M E R L S V D Y G K K S K L E F S I Y P A P Q V S T A V V E P Y N S I L T T H T T L E H S D C
human (bα1)
pig
rat (λαT14)
chicken (pT1)                                       R


                          210           220           230           240           250
human (kα1)   A F M V D N E A I Y D I C R R N L D I E R P T Y T N L N R L I S Q I V S S I T A S L R F D G A L N V
human (bα1)                                                      G
pig                                                              G
rat (λαT14)                                                      G
chicken (pT1)                                                    G


                          260           270           280           290           300
human (kα1)   D L T E F Q T N L V P Y P R I H F P L A T Y A P V I S A E K A Y H E Q L S V A E I T N A C F E P A N
human (bα1)
pig                              /G/I        /R/F/B
                                 (A)
rat (λαT14)
chicken (pT1)
urchin (pa2)                                                            ‖


                          310           320           330           340           350
human (kα1)   Q M V K C D P R H G K Y M A C C L L Y R G D V V P K D V N A A I A T I K T K R T I Q F V D W C P T G
human (bα1)
pig                                                                 /S
rat (λαT14)
rat (pT25)        ‖                                                  S
chicken (pT1)
urchin (pa2)                         M


                          360           370           380           390           400
human (kα1)   F K V G I N Y Q P P T V V P G G D L A K V Q R A V C M L S N T T A I A E A W A R L D H K F D L M Y A
human (bα1)
pig               E
rat (λαT14)
rat (pT25)
chicken (pT1)
urchin (pa2)


                          410           420           430           440           450
human (kα1)   K R A F V H W Y V G E G M E E G E F S E A R E D M A A L E K D Y E E V G V D S V E G E G E E E G E E Y
human (bα1)
pig
rat (λαT14)
rat (pT25)
chicken (pT1)
urchin (pa2)                          L                                          A
```

Fig. 2.1. Comparison of known amino acid sequences of α-tubulin. Data from Cowan *et al.* 1983 (human): Krauhs *et al.* 1981 (pig): Lemischka *et al.* 1981 (rat $\lambda\alpha$T14); Ginzburg *et al.* 1981 (rat pT25); Valenzuela *et al.* 1980 (chicken); Alexandraki and Ruderman 1983 (sea urchin). Where data was obtained from cDNA clones of incomplete length, the symbol ‖ indicates the 5′-limit of the amino acid sequence. Where protein sequence data showed internal heterogeneity, each alternative is shown in the figure.

```
                      10            20            30            40            50
human (Dß-1)  M R E I V H I Q A G Q C G N Q I G A K F W E V I S D E H G I D P T G T Y H G D S D L Q L D R I S V Y
pig                                                                     S  /V              E    /N
chicken (ß2)                                                            S                  E    N
chicken (ß4)                                                          S  N   V             E
yeast         I     S     Y          A        T  C G        L   F W          H D   I   K E   L W

                      60            70            80            90           100
human (Dß-1)  Y N E A T G G K Y V P R A I L V D L E P G T M D S V R S G P F G Q I F R P D N F V F G Q S G A G N N
pig           A/S/SN/H
chicken (ß2)          N
chicken (ß4)  S S H
yeast         F     S S     T        S   N           W   I   A     N S A I   N L        Y I        S        V

                     110           120           130           140           150
human (Dß-1)  W A K G H Y T E G A E L V D S V L D V V R K E A E S C D C L Q G F Q L T H S L G G G T G S G M G T L
pig                                               S
chicken (ß2)                                      S
chicken (ß4)                                      C   N
yeast                                   M     I R       G   S        I

                     160           170           180           190           200
human (Dß-1)  L I S K I R E E Y P D R I M N T F S V V P S P K V S D T V V E P Y N A T L S V H Q L V E N T D E T Y
pig
chicken (ß2)                             M
chicken (ß4)      V                                                              I
yeast         F     K     L     M   A        L       T                              H S           F

                     210           220           230           240           250
human (Dß-1)  C I D N E A L Y D I C F R T L R L T T P T Y G D L N H L V S G T M E C V T T C L R F P G Q L N A D L
pig                                   K                           A     S G
chicken (ß2)                          K                           A     S G
chicken (ß4)                          K   A                       A     S G        S
yeast                         Q       K   N Q   S           N     S V   S G        S     Y           S

                     260           270           280           290           300
human (Dß-1)  R K L A V N M V P F P R L H F F M P G F A P L T S R G S Q Q Y R A L T V P D L T Q Q V F D A K N M M
pig                                               /A                        C       M
chicken (ß2)                                                               E       M   S
chicken (ß4)                                      R                        E       M   A        .
urchin (pß3)                                                               S E     M
yeast                L                       V   Y       A I       S F   S   E       M   E

                     310           320           330           340           350
human (Dß-1)  A A C D P R H G R Y L T V A A V F R G R M S M K E V D E Q M L N V Q N K N S S Y F V E W I P N N V K
pig
chicken (ß2)                          I
chicken (ß4)                          T                         . A I   S
urchin (pß3)                          I
urchin (pß1)                                                                                        ‖        Q
yeast         A     N           F       K V   V       E D E   H K     S       D

                     360           370           380           390           400
human (Dß-1)  T A V C D I P P R G L K M A V T F I G N S T A I Q E L F K R I S E Q F T A M F R R K A F L H W Y T G
pig                                   S A
chicken (ß2)                          S S
chicken (ß4)  V                       S S
urchin (pß3)                          S A
urchin (pß1)                          S A
yeast               S V A   Q     D   A       A       S           V G D       S       K                 S

                     410           420           430           440
human (Dß-1)  E G M D E M E F T E A E S N M N D L V S E Y Q Q Y Q D A T A E E E E D F G E E A E E E A.
human (5ß)                                                          *   Q G E     E              V A.
pig                                                                 D   Q G E     E        G     D E A.
chicken ß2(=ß1)                                                     D   Q G E     E        G     D E A.
chicken (ß3)                                                            G E   E                  E.
chicken (ß4)                                                            G E M Y        D D       S E Q G A K.
urchin (pß3)                                                            G E   D        E G D E E A A.
urchin (pß1)                                                                           E G E D E E A A.
yeast         L     S                                        E     V   D D   E V D   N G D F G   P Q N Q D E P I T E N F E.
```

Fig. 2.2. Comparison of known amino acid sequences of β-tubulin. Data from Gwo-Shu Lee *et al.* 1983 (human Dβ-1); Hall *et al.* 1983 (human 5β); Ponstingl 1981 (pig); Sullivan *et al.* 1984 (chicken β2 and β4); Alexandraki and Ruderman 1983 (sea urchin): Neff *et al.* 1983 (yeast). Where data was obtained from cDNA clones of incomplete length, the symbol ‖ indicates the 5′-limit of the amino acid sequence. Where protein sequence data showed internal heterogeneity, each alternative is shown in the figure.

ing more than one different α- and β-tubulin gene will contain a mixture of tubulin gene products and, as such, has the potential for internal sequence heterogeneity. This, in addition to its labour-intensive nature, makes amino acid sequencing an arduous task in defining tubulin gene complexity. A simpler and therefore more attractive approach has been via the construction and sequence analysis of tubulin-specific cDNA clones, not least because such probes provide the additional potential for the isolation, characterization and chromosomal mapping of the genes themselves (see below).

The tubulin multigene families. The first α- and β-tubulin cDNA clones were constructed using embryonic chicken brain as the source of mRNA. Analysis of chicken α- and β-tubulin mRNAs by cell-free translation showed them to be indistinguishable in size, though a partial resolution could be obtained under native (non-denaturing) conditions, a result presumably ascribable to differences in secondary structure (Cleveland, Kirschner and Cowan 1978). Using this material as substrate, cDNA clones corresponding to about 75 per cent and >90 per cent of the sequences present in chicken α- and β-tubulin mRNA were obtained (Cleveland, Lopata, Cowan, McDonald, Rutter and Kirschner 1980). Although there is significant homology between α- and β-tubulin at the amino acid level, no cross-hybridization is detectable between the two probes. On the other hand, both chicken tubulin cDNA probes do cross-hybridize with genomic sequences from all eukaryotic species tested (with the exception of yeast) under conditions of high stringency. Yeast tubulin sequences are detectable with the chicken sequences under lower stringency conditions (Neff, Thomas, Grisafi and Botstein 1983). Use of the chicken cDNA probes in Southern blot experiments with genomic DNA from different eukaryotic species gives a surprisingly varied picture. In the homologous case, that is, chicken, about four bands are detectable with a given restriction enzyme. This figure seems to represent the number of genes, since four distinct β-tubulin sequences have been isolated from the chicken genome as recombinant fragments (Lopata, Havercroft, Chow and Cleveland 1983). By contrast, sea urchin, mouse, rat and human DNA all contain much larger multigene families, with about 15–20 members each. The significance of the large multigene families in mammals is discussed below.

Since the construction of the chicken α- and β-tubulin cDNA probes, others have been obtained from several species, including rat (Lemischka, Farmer, Racaniello and Sharp 1981; Ginzburg, Behar, Givol and Littauer 1981), human (Cowan, Dobner, Fuchs and Cleveland 1983; Hall, Dudley, Dobner, Lewis and Cowan 1983), sea urchin (Alexandraki and Ruderman 1981, 1983), and *Chlamydomonas* (Silflow and Rosenblum 1981). The majority of these clones have been sequenced, yielding either complete or partial amino acid sequence data; in addition, complete sequences have been determined for two expressed chicken β-tubulin genes (Sullivan, Lau and Cleveland 1984), an expressed human β-tubulin gene (Gwo-Shu Lee, Lewis, Wilde and Cowan 1983), an expressed rat α-tubulin gene (Lemischka and Sharp 1982), and the single β-tubulin gene present in yeast (Neff *et al.* 1983).

Tubulin isotypes. Inspection of the amino acid sequence data for α-tubulins derived either directly (pig) or via cDNA or genomic clones (human, rat, chicken, sea urchin) reveals very extensive homology (Fig. 2.1). Indeed, among the mammalian sequences (human, pig, and rat) there is variability at only five (out of a total of 451) amino acid residues. The sea urchin sequence is equally remarkably conserved. Within the 161 C-terminal amino acids encoded by a sea urchin cDNA clone, there are three substitutions compared with corresponding human sequences. Comparison of two complete intraspecies sequences (i.e. human kα1 and bα1) reveals an even stricter conservation: here, only a single substitution appears (glycine $\rightarrow$ serine) at position 232.

An interesting feature of all the α-tubulin cDNA-derived sequences is the existence of a tyrosine codon immediately preceding the termination codon. An α-tubulin-specific enzyme that adds tyrosine to the protein, requires ATP and functions in the presence of protein synthesis inhibitors has been reported (Raybin and Flavin, 1977). However, the C-terminal tyrosine codon present in all α-tubulin cDNAs thus far sequenced shows that the primary post-translational event is the enzymatic removal, rather than the addition, of tyrosine (Valenzuela, Quiroga, Zaldivar, Rutter, Kirschner and Cleveland 1981; Lemischka *et al.* 1981; Cowan *et al.* 1983). The functional significance of this enzyme is not known.

In the case of β-tubulin, the picture is significantly different. Although there is still a very high degree of conservation, there is greater overall divergence between β-tubulin amino acid sequences. Several of these differences are scattered throughout the chain, but, in addition, there is a conspicuous lack of homology in the carboxyterminal regions as well as differences in the length of the peptides. The lack of C-terminal homology applies to β-tubulin sequences both within a single species (Hall *et al.* 1983; Sullivan *et al.* 1984) as well as across species boundaries (see Fig. 2.2). Within a species, each distinctively different β-tubulin gene product has been termed an isotype (Hall *et al.* 1983). In view of the C-terminal variability that contributes to the distinction between different isotypes, and because of known differences in the level of expression of different tubulin genes among various tissues and cell types (see section on 'Tubulin gene expression and its regulation' below), it is tempting to speculate that the C-terminus may contribute to the determination of particular kinds of microtubule function. The acidic nature of the C-terminal sequences suggests their location on the exterior of the folded peptide, making it available for further interactions. It remains to be seen whether different kinds of microtubule are enriched in one or more β-tubulin isotype, or, if not, whether secondary isotype-specific interactions contribute to functional specificity. These alternatives should now be open to experimental test, since the β-tubulin C-terminal differences are probably sufficient to permit their use as peptide haptens for the generation of monoclonal antisera. Such sera might then be used as fluorescent probes for assessing the contribution of distinct isotypes to functionally distince microtubules within a single cell.

Features of the 3'-untranslated regions. No recognizable homology can be found when comparing the 3'-untranslated regions of any α-tubulin cDNA with any β-tubulin cDNA, either within or across species boundaries; nor is there homology between these regions among α- and β-tubulin cDNAs from within the same species. Remarkably, however, comparison of the 3'-untranslated regions of each of two human α-tubulin cDNA clones with the corresponding regions of two rat α-tubulin cDNA clones reveals extensive (65 per cent and 80 per cent) interspecies homology (Cowan *et al.* 1983) (Fig. 2.3). The function of the 3'-untranslated region of eukaryotic mRNAs, other than to signal the addition of polyA, is unknown. The unexpected interspecies 3'-untranslated region homology implies the existence of selective constraints that have maintained sequence homology following species divergence: indeed, a residual 3'-untranslated region homology extending over a 27 bp region exists between human (bα1) and chicken (pT1) β-tubulin cDNA. No open reading frames exist in any of the 3'-untranslated regions, and the functional significance of these interspecies homologies in unclear.

Expressed and non-expressed tubulin genes

The size of the multigene families encoding tubulin varies considerably among different species. An important question therefore concerns the structural diversity and role of multiple genomic tubulin sequences. One possible approach to this issue is to search for different cDNA clones and by sequence analysis, to establish the number of transcribed genes. However, because cDNA libraries are usually constructed using mRNA isolated from a particular tissue and/or developmental stage, it is difficult to make such a search exhaustive. An alternative approach is to isolate tubulin-specific genomic sequences by screening recombinant libraries. A combination of sequence analysis together with DNA and RNA blot transfer experiments may then be performed to determine whether the gene is a candidate for functional transcription.

TUBULIN PSEUDOGENES

Reintegrated copies of processed mRNA. A major factor contributing to the large tubulin multigene family present in mammals has recently become

```
                    10        20        30        40
pT1         GAGTTCACAACGGTGCTGCTCGTACAGGGAACAA
                   :::::: ::::::::::: :::::::::::
bα1         AGTTAAAACGTCACAAAGGTGCTGCTTTTACAGGGAAGCT
            : :: ::: ::::: :::::::::::::: ::::::: : :
pILαT1      A-TT-AAATGTCAC-AAGGTGCTGCTTTCACAGGGATGTT

                    50        60        70        80
bα1         TATTCTGTTTTAAACATTGAAAATGTTGTGGTCTGATCAG
            ::::::: : ::::: :::: :::::::::::::::::
pILαT1      TATTCTG-GTCCAACATAGAAA--GTTGTGGGCTGATCAG

                    90       100       110       120
bα1         TTAATTTGTATGTAGCAGTGTATCGCTCTCATATACAATT
            ::::::::::::::: ::: ::: :  : ::::: :   ::
pILαT1      TTAATTTGTATGTGGCAATGTGTGCTG-TCATACAG--TT

                   130       140       150       160
bα1         AGCTGACCTATGCTCTAAAACTGAATGCCTTTGTTACAGA
            : ::::: :       :::  :::::: ::::: : :::
pILαT1      A-CTGACTT------TAAGTGTGAATGA-TTTGTCAGAGA

                   170       180       190       200
bα1         CCCAAGCTGTCCATTTCTGTGATGGGTTTTGAATAAAGTA
            ::: ::: :::::  :::  :::::::::: :::::: ::
pILαT1      CCCGAGCCGTCCACTTCACTGATGGGTTTTAAATAAAATA

                   210
bα1         TTCCCTGTCTTAAATG
            :::::::::::::
pILαT1      CTCCCTGTCTTA
```

```
                    10        20        30        40
kα1         TTATCCATTCCTTTTGGCCCTGCAGCATGTCATGCTCCCA
            : ::: :::: : ::::: : ::::::: :::
pT25        ---TTCACTCCTGCAGTCCCTGTATCATGTCAAACTC---

                    50        60        70        80
kα1         GAATTTCAGCTTCAGCTTAA-CTGACAGATGTTAAAGCTTT
            ::: : :::::: :::: : ::: :::  :  : ::::
pT25        -AACTCCAGCTCCAGCACTAGCTG-CAGGCATCGATGCTT-

                    90       100       110       120
kα1         CTGGTTAGATTGTTTTCACTTG-GTGATCATGTCTTTTCCA
            ::   :   :::: ::: :::::::::::::: ::::
pT25        CTATGCTG-----TTTCCCTTCTGTGATCATGTCTTCTCCA

                   130       140       150       160
kα1         TGTGTACCTG-TAATATTTTTCCATCATATCTCAAAGTAAA
            :::::::::: :::  :::::::::
pT25        TGTGTACCTCTTAAG--TTTTCCAT

                   170
kα1         GTCATTAACATCA

pT25
```

Fig. 2.3. Interspecies conservation of the 3′-untranslated regions of α-tubulin genes. The optimum alignments of the 3′-untranslated regions from pT1 (chicken), bα1 (human) and rat (pILαT1) are shown in the top half of the figure. Optimum alignments of the 3′-untranslated regions from kα1 (human) and pT25 (rat) are shown below. Data from Cowan *et al* 1983.

clear. The discovery that a significant proportion of the tubulin sequences present in the human genome are pseudogenes stemmed from an initial characterization of sequences isolated by screening recombinant genomic lambda libraries using chicken tubulin cDNA probes. Twelve non-over-lapping regions of β-tubulin-specific regions were obtained, accounting for about two-thirds of the β-tubulin multigene family detected by genomic Southern blot analysis (Cowan, Wilde, Chow and Wefald 1981). These re-combinants were restriction mapped and the location of tubulin-specific sequences defined by Southern blot experiments using the chicken β-tubulin cDNA probe. Many of the β-tubulin-specific regions were surprisingly short—of the order of 1.5 Kb. Previous work (Cleveland *et al.* 1978, 1980) had shown by RNA blot transfer experiments, that β-tubulin mRNA is typically about 1.8 Kb in size. In addition, sequence analysis of the chicken β-tubulin cDNA clone, pT2, showed the coding region to contain 445 amino acids (Valenzuela *et al.* 1981). This figure varies by only a few residues (depending upon the species and/or isotype—see Fig. 2.2), and the formal coding requirement for the polypeptide is therefore around 1335 base pairs. The difference between this figure and the observed size of cytoplasmic β-tubulin mRNA is accounted for in part by the 3'-polyA tract (about 200 bases) and in part by the 5'- and 3'-untranslated regions. The discovery that several genomic β-tubulin sequences are equal or almost equal in size to the mature cytoplasmic mRNA came as a surprise because, with very few ex-ceptions, all eukaryotic genes are interrupted by one or more intervening sequences. These sequences vary considerably in size, are transcribed coli-nearly with the coding regions, and are subsequently removed by an RNA splicing mechanism. In view of the small size of many genomic human β-tubulin sequences, it became evident that the intervening sequence(s) were either unusually short, or altogether absent (Cowan *et al.* 1981).

The nature of the truncated β-tubulin genomic sequences has now been established. As expected on the basis of restriction mapping, DNA sequenc-ing of a 'prototype' short β-tubulin gene, 46β, revealed that there are no intervening sequences (Fig. 2.4). In addition, the gene is rendered non-func-tional because the coding region contains an in-frame termination codon (Ser TCG→TAG) as a result of the substitution of an A-residue in place of a C-residue in the second codon position. In addition, at amino acid position 270, the third base of the phenylalanine codon (TTC) is missing, resulting in a frameshift leading to a termination codon shortly downstream. This pseudogene (a generic term for sequences bearing extensive homology to expressed genes, but 'crippled' by genetic lesions) has two further remark-

Fig. 2.4. Sequence of an expressed human β-tubulin gene (M40) and a closely related processed pseudogene (46β) The polyA tracts and polyA addition signals are underlined; the flanking direct repeats are doubly underlined. Internal in-frame ter-mination codons are boxed; the asterisk indicates a deleted base. Positions of inter-vening sequences in M40 are marked ($\blacktriangledown$). Data from Gwo-Shu Lee *et al.* 1983.

M40
21s

```
                                                            ACCGCGCCCCGCCCAGCCTCCTTTCCTCGCCGCCCTCCCTCTCCTTTCTCCCTCTCAGAAC
                                                            CCAGGCTGGTAGCATATGCCTGTAAGTCCCGGCTACTCAAGAAGCTGAGGTGTCG*      A
```

M40
21s

```
CTTCCTGCCGTCGCGTTTGCACCTCGCTGCTCCAGCCTCTGGGGCGCATTCCAACCTTCCAGCCTGCGACCTGGGAGAAAAAAAATTACTTATTTTCTTGCCCCATACATACCTTGAGGC
      A  C C*  C        C    A      A   A   AT   *        *      A                        G           A T
```

```
                                    Met Arg Glu Ile Val His Ile Gln Ala Gly Gln Cys Gly Asn Gln Ile Gly Ala Lys Phe Trp Glu Val Ile
                                                                                                        10                    20
M40   GAGCAAAAAAATTAAATTTTAACC ATG AGG GAA ATC GTG CAC ATC CAG GCT GGT CAA TGT GGC AAC CAG ATC GGT GCC AAG TTC TGG GAG GTG ATC
21s                                                                 G C                                                      C
```

```
      Ser Asp Glu His Gly Ile Asp Pro Thr Gly Thr Tyr His Gly Asp Ser Asp Leu Gln Leu Asp Arg Ile Ser Val Tyr Tyr Asn Glu Ala
            30                    40                    50
M40   AGT GAT GAA CAT GGC ATC GAC CCC ACC GGC ACC TAC CAC GGG GAC AGC GAC CTG CAG CTG GAC CGC ATC TCT GTG TAC TAC AAT GAA GCC
21s        G                                                                           C                    G
```

```
      Thr Gly Gly Lys Tyr Val Pro Arg Ala Ile Leu Val Asp Leu Glu Pro Gly Thr Met Asp Ser Val Arg Ser Gly Pro Phe Gly Gln Ile
            60                    70                    80
M40   ACA GGT GGC AAA TAT GTT CCT CGT GCC ATC CTG GTG GAT CTA GAA CCT GGG ACC ATG GAC TCT GTT CGC TCA GGT CCT TTT GGC CAG ATC
21s    T CA          A                          A       G
```

```
      Phe Arg Pro Asp Asn Phe Val Phe Gly Gln Ser Gly Ala Gly Asn Asn Trp Ala Lys Gly His Tyr Thr Glu Gly Ala Glu Leu Val Asp
                  90                    100                   110
M40   TTT AGA CCA GAC AAC TTT GTA TTT GGT CAG TCT GGG GCA GGT AAC AAC TGG GCC AAA GGC CAC TAC ACA GAG GGC GCC GAG CTG GTT GAT
21s                                                 C
```

```
      Ser Val Leu Asp Val Val Arg Lys Glu Ala Glu Ser Cys Asp Cys Leu Gln Gly Phe Gln Leu Thr His Ser Leu Gly Gly Gly Thr Gly
            120                   130                   140
M40   TCT GTC CTG GAT GTG GTA CGG AAG GAG GCA GAG AGC TGT GAC TGC CTG CAG GGC TTC CAG CTG ACC CAC TCA CTG GGC GGG GGC ACA GGC
21s                                              C                            C               T  C
```

```
      Ser Gly Met Gly Thr Leu Leu Ile Ser Lys Ile Arg Glu Glu Tyr Pro Asp Arg Ile Met Asn Thr Phe Ser Val Val Pro Ser Pro Lys
            150                   160                   170
M40   TCT GGA ATG GGC ACT CTC CTT ATC AGC AAG ATC CGA GAA GAA TAC CCT GAT CGC ATC ATG AAT ACC TTC AGT GTG GTG CCT TCA CCC AAA
21s
```

```
      Val Ser Asp Thr Val Val Glu Pro Tyr Asn Ala Thr Leu Ser Val His Gln Leu Val Glu Asn Thr Asp Glu Thr Tyr Cys Ile Asp Asn
            180                   190                   200
M40   GTG TCT GAC ACC GTG GTC GAG CCC TAC AAT GCC ACC CTC TCC GTC CAT CAG TTG GTA GAG AAT ACT GAT GAG ACC TAT TGC ATT GAC AAC
21s                                   A        T        T  G                     C
```

```
      Glu Ala Leu Tyr Asp Ile Cys Phe Arg Thr Leu Arg Leu Thr Thr Pro Thr Tyr Gly Asp Leu Asn His Leu Val Ser Gly Thr Met Glu
            210                   220                   230
M40   GAG GCC CTC TAT GAT ATC TGC TTC CGC ACT CTG AGG CTG ACC ACA CCA ACC TAC GGG GAT CTG AAC CAC CTT GTC TCA GGC ACC ATG GAG
21s                                        G             C       T       C     T C G A A
```

```
      Cys Val Thr Thr Cys Leu Arg Phe Pro Gly Gln Leu Asn Ala Asp Leu Arg Lys Leu Ala Val Asn Met Val Pro Phe Pro Arg Leu His
                  240                   250                   260
M40   TGT GTC ACC ACC TGC CTC CGT TTC CCT GGC CAG CTC AAT GCT GAC CTC CGC AAG TTG GCA GTC AAC ATG GTC CCC TTC CCA CGT CTC CAT
21s                         C                                            T
```

```
      Phe Phe Met Pro Gly Phe Ala Pro Leu Thr Ser Arg Gly Ser Gln Gln Tyr Arg Ala Leu Thr Val Pro Glu Leu Thr Gln Gln Val Phe
            270                   280                   290
M40   TTC TTT ATG CCT GGC TTT GCC CCT CTC ACC AGC CGT GGA AGC CAG CAG TAT CGA GCT CTC ACA GTG CCG GAC CTC ACC CAG CAG GTC TTC
21s        C        CT  *                       A                   A AG
```

```
      Asp Ala Lys Asn Met Met Ala Ala Cys Asp Pro Arg His Gly Arg Tyr Leu Thr Val Ala Ala Val Phe Arg Gly Arg Met Ser Met Lys
            300                   310                   320
M40   GAT GCC AAG AAC ATG ATG GCT GCC TGT GAC CCC CGC CAC GGC CGA TAC CTC ACC GCT GCT GTC TTC CGT GGT CGG ATG TCC ATG AAG
21s             G                       C T   G                       A
```

```
      Glu Val Asp Glu Gln Met Leu Asn Val Gln Asn Lys Asn Ser Ser Tyr Phe Val Glu Trp Ile Pro Asn Asn Val Lys Thr Ala Val Cys
            330                   340                   350
M40   GAG GTC GAT GAG CAG ATG CTT AAC GTG CAG AAC AAG AAC AGC AGC TAC TTT GTG GAA TGG ATC CCC AAC AAT GTC AAG ACA GCC GTC TGT
21s                        T                                                          A            T
```

```
      Asp Ile Pro Pro Arg Gly Leu Lys Met Ala Val Thr Phe Ile Gly Asn Ser Thr Ala Ile Gln Glu Leu Phe Lys Arg Ile Ser Glu Gln
            360                   370                   380
M40   GAC ATC CCA CCT CGT GGC CTC AAG ATG GCA GTC ACC TTC ATT GGT AAT AGC ACC GCC ATC CAG GAG CTC TTC AAG CGC ATC TCG GAG CAG
21s                              C     G        G                                              A
```

```
      Phe Thr Ala Met Phe Arg Arg Lys Ala Phe Leu His Trp Tyr Thr Gly Glu Gly Met Asp Glu Met Glu Phe Thr Glu Ala Glu Ser Asn
            390                   400                   410
M40   TTC ACT GCC ATG TTC CGC CGG AAG GCC TTC CTC CAC TGG TAC ACA GGC GAG GGC ATG GAC GAG ATG GAG TTC ACC GAG GCT GAG AGC AAC
21s                                                                                                                     C
```

```
      Met Asn Asp Leu Val Ser Glu Tyr Gln Gln Tyr Gln Asp Ala Thr Ala Glu Glu Glu Glu Asp Phe Gly Glu Glu Ala Glu Glu Glu Ala
            420                   430                   440
M40   ATG AAC GAC CTC GTC TCT GAG TAT CAG CAG TAC CAG GAT GCC ACC GCA GAA GAG GAG GAT TTC GGT GAG GAG GCC GAA GAG GAG GCC
21s                                                                               G                        A
```

```
      Op
M40   TAAGGAGAGCCCCCATCACCTCAGGCTTCTCAGTTCCCTTAGCCGTCTTACTCAACTGCCCCTTTCCTCTCCCTCAGAATTTGTGTTTGCTGCCTCTATCTTGTTTTTTGTTTTTTCTT
21s        A                                                                      G
```

```
M40   C.TGGGGGGGGGTCTAGAATTCCAGAACAGTGCCTGGCAATAGTAGGCGCTCAATAAATACTTGTTTGTTGAATCTCTCCTCTCTCTTTCCACTCTGGGAAACCTAGGTTTCTGCCATTCT
21s          A         ********  *                            A    _____                     GAAAAAAAAAAAAAAAAGGCTGAGGTGTCAGGATCCCTTGAGCCTGGGCA
```

able features. Shortly downstream from the hexanucleotide AATAAA that signals the addition of polyA to eukaryotic mRNAs there appears a long uninterrupted tract of A-residues. Finally, the entire sequence is flanked by a short directly repeated sequence. In accounting for the origin of processed pseudogenes, the acquisition of genetic lesions, the flanking direct repeat, the absence of intervening sequences (which do exist in expressed tubulin genes) (see section on 'Structure of expressed tubulin genes' below) and the 3'-polyA tract must all be adequately explained.

Both the addition of A-residues to mRNA molecules and the removal of intervening sequences are post-transcriptional events. Thus, the discovery of an intronless sequence with a 3'-polyA tract in genomic DNA suggests the reverse transcription of a polyadenylated mRNA to form cDNA, and the integration of this reverse transcript into the genome. The known poly-merases capable of synthesizing cDNAs all require primers for the initiation of both plus and minus strands. One way in which priming can occur is for the RNA template strand to fold back upon itself (Bernstein, Mount and Weiner 1983), a mechanism which has been proposed to explain the genera-

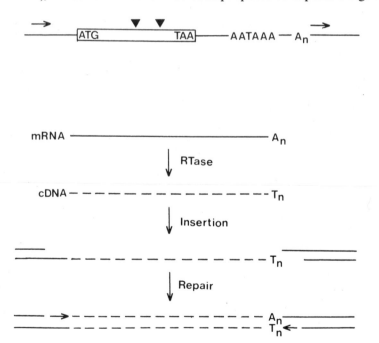

Fig. 2.5. Features of an intronless polyA-containing pseudogene and its possible mode of integration into the host chromosome. Top: mRNA-derived pseudogene showing the intronless coding region (boxed) containing internal genetic lesions (▼), the AATAAA polyadenylation signal, polyA tract and flanking direct repeats. Below: possible mechanism for the insertion of a cDNA intermediate into a staggered host chromosomal break.

tion of some human U3 RNA pseudogenes. However, self-priming of this kind necessarily leads to incomplete copies, and therefore cannot explain the generation of human tubulin pseudogenes. Thus, the nature of first and second strand priming is unknown, as are the enzymes involved. Nonetheless, given the rarity of successful integration, it is conceivable that known polymerases might accomplish successful transcription of mRNA templates. How the cDNA sequence became integrated into the genome is also a matter of speculation. One possible explanation is that insertion took place at a staggered host chromosomal break; flanking direct repeats could then be generated by repair at the target site (Van Arsdell, Denison, Bernstein, Weiner, Manser and Gesteland 1981) (Fig. 2.5).

. Several intronless polyA-containing human β-tubulin sequences have now been characterized (Wilde, Crowther, Cripe, Gwo-Shu Lee and Cowan 1982a; Wilde, Crowther and Cowan 1982b; Gwo-Shu Lee et al. 1983). All share the same mRNA-like features and flanking direct repeats, though these sequences are not related to one another. Thus, successful integration does not seem to depend upon the presence of a common target site. Inspection of the sequence data within the coding regions reveals a broad range of divergence relative to the parental expressed sequence, varying from a few residues to multiple substitutions, insertions and deletions that significantly reduce the overall homology. Because the homology with the expressed sequence never extends 5' to the cap site, and in the absence of recognizable upstream promoter signals, it seems likely that the integrated transcripts are not themselves transcribed. In that case, their rate of divergence from the prototype sequence should be the average rate (about 0.7 per cent per 10^6 years; Perler, Efstratiadis, Lomedico, Gilbert, Kolodner and Dodgson 1980) for a region of DNA not subject to selective pressure (Fig. 2.6). Ultimately, therefore, mRNA-derived pseudogenes may lose all resemblance with respect to the parental gene as they decay into the genomic background; indeed, the genome probably contains many such elements in varying stages of degeneration. Experimental evidence that this is in fact the case comes from Southern blot experiments performed with a β-tubulin cDNA probe: as the stringency conditions are lowered, the number of detectable bands increases.

The existence of mRNA-derived pseudogenes is not unique to the tubulin multigene families. Sequences with the same hallmarks of RNA processing have also been noted in the human metallothionein (Karin and Richards 1982) and dihydrofolate reductase multigene families (Chen, Shimada, Moulton, Harrison and Nienhuis 1982). In principle, the synthesis and chromosomal integration of cDNA copies could occur in any cell type; however, only integration events occurring in germ-line cells will be propagated, and one might therefore expect the bulk of mRNA-derived pseudogenes to involve sequences that are transcribed in germ-cell tissues. In addition, the successful propagation of integrated sequences requires

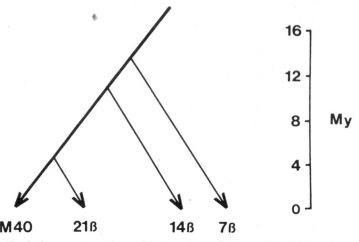

Fig. 2.6. Evolutionary tree: time of integration of three related intronless pseudo-genes into the host germ-line. Based on the data of Gwo-Shu Lee *et al.* 1983.

that there be no significant deleterious effect on the proper functioning of the cell.

Other tubulin pseudogenes. Not all the pseudogenes present in the human tubulin multigene families were derived via an mRNA intermediate. At least one human β-tubulin pseudogene contains a short intervening sequence, interrupting the coding region at Gly93, where the third intervening sequence occurs in a functionally expressed β-tubulin gene (Wilde, Crowther and Cowan 1982*b*; Gwo-Shu Lee *et al.* 1983). However, there are two single-base deletions in the first codon positions of Gly269 and Gly400, that quickly lead to in-phase termination codons at amino acid positions 361 and 405. Furthermore, no sequences encoding amino acids 5′ to threonine (55) could be detected, at least within 15 Kb of the remainder of the coding region, using a β-tubulin-specific cDNA probe. Although the existence of an inter-vening sequence greater than 15 Kb cannot be ruled out, it seems more likely that some DNA rearrangement (such as deletion, inversion or re-combination) with a break-point upstream from amino acid 55 resulted in the loss of N-terminal sequences in this gene.

STRUCTURE OF EXPRESSED TUBULIN GENES

Complete sequence information is currently available for the expressed tub-ulin genes listed in Table 2.1. Because of the extensive nature of the data, the reader is referred to the original publications for restriction maps and nucleotide sequences; amino acid sequences are shown in Figs 2.1 and 2.2. The following comparative observations are noteworthy.

Table 2.1

Data source for sequences of α- and β-tubulin genes.

Species	Clone designation	Reference
Rat (α)	λαT14	Lemischka and Sharp (1982)
Human (β)	M40	Gwo-Shu Lee *et al.* (1983)
Chicken (β)	β2	Sullivan *et al.* (1984)
Chicken (β)	β4	
Yeast (β)	TUB2	Neff *et al.* (1983)

For both α- and β-tubulin genes thus far sequenced, there is a general conservation in the number and position of coding regions (exons) (Fig. 2.7). All
vertebrate tubulin genes appear to contain three intervening sequences. In β-
tubulins, the interruptions in the coding regions occur immediately following
Lys19 and at Gly56 and Gly93 (the latter two codons being split by the
second and third intervening sequences, respectively). In α-tubulin genes,
interruptions appear immediately following the initiator Met residue, as
well as splitting the codon specifying Asp76 and following Leu125. The
sequences flanking the introns in all cases comply with consensus splice
junction sequences, but the introns themselves vary considerably in size. In
the case of human tubulin genes, some of the intervening sequences contain
interesting features. Both M40 (Gwo-Shu Lee *et al.* 1983) and 5β (Gwo-Shu
Lee *et al.* 1984) contain one (M40) or ten (5β) *Alu* elements in the first
(M40) and third (5β) introns, respectively. These middle repetitive sequences
are present in the human genome at a frequency of about 3×10^5, and have
the characteristics of transposable elements (Jelinek and Schmid 1982). A
human α-tubulin gene, bα1, contains two regions of multiple repeats of the
dinucleotide GT, one eighteen and the other ten units in length. It has been

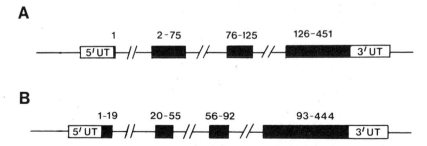

Fig. 2.7. Conservation of exon size among tubulin genes. Diagram (not to scale)
showing the exon pattern common to (a) α-tubulin and (b) β-tubulin genes. Numbers
indicate amino acids encoded by each exon (note, however, that some codons are
split by intervening sequences—see text). The number of amino acids encoded in the
C-terminal exon also varies (see Figs. 2.1 and 2.2) depending on the isotype.

50   Nicholas J. Cowan

speculated that these regions of DNA may exist in the Z conformation, but their functional significance *in vivo*, if any, is unknown. Curiously, not all tubulin genes contain the so-called TATA sequence commonly found in eukaryotic genes at position-35 relative to the cap site; this is the case for at least one human β-tubulin gene (M40; Gwo-Shu Lee *et al.* 1983), as well as a chicken β-tubulin gene (Sullivan *et al.* 1984). The significance of these unusual promoter sequences is not clear.

With the exception of the interspecies conservation of 3'-untranslated regions in two α-tubulin genes (see previously) there appear to be no lengthy homologies between the untranslated regions of tubulin genes. In addition, while the mRNAs for α-tubulin do not appear to vary in size, the length of mature cytoplasmic mRNAs encoding β-tubulin depends upon the gene in question. One human β-tubulin gene generates two mRNA species of 1.8 and 2.6 Kb as a result of alternative polyadenylation sites (Gwo-Shu Lee *et al.* 1983). Different chicken β-tubulin genes also yield characteristically sized mRNAs (Table 2.2). The location of sequences that may be important in determining tissue-specific expression is as yet unknown, but it is intriguing

Table 2.2

Differential expression of β-tubulin genes in chicken cells and tissues (Havercroft and Cleveland, 1984). E = embryo; A = adult.

mRNA size (Kb)	β1 4.0	β2 1.8	β3 1.8	β4 3.5–3.7	E
CELLS:					
fibroblast	+	+	+ +	+	E
chondroplasts	+	+ +	+	+	E
skeletal muscle	+ +	+	+ +	+	E
smooth muscle	+	+	+ +	+	E
neurons	+	+	+ + +	+	E
glia	+	+	+ +	+	E
hepatocytes		+ + +		+	A
primitive RBC's		+ + +		+	E
TISSUES:					
Lung	+	+	+ +	+	A
Oesophagus	+	+ +	+	+ +	A
Oviduct	+	+ +		+ +	A
Liver		+ + +		+	A
Brain	+	+	+ +	+	A
Brain	+	+	+ + + +		E
Gut		+ + +		+ +	A
Spleen		+ + +	+	+	A
Bursa		+ + +		+ +	A
Thymus		+ + +		+ +	A
Testis	+			+ + + + + +	A

to speculate that regions analogous to the so-called identifier sequences, alleged to specify tissue-specific expression in brain-specific genes (Sutcliffe, Milner, Bloom and Lerner 1982), might be found in at least some tubulin genes.

EVOLUTIONARY RELATIONSHIPS WITHIN TUBULIN MULTIGENE FAMILIES

Structural analysis of cloned human α- and β-tubulin genes has shown that, of the 15 or so sequences present in the genome, the majority are pseudogenes, mostly of the processed type (see above). This picture seems likely to be typical of mammalian species, where the tubulin multigene families are of similar size. The extent of sequence conservation within the coding regions is such that coding region probes cannot be used to distinguish among them. On the other hand, the untranslated regions, at least in the case of β-tubulin, show no evidence of extensive regions of conservation, either within or across species boundaries. (Curiously, the same does not hold true in the case of α-tubulin; see above). If 3'-untranslated regions are largely free from selective pressure, they can undergo random change; sequence homologies among them may then be taken as evidence of a recent common ancestor.

An approach based on 3'-untranslated region homologies has been successfully used for the dissection of the human β-tubulin multigene family. A subcloned 3'-untranslated region probe derived from a human β-tubulin cDNA (Hall et al. 1983) was used to identify homologous sequences in human genomic DNA in a Southern blot experiment (Gwo-Shu Lee et al. 1983). The pattern of bands obtained was relatively simple compared with the total β-tubulin gene complement identified with the intact cDNA probe; only about four bands were visible per restriction digest. Because the subcloned 3'-untranslated region probe was relatively short and contained no site for any of the restriction enzymes used, this figure must represent the number of genomic sequences bearing sequence relatedness. All four genomic sequences were subsequently isolated by screening recombinant λ genomic libraries. Each contained a distinct β-tubulin hybridizing region. One of the recombinants contained an expressed β-tubulin gene because within the coding regions there is perfect homology with the cDNA clone Dβ-1. All three remaining sequences were intronless polyA-containing pseudogenes (see before). With the exception of third codon position changes that do not affect the amino acid sequence, the coding regions of the parental expressed β-tubulin gene have remained essentially fixed through time. Comparison with the pseudogene coding sequences therefore allows an estimate to be made of the time at which they became integrated into the germ-line (Fig. 2.6). The existence of a parental expressed gene and a set of progeny RNA-mediated pseudogenes in varying stages of divergence is probably typical of the entire β-tubulin gene family in humans and, indeed, other mammalian species also. The absence of a corresponding multigene family infrastructure in chickens is a curiosity; possibly these animals lack one or more of the enzymes necessary for the generation and/or integration of cDNA intermediates.

CHROMOSOMAL LOCALIZATION OF TUBULIN GENES

Most species thus far examined display a dispersed arrangement of tubulin genes. In *Drosophila melanogaster*, for example, where *in situ* hybridization of ^{3}H-cDNA to polytene chromosomes allows direct visualization of each locus, α- and β-tubulin genes are found on different chromosomes (Sanchez, Natzle, Cleveland, Kirschner and McCarthy 1980; Mischke and Pardue 1982). In chickens, too, the tubulin gene families are dispersed (Cleveland, Hughes, Stubblefield, Kirschner and Varmus 1981). In these experiments, chromosomes were fractionated on sucrose gradients and by flow micro-fluorimetry; this enabled the unambiguous assignment of α-tubulin genes to chromosomes 1 and 8, and two of the β-tubulin genes to chromosome 2.

Because of the much larger size of the mammalian tubulin multigene families, their chromosomal assignment is more difficult. One approach to the assignment of human tubulin genes is to use mouse/human hybrid cell lines that contain limited subsets of human chromosomes. In such experiments, some means must be found of distinguishing between mouse and human tubulin sequences. This can be achieved either by exploiting the lack of interspecies homology in regions flanking the genes of interest or, more simply, by using a tubulin 3′-untranslated region probe unique to human DNA. Experiments using the latter approach show that M40, an expressed human β-tubulin gene (Gwo-Shu Lee *et al.* 1983) is located on the short arm of chromosome 6; the processed pseudogenes bearing 3′-homology to M40 are dispersed (DeMartinville, Cowan and Francke 1985).

The known chromosomal assignments of tubulin genes are listed in Table 2.3.

Tubulin gene expression and its regulation

Virtually all eukaryotic cells synthesize tubulin, but there is extensive functional diversity among different kinds of microtubule, depending on the cell type and its state of differentiation. Tubulin gene transcription might therefore be either constitutive, with post-translational factors influencing synthetic rates, functional distinction and assembly; or transcription itself might be regulated by functional demand. A key observation in this regard is that the level of unpolymerized tubulin influences the level of tubulin mRNAs, and hence, the rate at which new tubulin is synthesized (Ben Ze'ev, Farmer

Table 2.3

Chromosomal assignment of α- and β-tubulin genes.

Species	Sub-unit	Gene designation	Chromosomal localization/ number	Reference
D. melanogaster	α	Tα1	67C4–6	Kalfayan and Wensink
	α	Tα2	84B3–C8	1981; Mischke and
	α	Tα3	84D5–8	Pardue 1982
	α	Tα4	85E6–15	
	β	B2t	60A/B	Sanchez et al.
	β		85D4–7	1980; Kemphues et al. 1980
Chicken	α		1	Cleveland et al.
	α		8	1980
	β		2 (two genes)	
Human	β	M40	6 (short arm)	DeMartinville et
	β	46β	8	al. 1985

and Penman 1981; Cleveland, Lopata, Sherline and Kirschner 1981b, Cleveland and Kirschner 1982). Thus, when cells are exposed to colchicine so that the intracellular monomer pool is dramatically raised, there is a rapid decrease in tubulin synthesis (Fig. 2.8). Exposure to taxol or vinblastine, on the other hand (both drugs that maintain microtubules in polymerized form) does not affect rates of tubulin synthesis. The decline in tubulin synthesis that accompanies drug-induced depolymerization coincides with a reduction in the level of cytoplasmic tubulin-specific mRNA. Controls performed to concomitantly measure actin mRNA levels showed no corresponding reduction, implying a relatively short half-life for tubulin mRNA. The modulation of tubulin synthesis observed in these experiments does not seem to be an artifact of colchicine treatment, since microinjection of unpolymerized tubulin into CHO cells has a similar effect on *de novo* synthesis (Cleveland, Pittenger and Feramisco 1983). In theory, regulation of tubulin mRNA levels in response to relative tubulin monomer/polymer concentration could occur either transcriptionally, or post-transcriptionally at a number of steps including polyadenylation, splicing, transport to the cytoplasm or sequestration of mRNA. Current evidence suggests that the mechanism may not be transcriptional, since transcriptional rates measured by 'run off' experiments using nuclei incubated with ^{32}P-UTP *in vitro* showed no conspicuous difference between colchicine treated cells and untreated controls (Cleveland and Havercroft 1983). A definitive approach to understanding the mechanism of this regulatory phenomenon will require the manipulation of cloned fragments containing tubulin genes, so as to identify the genetic elements that are critical in the response to changes in monomer concentration.

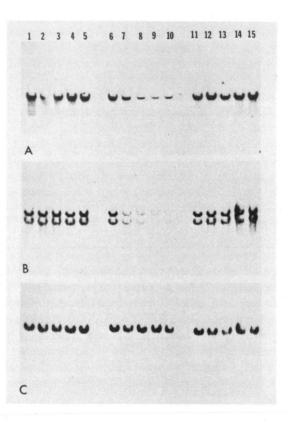

Fig. 2.8. Effect of colchicine on tubulin synthesis in CHO cells. CHO cells were incubated for 0–6 h without drug (lanes 1–5), with 10 μM colchicine (lanes 6–10) or with 1 μM taxol (lanes 11–15). Cytoplasmic RNA was prepared for each time-point and an RNA blot transfer experiment performed. Probes used were A. cloned α-tubulin, B. cloned β-tubulin and C. cloned β-actin. Data from Cleveland *et al.* 1981*b*.

Fluctuations in tubulin mRNA levels have also been the subject of study in a number of lower eukaryotic species including *Chlamydomonas*, *Naegleria*, *Tetrahymena* and *Polytomella* (Guttman and Gorovsky 1979; Brown and Rogers 1978; Fulton and Kowit 1975). These organisms offer a useful model for the study of tubulin gene expression because the experimental amputation of cilia or flagella results in a stimulation of *de novo* tubulin synthesis. A rise in the level of translatable tubulin mRNAs accompanies this enhanced protein synthesis; Lai, Walsh, Wardell and Fulton 1979;

Minami, Collis, Young and Weeks 1981; Lefebvre, Silflow, Wieben and Rosenblum 1980), suggesting an elevated tubulin gene transcription rate in response to deflagellation. It is not clear whether an alteration in the tubulin monomer pool size that might occur following flagellar removal in these organisms can influence tubulin mRNA levels in a manner analogous to that observed in most mammalian cells.

In addition to intracellular modulation of tubulin mRNA levels as a function of tubulin monomer concentration, there is evidence of differential tubulin gene expression during development. *Drosophila melanogaster*, for example, has four α-tubulin genes, all located at different sites on the third chromosome (Kalfayan and Wensink 1981). RNA blot transfer experiments using 3′-probes from genomic sequences revealed distinct patterns of mRNA levels depending upon the developmental stage, including some differences that are sex-specific (Kalfayan and Wensink 1982). At least one β-tubulin gene product, designated β3, appears to be expressed only transiently during embryogenesis (Raff, Fuller, Kaufman, Kemphues, Rudolf and Raff 1982). A second electrophoretically distinct β-tubulin subunit, designated β2, is expressed only in testis, and has been shown by genetic analysis to be encoded by a unique structural gene (Kemphues, Raff, Kaufman and Raff 1979; Kemphues, Raff, Raff and Kaufman 1980). The implications of this interesting mutant are discussed below.

In chickens, where four genes encode α-tubulin and probably six encode β-tubulin (Cleveland *et al.* 1980; D. W. Cleveland, personal communication), 3′-derived fragments from four of the β-tubulin genomic sequences have been used to examine the expression of β-tubulin mRNAs (Lopata *et al.* 1983; Havercroft and Cleveland 1984). Each probe detects a distinct subset of mRNAs, some of them of unexpectedly large size, with a complex pattern of expression among different tissues and cell lines (Table 2.2). Developmental changes in β-tubulin gene expression have also been identified in the developing rat, with the programmed appearance of a 2.5 Kb β-tubulin mRNA (Bond and Farmer 1983). A large (2.6 Kb) mRNA is also transcribed from an expressed human β-tubulin gene, designated M40, as a consequence of readthrough of the AATAAA sequence that specifies the polyadenylation of a 1.8 Kb mRNA transcribed from the same gene (Gwo-Shu Lee *et al.* 1983). The extended 3′-untranslated region of the 2.6 Kb mRNA does not appear to affect translational efficiency, and both 1.8 Kb and 2.6 Kb mRNA species are detectable in a variety of human cell lines. Not withstanding possible changes in expression during development (a difficult experimental problem because of ethical considerations) this gene appears to be expressed constitutively in human cells (Gwo-Shu Lee *et al.* 1983). A human α-tubulin cDNA clone, kα1, isolated from a keratinocyte cDNA library, also appears to be widely expressed (Cowan *et al.* 1983). In contrast, a second human α-tubulin cDNA clone, bα1, isolated from a foetal brain cDNA library, is expressed preponderantly in tissue of neuronal origin, and only at negligible levels elsewhere (Table 2.4). In summary, tubulin gene transcription in several species shows both quantitative modulation (in response to monomer levels and/or as a function of development) and, in a number of cases, tissue specificity.

Table 2.4

Expression of a human α-tubulin gene, bα1, in various human cell lines and in human brain.

HeLa Cells	—	Neuroblastoma CHP 126	—
Diploid fibroblasts	—	Neuroblastoma IMR 32	+ +
Epidermal cells	—	Neuroblastoma CHP 134	+ +
Squamous cell carcinoma SCC-15	—	Glioma 132	δ+
Brain (foetal)	+ + +	Retinoblastoma Y 79	—
Fibrosarcoma	—	Myeloma CM 1500A	—
		Hepatoma PLC/PRF 15	—

Concluding remarks

Comparison of the number and arrangement of tubulin genes between various species reveals a rather remarkable variation. In yeast, there is a single and essential β-tubulin gene (Neff *et al.* 1983). *Chlamydomonas* contains two genes each for α- and β-tubulin (Silflow and Rosenblum 1981), all of which are probably expressed (Brunke, Young, Buchbinder and Weeks 1982). In *Drosophila* and chickens there are minimally four α- and four β-tubulin genes; at least in chickens, all are expressed (Lopata *et al.* 1983). In mammalian species, on the other hand, the multigene families are much larger: a significant (and perhaps the majority) of the members being pseudogenes generated by integration of a cDNA intermediate into the host chromosome (Wilde *et al.* 1982*a*; Wilde, Crowther and Cowan 1982*b*; Gwo-Shu Lee *et al.* 1983; Lemischka and Sharp 1982). There is a corresponding variation in the chromosomal arrangement of the multigene families among different species. In most instances, the genes are dispersed (Table 2.1). In sea urchins, however, there is evidence that some genes within the same family are clustered (Alexandraki and Ruderman 1981). Finally, in Trypanosomes, a series of gene duplication events seems to have led to the existence of tandem arrays (Thomashow, Milhausen, Ruther and Agabian 1983) containing 13–17 copies per haploid genome of alternating α- and β-tubulin sequences. Tandem arrangements of α- and β-tubulin genes are also a feature of the *Leishmania* genome (Landfear, McMahon-Pratt and Wirth 1983).

In contrast to the variability in the number and arrangement of tubulin genes between species, the sequences of the proteins themselves are extensively conserved. With the exception of yeast, where the amino acid sequence diverges by about 30 per cent, all other complete β-tubulin sequences thus far determined are quite similar, though even within a species (e.g. chicken $\beta2$ and $\beta4$, Table 2), there can be substantial (34 out of about 445) differences. These differences are especially marked at the C-terminal end, and serve to define isotypes whose expression is at least in some cases tissue-specific. Although tissue-specificity is also (at least in some cases) a feature of α-tubulin gene expression, the extent of coding region conservation appears much more rigid. On the presently available data, with only a single amino acid difference between α-tubulin gene products from the same species, it does not seem appropriate to claim these as isotypes, though a single substitution could conceivably influence function. Certainly there is no evidence of α-tubulin C-terminal non-homologies analogous to those that define β-tubulin isotypes.

The existence of multiple expressed α- and β-tubulins in multicellular organisms, and the evidence for several β-tubulin isotypes, entails the genetic potential for subunit diversity. It is at present uncertain whether all isotypes contribute to different microtubules, or whether there is selective enrichment, and the resolution of this matter must await the generation of isotype-specific antisera. However, two observations raise doubt as to the contribution of genetic variability to the synthesis of functionally different microtubules within a single cell. First, in *Drosophila*, a structural mutation in a β-tubulin gene has been described (Kemphues *et al.* 1979, 1980) whose expression is restricted to the testis. The consequences of this mutation are far-reaching and affect the meiotic spindle, the cytoplasmic microtubular network and the axonemal microtubule of the sperm tail. Second, in *Aspergillus*, Oakley and Morris (1981) have described a temperature-sensitive β-tubulin gene mutant in which the effects on microtubule-mediated functions are wide-ranging. These data imply the assembly of multiple (and probably distinct) tubulin gene products into functionally different microtubules. If this is the case in general, then we might expect functional diversity to be a consequence of secondary interaction, that is, interaction of one or more tubulin isotypes with a factor or factors that determines the intracellular role of a given microtubule.

References

Alexandraki, D. and Ruderman, J. V. (1981). Sequence heterogeneity, multiplicity and genomic organization of α- and β-tubulin genes in sea urchins. *Mol. Cell. Biol.* **1**, 1125–1137.
—— and Ruderman, J. V. (1983). Evolution of α- and β-tubulin genes as inferred by the nucleotide sequences of sea urchin cDNA clones. *J. Mol. Evol.* in press.
Ben Ze'ev, A., Farmer, S. R., and Penman, S. (1979). Mechanisms of regulating tubulin synthesis in cultured mammalian cells. *Cell* **17**, 319–325.
Bernstein, L. B., Mount, S. M., and Weiner, A. (1983). Pseudogenes for human small

58 Nicholas J. Cowan

nuclear RNA U3 appear to arise by integration of self-primed reverse transcripts of the RNA into new chromosomal sites. *Cell* **32**, 461–472.

Bond, J. F. and Farmer, S. R. (1983). Regulation of tubulin and actin mRNA production in rat brain: expression of a new β-tubulin mRNA with development. *Mol. Cell. Biol.* **3**, 1333–1342.

Brown, D. L. and Rogers, K. (1978). Hydrostatic pressure-induced internalization of flagellar axonemes, disassembly, and reutilization during flagellar regeneration in *Polytomella*. *Exp. Cell. Res.* **117**, 313–324.

Brunke, K. J., Young, E. E., Buchbinder, B. U., and Weeks, D. P. (1982), Coordinate regulation of the four tubulin genes of *Chlamydomonas reinhardi*. *Nucleic Acids Res.* **10**, 1295–1310.

Chen, M-J., Shimada, T., Moulton, A. D., Harrison, M., and Nienhuis, A. W. (1982). Intronless human DHFR genes are derived from processed RNA molecules. *Proc. Natl. Acad. Sci. U.S.A.*, **79**, 7435–7439.

Cleveland, D. W., Kirschner, M. W., and Cowan, N. J. (1978). Isolation of separate mRNAs for α- and β-tubulin and characterization of the corresponding *in vitro* translation products. *Cell* **15**, 1021–1031.

—— Lopata, M. A., Cowan, N. J., McDonald, R. J., Rutter, W. J., and Kirschner, M. W. (1980). A study of the number and evolutionary conservation of genes coding for α- and β-tubulin and β- and γ-cytoplasmic actin using cloned cDNA probes. *Cell* **20**, 95–105.

—— Hughes, S. H., Stubblefield, E., Kirschner, M. W., and Varmus, H. E. (1981). Multiple α and β-tubulin genes represent unlinked and dispersed gene families. *J. Biol. Chem.* **256**, 3130–3134.

—— Lopata, M. A., Sherline, R., and Kirschner, M. W. (1981b). Unpolymerized tubulin modulates the level of tubulin mRNAs. *Cell* **25**, 537–546.

—— Pittenger, M. F., and Feramisco, J. R. (1983). Elevation of tubulin levels by microinjection suppresses new tubulin synthesis. *Nature* **305**, 738–740.

—— and Kirschner, M. W. (1982). Autoregulated control of the expression of α- and β-tubulins: implications for microtubule assembly. Cold Spring Harbor Symp. *Quant. Biol.* **44**, 171–183.

—— and Havercroft, J. C. (1983). Is apparent autoregulatory control of tubulin synthesis nontranscriptionally regulated? *J. Cell. Biol.* **97**, 919–924.

Cowan, N. J., Dobner, P. R., Fuchs, E. V., and Cleveland, D. W. (1983). Expression of human α-tubulin genes: interspecies conservation of 3′ untranslated regions. *Mol. Cell. Biol.* **3**, 1738–1745.

—— Wilde, C. D., Chow, L. T., and Wefald, F. C. (1981). Structural variation among human β-tubulin genes. *Proc. Natl. Acad. Sci. U.S.A.* **78**, 4877–4881.

DeMartinville, B., Cowan, N. J., and Francke, U. (1985). Dispersed chromosomal localization of a human β-tubulin gene subfamily. Manuscript in preparation.

Fulton, C. and Kowit, J. D. (1975). Programmed synthesis of flagellar tubulin during cell differentiation in *Naegleria*. *Ann. N.Y. Acad. Sci.* **253**, 318–332.

Ginzburg, I., Behar, L., Givol, D., and Littauer, U. Z. (1981). The nucleotide sequence of rat α-tubulin: 3′ end characteristics and evolutionary conservation. *Nucleic Acids Res.* **9**, 2691–2697.

Guttman, S. D. and Gorovsky, M. A. (1979). Cilia regeneration in starved *Tetrahymena*: an inducible system for studying gene expression and organelle biogenesis. *Cell* **17**, 307–317.

Gwo-Shu Lee, M., Lewis, S. A., Wilde, C. D., and Cowan, N. J. (1983). Evolutionary history of a multigene family: an expressed human β-tubulin gene and three processed pseudogenes. *Cell* **33**, 477–487.

—— Loomis, C., and Cowan, N. J. (1984). Sequence of an expressed human β-tubulin gene containing ten *Alu* family members. *Nucleic Acids Res.* **12**, 5823–5836.

Hall, J. L., Dudley, L., Dobner, P. R., Lewis, S. A., and Cowan, N. J. (1983). Identification of two human β-tubulin isotypes. *Mol. Cell. Biol.* **3**, 854–862.

Havercroft, J. C. and Cleveland, D. W. (1984). Submitted to *J. Cell Biol.*

Jelinek, W. R. and Schmid, C. W. (1982). Repetitive sequences in eukaryotic DNA and their expression. *Ann. Rev. Biochem.* **51**, 813–844.

Kalfayan, L. and Wensink, P. C. (1981) α-Tubulin genes of *Drosophila. Cell* **21**, 97–106.

—— and Wensink, P. C. (1982). Development and regulation of *Drosophila* α-tubulin genes. *Cell* **29**, 91–98.

Karin, M. and Richards, R. I. (1982). Human metallothionein genes—primary structure of the metallothionein II gene and a related processed gene. *Nature* **299**, 797–802.

Kemphues, K. J., Raff, R. A., Kaufman, T. C., and Raff, E. C. (1979). Mutation in a structural gene for a β-tubulin specific to testis in *Drosophila melanogaster. Proc. Natl. Acad. Sci. U.S.A.*, **76**, 3993–3995.

—— Raff, E. C., Raff, R. A., and Kaufman, T. C., (1980). Mutation in testis-specific β-tubulin *Drosophila*: analysis of its effect on meiosis and map location of the gene. *Cell* **21**, 445–451.

Krauhs, E., Little, M., Kempf, T., Hofer-Warbinek, R., Ade, W., and Ponstingl, H. (1981). Complete amino acid sequence of β-tubulin from porcine brain. *Proc. Natl. Acad. Sci. U.S.A.* **78**, 4156–4160.

Lai, E. Y., Walsh, C., Wardell, D., and Fulton, C. (1979). Programmed appearance of translatable flagellar tubulin mRNA during cell differentiation in *Naegleria. Cell* **17**, 867–878.

Landfear, S. M., McMahon-Pratt, D., and Wirth, D. (1983). Tandem arrangement of tubulin genes in the protozoan parasite *Leishmania enriettii. Mol. Cell. Biol.* **3**, 1070 1076.

Lefebvre, P. A., Silflow, C. D., Wieben, E. D., and Rosenblum, J. L. (1980). Increased levels of mRNAs for tubulin and other flagellar proteins after amputation or shortening of *Chlamydomonas* flagella. *Cell* **20**, 469–477.

Lemischka, I. R., Farmer, S., Racaniello, V. R., and Sharp, P. A. (1981). Nucleotide sequence and evolution of a mammalian α-tubulin messenger RNA. *J. Mol. Biol.* **15**, 101–120.

—— and Sharp, P. A. (1982). The sequences of an expressed rat α-tubulin gene and a pseudogene with an inserted repetitive element. *Nature* **300**, 330–335.

Lopata, M. A., Havercroft, J. C., Chow, L. T., and Cleveland, D. W. (1983). Four unique genes required for β-tubulin expression in vertebrates. *Cell* **32**, 713–724.

Luduena, F. R. and Woodward, D. O. (1973). Isolation and partial characterization of α- and β-tubulin from outer doublets of sea urchin sperm and microtubules of chick embryo brain. *Proc. Natl. Acad. Sic. U.S.A.* **70**, 3594–3598.

Minami, S. A., Collis, P. S., Young, E. E., and Weeks, D. P. (1981). Tubulin induced in *C. reinhardii*: requirement for tubulin mRNA synthesis. *Cell.* **24**, 89–95.

Mischke, D. and Pardue, M. L. (1982), Organization and expression of α-tubulin genes in *Drosophila melanogaster. J. Mol. Biol.* **156**, 449–446.

Neff, N. F., Thomas, J. H., Grisafi, P., and Botstein, D. (1983). Isolation of the β-tubulin gene from yeast and demonstration of its essential function *in vivo. Cell* **33**, 211–219.

Oakley, B. R. and Morris, N. R. (1981). A β-tubulin mutation in *Aspergillus nidulans* that blocks microtubule function without blocking assembly. *Cell* **12**, 561–571.

Osborne, M. and Weber, K. (1977). The display of microtubules in transformed cells. *Cell* **12**, 561–571.

Perler, F., Efstratiadis, A., Lomedico, P., Gilbert, W., Kolodner, R., and Dodgson, J. (1980). The evolution of genes: the chicken preproinsulin gene. *Cell* **20**, 555–566.

Ponstingl, H., Little, M., Krauhs, E., and Kempf, T. (1981). Complete amino acid sequence of α-tubulin from porcine brain. *Proc. Natl. Acad. Sci. U.S.A.* **78**, 2757–2761.

Raff, E. C., Fuller, M. T., Kaufman, T. C., Kemphues, K. J., Rudolph, F. E., and Raff, R. A. (1982). Regulation of tubulin gene expression during embryogenesis in *Drosophila melanogaster. Cell* **28**, 33–40.

Raybin, D. and Flavin, M. (1977). Enzyme which specifically adds tyrosine to the α-chain of tubulin. *Biochemistry* **16**, 2189–2194.

Sanchez, F., Natzle, J. E., Cleveland, D. W., Kirschner, M. W., and McCarthy, B. J. (1980). A dispersed multigene family encoding tubulin in *Drosophila melanogaster. Cell.* **22**, 845–854.

Silflow, C. D. and Rosenblum, J. L. (1981). Multiple α and β tubulin genes in *Chlamydomonas* and regulation of tubulin mRNA levels after deflaggelation. *Cell* **24**, 81–88.

Sullivan, K., Lau, S., and Cleveland, D. W. (1984) Submitted to *J. Cell. Biol.*

Sutcliffe, J. G., Milner, R. J., Bloom, F. E., and Lerner, R. A. (1982). Common 82-nucleotide sequence unique to brain RNA. *Proc. Natl. Acad. Sci. U.S.A.* **79**, 4942–4946.

Thomashow, L. S., Milhausen, M., Rutter, W. J., and Agabian, N. (1983). Tubulin genes are tandemly linked and clustered in the genome of *Trypanosoma brucei. Cell* **32**, 35–43.

Valenzuela, P., Quiroga, M., Zaldivar, J., Rutter, W. J., Kirschner, M. W., and Cleveland, D. W. (1981). Nucleotide and corresponding amino acid structure encoded by α- and β-tubulin mRNA. *Nature* **289**, 650–655.

Van Arsdell, S. W., Denison, R. A., Bernstein, L. B., Weiner, A. M., Manser, T., and Gesteland, R. F. (1981). Direct repeats flank three small nuclear RNA pseudogenes in the human genome. *Cell* **26**, 11–17.

Wilde, C. D., Crowther, C. E., Cripe, T. P., Gwo-Shu Lee, M., and Cowan, N. J. (1982*a*). Evidence that a human β-tubulin pseudogene is derived from its corresponding mRNA. *Nature* **292**, 83–84.

—— Crowther, C. E., and Cowan, N. J. (1982*b*). Diverse mechanisms in the generation of human β-tubulin pseudogenes. *Science* **217**, 549–552.

3 Structural and Functional Analyses of *Drosophila melanogaster* Actin Genes

ERIC A. FYRBERG

Introduction

Technical advances made during the last decade have markedly improved our ability to investigate the structure and function of metazoan genes. It is presently possible to isolate virtually any segment of eukaryotic chromosomal DNA and to rapidly detail both its global organization and nucleotide sequence. Hybridization of such purified DNA fragments *in situ* to intact chromosomes or tissue sections can establish, in turn, their genomic locations and the constellations of tissue types in which they are transcribed to form stable messenger RNAs.

Genetic functions of isolated DNA segments can be investigated more directly using the technique of DNA mediated transformation. A variety of methods permit introduction of cloned DNA fragments into eukaryotic chromosomes. Frequently such transfected sequences are regulated in a manner indistinguishable from the 'resident' counterparts. The ability to manipulate DNA in this fashion represents a significant advance in genetic technique, since it allows one to systematically and efficiently generate a series of 'alleles' using *in vitro* mutagenesis and to subsequently test the ability of each to function in a normal manner within the context of living cells and tissues.

As a consequence of these developments contemporary genetic techniques offer a fresh approach by which to investigate the synthesis and assembly of eukaryotic structural proteins. Previous genetic investigations have contributed a great deal to our understanding of enzyme structure and function, but relatively little to our knowledge of structural proteins (O'Brien and MacIntyre, 1978). This disproportion is likely attributable to several factors, most notably the difficulties inherent to devising efficient screens for structural protein mutants. In particular, in the absence of convenient functional (i.e. enzymatic activity) assays it is sometimes impossible to recognize mutations affecting a particular gene. Furthermore, if mutations affecting synthesis and assembly of structural proteins are frequently dominant or semi-dominant lethals then they may be only rarely recovered in genetic screens. Despite these drawbacks, it is presently possible to systematically investigate biochemical, developmental and physiological aspects of structural protein function using a combination of molecular and/or classical genetic techniques. Data obtained in this fashion will increasingly afford new insights into long standing biological questions (Kemphues, Raff, Raff and Kaufman 1980; Spradling and Mahowald, 1981; Mishina *et al.* 1984).

In this chapter I review our progress in defining the structure and function of genes which encode actins of the fruit fly, *Drosophila melanogaster*. From the inception of this work our goal has been to characterize the genes encoding a major structural component of eucaryotic cells and thus facilitate understanding the epigenesis and function of cytoskeletal structures. While my preoccupations are occasionally those of one attempting to characterize one small fraction of a metazoan genome, my broader viewpoint is that actin genes and proteins are of interest to a large audience including those concerned with genetic regulatory mechanisms, muscle biochemistry, and organismal evolution.

Structural Studies of *Drosophila* Actin Genes

DETERMINATION OF ACTIN GENE NUMBER

Characterization of *Drosophila* genomic DNA has revealed that actins of the fly are encoded by a family of six nonallelic genes. Initially *Drosophila* actin genes were independently isolated by two laboratory groups (Tobin, Zulauf, Sanchez, Craig and McCarthy 1980; Fyrberg, Kindle, Davidson and Sodja 1980) by probing genomic DNA libraries with the B-1 *Dictyostelium* actin cDNA clone isolated by Bender, Davidson, Kindle, Taylor, Silverman and Firtel (1978). Because the primary amino acid sequence of actin is highly conserved the *Dictyostelium* probe hybridizes to all of the *Drosophila* genes even under moderately stringent conditions. Restriction mapping of the isolated *Drosophila* clones revealed that they comprised six classes of overlapping DNA segments, indicating that there were probably six closely related genes.

To directly demonstrate that these six classes of clones accounted for all members of the *Drosophila* actin gene family Fyrberg, Bond, Hershey, Mixter and Davidson (1982) performed the Southern blotting experiment, shown in Fig. 3.1. Representatives of each class of isolated *Drosophila* actin gene were digested with Eco RI, and the resulting fragments were separated by electrophoresis on agarose gels. In an adjacent lane of the same gel an Eco RI digest of genomic *Drosophila* DNA was electrophoresed. DNA fragments were then blotted to nitrocellulose and hybridized with a labelled actin gene probe, in this case the protein coding region of the DmA2 *Drosophila* actin gene. As can be seen in Fig. 3.1, the seven prominent bands of the genomic Eco RI digest can all be accounted for by the six cloned segments. We originally designated these genes DmA1-DmA6 on the basis of decreasing sizes of their hybridizing Eco RI fragments. Each of the phages contains a single hybridizing Eco RI fragment except λDmA6, which contains two. To be certain that each hybridizing band contains only one gene (or a portion thereof) blot-reconstruction experiments were performed by

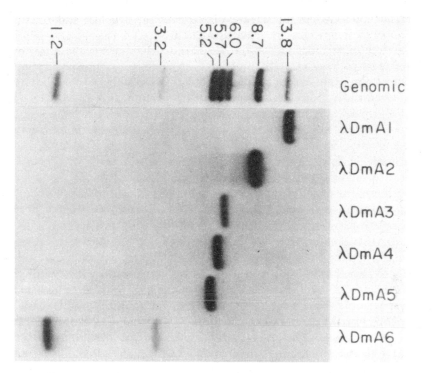

Fig. 3.1. Blot-hybridization Analysis of λDmA1–λDmA6. An *Eco* RI digest of geno-mic *Drosophila* DNA (left lane) was electrophoresed in parallel with *Eco* RI digests of λDmA1–λDmA6. Hybridization to a probe containing the actin protein coding region of the λDmA2 clone reveals that these six phages contain all of the *Drosophila* actin genes

Fyrberg *et al.* (1980). Results of these experiments confirm that there is a single gene within each chimeric phage.

CHROMOSOMAL LOCATIONS OF ACTIN GENES

To investigate the chromosomal locations of *Drosophila* actin genes each was hybridized *in situ* to larval polytene chromosomes using the technique of Gall and Pardue (1971). The observation that the six genes were contained within nonoverlapping chromosome segments was an initial indication that the genes might be unlinked. *In situ* hybridization confirmed that these genes reside within six widely dispersed chromosome subdivisions; DmA1 within subdivision 88F of the third chromosome, DmA2 within 5C of the X, DmA3 and DmA4 within (respectively) 42A and 57A of the second, and DmA5 and DmA6 within 87E and 79B of the third chromosome. Since their chro-mosome locations represent more meaningful designations for particular genes than did our previous convention the *Drosophila* actin genes have been renamed act88F, act5C, act42A, act57A, act87E and act79B by Zau-lauf, Sānchez, Tobin, Rdest and McCarthy (1981).

The biological significance of the dispersed gene arrangement is not entirely understood, but most likely reflects the evolutionary history of actin genes within the genus *Drosophila*. Actin genes within organisms of other phyla are frequently linked *and* dispersed, as in nematodes (Files, Carr and Hirsch 1983) and sea urchins (Scheller, McAllister, Crain, Durica, Posakony, Britten and Davidson 1981). To date there is no compelling reason to believe that these variable chromosome arrangements are correlated with any aspect of actin gene function, although formally this remains a viable hypothesis. It is more probable that the chromosome arrangement of any series of related genes is the result of the timing and/or mechanism of gene duplica-tion in relation to events which serve to rearrange the genome, such as chromosome inversions and translocations. Supporting this notion is the observation that both linkage and number of α-like and β-like globin genes has changed rapidly during the interval following the separation of am-phibian and mammalian ancestral lines (Wood and Weatherall 1983). The extreme dispersal of actin genes in *Drosophila* may indicate primarily that there have been no *recent* tandem duplications of actin genes in this genus. Comparisons of 3' untranslated and flanking regions have in fact indicated that no pair of *Drosophila* actin genes is the product of a recent duplication event (refer to following sections). Further insight into the issue of actin gene arrangement may come from comparisons of actin gene location within other Diptera.

COMPARATIVE ANATOMY OF DROSOPHILA ACTIN GENES

Two aspects of actin genes make them especially well suited for comparative structural studies. The first is their evolutionary conservation. Because actin is a highly conserved and ubiquitous protein the structure of these genes can be examined across very large evolutionary distances (Pollard and Weihing 1974; Firtel 1981). This factor facilitates investigation of the mech-anisms whereby genetic information is preserved and changed. The second aspect concerns the complexities of actin gene function. Actin synthesis is highly regulated in eukaryotes. As muscle and nonmuscle cells of a par-ticular metazoan divide and differentiate they initiate and/or terminate syn-thesis of particular actin isoforms, presumably by activating and repressing the activities of the corresponding genes (Buckingham and Minty 1983; Schwartz, this volume). By comparison of the structures of members of actin gene families *within* an organism it is possible to investigate both the functional specializations of each protein coding region and the mechanisms by which actin gene expression is regulated.

Comparisons of the protein coding regions of both *Drosophila* and *non-Drosophila* actin genes have demonstrated that they typically encode distinct but closely related isoforms. To date, protein coding regions of two *Drosophila* actin genes (act79B and act88F) have been completely sequenced and those of the remaining four genes partially sequenced (Fyrberg, Bond, Hershey, Mixter and Davidson 1981; Sanchez, Tobin, Rdest, Zulauf and McCarthy 1983). These composite data have shown that the six genes encode at least five distinct proteins. All of the *Drosophila* genes are closely related, however. For example, nucleotide sequences of the act79B and act88F protein coding regions are 88 per cent homologous, while amino acid sequences of the isoforms encoded by these respective genes are 95 per cent conserved. Comparisons of the *Drosophila* actin genes to those of distantly related organisms have revealed a similar degree of homology. Cooper and Crain (1982) reported that the nucleotide sequence of the coding region of a sea urchin actin gene is 83 per cent homologous to the act79B and act88F sequences, and that the amino acid sequence of the encoded isoform is 94 per cent homologous to the *Drosophila* sequences. From comparison of these sequences it is clear that almost all selective pressure is exerted at the level of the protein sequence (Buckingham and Minty 1983).

Since particular *Drosophila* actin genes encode slightly different protein isoforms, the observed amino acid replacements may have a selective value. An obvious and intriguing possibility is that these amino acid replacements make certain *Drosophila* actin isoforms better suited for particular epigenetic roles. However, it is not yet possible to say whether or not this is the case. What is clear is that the list of potential candidates for such meaningful replacements is quite small. Sequence comparison of proteins encoded by act79B and act88F, for example, have revealed only 17 amino acid replacements in 377 residues. Of these 17, 8 must be considered extremely conservative (glu vs. asp, val vs. ile, ser vs. thr, gln vs. asn, met vs. ile, or tyr vs. phe) and are likely to be neutral replacements. Of the remaining nine, at least five represent either polymorphisms or sequencing errors (Sanchez *et al.* 1983) since we have been unable to confirm them in the course of independent sequence analyses. Some of the final four replacements (for example cys vs. ser at amino acid 52; asn vs. ser at amino acid 296) could conceivably have selective value. However, it is equally probable that these amino acids are of no functional consequence. In a following section an experimental approach to test the biological significance of these amino acid replacements is discussed.

Comparisons of *Drosophila* actin genes to those of other organisms have revealed two very interesting aspects of the actin amino terminus. Sequence comparisons of vertebrate actins previously demonstrated that the amino-terminal tryptic peptide of actin has a relatively high percentage of amino acid replacements and that sequence divergences tend to be tissue-specific, rather than species specific. Thus, skeletal muscle actins from several vertebrates species are identical in amino acid sequence but differ in sequence from the cytoplasmic actins isolated from these same species (Vandekerckhove

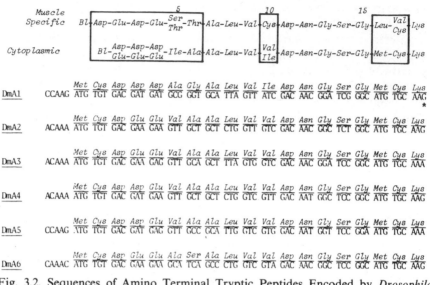

Fig. 3.2. Sequences of Amino Terminal Tryptic Peptides Encoded by *Drosophila* Actin Genes. The sequence of each encoded protein is aligned with the composite sequence of vertebrate muscle-specific and cytoplasmic actins. Within the boxed regions are the replacements which distinguish the vertebrate muscle specific actins from their cytoplasmic counterparts. Each of the *Drosophila* sequences resembles the vertebrate cytoplasmic actins, partial exceptions being act88F and act79B, where amino acid number 6 is glycine or serine (respectively). Each of the derived *Drosophila* sequences encodes a cysteine that immediately follows the initiator methione, however cysteine does not occur at this position in mature vertebrate or invertebrate actins.

and Weber 1978). Since these differences are so well conserved within vertebrates it was thought that these amino acid replacements might be involved in specific functions of muscle as opposed to non-muscle actins. It was therefore surprising to find that all six *Drosophila* actin genes encode proteins which resemble vertebrate cytoplasmic actins at their amino-termini (Fyrberg *et al.* 1981). These sequences are summarized in Fig. 3.2. As can be seen by inspection of this data, all actin isoforms encoded by *Drosophila* genome have sequences resembling vertebrate cytoplasmic isoforms. This finding takes on a greater significance when one considers that at least three and possibly four of these *Drosophila* genes encode muscle-specific isoforms (refer to following sections).

Sequencing of actin genes in other invertebrates such as nematodes and sea urchins has revealed that they too encode isoforms which resemble the cytoplasmic actins of vertebrates. In no case has the counterpart of a vertebrate skeletal muscle actin gene been found in an invertebrate species. Collectively, these observations support the hypothesis that the amino acid replacements observed in vertebrate muscle-specific actin isoforms are not requisite for muscle function *per se*. Rather, these replacements may facilitate some aspect of sarcomeric actin function which is unique to vertebrates.

Analysis of the amino-terminal sequences encoded by particular actin genes have revealed one additional feature of interest, namely that the initiator methionine codons are followed, in each case, by a cysteine residue (refer to Fig. 3.2). Subsequently, an analogous cysteine codon has been discovered in all actin genes except those of protists and the genes which encode the cytoplasmic isoforms of human actins (Gunning, Ponte, Okayama, Engel, Blau and Kedes 1983a). Since cysteine is never found at this position in actin polypeptides it must be removed by post-translational processing. This suggests that the residue plays a regulatory role during actin synthesis and/or assembly. However, definitive evidence to indicate that this is the case must await *in vivo* tests of function.

NONCODING AND FLANKING REGIONS

Noncoding and flanking regions are essential portions of eukaryotic genes, but as yet their precise roles have not been determined. Multigene families represent convenient paradigms for investigating the role(s) of these sequences. Assuming that particular sequences lying outside of protein coding regions are requisite for regulated gene function it logically follows that these regions would not diverge a maximum rates following gene duplication. Comparisons of sequences surrounding protein coding regions of respective members of multigene families can reveal conserved segments and allow tentative conclusions regarding their function to be formed. Such an approach resulted in the discoveries of the CCAAT and ATA box sequences which flank most eucaryotic genes (Goldberg 1979; Efstratiadis *et al.* 1980).

From the structural characterizations carried out to date we can reasonably conclude that there are no long and well conserved blocks of sequence outside of protein coding regions of *Drosophila* actin genes. The initial indication that this was the case came from heteroduplex experiments of Fyrberg *et al.* (1981), but not all combinations of actin gene pairs were analyzed in these experiments. In subsequent investigations of actin gene structure and expression the 3' untranslated and flanking regions of all six genes have been subcloned and characterized (Sanchez *et al.* 1983; Fyrberg, Mahaffey, Bond and Davidson 1983). Cross-hybridization experiments and DNA sequencing have demonstrated that each is unique. These results contrast that of Ponte, Gunning, Blau and Kedes (1983) who found that 3' untranslated regions of several human cytoskeletal actin genes are very homologous. This latter discovery likely indicates that the human cytoskeletal actin gene subfamily has recently expanded by a duplication or amplification event. Since no such 3' untranslated region homology is found in *Drosophila* we presume that all of the gene duplication events which generated the *Drosophila* actin multigene family are comparatively ancient.

Analyses of 5′ untranslated and flanking segments have likewise failed to reveal substantial homology between the *Drosophila* actin genes. To date, very little nucleotide sequence data is available but comparisons have not revealed any homology except the ATA or TATA (Goldberg-Hogness) box. From the Southern blotting experiments performed previously it is reasonable to conclude that any sequence conservation in these regions will involve very short stretches of nucleotides.

ANALYSES OF INTRON LOCATIONS

Analysis of the exon-intron arrangement of *Drosophila* actin genes has revealed that not all of the genes have identical structural organizations. Lomedico, Rosenthal, Efstratiadis, Gilbert, Kolodner and Tizard (1979) first reported that one of the two nonallelic insulin genes of rats had lost an intron. Subsequent surveys of gene structure have, however, indicated that such structural variability is relatively rare among multigene family members

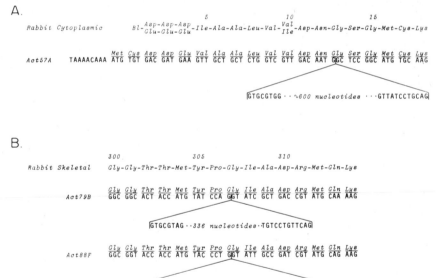

Fig. 3.3. Interruptions within Protein Coding Regions of *Drosophila* Actin Genes. Panel A illustrates an intron within the act57A protein coding region. Codon 13 of this gene is interrupted by an untranslatable sequence of approximately 630 nucleotides, but none of the remaining five genes has an intron at the identical position. Panel B illustrates that act88F and act79B each have an intron within codon 307, and that they have sizes of 60 and 360 nucleotides, respectively. None of the remaining four genes are believed to have introns in this location, although this has been confirmed by nucleotide sequencing in only two cases (those of act5C and act42A). Inspection of the sequences at the 5′ and 3′ ends of all three interruptions reveals that they conform to the 'GT-AG' rule of Breathnach, Benoist, O'Hare, Gannon and Chambon (1978).

and that more frequently all members of a multigene family have analogous intron-exon arrangements. In contrast, within the *Drosophila* actin multigene family the positions of introns are rather variable, as can be seen by inspection of Fig. 3.3. Panel A of this figure illustrates the nucleotide sequence of the 5′ end of the act57A protein coding region. Inspection of this sequence reveals that an intron splits the first two G's of the glycine codon at position 13. Surprisingly, an intron is not found at this location in any of the other five genes (Fyrberg *et al.* 1981). Panel B demonstrates that both act79B and act88F have an intron within glycine codon number 307. However, none of the remaining four genes are believed to have introns at this location, although in only two cases (act5C and act42A) has this been directly demonstrated by sequencing the corresponding region.

A broader perspective of these unexpected findings has resulted from comparison of actin gene structure in a variety of eukaryotes. This data has been reviewed by Buckingham and Minty (1983) and can be summarized as follows. Intron positions within actin genes are highly variable both within and between species. A total of 14 distinct positions have been documented so far, and it is likely that several more remain to be discovered. In four cases, the positions of particular introns are conserved over relatively large evolutionary distances. One intron location within a plant actin gene (between codons 18 and 19 of corn and soybean actin genes) is also found within the actin IV gene of nematodes. A second plant actin gene location is apparently conserved in vertebrate species. Actin genes of soybean, corn, chickens, rats and humans all have an intron within a glycine codon at position 150. In addition, four intron locations within sea urchin actin genes (between codons 41 and 42, 121 and 122, 327 and 328 and within codon 204) are found in various vertebrate actin genes. These composite results seem to support best the notion that the primordial actin gene contained at least 14 introns, and that most of these have been deleted from any particular actin gene, whether derived from genomes of plants, protosomes or deuterostomes. The ramifications of such a hypothesis have been discussed recently by Blake (1983). The only point worth adding to his thorough and lucid discussion is that if the primordial actin gene did indeed contain more than 14 exons some of them would have encoded peptides consisting of only a few amino acid residues (five in the case of the smallest 'primordial' exon).

Functional Studies

BLOT-HYBRIDIZATION ANALYSES OF *DROSOPHILA* ACTIN GENE EXPRESSION

There are at least two approaches by which to establish the functional roles of particular *Drosophila* actin genes. The first involves using DNA-RNA hybridization to examine the temporal and anatomical distribution of actin mRNAs during normal Drosophila development. Utilizing data generated in this fashion it is possible to deduce the major functional role of each gene. A second approach utilizes classical genetic techniques to recover defective alleles of each gene. By analyzing the phenotype associated with each such mutation one can learn the functions of the corresponding gene. Both techniques have significant advantages and drawbacks and it is most appropriate to employ both approaches simultaneously.

Before describing results of DNA-RNA hybridization experiments it is necessary to mention one technical problem associated with this approach. As has been already detailed, the protein coding regions of *Drosophila* actin genes are approximately 85 per cent homologous at the level of nucleotide sequence, and cross-hybridize efficiently even under moderately stringent conditions. To circumvent the potential ambiguities generated by cross-hybridization of nonhomologous actin genes and mRNAs we and others have constructed specific hybridization probes for transcripts of individual actin genes by subcloning the region of each that is complementary to the 3′ untranslated region of the homologous mRNA (Fyrberg *et al.* 1983; Sanchez *et al.* 1983). In control experiments it was shown that each such probe hybridizes only to transcripts of the homologous gene. Using such subcloned fragments it is possible to unambiguously investigate the expression of each member of the actin multigene family.

Experiments utilizing these hybridization probes strongly imply that all six *Drosophila* actin genes are functional, and that none are pseudogenes. RNA blotting experiments of Fyrberg *et al.* (1983) have shown that each gene directs formation of mRNA of 1.6–2.1 kb, sufficient to encode the 375 aa actin polypeptide. When these mRNAs are translated *in vitro* each directs the synthesis of a polypeptide having the molecular weight and isoelectric point of actin. These composite hybrid-selection data strongly indicate that each of the six *Drosophila* actin genes is transcribed to form stable and functional messenger RNA *in vivo*.

These same hybridization probes were used to study variation in steady state levels of actin gene transcripts during the *Drosophila* life cycle. Poly(A)$^+$ RNA was prepared from several developmental stages, ranging from early embryos to adults, and also from several permanent *Drosophila* cell lines. After fractionation of these RNA preparations on denaturing agarose gels they were blotted to nitrocellulose and hybridized to ^{32}P-labeled actin gene-specific probes. Results of these experiments have revealed that the accumulation of particular RNAs is temporarily modulated, as can be seen by inspection of the blots displayed in Fig. 3.4. The main conclusions of these RNA blotting experiments can be summarized as follows.

RNA complementary to act5C and act42A is present during all stages of development examined. Levels of mRNAs transcribed from these genes peak

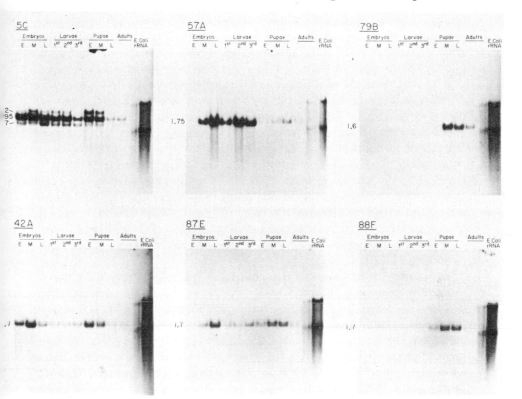

Fig. 3.4. Developmental Patterns of Transcripts for the Six Actin Genes. 1 µg of poly(A)⁺ RNA from different developmental stages was subjected to electrophoresis on formaldehyde-agarose gels and blotted to nitrocellulose. Six filters, identically prepared, were hybridized to the six nick-translated actin gene specific probes. The lengths of the transcripts from each gene are indicated to the left of each panel. The early (E), and mid (M), and late (L) embryo RNAs were made from embryos which had been aged for 0–4, 8–12, and 6–20 h, respectively, after egg laying. The 1st, 2nd and 3rd instar larval RNAs were made from animals aged 32–37, 48–51, and 89–99 h, respectively, after egg laying. The pupae were selected 21–27 h (early) and 48—58 h (mid) after the onset of pupal development. The late pupal RNA sample was made just after the first few animals had eclosed (emerged as adults). The adult RNA was made from both males and females < 5 days old.

E. coli 16S and 23S ribosomal RNAs were used as a standard to determine the length of the actin transcripts. Nick-translated pKK2361 (a gift from Harry Noller and Mary Alice Raker) that contains the entire E. coli rrnB ribosomal RNA operon was hybridized to the lanes containing the standard.

during early to mid embryogenesis, decrease during late embryogenesis and the larval instars, and rise again during early pupal development. This pattern of expression is not correlated with *Drosophila* muscle differentiation, which occurs during late embryogenesis and late in pupal development as well (Poulson 1950; Bodenstein 1950). Furthermore, using either RNA gel blots or dot blots (described below), we find that in several undifferentiated permanent *Drosophila* cell lines all actin mRNA is transcribed from either act5C or act42A. Both of the aforementioned observations imply that act5C and act42A encode cytoplasmic or cytoskeletal actins. Finally it is of interest to note that the act5C specific probe hybridizes to three different size classes of mRNA, and the relative levels of these three classes change somewhat during development. This aforementioned size heterogeneity could be generated by either differential processing of a primary transcript, or by the fact that the transcribed region utilizes more than one point of initiation or termination. Recent S1 and exonuclease 7 mapping experiments by B. J. Bond (personal communication) indicate that the length heterogeneity of these mRNAs resides within their 3′ untranslated regions. The preliminary indication is that the observed heterogeneity results from utilization of multiple transcription termination signals. Presumably, the relative efficiency with which each termination signal is recognized varies as a function of developmental stage.

Transcripts from genes act57A and act87E are most abundant during late embryogenesis. Both transcripts are present at reduced levels throughout larval growth, although the reduction is more marked for act87E. Rather low levels of both transcripts are found during the larval-pupal transition, and these subsequently rise to moderate levels during late pupal development. Periods during which these two mRNAs are abundant are correlated with the differentiation of larval musculature and its subsequent restructuring during late pupation to form adult muscles (Poulson 1950; Crossley 1978).

Messenger RNAs encoded by the final two genes, act79B and act88F, occur at maximal levels during mid to late pupal development, and remain high in newly enclosed adults. Additionally, we detect very low levels of act79B transcripts during late embryogenesis and throughout larval growth. As will be described in more detail in the following paragraph, the timing and location of act79B and act88F mRNA accumulation during pupal development is precisely correlated with differentiation of adult leg and thoracic musculature (Crossley 1978).

The above described experiments demonstrate that the six *Drosophila* actin genes can be grouped into three pairs, with members of each pair similarly regulated and possibly functionally related. For independent tests of these assignments we have hybridized dot blot strips containing specific probe DNAs to ^{32}P-labelled cDNAs representing poly (A)$^{+}$ RNA of particular body parts. To date, RNAs from heads, thoraces, legs and abdomens of late pupae, and ovaries of newly eclosed adults have been tested. Results of these experiments are illustrated in Fig. 3.5 and discussed in the following paragraphs.

Once again, we observe similar patterns of mRNA expression for particular pairs of actin genes. Act57A and act87E transcripts are present primarily in the head and abdomen. This observation strengthens the con-

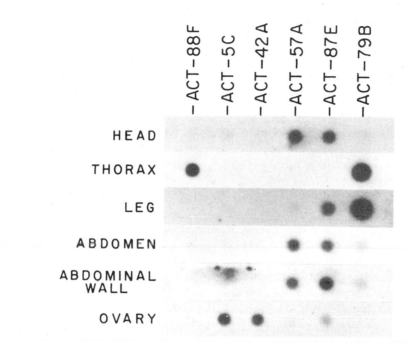

Fig. 3.5. Dot Blots of Actin Gene-specific Probes to Spatially Localized ^{32}P-labelled cDNAs. Nitrocellulose strips containing 'dots' of actin gene specific probe DNAs were hybridized to ^{32}P-labelled cDNAs representing spatially localized preparations of poly(A)$^+$ RNA. Heads, thoraces, legs and abdomens were isolated from late pupae. Abdominal wall RNA was prepared from abdomens which were emptied of organs using pressure from a small rolling pin. Ovaries were dissected from newly eclosed adult females. Note the striking paired expression of genes.

clusion that act57A and act87E are expressed during the differentiation and restructuring of larval muscle, since much of the cephalic and abdominal musculature of *Drosophila* is comprised of restructured larval muscle (Crossley 1978). Low but significant amounts of act87E are also found in legs and ovaries. In the thorax, where the indirect flight muscles are the largest structures, we detect only act88F and act79B transcripts. Act 79B transcripts are also abundant in legs. Since thoracic and leg musculature both are derived primarily from imaginal discs (Crossley 1978; Lawrence 1982), this observation supports the notion that both genes are activated during the differentiation of imaginal myoblasts.

When the head, thorax or abdomen blots are exposed for longer periods, we detect low to moderate levels of act5C and act42A transcripts, indicating they are not associated with any particular organ or muscle type. In fact, these transcripts predominate only in adult ovaries and in several permanent *Drosophila* cell lines examined. Since act5C and act42A RNAs are present very early in embryogenesis, they are probably components of maternal mRNA (Anderson and Lengyel 1979). It seems reasonable to assume that these ovarian transcripts are transcribed in polyploid nurse cells and transported to the oocyte for use during early embryogenesis.

Collectively, these nucleic acid hybridization experiments have conclusively demonstrated that the task of *Drosophila* actin synthesis is divided between six nonallelic genes, each of which is activated only in particular epigenetic situations (i.e. during particular developmental stages or in particular cell lineages and tissue types). In the future, our understanding of temporal and spatial specificity of actin gene activity will continue to be refined by application of more sophisticated techniques (i.e. *in situ* hybridization of actin gene probes to RNAs present in tissue sections of developing organisms), and by analyses of mutations which affect particular actin genes. Nevertheless, our present understanding of actin mRNA accumulation is sufficient to allow particular models of gene regulation to be tested and also to form reasonable predictions of the types of phenotypic defects which would result from mutations of particular actin genes.

Before turning to the subject of genetic investigation of actin gene function, at least three topics warrant brief discussion. The first concerns the observation that *Drosophila* actin synthesis seems always to be directed by similarly regulated pairs of genes. More specifically act5C and act42A; act57A and act87E and act88F and act79B form gene pairs which are always coexpressed, the one exception being leg muscle, where act79B and act87E are coexpressed. The meaning of this coexpression phenomenon is by no means clear, however, it is certainly not unique to *Drosophila*. Recent analyses by Gunning *et al.* (1983*b*) have revealed that human actin gene expression always involves pairs of genes. For example, during cardiac muscle differentiation genes encoding cardiac and skeletal muscle actins are coexpressed, while undifferentiated cells coexpress the α and β cytoplasmic actin genes. The possible physiological significance of these findings (Gunning *et al.* 1983*b*) may involve a requisite interaction of two or more actin isoforms in order to form thin filaments in a regulated manner. Previous observations have revealed that pairs of myosin isoforms are coordinately synthesized during nematode muscle development (Garcea, Schachat and Epstein 1978) and these authors have discussed the possibility that regulated formation of thick filaments requires interaction of multiple myosin species.

Both of the remaining two topics involve mechanisms by which synthesis of actin and non-actin contractile proteins is orchestrated. The first concerns the various means by which contractile protein isoforms are encoded. Investigations of the structural details of non-actin contractile protein genes of *Drosophila* have revealed they all generate multiple protein isoforms by differential splicing of a primary transcript. The single myosin heavy chain gene, for example, is differentially spliced so as to generate three overlapping transcripts, and the accumulation of each of these RNAs is developmentally regulated (Rozek and Davidson 1983). DNA sequencing of cDNA clones representing these myosin heavy chain messengers has revealed that they encode proteins which differ in their primary amino acid sequences only over the carboxy-terminal 22–27 amino acids (C. Rozek and N. Davidson, personal communication). A similar phenomenon has been documented for myosin light chain genes (S. Falkenthal, personal communication) and tropomyosin and tropomyosin-related genes (Karlik, Mahaffey, Coutu and Fyrberg 1984). These results clearly demonstrate that two distinct mechanisms may be employed to generate contractile protein isoforms of *Drosophila*. In the first, which is typified by the actin genes, a set of related proteins is encoded by a family of related genes, the activities of which are probably regulated at the level of transcription. In the second, typified by the other contractile protein genes of the fly, a single transcribed region generates multiple mRNAs and proteins by alternate patterns of RNA splicing and processing. Clearly, the coordinated activation of contractile protein synthesis in *Drosophila* involves both mechanisms, and therefore, to ultimately understand the genetic programme of differentiating muscle cells we must understand both mechanisms and learn how each is regulated.

The final topic concerns the relationship of contractile protein gene regulation to chromosomal linkage. Previously there has been much speculation that coordinately regulated genes might be clustered within particular chromosome regions. Activation of series of coordinately regulated genes would by achieved by changing molecular conformation of the chromosome 'domain' including such a gene cluster. While the simplicity of such a model is enticing, the linkage arrangement of *Drosophila* contractile protein genes, which is summarized in Fig. 3.6, lends absolutely no credence to it. In no case is more than one type of contractile protein gene functionally linked in the *Drosophila* genome. The closest observed linkage is that of the act88F actin gene to a tropomyosin gene. However the distance separating these two genes is too great (~150 kb) to imply the linkage is functional (Karlik *et al.* 1984). In fact we have recently tested this directly by introducing the act88F gene into four new chromosomal locations using DNA mediated transformation (J. W. Mahaffey, unpublished). Despite the fact that the linkage arrangement of the gene has changed, in all cases the regulated function appears normal since act88F transcripts continue to accumulate only within thoracic muscles. Thus, we are led to conclude that activation of particular *Drosophila* contractile protein genes must be mediated by interactons of trans-acting factors with cis-linked regulatory sequences.

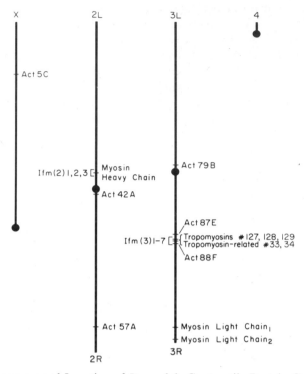

Fig. 3.6. Chromosomal Location of *Drosophila* Contractile Protein Genes. The diagram schematically represents the four chromosomes (X, 2, 3, and 4) of diploid *Drosophila* cells. Locations of particular contractile protein genes are indicated along the right side of each chromosome. On the left sides the approximate locations of two clusters of dominant flightless mutations are bracketed (Mogami and Hotta 1981; and the text).

Locations of each of these genes on the cytological (salivary chromosome) map have been determined in all cases. The six actin genes are named according to these locations, as described in the text. Cytological locations of other genes are as follows; myosin heavy chain; 36B (Rozek and Davidson 1983; Bernstein *et al.* 1983); tropomyosin and tropomyosin-related genes; 88F (Bautch *et al.* 1982; Karlik *et al.* 1984); myosin light chain$_1$ (alkali light chains), 98B; myosin light chain$_2$ (essential light chains), 99E.

GENETIC INVESTIGATIONS OF *DROSOPHILA* ACTIN GENE FUNCTION

While formal genetic studies of *Drosophila* actin genes are presently in their infancy, relative the already described molecular work, such investigations promise to further elucidate particular aspects of actin synthesis, assembly and function. In theory, it should be straightforward to generate large numbers of mutant alleles of actin genes using conventional mutagenesis and screening techniques, and to establish the molecular defect within each by isolating and sequencing the appropriate segment of chromosomal DNA. Functional properties of polypeptides encoded by respective alleles can be deduced by investigating the anatomy and physiology of the mutant muscle fibres or by characterizing isolated mutant actin isoforms using biochemical and biophysical techniques. Additional features of regulated actin gene function can be investigated by classical genetic techniques. For example, we should gain important insights into the interactions of actin polypeptides (both with themselves and with other macromolecules) by studying the complementation of various actin alleles, or by isolating and characterizing revertants of actin gene mutants.

The most convenient manner to proceed with such an investigation is to focus efforts on an actin gene which lends itself particularly well to the classical genetic approach. We consider the act88F actin gene the best possible candidate due to the fact that this gene is expressed only within indirect flight muscles of the adult, which in turn offer a number of experimental advantages. It is appropriate at this point to briefly describe this system of muscle fibres and point out some of these advantages.

The indirect flight muscles (IFM) of *Drosophila* comprise a series of 26 large muscle fibres occupying roughly 50 per cent of the volume of the adult thorax. These are by far the largest muscle fibres of the adult, and this factor facilitates investigations of their morphology and biochemistry (Deak 1977; Deak, Bellamy, Bienz, Dubuis, Fenner, Gollin, Rahmi, Ramp, Reinhardt and Cotton 1982; Mogami, Nonomura and Hotta 1981). Functionally, these muscles have evolved to vibrate the wings rapidly (*Drosophila* can beat its wings at up to 300 times per second) and this entails a number of structural specializations, some of which are apparent in flight muscles of other insects as well (Bullard 1983). However, the basic organization and biochemistry of these fibres is in many respects similar to that of the more familiar vertebrate skeletal muscle.

From the technical standpoint, the most noteworthy aspect of these muscle fibres is that they are utilized only for flight; they are not required for either viability or fertility. This is a great experimental advantage, since mutations which disrupt the integrity of these fibres can survive as homozygotes thereby facilitating characterization of their phenotype. An additional experimental advantage is that such mutants are almost always flightless and, frequently, hold their wings in abnormal positions. Since both of these traits are easy to recognize, screens for such mutants are very straightforward, and in the course of previous decades many mutations which affect IFM myofibrillar structure have been isolated and partially characterized.

Since so many mutations affecting IFM myofibrillar structure have been isolated previously, it seems most appropriate to focus present efforts on ascertaining which of these affect particular contractile protein genes. This task is facilitated by comparing the chromosomal locations of particular mutations, relative to the known locations of contractile protein genes within the *Drosophila* genome (summarized in Fig. 3.6). Such comparisons have recently revealed a striking correlation between the positions of mutations and genes. Mogami and Hotta (1981) isolated and characterized 26 dominant flightless mutations and showed that each disrupts myofibrils of indirect flight muscle. Unexpectedly, most of these mutations map within either of two small chromosome regions. One such region is located on the left arm of chromosome 2, coincident with the position of the *Drosophila* myosin heavy chain gene (Rozek and Davidson 1983; Bernstein, Mogami, Donady and Emerson 1983). The other region is on the right arm of chromosome 3 between the cytological markers *red* and *spineless aristapedia* (Doane and Treat-Clemons 1982; Lindsley and Grell 1968). This location coincides with those of tropomyosin and tropomyosin-related genes (Bautch, Storti, Mischke and Pardue 1982; Karlik *et al.* 1984) and the act88F actin gene, which is expressed during the differentiation of flight muscles (Fyrberg *et al.* 1983). These coincidences strongly imply that several of these mutants result from lesions within the respective contractile protein genes.

Recently we have succeeded in demonstrating that one of the third chromosome mutants of Mogami and Hotta is the result of a defective allele of the act88F actin gene. This mutant, referred to as Ifm(3)7 is ethylmethanesulphonate-induced and (to reiterate) maps to a location on the third chromosome coincident with the act88F actin gene. Biochemical evidence implying that the mutant might carry a defective act88F allele came from two-dimensional gel electrophoresis of Ifm(3)7 thoracic proteins. Analyses by Mogami and Hotta (1981) and Fyrberg *et al.* (submitted for publication), revealed the presence of a protein having a molecular weight slightly less than actin, and an isoelectric point that was slightly more acidic. Hybrid selection and translation of act88F complementary RNA derived from Ifm(3)7 flies demonstrated that this protein was encoded by the act88F gene, thereby directly proving that it was a defective actin isoform.

To examine the molecular nature of the gene defect we have cloned and sequenced that act88F allele of Ifm(3)7. Bam HI digested fragments of Ifm(3)7 genomic DNA were inserted into the Charon 28 bacteriophage vector (Maniatis, Fritsch and Sambrook 1982) and the recombinant molecules were packaged *in vitro* to form viable phage. The particular bacteriophage which carries the act88F sequence was isolated by screening approximately 1×10^6 phages using the technique of Benton and Davis (1977), and the act88F protein coding region was subcloned in plasmid vectors and sequenced by the procedure of Maxam and Gilbert (1980). The key result of these studies is shown in Fig. 3.7. Inspection of the illustrated sequencing ladder demonstrates that a single G > A transition within codon 355 has converted a tryptophan (TGG) codon to an opal (TGA) terminator. As a result this allele would be expected to encode a truncated actin polypeptide which would lack the carboxy-terminal 20 amino acids.

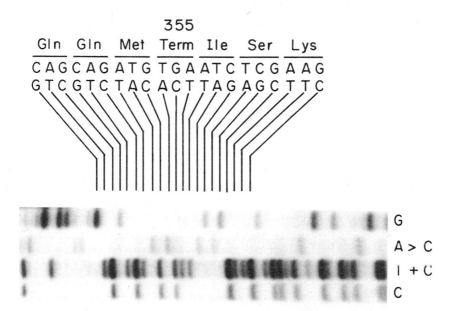

Fig. 3.7. Nucleotide Sequence of the Nonsense Mutation within the Act88F Actin Gene of Ifm(3)7. The autoradiogram is that of an acrylamide gel used to determine the sequence of codons 333–375 of the Ifm(3)7 act88F gene. The sequence of the noncoding (lower) strand can be read directly from the gel. As can be seen by inspection, the normal codon 355 (TGG, tryptophan) has been converted to an opal terminator by a single G > A transition. The mutated gene therefore specifies an actin isoform having the carboxy-terminal 20 amino acids deleted.

Our explanation of the relationship of the gene defect to the aberrant phenotype of indirect flight muscles of Ifm(3)7 takes into consideration several experimental observations. First, the abnormal protein, although truncated, is sufficiently stable to be visualized on Coomassie blue stained two dimensional gels. We interpret this to mean that the protein is present at high concentration within developing muscle fibres. This is an indication (although by no means compelling evidence) that the mutant isoform may be participating in at least some aspects of actin binding and/or polymerization. Supporting this supposition is a second observation, namely that at least two monoclonal anti-*Drosophila* actin antibodies recognize the truncated Ifm(3)7 isoform. This is once again an indication, albeit an indirect one, that the mutant actin polypeptide is sufficiently normal to participate in some stages of actin binding or assembly. Third, observation of fibres of Ifm(3)7 using transmission electron microscopy has revealed that while myofibrillar structure is grossly disrupted, the integrity of thin (actin-containing) filaments and Z-discs is affected more profoundly than that of thick (myosin-containing) filaments. Collectively, these observations support the notion that the truncated actin polypeptide is sufficiently normal to participate in some aspects of actin function or assembly but that at some point in muscle differentiation the abnormal structure of the protein disrupts myofibrillar integrity. This proposed scenario would explain the dominance of the Ifm(3)7 allele, since the haploid gene dosage would be sufficient to 'poison' myofibrillar assembly in affected muscles.

In the near future several additional aberrant act88F alleles should be available for experimentation. Characterization of other flightless mutants mapping in the same chromosome region as Ifm(3)7 will likely reveal that some have missense mutations within the act88F actin gene. Classical genetic analyses of these and other alleles should be most informative. For example, it should be possible to isolate and characterize EMS or gamma-ray-induced revertants of particular actin gene mutations. This approach may demonstrate that mutations in genes encoding proteins which interact with that actin isoform can offset effects of the actin lesion, and thus reveal that previously unsuspected protein-protein interactions are requisite for myofibril formation. Analyses of null (no RNA) alleles will reveal whether or not act88F is a haplo-insufficient gene. Analysis of such an allele, in conjunction with analyses of flies having supernumerary copies of the act88F gene will demonstrate the degree to which myofibrillar assembly is dependent upon precise stoichiometry of contractile protein synthesis.

GERMLINE TRANSFORMATION EXPERIMENTS

Rubin and Spradling have developed a highly efficient technique for introducing cloned DNA segments into Drosophila germline chromosomes. Integration of the cloned DNA is catalyzed by particular elements of a genetically regulated system of DNA transposition which is responsible for the phenomenon of P-M hybrid dysgenesis (Kidwell, Kidwell and Sved 1977). In this technique cloned DNA sequences to be integrated are first inserted within a plasmid vector containing a Drosophila transposable element (termed a P element) using standard recombinant DNA methodology. Injection of such a chimeric plasmid (in concert with one containing the gene which encodes the P element-specific transposase) into germ plasm of M cytotype embryos results in the integration of cloned sequences into germline chromosomes. Chromosomes which contain the integrated sequences are stably inherited by subsequent generations. Detailed explanations of these methods have been published by Spradling and Rubin (1982), and Rubin and Spradling (1982).

The germline transformation technique has several applications for further studies of actin gene function in Drosophila. Perhaps the most obvious is to provide a means by which to reintroduce *in vitro*-mutagenized genes into the genome, thereby enabling the effects of particular actin amino acid replacements to be investigated in the context of living cells. A second useful application is to provide a straightforward strategy for defining cis-linked regions requisite for regulated actin gene expression. One can integrate the protein coding region of a particular actin gene with varying amounts of 5′ and 3′ 'flanking' sequence and subsequently ascertain whether or not the gene functions normally. This general approach should ultimately allow regulatory sequences to be localized precisely. Preliminary analyses of several *Drosophila* structural genes have indicated that such regions constitute relatively short (200–1000 nucleotides) sequences located immediately upstream from the start point of transcription and that these sequences will function properly within a variety of chromosomal contexts (Scholnick, Morgan and Hirsh 1983; Spradling and Rubin 1983; Goldberg, Posakony and Maniatis 1983).

Assuming that regulatory regions of actin genes are as small and autonomously acting as preliminary results indicate, a third line of experiments will be possible using germline transformation. By joining the 'regulatory' region of one actin gene to the protein coding region of another and introducing the resulting chimera into the genome, it should be possible to induce synthesis of particular actin isoforms in new epigenetic situations. For example, by fusing the regulatory sequence of the Ifm specific act88F actin gene to the protein coding region of the cytoplasmic act5C gene it should be possible to induce synthesis of cytoplasmic actin during indirect flight muscle development and to assess the effect of this abnormal protein synthetic pattern. In this manner one should be able to systematically investigate the selective value of actin isoforms, and thus better understand the apparent genetic redundancy of the six similar genes. A conceptually similar approach is being used by Gunning, Ponte, Kedes, Hickey and Skoultchi (1984) to investigate aspects of human actin isoform function.

To enhance our ability to systematically construct such chimeric transcription units we have recently initiated experiments designed to define the regulatory region of the act88F actin gene. Quite by accident we recently discovered that an indirect flight muscle mutant referred to as *raised* (Ives 1945; Lang, Wyss and Eppenberger 1981) could be 'rescued' by integrating extra copies of the wild type (Canton-special strain) act88F gene into its chromosomes. The molecular basis of this phenomenon is not yet clear (i.e. we do not yet know the nature of the defect within the *raised* act88F gene), however all indications are that the rescue involves regulated expression of the supernumerary copies of the act88F gene, since actin synthesis is markedly enhanced within thoraces of the transformed *raised* strains (J. W. Mahaffey, unpublished observations). As a result of the expression of these supernumerary actin genes wing position is normal in the transformed flies and they are capable of flight, although it is not clear that they fly as strongly as the wild type strain. The protocol for transforming *raised* flies (and for recognizing transformants) is illustrated in Fig. 3.8.

This simple transformation assay is facilitating precise definition of the regulatory region of the act88F actin gene. By attempting to rescue the *raised* mutant with act88F actin genes in which 5′ flanking sequences have been progressively deleted we have established that no more than 1350 nucleotides of 5′ flanking DNA is required for regulated expression (P. K. Geyer, unpublished observations). By recombining this flanking segment with protein coding regions of other *Drosophila* actin genes it should soon

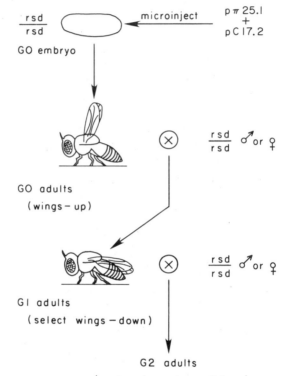

Fig. 3.8. Protocol for Rescue of the *Raised* Mutation Using the Cloned Act88F Actin Gene. Germ plasm of homozygous *raised* embryos is injected with a mixture of two plasmids. One of these (pC17.2) contains the act88F actin gene which has been inserted within a 'P' transposable element. The other (p25.1) encodes proteins which will catalyze integration of P element containing sequences into germline chromosomes (O'Hare and Rubin 1983). Adults which develop from the injected embryos (generation O, or GO) occasionally produce gametes carrying the supernumerary act88F copies and when mated to *raised* homozygotes will bear flightless G1 adults having wings-down (partially corrected phenotype). G1 adults can be crossed to *raised* homozyotes, and sibs of the succeeding generation can be mated to homozygose chromosomes carrying the supernumerary actin gene copies. These homozygous G2 offspring are frequently capable of flight.

be possible to induce expression of any *Drosophila* actin isoform within developing indirect flight muscle fibres. By testing whether these isoforms can rescue the raised homozygotes or (alternatively) null alleles of act88F, we hope to clarify the biological significance of actin isoforms.

Concluding Remarks

All things considered, the prospects for further elucidation of actin gene function in *Drosophila* are very favourable. The ability to combine molecular and classical genetic approaches, coupled with the biological advantages of the indirect flight muscles permits a more systematic approach than is possible in most other biological systems. At this time I see no reason why the experimental approaches discussed herein cannot be successfully applied to the other contractile protein genes of *Drosophila*.

Acknowledgements

Work from the author's laboratory has been supported by grants from the National Institutes of Health and the Muscular Dystrophy Association. I thank numerous colleagues for enlightening discussions and unpublished results. *Add:* Figures 3:1, 3:2, 3:3, 3:4, 3:5, 3:8 reproduced with permission from M.I.T. Press.

References

Anderson, K. V. and Lengyel, J. A. (1979). Rates of synthesis of major classes of RNA in *Drosophila* embryos. *Dev. Biol.* **70**, 217–231.

Bautch, V. L., Storti, R. V., Mischke, D., and Pardue, M. L. (1982). Organization and expression of *Drosophila* tropomyosin genes. *J. Mol. Biol.* **162**, 231–250.

Bender, W., Davidson, N., Kindle, K. L., Taylor, W. C., Silverman, M., and Firtel, R. A. (1978). The structure of M6, a recombinant plasmid containing *Dictyostelium* DNA homologous to actin messenger RNA. *Cell* **15**, 779–788.

Benton, W. D. and Davis, R. W. (1977). Screening *λ*gt recombinant clones by hybridization to single plaques *in situ*. *Science* **196**, 180–182.

Bernstein, S., Mogami, K., Donady, J., and Emerson, C. (1983). *Drosophila* myosin heavy chain is encoded by a single gene located in a chromosomal region of other muscle genes. *Nature* **302**, 393–397.

Blake, C. (1983). Exons – present from the beginning? *Nature* **306**, 535–537.

Bodenstein, D. (1950). The postembryonic development of *Drosophila*. In *Biology of Drosphila* (ed. M. Demerec) pp. 278–282. John Wiley and Sons, New York.

Breathnach, R., Benoist, C., O'Hare, K., Gannon, F., and Chambon, P. (1978). Ovalbumin gene: Evidence for a leader sequence in mRNA and DNA sequences at the exon-intron boundaries. *Proc. Natl. Acad. Sci. U.S.A.* **75**, 4853–4857.

Buckingham, M. E. and Minty, A. J. (1983). Contractile protein genes. In *Eukaryotic Genes: Their Structure, Activity and Regulation* (ed. a. Flavell, S. P. Gregory, and N. MacLean) Butterworths.

Bullard, B. (1983). Contractile proteins of insect flight muscle. *Trends in Biomedical Science*, February, 1983. Elsevier Biomedical Press.

Cooper, A. D. and Crain, W. R. (1982). Complete nucleotide sequence of a sea urchin actin gene. *Nucleic Acids Res.* **10**, 4081–4092.

Crossley, A. C. (1978). The morphology and development of the *Drosophila* muscular system. In *The Genetics and Biology of Drosophila*, Vol. 2b (ed. M. Ashburner and T. R. F. Wright) pp. 499–560. Academic Press, New York.

Deak, I. I. (1977). Mutations of *Drosophila melanogaster* that affect muscles. *J. Embryol. exp. Morph.* **40**, 35–63.

—— Bellamy, P. R., Bienz, M., Dubuis, Y., Fenner, E., Gollin, M., Rahmi, A., Ramp, T., Reinhardt, C. A., and Cotton, B. (1982). Mutations affecting the indirect flight muscles of *Drosophila malanogaster*. *J. Embryol. exp. Morph.* **69**, 61–81.

Doane, W. W. and Treat-Clemons, L. G. (1982). Biochemical loci of the fruit fly (*Drosophila melanogaster*). *Dros. Inf. Serv.* **58**, 41–60.

Efstratiadis, A. *et al.* (1980). The structure and evolution of the human β-globin gene family. *Cell* **21**, 653–668.

Files, J. G., Carr, S., and Hirsh, D. (1983). Actin gene family of *Caenorhabditis elegans*. *J. Mol. Biol.* **164**, 355–375.

Firtel, R. A. (1981). Multigene families encoding actin and tubulin. *Cell* **24**, 6–7.

Fyrberg, E. A., Kindle, K. L., Davidson, N., and Sodja, A. (1980). The actin genes of *Drosophila*: A dispersed multigene family. *Cell* **19**, 365–378.

—— Bond, B. J., Hershey, N. D., Mixter, K. S., and Davidson, N. (1981). The actin genes of *Drosophila*: Protein coding regions are highly conserved but intron positions are not. *Cell* **24**, 107–116.

—— Bond, B. J., Hershey, N. D., Mixter, K. S., and Davidson, N. (1982). Structural studies of the *Drosophila malanogaster* actin genes. In *Muscle Development: Molecular and Cellular Control* (ed. M. L. Pearson and H. F. Epstein) Cold Spring Harbor Laboratory.

—— Mahaffey, J. W., Bond, B. J., and Davidson, N. (1983). Transcripts of the six *Drosophila* actin genes accumulate in a stage- and tissue-specific manner. *Cell* **33**, 115–123.

—— Karlik, C. C., and Coutu, M. D. A nonsense mutation in the act88F actin gene disrupts myofibril formation in *Drosophila* flight muscle. *Cell* **38**, 711–719.

Gall, J. G. and Pardue, M. L. (1971). Nucleic acid hybridization to cytological preparations. *Methods Enzymol.* **21**, 470–480.

Garcea, R. L., Schachat, F., and Epstein, H. F. (1978). Coordinate synthesis of two myosins in wild type and mutant nematode muscle during larval development. *Cell* **15**, 421–428.

Goldberg, D. A., Posakony, J. W., and Maniatis, T. (1983). Correct developmental expression of a cloned alcohol dehydrogenase gene transduced into the *Drosophila* germ line. *Cell* **34**, 59–73.

Goldberg, M. (1979). Ph.D. Thesis. Stanford University, Stanford, California.

Gunning, P., Ponte, P., Okayama, H., Engel, J., Blau, H., and Kedes, L. (1983a). Isolation and characterization of full length cDNA clones for human α, β and γ-actin mRNAs: Skeletal but not cytoplasmic actins have an amino-terminal cysteine that is subsequently removed. *Mol. Cell. Biol.* **3**, 787–795.

—— Ponte, P., Blau, H., and Kedes, L. (1983b). α-Skeletal and α-cardiac actin genes are co-expressed in adult human skeletal muscle and heart. *Mol. Cell. Biol.* **3**, 1985–1995.

—— Ponte, P., Kedes, L., Hickey, R. J., and Skoultchi, A. I. (1984). Expression of human cardiac action in mouse L cells: a sarcomeric actin associates with a non-muscle cytoskeleton. *Cell* **36**, 709–715.

Ives, P. T. (1945). *Dros. Inf. Serv.* **19**, 46.

Karlik, C. C., Mahaffey, J. W., Coutu, M. D., and Fyrberg, E. A. (1984). Organization of contractile protein genes within the 88F subdivision of the *Drosophila melanogaster* third chromsome. *Cell* **37**, 469–481.

Kemphues, K. J., Raff, E. C., Raff, R. A., and Kaufman, T. C. (1980). Mutation in a testis-specific β-tubulin in *Drosophila*: Analysis of its effects on meiosis and map location of the gene. *Cell* **21**, 445–451.

Kidwell, M. G., Kidwell, J. F., and Sved, J. A. (1977). Hybrid dysgenesis in *Drosophila melanogaster*: A syndrome of aberrant traits including mutation, sterility and male recombination. *Genetics* **86**, 813–833.

Lang, A. B., Wyss, C., and Eppenberger, H. M. (1981). Lack of actin III in fibrillar flight muscle of flightless *Drosophila* mutant *raised. Nature* **291**, 506–508.

Lawrence, P. A. (1982). Cell lineage of the thoracic muscles of *Drosophila. Cell* **29**, 493–503.

Lindsley, D. L. and Grell, E. H. (1968). Genetic variations of *Drosophila melanogaster. Carnegie Inst. Wash.* Publ. no. 627.

Lomedico, P., Rosenthal, N., Efstratiadis, A., Gilbert, W., Kolodner, R., and Tizard, R. (1979). The structure and evolution of the two nonallelic rat prepoinsulin genes. *Cell* **18**, 545–558.

Maniatis, T., Fritsch, E. F., and Sambrook, J. (1982). *Molecular cloning*. Cold Spring Harbor Laboratory, Cold Spring Harbor, New York.

Maxam, A. and Gilbert, W. (1980). Sequencing end-labelled DNA with base-specific chemical cleavages. *Meth. Enzymol.* **65**, 499–560.

Mishina, M. *et al.* (1984). Expression of functional acetylcholine receptor from cloned cDNAs. *Nature* **307**, 604–608.

Mogami, K. and Hotta, Y. (1981). Isolation of *Drosophila* flightless mutants which affect myofibrillar proteins of indirect flight muscle. *Mol. Gen. Genet.* **183**, 409– 417.

—— Nonomura, Y., and Hotta, Y. (1981). Electron microscopic and electrophoretic studies of a *Drosophila* muscle mutant *Wings-up B. Jpn. J. Genet.* **56**, 51–65.

O'Brien, S. J. and MacIntyre, R. J. (1978). Genetics and biochemistry of enzymes and specific proteins of *Drosophila*. In *The Genetics and Biology of* Drosophila (ed. M. Ashburner and T. R. F. Wright) Vol. 2a, pp. 395–551. Academic Press, New York.

O'Hare, K. and Rubin, G. M. (1983). Structure of P transposable elements of *Drosophila melanogaster* and their sites of insertion and excision. *Cell* **34**, 25–35.

Pollard, T. D. and Weihing, R. R. (1974). Actin and myosin and cell movement. *CRC Crit. Rev. Biochem.* **2**, 1–65.

Ponte, P., Gunning, P., Blau, H., and Kedes, L. (1983). Human actin genes are single copy for α-skeletal and α-cardiac actin but multicopy for β- and γ-cytoskeletal genes: 3′ untranslated regions are isotype specific but are conserved in evolution. *Mol. Cell. Biol.* **3**, 1783–1791.

Poulson, D. F. (1950). Histogenesis, organogenesis and differentiation of the embryo of *Drosophila melanogaster* meigen. In *Biology of Drosophila* (ed. M. Demerec) pp. 168–181. John Wiley and Sons, New York.

Rozek, C. E. and Davidson, N. (1983). *Drosophila* has one myosin heavy chain gene with three developmentally regulated transcripts. *Cell* **32**, 23–34.

Rubin, G. M. and Spradling, A. C. (1982). Genetic transformation of *Drosophila* with transposable element vectors. *Science* **218**, 348–353.

Sánchez, F., Tobin, S. L., Rdest, U., Zulauf, E., and McCarthy, B. J. (1983). Two *Drosophila* actin genes in detail: Gene structure, protein structure and transcription during development. *J. Mol. Biol.* **163**, 533–551.

Scheller, R. H., McAllister, L. B., Crain, W. R. Jr., Durica, D. S., Posakony, J. W., Britten, R. J., and Davidson, E. H. (1981). Organization and expression of multipole actin genes in the sea urchin. *Mol. Cell. Biol.* **7**, 609–628.

Scholnick, S. B., Morgan, B. A., and Hirsh, J. (1983). The cloned dopa decarboxylase gene is developmentally regulated when reintegrated into the *Drosophila* genome. *Cell* **34**, 37–45.

Spradling, A. C. and Mahowald, A. P. (1981). A chromosome inversion alters the pattern of specific DNA replication in *Drosophila* follicle cells. *Cell* **27**, 203–209.

Spradling, A. C. and Rubin, G. M. (1982). Transposition of cloned P elements into *Drosophila* germline chromosomes. *Science* **218**, 341–347.

Spradling, A. C. and Rubin, G. M. (1983). The effect of chromosomal position on the expression of the *Drosophila* xanthine dehydrogenase gene. *Cell* **34**, 47–57.

Tobin, S. L., Zulauf, E., Sánchez, F., Craig, E. A., and McCarthy, B. (1980). Multiple actin-related sequences in the *Drosophila melanogaster* genome. *Cell* **19**, 121–131.

Vandekerckhove, J. and Weber, K. (1978). Mammalian cytoplasmic actins are the products of at least two genes and differ in primary structure in at least 25 identified positions from skeletal muscle actins. *Proc. Natl. Acad. Sci. U.S.A.* **75**, 1106–1110.

Wood, W. G. and Weatherall, D. J. (1983). Developmental genetics of the human hemoglobins. *Biochem. J.* **215**, 1–10.

Zulauf, E., Sánchez, F., Tobin, S. L., Rdest, U., and McCarthy, B. J. (1981). Developmental expression of a *Drosophila* actin gene encoding actin I. *Nature* **292**, 556–558.

4 Expression of proviral DNA of mouse mammary tumour virus and its transcriptional control sequences

B. GRONER, B. SALMONS,
W. H. GÜNZBURG, N. E. HYNES AND
H. PONTA

Introduction

The study of retroviral systems has contributed extensively to the understanding of eukaryotic gene expression. Although a wide variety of different
retroviruses exist which are harboured by many different hosts, their basic
characteristics are similar (Weiss, Teich, Varmus and Coffin 1982). There
are a number of unique features which distinguish other cellular genes from
retroviruses and there are features which are common to all cellular and
retroviral genes. The distinctive characteristic of retroviral genes is their
dual mode of transmission. As part of the genome they are present in the
germ line of many animals and transmitted from one generation to the
next. These endogenous proviral genes are part of the genetic information
of all somatic cells. In addition to the vertical transmission of endogenous
proviral gene copies a horizontal mode exists. This retroviral life cycle
includes transcription of proviral DNA, translation and virus maturation,
release of virus particles, infection of new host cells, reverse transcription
and integration into the genome of the infected cells. These steps amount
to a transposition event and thus distinguish proviral genes from other
cellular genes (Varmus 1983). Why are these seemingly atypical genes a rich
source of investigation for the molecular biologist? If we again consider the
vertically transmitted endogenous proviruses, one aspect is prominent:
endogenous proviruses have been found in a large number of vertebrates.
Avian viruses such as the avian leukaemia virus, and murine viruses such as
the murine leukaemia and murine mammary tumour virus, have been extensively investigated (Coffin 1982). The endogenous proviruses of mouse
mammary tumour virus are present in multiple copies (two to six copies) in
the genomes of most inbred mouse strains (Traina-Dorge and Cohen 1983).
The proviral DNA was probably acquired by infrequent germ line infection
events which have taken place after speciation. No apparent specificity for
integration into the host genome has been detected, since proviral genes are
found at different genomic locations in different mouse strains. Different
endogenous proviral MMTV genes have been found to have different biological properties with respect to the control of their expression and their involvement in tumour formation (Hynes, Groner and Michalides 1984). The
presence of a particular gene in different locations of the genome provides

an excellent opportunity to study effects on gene expression which go beyond the primary sequence of a gene and its regulatory sequences (Feinstein, Ross and Yamamoto 1982). These effects include chromatin conformation, methylation of DNA or other factors regulating domains of the genome and tissue specific expression. The correlation between proviral DNA methylation and tissue specific expression will be discussed.

Horizontally transmitted proviral genes of MMTV have helped in the elucidation of several questions:

A. The process of reverse transcription creates a DNA molecule which is flanked at both ends by long terminal repeats (LTR). These LTRs contain sequence information from the 5' (U5) and the 3' (U3) ends of the viral genomic RNA which is present in virus particles. The integration event into the host cellular DNA leaves the direct repeats of several hundred nucleotides intact, i.e. no circular permutations occur and the integration event is specific with respect to the 5' end and 3' end of the proviral DNA. The process of reverse transcription and integration precisely defines the borders of the proviral gene. This definition is particularly useful when transcriptional control sequences located 5' of the promoter sequence are being investigated. If the proviral DNA provides its own transcription regulation signals they have to be located within several hundred nucleotides of the U3 region of the LTR. Studies on the hormonal control of proviral transcription and enhancer activity found in the MMTV LTR will be described below.

B. The proviral DNA is flanked by LTR sequences generated during the process of reverse transcription (Varmus 1983). Sequence analysis of the LTRs and their flanking host DNA has revealed a number of features which resemble the sequence organization at the ends of transposable elements found in bacteria, yeast, and *Drosophila*. Since integration of DNA into the host genome is the least common denominator between these elements and proviral DNA, insight into the recombination process may be gained. A circular intermediate in which both LTRs are joined in tandem has been shown to serve as a substrate for integration (Panganiban and Temin 1984). Two base pairs are lost from the 5' and 3' ends of the provirus during the integration event. The host DNA sequence into which the proviral integration occurs is duplicated during this process. Four to six nucleotides found once in the genomic DNA are present on both sides of the provirus. Three to 22 pairs of inverted repeat sequences flank the LTR sequences themselves. These features of provirus integration allow an approach to the enzymatic description of DNA recombination in mammalian cells.

C. A third important field of investigation accessible through horizontally transmitted retroviruses is the mechanism of cellular transformation. Retroviruses can be distinguished into two groups, one containing the genetic information required for cellular transformation (v-onc) and one which transforms cells by an indirect mechanism related to insertional mutagenesis by the proviral DNA. Since MMTV does not seem to contain an oncogene, attention has focussed on the host DNA with which the proviral DNA associates in mammary tumours. The discovery of domains within the genome of mammary tumour cell DNA which harbour proviral DNA and the activation of cellular transcripts from these domains has provided a first hint of a link between insertion and transformation (Nusse and Varmus 1982; Peters, Brookes, Smith and Dickson 1983). It is, however, still unclear if the activated cellular gene has a role in the transformation process. The identification of the function of the MMTV activated gene remains an important question. How does the provirus exert its activating influence? Molecular details about the regulatory DNA sequences contained in the MMTV LTR and their possible involvement in the activation of genes over a distance will be discussed. Properties analogous to enhancer sequences seem to be involved and present in the MMTV LTR sequence.

Expression of endogenous proviral DNA and a hybrid of proviral variants

The presence of proviral MMTV at many different locations within the mouse genome has been extensively studied (Traina, Taylor and Cohen 1981; Callahan, Gallahan and Kozak 1984; MacInnes, Morris, Flintoff and Kozak 1984). Seventeen loci containing MMTV genes which are characterized by unique host sequences flanking the proviral DNA have been described in different inbred mouse strains (Traina-Dorge and Cohen 1983). At least five of these MMTV proviral loci are present in the GR mouse (Groner, Buetti, Diggelmann and Hynes 1980). These are dispersed over five chromosomes and can be distinguished with respect to their biological properties. One of the five endogenous MMTV proviruses (Mtv-2) controls the expression of high levels of MMTV in the milk of lactating females and the high incidence of pregnancy-dependent tumours in the GR mouse strain. The Mtv-2 locus is present on chromosome 18 (Michalides, van Nie, Nusse, Hynes and Groner 1981). A second proviral locus (Mtv-3) of the GR mouse is responsible for the synthesis of MMTV specific RNA and protein. This Mtv-3 locus on chromosome 11, however, directs only p27 expression and no envelope glycoproteins are found. Since the proper mRNA of 35S and 24S are found in lactating mammary glands of GR-Mtv-2$^-$ mice (lacking the Mtv-2 locus and only expressing the Mtv-3 locus) it is reasonable to assume that the Mtv-3 provirus is mutated (Hynes, Groner and Michalides 1984). Mtv-8 and Mtv-19, also present in the genome of the GR mouse, seem to be silent copies. Mtv-20 appears to be expressed at least in the spleen (Günzburg, unpublished results).

What is the basis for the difference in the biological activity of different endogenous proviral copies? Molecular cloning and the comparison of the restriction enzyme sites present in the proviral DNA have shown that the gene copies are very similar but that they are not identical (Herrlich, Hynes,

Ponta, Rahmsdorf, Kennedy and Groner 1981). Could a slight sequence variation be the reason for inactivation of the MMTV proviral genes? This possibility was investigated. An entire proviral gene containing cellular flanking sequences on both sides was molecularly cloned and identified as Mtv-8. Transfection of this clone (pGR 16, Fig. 4.1) into mouse L cells (Hynes, Kennedy, Rahmsdorf and Groner 1981a; Diggelman, Vessaz and Buetti 1982), rat XC cells (Ponta, Kennedy, Herrlich, Hynes and Groner 1983) or cat kidney cells (B. Salmons, unpublished results) showed that the transfected DNA can be stably acquired by all three cell types, transcribed into 35S and 24S RNA and that its transcription is induced by the addition of glucocorticoid hormone to the growth medium. No virus particles, however, were found in the tissue culture supernatant of the transfected cells. The provirus Mtv-8 has been found in most mouse strains and a high degree of methylation of the provirus has been detected. Gene cloning resulting in non-methylated proviral DNA and reintroduction into cultured cells led to transcriptional activation. The absence of virus production, however, indicated a defect in the coding potential of the provirus.

· The viral glycoproteins gp52 and gp36 are part of the membrane surrounding the virus particle and are encoded by a 24S mRNA which is transcribed from the 3′ proximal env portion of the provirus (Bentvelzen 1982). Both glycoproteins are synthesized as a 73 kd precursor protein which

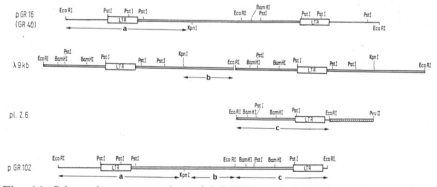

Fig. 4.1. Schematic representation of MMTV proviral DNAs and recombinant DNAs used in transfection experiments.

Inserts cloned into the Eco RI site, or the Eco RI and PvuII sites of pBR322 (prefix p), or lambda (prefix λ) vectors, are shown. Mouse genomic DNA is indicated by a single line, MMTV sequences by a double line and thymidine kinase sequences by a double line with dots. The MMTV long terminal repeat sequence is marked LTR.

The hybrid provirus, pGR102, consists of the *gag* region (a), of the endogenous provirus GR40, and the *pol* and *env* regions (b and c, respectively) of exogenous type MMTV DNA.

The molecular clones shown have been described before: pGR16 (GR40) by Hynes *et al.* 1981a, and Ponta *et al.* 1983; λ9 kb by Buetti and Diggelmann 1981; p1 2.6 by Hynes *et al.* 1983).

is cleaved post-translationally into gp52 and gp36. This precursor (Pr73^{env}) can be visualized by immunoprecipitation of labeled cellular proteins with an antiserum specifically raised against gp52 (Dickson and Atterwill 1980; Sarkar and Racevskis 1983). Figure 4.2, lane 7, shows the proteins precipitated from a mammary tumour cell line (GR) which produces a large amount of virus particles. The Pr73^{env} as well as the mature gp52 can be seen. Cat kidney cells can be infected with MMTV and are able to support virus production (Lasfargues, Kramarsky, Lasfargues and Moore 1974). When these cells transfected with the cloned Mtv-8 DNA were investigated for Pr73^{env} and gp52 expression, only a protein of 68 kd could be precipitated with an anti-gp52 serum (Fig. 4.2, lane 1). No processed, mature gp52 protein was found. The nucleotide sequence of the env genes of the proviral copy expressed in GR cells (Mtv-2) and the molecularly cloned copy which was transfected into the cat kidney cells (Mtv-8) have been obtained (Redmond

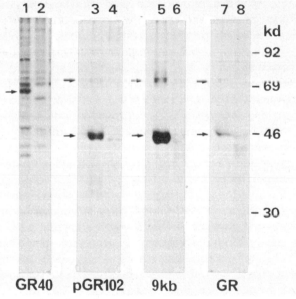

Fig. 4.2. Immunoprecipitation of MMTV specific env proteins with anti-gp52 serum.
   Transfected cat kidney cells were labeled overnight in ^{35}S methionine-containing medium. Cell extracts were prepared and immunoprecipitated with anti-gp52 serum (lanes 1,3,5,7) which recognizes Pr73^{env} and gp52 (indicated by arrows in lanes 3,5,7) and Pr68^{env} (arrowed lane 1). The immunoprecipitates were recovered using Protein A sepharose and analysed by SDS-polyacrylamide electrophoresis. As a control, the same cell extracts were immunoprecipitated with normal rabbit serum (lanes 2,4,6,8).
Lanes 1 and 2: Cells transfected with the endogenous provirus GR40 (Mtv-8).
Lanes 3 and 4: Cells transfected with the hybrid construct pGR102 (Fig. 4.1).
Lanes 5 and 6: Cells transfected with concatenates of exogenous (Mtv-2) DNA (λ9 kb, Fig. 4.1).
   Env-specific MMTV proteins were also immunoprecipitated from a labeled cell lysate prepared from virus-producing GR cells (lanes 7 and 8).

and Dickson 1983; Majors and Varmus 1983*a*; Knedlitschek, unpublished results). The Mtv-2 env protein extends into the 3′ LTR region and the carboxyl terminus of gp36 is encoded by a sequence extending through a polypurine tract (priming site for positive strand synthesis) 53 nucleotides into the 3′ LTR (Henderson, Sowder, Smythers and Oroszlan 1983). The env gene of Mtv-8 has a stop codon in the env precursor reading frame located 152 nucleotides 5′ of the LTR border and codes for a shorter precursor protein of 68 kd (Pr68^{env}). The loss of 68 amino acids at the carboxyl terminus results in the loss of a hydrophobic region and seems to inhibit the proper processing.

The major structural component of the viral core is the phosphoprotein p27. This protein is synthesized from 35S mRNA and is encoded in the 5′ gag portion of the provirus. Similar to the env gene products, the gag gene products (p27, pp21, p14 and p10) are translated as a polyprotein precursor of 77 kd (Pr77^{gag}) which is processed post-translationally (Dickson and Atterwill 1978). Using an antiserum against p27 the Pr77^{gag} and mature p27 was found in Mtv-8 transfected cells (Salmons, unpublished results). This result indicates that Mtv-8 can support the synthesis and maturation of the viral core proteins.

A molecular clone which can support a 'productive transfection' would be very valuable for the 'reverse genetics' of MMTV. Introduction of targeted lesions and their phenotypic consequence could be studied.

Attempts to molecularly clone the intact Mtv-2 proviral DNA were not successful. Changes in the molecular weight of the PstI fragment located in the gag region of the provirus just 3′ of the left LTR ('poison sequence') were consistently observed upon introduction into prokaryotic vectors (Majors and Varmus 1981; Groner *et al.* 1980). It was, however, possible to obtain molecular clones of Mtv-2 and of other horizontally transmitted proviral genes which only contain the 3′ portion encoding the env information. Since the defect of the Mtv-8 copy is suspected to be in the env region, a hybrid provirus was constructed *in vitro* which comprises the gag region of Mtv-8 (Hynes *et al.* 1981*a*, region a in Fig. 4.1), the pol region derived from a Mtv-2 related clone (Buetti and Diggelmann, 1981), a molecular clone of a circular intermediate of proviral integration which contains only a single LTR (Kpn I to EcoRI, region b in Fig. 4.1) and the env gene region of an Mtv-2 related horizontally transmitted provirus (Groner *et al.* 1980) (region c in Fig. 4.1). This *in vitro* recombined proviral gene (pGR102, Fig. 4.1) was transfected into cat kidney cells and gp52 related proteins were immunoprecipitated. Authentic Pr73^{env} and gp52 were synthesized (Fig. 4.2, lane 3). The same result could be observed when the 9 kb circular permutated proviral DNA (Fig. 4.1, 9 kb, Buetti and Diggelmann 1981) was separated from its prokaryotic vector DNA, concatenated by ligation and transfected (Fig. 4.2, lane 5). Table 4.1 summarizes the proteins detected with anti-gp52 and anti-p27 sera in cells transfected with different proviral DNA constructs.

Table 4.1

MMTV-specific proteins synthesized in transfected cells

Transfected proviral DNA	Proviral variant	Reference	MMTV proteins synthesized in transfected cells		Virus production
			env-related	gag-related	
pGR16	Endogenous GR40 (Mtv-8)	Hynes *et al.* 1981*a*	Pr68	Pr77^{gag}, p27	—
9kb	Concantenated 9kb Exogenous (Mtv-2 related)	Buetti and Diggelmann 1981	gPr73^{env}, gp52	Pr77^{gag}, p27	+
pGR102	Endogenous gag Exogenous pol/env	Salmons *et al.* manuscript in prep.	gPr73^{env}, gp52	Pr77^{gag}, p27	+
GR, MMTV producing cell line		Ringold 1979	gPr73^{env}gp52	Pr77^{gag}, p27	+

Virus particles were found in the tissue culture medium of pGR102 transfected cat kidney cells which contained correctly processed gp52 and p27
and which banded at the expected density of 1.17 g/cm^3 in a sucrose gradient. This result indicates that the gag region of Mtv-8, although slightly
different from the one of Mtv-2 as judged by restriction sites polymorphisms, is functional and can support core protein production. Mutations
in the env region of Mtv-8 prevent the synthesis of mature glycoproteins.
These experiments define one level, differences in nucleotide sequence, which
is responsible for the different biological properties of the endogenous
MMTV proviruses.

Methylation of proviral DNA and its effect on transcription

The cloned Mtv-8 provirus introduced into mouse L cells by transfection is
transcriptionally active and can be hormonally induced. This is in contrast
to a copy of Mtv-8 present in untransfected L cells which is transcriptionally
silent and not inducible (Hynes et al. 1981b). What could be the basis for
the difference in transcriptional activity between the endogenous resident
gene and the transfected cloned gene? DNA methylation has been implicated
in the regulation of gene expression (Ehrlich and Wang 1981; Cooper 1983).
Several examples have been described in which genes are undermethylated
in tissues where they are expressed and hypermethylated in tissues where
they are silent (Razin and Friedman 1981). The use of methylation-sensitive
restriction enzymes recognizing 5' CpG 3' has been used to study endogenous proviral MMTV genes (Breznik and Cohen 1982; Hu, Fanning and
Cardiff 1984). The Mtv-8 copies endogenous to mouse L cells are highly

Fig. 4.3. a. Analysis of the extent of methylation of MMTV proviral genes by Southern blotting visualisation of restriction fragments.

   DNA was digested with the restriction enzymes Eco RI (lanes 1,3,5) or Eco RI
and Hpa II (lanes 2,4,6). After size separation by gel electrophoresis, the DNA frag-
ments were transferred to a nitrocellulose filter and hybridized to a ^{32}P-labeled,
nick-translated MMTV probe.
Lanes 1 and 2: DNA from livers of GR mice.
Lanes 3 and 4: DNA from GR liver cells immortalized by transfection with SV40
DNA.
Lanes 5 and 6: DNA from SV40 immortalized GR liver cells treated with 5-azacy-
tidine.
b. Quantitation of MMTV-specific transcripts by dot blot analysis.
   RNA prepared from various cells was dotted onto a nitrocellulose filter, and
MMTV-specific transcripts visualized by hybridization to the ^{32}P-labeled MMTV
probe.
Lane 1: RNA from livers of GR mice.
Lane 2: RNA from GR liver cells immortalized by transfection of SV40 DNA.
Lane 3: RNA from SV40 immortalized GR liver cells treated with 5-azacytidine.
Lane 4: As in lane 3, after treatment with glucocorticoid hormone.
   A quantitation of the transcripts is shown in Table 4.2.

methylated; cloned, transfected Mtv-8 copies are non-methylated (Hynes *et al.* 1981*b*). To correlate MMTV DNA methylation and transcription in a less artificial situation, the state of methylation of proviral genes in organs of the GR mouse strain was investigated (Günzburg and Groner 1984). All somatic cells of this inbred mouse strain contain at least five copies of endogenous MMTV proviruses present at different chromosomal locations on five different chromosomes (R. Michalides, personal communication). We derived an experimental approach which allows us to probe the state of methylation of all proviral genes independently from each other. This protocol is based on the detection of the endogenous proviral gene copies by

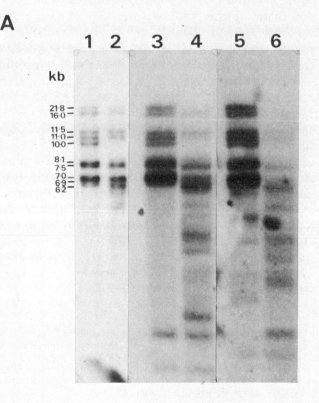

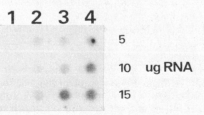

visualization of locus-specific EcoRI fragments. Each EcoRI fragment contains several recognition sites for the restriction enzyme HpaII which is selectively inhibited by the methylation of the second cytosine of the palindromic recognition sequence. Double digestion of genomic DNA with EcoRI and HpaII allows us to distinguish fully and hypomethylated proviral genes. We find that specific methylation states are associated with different proviral loci and that these patterns are specific for different tissues. Furthermore the methylation of individual proviral genes is stable over many mouse generations and may extend over genomic domains (Günzburg and Groner 1984; Günzburg, Hynes and Groner 1984).

The investigation of MMTV proviral locus methylation can be combined with expression studies. Figure 4.3, lanes 1 and 2 show the comparison of GR liver DNA digested with EcoRI (lane 1) or with EcoRI and HpaII (lane 2). The persistence of all bands except those of 10.0 and 8.1 kb shows that 4 proviral copies are fully methylated at the Hpa II recognition sites in

Table 4.2

MMTV-specific RNA present in cellular RNA from various mouse tissues or cells.

RNA Source	percentage MMTV-specific RNA × 10^3	Approx. no. of molecules/cells
GR liver	not detectable	<4
SV40-transformed GR liver cells	0.28	~11
SV40-transformed GR liver cells treated with 5-azacytidine	0.5	~20
SV40-transformed GR liver cells treated with 5-azacytidine and glucocorticoid hormone	0.92	~36
GR 5-day regenerating liver	0.65	~26

Values are calculated from RNA dot blot analysis in which MMTV viral RNA was also dotted as a standard. The approximate number of molecules was calculated assuming 1 molecule of MMTV RNA = 0.5×10^{-17} g and that one cell produces 2×10^{-5} ug total RNA.

Fig. 4.4. a. Analysis of the extent of methylation of MMTV proviral genes by Southern blotting visualization of restriction fragments.

DNA was digested with the restriction enzymes Eco RI (lanes 1 and 3), or Eco RI and Hpa II (lanes 2 and 4). MMTV-specific fragments were visualized as described in Fig. 4.3a.
Lanes 1 and 2: DNA from livers of GR mice.
Lanes 3 and 4: DNA from a 5-day regenerating GR mouse liver.
b. Quantitation of MMTV-specific transcripts by dot blot analysis.

RNA prepared from GR livers (lane 1), or 5-day regenerating GR liver (lane 2) was dotted onto a nitrocellulose filtre, and the MMTV-specific transcripts visualized by hybridization to the ^{32}P-labeled MMTV probe.

A quantitation of the transcripts is shown in Table 4.2.

liver cells and that a single copy (Mtv-20, characterized by EcoRI fragments of 10.0 and 8.1 kb) is hypomethylated. An RNA dot blot hybridization experiment showed that all five proviral copies are transcriptionally silent in liver tissue (Fig. 4.3b, lane 1 and Table 4.2). As in the case of the α-2

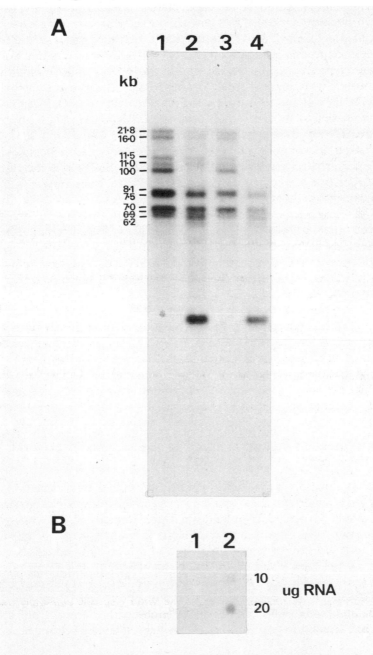

(1) collagen gene (McKeon, Ohkubo, Pastan and de Crombrugghe 1982) and the rat hepatoma cell albumin gene (Ott, Sperling, Cassio, Levilliers, Sala-Trepat and Weiss 1982) under-methylation of the Mtv-20 copy in liver cells *in vivo* is not a sufficient prerequisite for MMTV transcription.

Previous investigation of the methylation of horizontally transmitted, transcriptionally active MMTV showed that these proviral copies are hypo-methylated (Cohen 1980). Experimentally induced hypomethylation of endogenous proviral genes has an effect on MMTV transcription. GR liver cells were immortalized by transfection of SV40 DNA. Their establishment in culture led to a marked reduction in the extent of proviral methylation (Fig. 4.3a, lane 4) and to the transcriptional activation of endogenous pro-viral DNA (Fig. 4.3b, lane 2 and Table 4.2). SV40-immortalized liver cells were treated with 5-azacytidine. This compound is known to inhibit DNA methylation (Jones and Taylor 1980) and leads to a further hypomethylation of MMTV proviral genes (Fig. 4.3a, lane 6). The decrease in the extent of methylation was accompanied by increased MMTV transcription (Fig. 4.3b, lane 3) which was inducible by glucocorticoid hormone (lane 4). The quanti-tation of transcripts is shown in Table 4.2. Rapid growth of liver tissue is observed after removal of a part of the liver. Regenerating liver was compared to normal liver in its extent of proviral methylation. Fig. 4.4a, lane 4 demonstrates the reduction in the MMTV proviral gene methylation which is accompanied by the appearance of MMTV transcripts (Fig. 4.4b, lane 2 and Table 4.2).

Three regimens of treatment: transformation, azacytidine treatment or induction of proliferation by partial hepatectomy, have thus been shown to decrease the extent of MMTV gene methylation. The carefully controlled and maintained patterns of methylation observed in differentiated tissues are disrupted and accompanied by gene transcription. These experiments identify methylation as a second level of control which influences the diffe-rential transcription of proviral copies.

Enhancement of gene expression in the vicinity of proviral MMTV DNA

A basic assumption in the current concept of cellular transformation is the ability of a single or a few genes to trigger the pleiotropic biochemical events which distinguish a normal from a transformed cell. The concept was derived many years ago from experiments in which small viruses such as SV40, polyoma virus or RSV were used to transform cultured cells (reviewed by Bishop 1983 and Weinberg 1982). The identification and characterization of the genes involved in the transformation process, however, only became possible recently and led to the description of 18 viral oncogenes (Land, Parada and Weinberg 1983). These oncogenes are derived from cellular genes and have undergone various alterations when they became part of the proviral genome. Although the mechanism of action of these oncogenes is still poorly understood, it is reasonable to assume that the proviral directed expression of these genes is a sufficient prerequisite for transformation of certain cell types in culture. How do proviruses such as MMTV, which do not contain derivatives of cellular oncogenes, and which do not transform cells in culture, cause tumours? A possible mechanism could be based on the random integration of proviral DNA into the cellular genome. If the provirus integrates in the vicinity of a cellular gene which plays a role in cell proliferation, the insertion of transcriptional regulatory elements contained in the proviral DNA might affect its expression. This altered expression of a cellular gene with respect to quantity or timing might act as a trigger for transformation. Support for this hypothesis was found in two instances. First, the avian leukosis virus (ALV) causes bursal lymphomas in chickens and proviral DNA insertion was found in tumour cells near the c-myc locus. This integration of the proviral DNA led to increased c-myc transcription (Hayward, Neel and Astrin 1981; Payne, Bishop and Varmus 1982). The second example is the presence of MMTV proviral DNA in the vicinity of the int-1 locus in the majority of C3H mammary tumours (Nusse and Varmus 1982) and the int-2 locus in mammary tumours of the BR6 strain of mice (Peters, Brookes, Smith and Dickson 1983). The insertion of MMTV stimulates the expression of a cellular gene on chromosome 15 which is not expressed in non-tumour tissue (Nusse, van Ooyen, Cox, Fung and Varmus 1984). This effect of the proviral DNA must be conferred over a distance of several kilobases because the integration sites around the activated cellular gene are scattered over around 20 kb.

We have investigated the possibility that the MMTV proviral DNA contains sequences analogous to enhancers (Gruss 1984) and that the insertion of these sequences is the reason for the activation of the cellular int loci. For this purpose an indicator gene (thymidine kinase gene = tk) was recombined *in vitro* with the MMTV proviral DNA. Figure 4.5 shows four different constructs in which the tk gene was linked to the MMTV proviral gene either at its 5′ or 3′ side in both possible relative transcriptional orientations. The four constructs were transfected into mouse L cells and the cells were cultured in the absence and presence of glucocorticoid hormone. Figure 4.5 shows the quantitation of transcripts initiated at the cap site of the tk mRNA using the single strand specific nuclease protection procedure (S1 mapping) (Hynes, van Ooyen, Kennedy, Herrlich, Ponta and Groner 1983). Constructs 1 and 2 show a low level of tk mRNA expression in the absence of hormone and an appreciable increase by the addition of hormone to the growth medium. This induction of tk mRNA is due to the physical vicinity of the MMTV LTR which has previously been shown to confer hormonal sensitivity onto promoters which are otherwise not hormonally responsive (Hynes *et al.* 1983). Constructs 3 and 4 show a dramatic enhancement of the mRNA expression independent of the presence of hor-

Constructs:

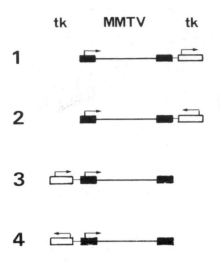

S₁ Mapping:

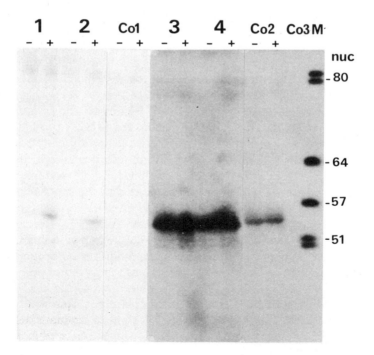

mone. These constructs link the tk gene either 5′ to the MMTV gene in the same transcriptional orientation (construct 3) or 5′ in the opposite transcriptional orientation (construct 4). The comparison of the transcriptional effects of MMTV proviral DNA on adjacent genes can therefore be of two types: a hormonal induction is observed when the indicator gene is linked 3′ to the MMTV gene and a strong hormone-independent enhancer effect is observed when the indicator gene is linked 5′ of the MMTV provirus. It is interesting to note that the proviral insertion in mammary tumours with respect to the int locus in nearly all cases is analogous to constructs 3 and 4 (Peters, Brookes, Smith and Dickson 1983; Nusse et al. 1984). The enhancer-like transcriptional activation might therefore play a role in the insertional mutagenesis and tumour formation.

The hormonal response sequence (HRE) of MMTV has enhancer-like properties

The hormonal regulation of gene expression has been an attractive feature for the study of mouse mammary tumour virus. Cultured mammary tumour cells producing MMTV respond to the addition of glucocorticoid hormone to their growth medium by an increase in viral RNA synthesis (Ringold 1979). Molecular cloning and recombination experiments have shown that the DNA sequence which is required for hormonal regulation is located within the proviral LTR region. Provision of the MMTV LTR with heterologous genes led to the hormone-responsive expression of these chimeric constructs in transfected cells (Groner et al. 1983a; Hager 1983; Ringold 1983). A combination of the LTR with the tk gene has proven very valuable. The precise sequence requirements for homonal induction, the interaction of the glucocorticoid receptor with the proviral DNA and certain functional aspects of the induction process were studied using the

Fig. 4.5. In vitro recombination of MMTV proviral DNA with the thymidine kinase (tk) gene.
   A molecular clone of MMTV proviral DNA (pGR21), similar to pGR102 (Fig. 4.1), was used for in vitro recombination. A 2.4 kb Eco RI fragment of the tk gene (Wilkie, Clements, Boll, Mantei, Lonsdale and Weissman 1979) was inserted into the Eco RI site located 222 bp 3′ of the right LTR in both of the possible orientations (constructs 1 and 2). A 3.6 kb Bam HI fragment of the tk gene was inserted into the Bam HI site located 1 kb 5′ of the left LTR in both of the possible orientations (constructs 3 and 4). The constructs were transfected into L cells and grown in the absence or presence of glucocorticoid hormone. Transcripts originating from the tk start were quantitated by S1 mapping analysis as described in Fig. 4.5. The numbers at the top of the autoradiograph refer to the constructs shown on the left. The controls refer to transfections with the cloned tk Eco RI fragment (co 1) and to the cloned tk Bam HI fragment (co 2) devoid of proviral DNA. No signal was observed when yeast RNA was introduced into the S1 mapping reaction (co 3).

A 184 bp LTR fragment confers hormone inducibility to the tk gene

A. Construction

B. S1 mapping of the tk transcript

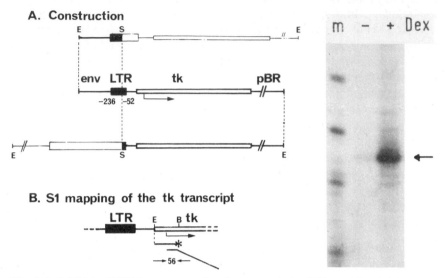

Fig. 4.6. A 184 bp LTR fragment confers hormone inducibility to the tk gene.

A 5′ deletion of pl 2.6 (Fig. 4.1) retaining 236 nucleotides 5′ of the LTR cap site (Hynes *et al.* 1983) was combined with a 3′ deletion of the same plasmid in which the LTR cap site and sequences to position −52 had been removed (Groner *et al.* 1984). Both deletions were cut at the LTR Sac I site at position −109 and recombined as indicated in A. The resulting construct (HRE-tk) was transfected into L cells and the cells were cultured in the presence and absence of glucocorticoid hormone. Transcripts initiated at the tk cap site were quantitated by the S1 mapping procedure schematically shown in B. The protected DNA fragments of 56 nucleotides, indicative of correctly initiated tk mRNA, are shown on the autoradiograph and are marked by the arrow.

LTR-tk gene (Hynes *et al.* 1983; Majors and Varmus 1983*b*; Buetti and Diggelmann 1983).

This chimeric gene originally contained the entire MMTV LTR sequence and was linked to an intact tk gene with its own promoter region (Hynes *et al.* 1983). Upon transfection into mouse L cells the RNA initiating both at the LTR and at the tk start sites were hormonally inducible, i.e. the physical vicinity of the LTR DNA was sufficient to subject the tk promoter to hormonal stimulation. Deletion mutants were constructed *in vitro* which removed defined sequences from the U3 region of the LTR and which helped to define the minimal sequence requirements on the 5′ side of the LTR promoter region. 202 nucleotides located 5′ of the LTR cap site proved to be sufficient for hormonal induction of the LTR and tk initiated transcripts (Hynes *et al.* 1983). The effect on the tk transcripts allowed a sequence delimitation for hormonal inducibility from the 3′ side. Targeted deletions removing the LTR cap site and TATA sequence were constructed and the hormonal inducibility of the tk transcripts was measured in transfected cells. This 3' deletion series defined the border of the required sequences at nucleotide -59, i.e. 59 nucleotides 5' of the LTR initiation site can be deleted without affecting the hormonal control element (Groner, Kennedy, Skroch, Hynes and Ponta 1984; Ponta et al. unpublished results).

The results from the 5' deletion and 3' deletion series can be combined to define a minimal element of 143 nucleotides (-59 to -202) which contains the necessary regulatory sequence information. This sequence element (HRE = hormone response element) was used in molecular recombination experiments to learn about its biological properties. Figure 4.6 shows a chimeric molecule in which the HRE (-52 to -236) was linked directly to the tk gene. As expected, the presence of the HRE is sufficient to confer hormonal inducibility onto the tk promoter. The hormonal induction effect observed in Fig. 4.6 is considerably more pronounced than in the construct containing two RNA initiation sites (Hynes et al. 1983).

Additional constructs were made to probe the effect of distance, promoter specificity and relative orientation of the HRE to the regulated promoter. Figure 4.7 shows the four constructs in which the α globin gene (Nishioka and Leder 1979) has been ligated to the HRE. The distance from the HRE to the α globin promoter is about 1.1 kb and the HRE has been linked at the 5' side (constructs 1 and 2) and the 3' side (constructs 3 and 4) of the α globin gene in both possible orientations. Transcription from the α globin cap site was quantitated in the mRNA of transfected cells by the S1 mapping procedure. Construct 1 (Fig. 4.7), in which the HRE is located 5' of the α globin gene in the same transcriptional orientation is similar to the construct HRE-tk shown in Fig. 4.6. The distance from the HRE to the affected initiation site is increased from 0.4 to 1.1 kb. All four constructs show hormone inducible transcription of α globin mRNA (Fig. 4.7, lanes 1–4). No hormonal induction is observed in the α globin gene construct which does not contain LTR sequences (lane 5). This observation indicates that the HRE can act in an orientation- and position-independent manner. These constructs and their transcriptional regulation show that there is no apparent specificity for the induced promoter. The distance over which the HRE can exert its effect can be varied. The mechanism of induction is functionally related to enhancer sequences which have been shown to be able to modulate transcriptional efficiency over a distance of several hundred nucleotides (de Villiers and Schaffner 1981). The hormonal requirement for enhancer function is unique to the HRE of MMTV and allows us to define hormone action as 'conditional enhancement'.

Discussion

Genetic approaches have been used to demonstrate that endogenous proviral genes, although similar in their information content, can exhibit differ-

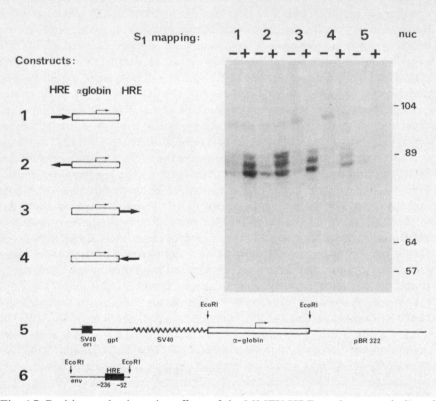

Fig. 4.7. Position and orientation effects of the MMTV HRE on the transcription of the mouse α-globin gene.

The mouse α-globin gene flanked by Eco RI sites (Nishioka and Leder 1979) was inserted into the pSV2 gpt vector (Southern and Berg 1982, construct 5). This plasmid was kindly provided by E. Wagner. A 774 bpEcoRI fragment containing 184 bp of LTR sequences (−236 to −52, construct 6) was inserted into an EcoRI site located 1.1 kb 5′ of the α-globin cap site in both of the possible orientations (constructs 1 and 2) or into an EcoRI site located 1.1 kb 3′ of the α-globin cap site (constructs 3 and 4). Mouse L cells were transfected with the constructs 1 to 5 and stable transfected clones were grown in mass culture in the presence or absence of hormone. Cellular RNA was hybridized to a 104 nucleotide, Hae III-PstI fragment, in which the Hae III site was 5′ end labelled. This fragment spans the transcription start of the globin gene. Accurately initiated α-globin mRNA protects a 98 nucleotide fragment. A slight heterogeneity in the initiating nucleotide can be observed resulting in the bands seen on the autoradiograph. The numbers at the top of the autoradiograph refer to the construct used for transfection shown on the left.

ent biological properties (Coffin 1982). DNA blotting, gene cloning and sequencing, and DNA-mediated gene transfer experiments have made it possible to define the levels that distinguish endogenous proviral gene copies from one another and factors or defects responsible for their differential behaviour. In the case of the endogenous proviral genes of mouse mammary tumour virus, at least two levels could be defined: sequence alterations and differences in the secondary modification of the proviral DNA.

The finding that the Mtv-8 proviral copy has a mutation in the env region which leads to the synthesis of a truncated env precursor protein and prevents the maturation of the precursor is the most likely explanation for the inability of Mtv-8 to support the production of virus particles. The *in vitro* exchange of the Mtv-8 env region with the Mtv-8 region restores the potential for virus production. By analogy, a rare gene conversion event *in vivo* could restore a competent proviral gene from defective endogenous copies. This could be responsible for late appearing mammary tumours in strains such as C3Hf and Balb/c. No intact proviral clone of Mtv-2 (responsible for virus production in the GR mouse) has been obtained and the availability of proviral DNA capable of 'productive transfection' permits *in vitro* mutagenesis to probe functional aspects of the proviral information. The U3 region of MMTV potentially encodes a 36 kd protein which is not a structural viral protein (Dickson and Peters 1983). It has been speculated that this 'orf' (open reading frame) protein might be implicated in the transforming ability of MMTV or play a role in the retroviral life cycle (Wheeler, Butel, Medina, Cardiff and Hager 1983; van Ooyen *et al.* 1983; Graham *et al.* 1984). Targeted mutations in this region of pGR 102 and reintroduction of the mutated provirus into cells will allow the observation of potential phenotypic consequences.

DNA methylation has been defined as a level at which proviral gene expression can be differentially controlled (Traina-Dorge and Cohen 1983). Proviral methylation is copy- and tissue-specific, and stringently maintained over many generations (Günzburg and Groner 1984). Experimental manipulation such as induced cellular proliferation by transformation with SV40 or partial hepatectomy or treatment of cultured cells with 5- azacytidine result in a decrease in the extent of proviral methylation. All three induced hypomethylated states can be correlated with an increase in the level of transcription. Not all proviral copies in the liver cells of the GR mouse are equally susceptible to hypomethylation. We noticed that Mtv-8 remains methylated. A comparison of many tissues in different mouse strains always reveals a fully methylated Mtv-8 (Günzburg, Hynes and Groner, 1984). Since Mtv-8 is located in a highly methylated chromosomal site it is possible that a differential susceptibility to hypomethylation influences exists and that certain chromosomal regions need to maintain their methylation pattern. A relative resistance of the Mtv-8 locus against DNAase I digestion of GR liver nuclei with respect to the other proviral copies has also been observed (Günzburg, unpublished results).

Transcriptional control sequences and their mechanism of action have been a main focus of MMTV research. The functional definition of a 143 nucleotide sequence (-59 to -202) was of great value for the description of the molecular details of steroid hormone action (Groner et al. 1984). Within the 143 nucleotide sequence specific binding sites for the glucocorticoid receptor have been mapped (Scheiderreit, Geisse, Westphal and Beato 1983; Pfahl, McGinnis, Hendricks, Groner and Hynes 1983). The induction process requires a functional hormone receptor complex, it is rapid and independent of simultaneous protein synthesis. The rate of transcription initiation is increased by the hormonal induction (Groner et al. 1983b). Sequence elements which exert a cis acting transcriptional enhancement effect on adjacent genes have been found in SV40 and polyoma virus (Gruss, Dhar and Khoury 1981; de Villiers and Schaffner 1981), in bovine papilloma virus (Lusky, Berg, Weiher and Botchan 1983), adenovirus (Weeks and Jones 1983) and in LTRs of retroviruses (Laimins, Gruss, Pozzalfi and Khoury 1984). Cellular genes have also been found to contain these regulatory sequences (Banerjee, Olson and Schaffner 1983; Gillies, Morrison, Di and Tonegawa 1983; Queen and Baltimore 1983). A feature noted in the definition of enhancer sequences was the preferential activation of proximal promoter sequences over more distal ones (Wasylyk, Wasylyk, Augerean and Chambon 1983) and the relative independence from position and orientation with respect to the enhanced gene. Similarities with the HRE are apparent. The HRE qualifies as an enhancer element since it increases transcription from the α-globin promoter in a orientation- and position-independent manner in the presence of hormone. These observations suggest a functional similarity between enhancers and the HRE or define the hormonal induction process as hormone-dependent enhancement. The enhancer quality of the HRE is also important in the context of tumorigenesis. Constructs linking indicator genes 5' of the proviral DNA showed a strong enhancement of transcription. Constructs with the indicator gene 3' of the proviral DNA showed hormonal induction. The potential to influence gene expression in the vicinity of the proviral integration site is an important facet in the model of retroviral (v-onc⁻) tumorigenesis. The relative orientation of tumour-specific proviral copies have been mapped with respect to the transcripts in the int loci (Nusse et al. 1984; Peters, Kozak and Dickson 1984). The orientations found with respect to the int transcripts and the properties of the proviral DNA tk and α-globin constructs suggest a mechanism for insertional activation. Hormone-independent enhancement and not promoter insertion or hormonal induction seems to be important in MMTV induced mammary tumorigenesis.

Acknowledgements

We thank U. Rahmsdorf and P. Butkeraitis for their excellent technical assistance and C. Wiedmer and T. Marti for help in preparation of the manuscript.

References

Banerjee, J., Olson, L., and Schaffner, W. (1983). A lymphocyte specific cellular enhancer is located downstream of the joining region in immunoglobulin heavy chain genes. *Cell* **33**, 729–740.

Bentvelzen, P. (1982). Interaction between host and viral genomes in mouse mammary tumors. *Ann. Rev. Gen.* **16**, 273–295.

Bishop, J. M. (1983). Cellular oncogenes and retroviruses. *Ann. Rev. Biochem.* **52**, 301–354.

Breznik, T. and Cohen, J. C. (1982). Altered methylation of endogenous viral promoter sequences during mammary carcinogenesis. *Nature* **295**, 255–257.

Buetti, E. and Diggelmann, H. (1981). Cloned mouse mammary tumor virus DNA is biologically active in transfected mouse cells and its expression is stimulated by glucocorticoid hormones. *Cell* **23**, 335–345.

——— and Diggelmann, H. (1983). Glucocorticoid regulation of mouse mammary tumor virus: identification of a short essential DNA region. *The EMBO Journal* **2**, 1423–1429.

Callahan, R., Gallahan, D., and Kozak, C. (1984). Two genetically transmitted Balb/c mouse mammary tumor virus genomes located on chromosomes 12 and 16. *J. Virol.* **49**, 1005–1008.

Coffin, J. (1982). Endogenous Viruses. In: *Molecular Biology of Tumor Viruses*. RNA Tumor Viruses. (ed. R. A. Weiss, N. Teich, H. E. Varmus, and J. M. Coffin) pp. 1109–1203. Cold Spring Harbor Lab, Cold Spring Harbor, New York.

Cohen, J. C. (1980). Methylation of milk borne and genetically transmitted mouse mammary tumor virus proviral DNA. *Cell* **19**, 653–662.

Cooper, D. N. (1983) Eukaryotic DNA methylation. *Human Genetics* **64**, 315–333.

Dickson C. and Atterwill, M. (1978). Polyproteins related to the major core protein of mouse mammary tumor virus. *J. Virol.* **26**, 660–672.

——— and Atterwill, M. (1980). Structure and processing of the mouse mammary tumor virus glycoprotein precursor pr73^{env}. *J. Virol.* **35**, 349–361.

Dickson, C. and Peters, G. (1983). Proteins encoded by mouse mammary tumor virus. In: *Current Topics in Microbiology and Immunology*, Vol. 106 (ed. P. K. Vogt and H. Koprowski) pp. 1–34, Springer Verlag, Berlin, Heidelberg.

Diggelmann, H., Vessaz, A. L., and Buetti, E. (1982). Cloned endogenous mouse mammary tumor virus DNA is biologically active in transfected mouse cells and its expression is stimulated by glucocorticoid hormones. *Virol.* **122**, 332–341.

Ehrlich, M. and Wang, R. Y. H. (1981). 5-methylcytosine in eukaryotic DNA. *Science* **212**, 1350–1357.

Feinstein, S. C., Ross, S. R., and Yamamoto, K. R. (1982). Chromosomal position effect determine transcriptional potential of integrated mouse mammary tumor virus DNA. *J. Mol. Biol.* **156**, 549–565.

Gillies, S. D., Morrison, S. L., Di, V. T., and Tonegawa, S. (1983). A tissue specific transcription enhancer element is located in the major intron of a rearranged immunoglobulin heavy chain gene. *Cell* **33**, 717–728.

Graham, D. E., Medina, D., and Smith, G. H. (1984). Increased concentration of an indigenous mouse mammary tumor virus long terminal repeat-containing transcript is associated with neoplastic transformation of mammary epithelium of C3H/Sm mice. *J. Virol.* **49**, 819–827.

Groner, B., Buetti, E., Diggelmann, H., and Hynes, N. E. (1980). Characterisation of endogenous and exogenous mouse mammary tumor virus proviral DNA with site specific molecular clones. *J. Virol.* **36**, 734–745.

——— Ponta, H., Beato, M., and Hynes, N. E. (1983a). The proviral DNA of mouse mammary tumor virus: its use in the study of the molecular details of steroid hormone action. *Mol. Cell. Endoc.* **32**, 101–116.

—— Hynes, N. E., Rahmsdorf, U., and Ponta, H. (1983*b*). Transcription initiation of transfected mouse mammary tumor virus LTR DNA is regulated by glucocorticoid hormones. *Nucleic Acids Res.* **11**, 4713–4725.

—— Kennedy, N., Skroch, S., Hynes, N. E., and Ponta, H. (1984). DNA sequences involved in the regulation of gene expression by glucocorticoid hormones. *Biochim. Biophys. Acta* **781**, 1–6.

Gruss, P., Dhar, R., and Khoury, G. (1981). Simian virus 40 tandem repeated sequences as on element of the early promoter. *Proc. Nat. Acad. Sci. U.S.A.* **78**, 943–947.

—— (1984). Magic enhancers. *DNA* **3**, 1–5.

Günzburg W. H. and Groner, B. (1984). The chromosomal integration site determines the tissue specific methylation of mouse mammary tumor virus proviral genes. *The EMBO Journal* **3**, 1129–1135.

Günzburg, W. H., Hynes, N. E., and Groner, B. (1984). The methylation pattern of endogenous mouse mammary tumor virus proviral genes is tissue specific and stably inherited. *Virology* **138**, 212–224.

Hager, G. (1983). Expression of a viral oncogene under control of the mouse mammary tumor virus promoter: A new system for the study of glucocorticoid regulation. *Prog. Nucl. Acids Res. Mol. Biol.* **29**, 193–203.

Hayward, W. S., Neel, B. G., and Astrin, S. M. (1981). Activation of a cellular onc gene by promoter insertion in ALV-induced lymphoid leukosis. *Nature* **290**, 475–480.

Henderson, L. E., Sowder, R., Smythers, G., and Oroszlan, S. (1983). Terminal amino acid sequences and prokolytic clearage sites of mouse mammary tumor virus env gene products. *J. Virol.* **48**, 314–319.

Herrlich, P., Hynes, N. E., Ponta, H., Rahmsdorf, U., Kennedy, N., and Groner, B. (1981). The endogenous proviral mouse mammary tumor virus genes of the GR mouse are not identical and only one corresponds to the exogenous virus. *Nucleic Acids Res.* **9**, 4981–4995.

Hu, W. S., Fanning, T. G., and Cardiff, R. D. (1984). Mouse mammary tumor virus: specific methylation patterns of proviral DNA in normal mouse tissues. *J. Virology* **49**, 66–71.

Hynes, N. E., Kennedy, N., Rahmsdorf, U., and Groner, B. (1981*a*). Hormone responsive expression of an endogenous proviral gene of mouse mammary tumor virus after molecular cloning and gene transfer into cultured cells. *Proc. Nat. Acad. Sci. U.S.A.* **78**, 2038–2042.

—— Rahmsdorf, U., Kennedy, N., Fabianni, L., Michalides, R., Nusse, R., and Groner, B. (1981*b*). Structure, stability, methylation, expression and glucocorticoid induction of endogenous and transfected proviral genes of mouse mammary tumor virus in mouse fibroblasts. *Gene* **16**, 307–317.

—— van Ooyen, A., Kennedy, N., Herrlich, P., Ponta, H., and Groner, B. (1983). Subfragments of the large terminal repeat cause glucocorticoid responsive expression of mouse mammary tumor virus and of an adjacent gene. *Proc. Nat. Acad. Sci. U.S.A.* **80**, 3637–3641.

—— Groner, B. and Michalides, R. (1984). Mouse mammary tumor virus: Transcriptional control and involvement in tumorigenesis. *Adv. Cancer Res.* **41**, 155–184.

Jones, P. A. and Taylor, S. M. (1980). Cellular differentiation, cytidine analogues, and DNA methylation. *Cell* **20**, 85–93.

Laimins, L. A., Gruss, P., Pozzalti, R., and Khoury, G. (1984). Characterisation of enhancer elements in the long terminal repeat of Moloney Murine Sarcoma Virus. *J. Virology* **49**, 183–189.

Land, H., Parada, L. F., and Weinberg, S. A. (1983). Cellular oncogenes and multistep carcinogenesis. *Science* **222**, 771–778.

Lasfargues, E. Y., Kramarsky, B., Lasfargues, J. C., and Moore, D. H. (1974). Detection of MMTV in cat kidney cells infected with purified B particles from RIII milk. *J. Nat. Cancer Inst.* **53**, 1831–1833.

Lusky, M., Berg, L., Weiher, H., and Botchan, M. (1983). Bovine Papilloma virus contains an activator of gene expression at the distal end of the early transcription unit. *Mol. Cell. Biol.* **3**, 1108–1122.

MacInnes, J. S., Morris, V. L., Flintoff, W. F., and Kozak, C. (1984). Characterisation and chromosomal location of endogenous mouse mammary tumor virus loci in GR, NFS, and DBA mice. *Virology* **132**, 12–25.

Majors, J. E. and Varmus, H. E. (1981). Nucleotide sequences at host proviral junctions for mouse mammary tumour virus. *Nature* **289**, 253–258.

—— and Varmus, H. E. (1983*a*). Nucleotide sequencing of an apparent proviral copy of env mRNA defines determinants of expression of the mouse mammary tumor virus env gene. *J. Virol.* **47**, 495–504.

—— and Varmus, H. E. (1983*b*). A small region of the mouse mammary tumor virus long terminal repeat confers glucocorticoid hormone regulation on a linked heterologons gene. *Proc. Nat. Acad. Sci. U.S.A.* **180**, 5866–5870.

McKeon, C., Ohkubo, H., Pastan, I., and de Crombrugghe, B. (1982). Unusual methylation pattern of the alpha-2(1) collagen gene. *Cell* **29**, 203–210.

Michalides, R., van Nie, R., Nusse, R., Hynes, N. E., and Groner, B. (1981). Mammary tumor induction loci in GR and DBAf mice contain one provirus of the mouse mammary tumor virus. *Cell* **23**, 165–173.

—— van Ooyen, A., and Nusse, R. (1983). Mouse mammary tumor virus expression and mammary tumor development. In: *Current Topics of Microbiology and Immunology*, Vol 106 (ed. S. K. Vogt and H. Koprowski) pp. 57–78. Springer Verlag, Berlin, Heidelberg, New York.

Nishioka, Y. and Leder, P. (1979). The complete sequence of a chromosomal mouse alpha-globin gene reveals elements conserved throughout vertebrate evolution. *Cell* **18**, 875–882.

Nusse, R. and Varmus, H. E. (1982). Many tumours induced by the mouse mammary tumor virus contain a provirus integrated in the same region of the host genome. *Cell* **31**, 99–109.

—— van Ooyen, A., Cox, D., Fung, Y. K. T., and Varmus, H. E. (1984). Mode of proviral activation of a putative mammary oncogene (int-1) on mouse chromosome 15. *Nature* **307**, 131–136.

Ott, M. O., Sperling, L., Cassio, D., Levilliers, J., Sala-Trepat, J., and Weiss, T. C. (1982). Undermethylation at the 5′ end of the albumin gene is necessary but not sufficient for albumin production by vat hepatome cells in culture. *Cell* **30**, 825–833.

Panganiban, A. T. and Temin, H. M. (1984). Circles with two tandem LTRs are precursors to integrated retrovirus DNA. *Cell* **36**, 673–679.

Payne, G. S., Bishop, J. M., and Varmus, H. E. (1982). Multiple arrangements of viral DNA and an activated host oncogene in bursal lymphomas. *Nature* **295**, 209–213.

Peters, G., Brookes, S., Smith, R., and Dickson, C. (1983). Tumorigenesis by mouse mammary tumor virus: Evidence for a common region for provirus integration in mammary tumors. *Cell* **33**, 369–377.

—— Kozak, C., and Dickson, C. (1984). Mouse mammary tumor virus integrated regions int-1 and int-2 map on different mouse chromosomes. *Mol. Cell. Biol.* **4**, 375–378.

Pfahl, M., McGinnis, D., Hendricks, M., Groner, B., and Hynes, N. E. (1983). Correlation of glucocorticoid receptor binding sites on MMTV proviral DNA with hormone inducible transcription. *Science* **222**, 1341–1343.

Ponta, H., Kennedy, N., Herrlich, P., Hynes, N. E., and Groner, B. (1983). A deletion mutant of mouse mammary tumour virus, lacking 516 nucleotides of the 5′ long terminal repeat sequence, can be expressed in a hormone responsive fashion. *J. Gen. Virol.* **64**, 567–577.

Queen, C. and Baltimore, D. (1983). Immunoglobulin gene transcription is activated by downstream sequence elements. *Cell* **33**, 741—748.

Razin, A. and Friedman, J. (1981). DNA methylation and its possible biological roles. *Prog. Nucl. Acids Res. Mol. Biol.* **25**, 33–52.

Redmond, S. M. S. and Dickson, C. (1983). Sequence and expression of mouse mammary tumor virus env gene. *The EMBO Journal* **2**, 125–131.

Ringold, G. M. (1979). Glucocorticoid regulation of mouse mammary tumour virus gene expression. *Bioch. Biophys. Acta* **560**, 487–507.

—— (1983). Regulation of mouse mammary tumor virus gene expression by glucocorticoid hormones. In: *Current Topics of Microbiology and Immunology*, Vol. 106 (ed. S. K. Vogt and H. Koprowski) pp. 79–103. Springer Verlag, Berlin, Heidelberg, New York.

Sarkar, N. H. and Racevskis, J. (1983). Expression and disposition of the murine mammary tumor virus (MuMTV) envelope gene products by murine mammary tumor cells. *Virology* **126**, 279—300.

Scheiderreit, C., Geisse, S., Westphal, H. M., and Beato, M. (1983). The glucocorticoid receptor binds to defined nucleotide sequences near the promoter of mouse mammary tumor virus. *Nature* **304**, 749–752.

Southern, P. J. and Berg, P. (1982). Transformation of mammalian cells to antibiotic resistance with a bacterial gene under control of the SV40 early region promoter. *J. Mol. Appl. Genet.* **1**, 327–341.

Traina, V. L., Taylor, B. A., and Cohen, J. C. (1981). Genetic mapping of endogenous mouse mammary tumor viruses: locus characterisation, segregation and chromosonal distribution. *J. Virology* **40**, 735–744.

Traina-Dorge, V. and Cohen, J. C. (1983). Molecular genetics of mouse mammary tumor virus. In: *Current Topics of Microbiology and Immunology*, Vol. 106 (ed. P. K. Vogt and H. Koprowski) pp. 35–56. Springer Verlag, Berlin, Heidelberg, New York.

van Ooyen, A. J. J., Michalides, R. J. A. M., and Nusse, R. (1983). Structural analysis of a 1.7 kilobase mouse mammary tumor virus specific transcript. *J. Virol.* **46**, 363–370.

Varmus, H. E. (1983). Retroviruses. In: *Mobile Genetic Elements* (ed. J. A. Shapiro) pp. 411–503. Academic Press, New York, London.

de Villiers, J. and Schaffner, W. (1981). A small segment of polyoma virus DNA enhances the expression of a cloned B globin gene over a distance of 1400 base pairs. *Nucl. Acids Res.* **9**, 6261–6264.

Wasylyk, B., Wasylyk, C., Augerean, P., and Chambon, P. (1983). The SV40 72 bp repeat preferentially potentiates transcription starting from proximal natural or substitute promoter elements. *Cell* **32**, 503–514.

Weeks, D. L. and Jones, N. C. (1983). E1A control of gene expression is mediated by sequences 5′ to the transcriptional starts of the early viral genes. *Mol. Cell. Biol.* **3**, 1222–1234.

Weinberg, R. A. (1982). Oncogenes of spontaneous and chemically induced tumors. *Adv. Can. Res.* **36**, 149–163.

Weiss, R. A., Teich, N., Varmus, H. E., and Coffin, J. M., eds. (1982). RNA Tumor Viruses. In: *Molecular biology of tumor viruses*. Cold Spring Harbor Laboratories, Cold Spring Harbor, New York.

Wheeler, D. A., Butel, J. S., Medina, P., Cardiff, R. D., and Hager, G. L. (1983). Transcription of mouse mammary tumor virus: Identification of a candidate mRNA for the long terminal repeat gene product. *J. Virol.* **46**, 42–49.

Wilkie, N. M., Clements, J. B., Boll, W., Mantei, N., Lonsdale, D., and Weissman C. (1979). Hybrid plasmids containing an active thymidine kinase gene of herpes simplex virus. *Nucl. Acids Res.* **7**, 859–877.

5   The *ras* gene family
ALAN HALL

The *ras* gene family

The last ten years has seen a dramatic increase in our understanding of the way in which animal retroviruses cause cancer. In particular one group, the acutely transforming RNA tumour viruses, has received much attention. Each of these viruses contains a gene, called the viral oncogene or v-*onc*, that is essential for its tumorigenic properties. The first *bona fide* v-*onc* to be characterized was v-*src*, the oncogene carried by the Rous Sarcoma Virus, which causes fibrosarcomas in chickens (Rous 1910; Vogt 1977). Since then around 18 different v-*oncs* have been described (for review see Bishop 1983). These have been identified in a range of viruses, infecting different animals including one, Simian Sarcoma Virus (carrying the oncogene v-*sis*) which has been isolated from a primate species (Gelmann, Wong-Staal, Kramer and Gallo 1981). Two members of this group of viral oncogenes, which are closely related to each other, form the starting point for this chapter. These are the Harvey *ras* (v-Ha-*ras*) and the Kirsten *ras* (v-Ki-*ras*) genes.

Over the last four years, it has been shown that for each of the viral oncogenes so far looked at there are related sequences present in the genomes of all vertebrates, including man (Bishop 1983). These sequences, known as proto-oncogenes (or c-*oncs* for cellular *onc*ogenes) have been the cause of the recent excitement concerning the molecular biology of the development of human cancer (for review see Weinberg 1983). It appears that at least some of these cellular oncogenes may play a role in the initiation or maintenance of the tumour phenotype. In particular the discovery that the c-*ras* genes (i.e. the cellular homologues of v-Ha-*ras* and v-Ki-*ras*) have been genetically altered in a variety of human tumours has focussed much attention on this gene family. The purpose of this chapter is to present a full account of the viral and cellular *ras* genes at the molecular level. The known properties of the *ras* gene product, the p21 protein, and the role of the *ras* genes in the development of human tumours will also be presented.

The viral *ras* genes

ISOLATION OF *ras* CONTAINING VIRUSES

In 1964 Harvey found that stocks of Moloney Murine Leukemia Virus (Mo-MuLV) routinely passaged in rats had acquired increased tumorigenicity (Harvey 1964). A variant form of Mo-MuLV was subsequently isolated and named Harvey Murine Sarcoma Virus (Ha-MuSV) and unlike the original Mo-MuLV was shown to form sarcomas rapidly when injected into newborn mice or rats. This was the first sarcoma virus isolated from mammals. Somewhat later Kirsten and Mayer followed Harvey's experiments and passaged Kirsten Murine Leukemia Virus (Ki-MuLV) through rats (Kirsten and Mayer 1967). They too obtained a preparation which had increased tumorigenicity and a virus clone [Kirsten Murine Sarcoma Virus (Ki-MuSV)] was isolated. Analysis of both these viruses showed that unlike the starting virus preparation they each contained an oncogene and that these oncogenes were somehow related to each other (Chien, Lai, Shih, Verma, Scolnick, Ray-Burman and Davidson 1979). Accordingly, they have been called viral Harvey ras (v-Ha-ras) and viral Kirsten ras (v-Ki-ras). Since then two other viral isolates have been obtained that contain ras related oncogenes; one, Rasheed Sarcoma Virus or RaSV, was isolated from a chemically transformed rat cell line and the other, Balb Sarcoma Virus (B-MuSV), was isolated from a BALB/c mouse carrying a spontaneous leukemia (Rasheed, Gardner and Heubner 1978; Peters, Rabstein, Van Vleck, Kelloff and Heubner 1974). It appears that in all four cases viruses initially lacking an oncogene have picked up the genetic information for sarcomagenesis from the cells through which they have been passaged. In the case of the Ha-, Ki-, and Ra-Sarcoma Viruses, this information is of rat origin whereas in B-MuSV it is of mouse origin. Furthermore the oncogenes picked up by these four independent isolates are related to each other and the generic term 'ras' has been adopted to describe them.

THE STRUCTURE OF THE ras CONTAINING VIRUSES

Most of the genetic analysis on the ras containing viruses has been carried out with the Harvey and Kirsten strains. The DNAs corresponding to the Ha-MuSV and Ki-MuSV RNA genomes have been cloned from virally-infected cells (Hager, Chang, Chan, Garon, Israel, Martin, Scolnick and Lowy 1979; Ellis, Defeo, Maryak, Young, Shih, Chang, Lowy and Skolnick 1981; Tsuchida and Uesugi 1981). Both Harvey and Kirsten virus isolates contain mainly rat cellular derived sequences (4.5 Kb for Harvey and 5.5 Kb for Kirsten) and only small stretches at either end, including the long terminal repeats (LTRs), are derived from MuLV sequences (see Figs 5.1a and 5.2a) (Anderson and Robbins 1976; Shih, Williams, Weeks, Maryak, Vass and Scolnick 1978). The ras oncogenes are encoded in less than 1.0 Kb and most of the rat sequence is derived from 30S RNA genes. These are rat cellular genes that are expressed in some rat cells as a 30S product and that are present in many copies in the rat genome (Tsuchida, Gilden and Hatanaka 1974). No specific function has been attached to these genes but their presence in both virus isolates suggests some mechanistic role in the evolution of the viruses. It is presumed that the 30S sequences and the ras sequences were incorporated in two separate events but the mechanism and the interrelationship between these sequences is not known (Ellis et al. 1980).

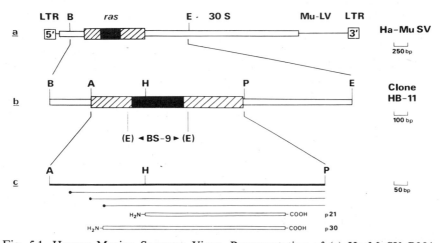

Fig. 5.1. Harvey Murine Sarcoma Virus. Representation of (*a*) Ha-MuSV RNA genome (5.5 Kb) and (*b*) clone HB-11 (Ellis *et al*. 1981) containing rat 30S cellular sequences, open box; Harvey specific *ras* sequences, shaded box; *ras* sequences shared by Harvey and Kirsten Viruses, black box; and MuLV sequences, single line. A subclone of HB-11, BS-9 (Ellis *et al*. 1980) is also shown and is often used to detect Harvey related cellular sequences. (*c*) AccI-PstI restriction fragment with known nucleotide sequence. Black dots represent putative RNA pol II transcription start sites and the locations of the p21 and p30 protein products are shown underneath. A, AccI; B, BamHI; E, EcoRI; (E), EcoRI-linkered DNA; H, HindIII; P, PstI.

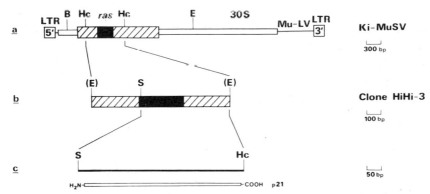

Fig. 5.2. Kirsten Murine Sarcoma Virus. (*a*) Ki-MuSV RNA genome (6.5 Kb) and (*b*) a subclone, Hi-Hi3 (Ellis *et al*. 1981) lacking rat 30S sequences and used to detect Kirsten-related cellular sequences. Rat 30S sequences, open box; Kirsten-specific *ras* sequences, shaded box; *ras* sequences shared by Harvey and Kirsten viruses, black box; and MuLV sequences, single line. (*c*) SstII/HincII restriction fragment sequenced. B, BamHI; E, EcoRI; (E), EcoRI-linkered DNA; Hc, HincII; S, SstII.

An *in vitro* transformation assay has been used to localize the *ras* oncogene within the rat 30S sequences of the cloned viruses. DNA from the intact virus and from deletion mutants was precipitated with calcium phosphate and added to NIH/3T3 cells in a transfection assay (Graham and Van der Eb 1973; Lowy, Rands and Scolnick 1978; Hager *et al.* 1979; Ellis, Defeo, Shih, Gonda, Young, Tsuchida, Lowry and Scolnick 1981). Foci of transformed 3T3 cells were only obtained when an intact 5′ LTR and sequences towards the 5′ end of the viruses were present (Chang, Ellis, Scolnick and Lowry 1980*a*; Ellis *et al.* 1980; Chang, Maryak, Wei, Shih, Shober, Cheung, Ellis, Hager, Scolnick and Lowy 1980*b*; Tsuchida, Ryder and Ohtsubo 1982). Further analysis using *in vitro* mutagenesis (primarily by insertion of linkers at various restriction sites) localized the transforming genes to the positions shown in Figs 5.1*b* and 5.2*b* (Wei, Lowy and Scolnick 1980).

The complete nucleotide sequences of the two *ras* genes have been reported (Dhar, Ellis, Shih, Oroszlan, Shapiro, Maizel, Lowy and Scolnick 1982; Tsuchida *et al.* 1982). The predicted amino acid sequence of the p21 product (189 amino acids) showed that 110 of the 120 N-terminal amino acids were identical in v-Ha-*ras* and v-Ki-*ras* whereas only 3 out of 22 amino acids at the C-terminus were the same. With an overall amino acid homology of 80 per cent this suggests a strong evolutionary conservation of these sequences. More detailed structural analysis of the four independent *ras* gene isolates is now presented.

v-*Ha*-ras

As shown in Fig. 5.1*c*, the Harvey *ras* gene has been localized to a 1 Kb AccI/PstI fragment which has since been completely sequenced (Dhar *et al.* 1982). Previous work had shown that the 5′ end of v-Ha-*ras* mRNA transcribed from an SV40/Ha-MuSV hybrid plasmid, mapped within the rat-derived sequences about 160 bp upstream of the HindIII site shown in Fig. 5.1 (Gruss, Ellis, Shih, Koenig, Scolnick and Khovry 1981). Transcription from this position is also observed in Ha-MuSV transformed cells though most *ras* mRNA is encoded within a larger transcript starting at the viral 5′-LTR. It is unusual for viral oncogenes to carry their own promoter in animal retroviruses. Analysis of the DNA sequence upstream of the ras coding region indicates three possible RNA polymerase II recognition sequences, i.e. Goldberg-Hogness boxes (TATAAA) at positions which would be consistent with this internal 5′ end of the message (Fig. 5.1*c*). A pol III promoter is also located in this region though there is no evidence that pol III transcribes this gene and its significance is not known. However, transfection experiments with DNA from deleted viruses have shown a requirement for the viral LTR (Chang *et al.* 1980*a*) and clearly the rat promoter is not sufficient on its own for efficient transcription. It is possible that the enhancer sequence in the MuSV-LTR (Levinson, Khovry, Vande Wonde and Gruss 1982) increases transcription from this internal promoter or more likely that transcription from the LTR and not from the internal promoter is biologically more important.

There are three potential AUG initiation codons, all in the same reading frame, at positions -52, -39 and $+1$ ($+1$ is the AUG which must be used to produce the major p21 product). If the other two initiation codons were used this would result in a p30 (initiation at -52) and a p29 (initiation at -39). There is some evidence for minor amounts of p30 in African green monkey kidney cells infected with an SV40/Ha-MuSV recombinant but no p29 has yet been detected (Gruss *et al.* 1981). Eukaryote mRNA's usually utilize the first AUG as the initiation codon; clearly in the case of v-Ha-*ras* the third is preferred. A model has been proposed to account for this observation based on a predicted secondary structure which would obscure, partially obscure and leave open, the AUG yielding p29, p30 and p21 respectively (Dhar *et al.* 1982). It has been shown that p30 is not required for transformation, since Ha-MuSV LTR fused only to sequences downstream of AUG at $+1$ are sufficient to transform cells in a transfection assay (Dhar *et al.* 1982). The amino acid sequence of the viral Ha-p21 is given later in Fig. 5.5.

v-*Ki*-ras

The v-Ki-*ras* coding sequence has been localized to a 600 bp Sst II/IIinc II fragment (see Fig. 5.2c) by making internal deletions downstream of the 5′ LTR (Tsuchida *et al.* 1982). Deletions between the LTR and the Sst II site did not affect transforming activity. The 600 bp fragment was then sequenced and the AUG ($+1$) initiation codon was found to be located 24 bp downstream from the Sst II site. Both Ki-*ras* and Ha-*ras* p21s are 189 amino acids in length (see Fig. 5.5). Since very little sequence information is reported upstream of AUG ($+1$) in Ki-*ras* it is not possible to say if other higher molecular weight protein products are predicted from the Kirsten virus. The 8 amino acids that would be predicted to precede the AUG initiation codon of Ki-*ras* p-21 bear no relationship to those predicted upstream of the Ha-*ras* p21.

Rasheed ras

The *ras* gene present in this isolate hybridizes much more strongly with v-Ha-*ras* than with v-Ki-*ras* (Gonda, Young, Elser, Rasheed, Talmadge, Nagashima, Li and Gilden 1982). The virus encodes a p29 protein which is a fusion protein of viral-*gag* sequences with the *ras* gene (Rasheed 1980; Gonda *et al.* 1982). The complete DNA sequence of this region of the virus has been published (Rasheed, Norman and Heidecker 1983). The first AUG codon has been assigned to position 610 at the 5′ end of the virus and is followed by 747 bp of open reading frame. The p21 *ras* contribution to the predicted protein is almost identical in sequence to v-Ha-*ras* except for amino acids corresponding to positions 59, 122, 123 and 150 of the Harvey protein. The fusion to *gag* sequences is such that, in addition to all the amino acids corresponding to v-Ha-*ras* p21, the preceeding 21 amino acids predicted from the DNA sequence of the v-Ha-*ras* gene are present in the p29. No p21 product, corresponding to initiation at the internal AUG, has been detected in cells infected with the Rasheed virus.

BALB/c ras

Southern blot analysis showed that, under stringent conditions, the *ras* sequence of Ha-MuSV was strongly related to the *onc* sequence present in BALB-MuSV, called v-*bas* (Andersen, Devare, Tronick, Ellis, Aaronson and Scolnick 1981). Molecular analysis of cloned viral DNAs shows that the oncogenes of Ha- and BALB-MuSV are located in different positions within the genome, the former being at the 5′ end (i.e. near the 5′ LTR, see Fig. 5.1*a*) whereas the latter is towards the 3′ end. Unlike Ha-and Ki-MuSV, which contain viral helper, *ras* gene and rat 30S sequences, BALB-MuSV contains only viral helper and *bas* sequences. The *bas* oncogene is thought to be derived from the mouse cellular homologue of v-Ha-*ras* (v-Ha-*ras* being derived from a rat c-Ha-*ras* gene). No sequence information has so far been reported for the *bas* isolate.

PROTEIN PRODUCTS OF THE VIRAL ras GENES

In vitro translation of both Ha-MuSV and Ki-MuSV viral RNA yields a 21 000 Dalton protein termed p21 (Parks and Scolnick 1977; Shih *et al.* 1978). The protein can also be detected at high levels in virally-transformed cells when antiserum from Ha-MuSV infected rats is used in an immunoprecipitation reaction (Shih, Weeks, Young and Scolnick 1979*a*). Furthermore mutants in the Kirsten virus which are temperature sensitive for transformation encode a thermolabile p21 protein and this is therefore supposed to correspond to the transforming protein (Shih *et al.* 1979*b*). The Ra-SV encoded *gag-ras* fusion protein (p29) has part of the *gag* protein fused to 21 K Dalton of *ras* (Rasheed 1980). Labelling B-MuSV transformed NIH/3T3 cells with ^{35}S methionine and using a rat antiserum raised against Ha-p21 revealed a virally-derived p21 in the cell extract (Andersen *et al.* 1981).

In cells transformed by Harvey and Kirsten viruses two protein products can be detected immunologically which have slightly different mobilities after SDS-polyacrylamide gel electrophoresis (Shih *et al.* 1979*a*); one migrating at 21 000 Daltons, the other migrating rather slower at 23 000 Daltons. The latter, which represents some 25 per cent of the total *ras* protein, has been shown to be a phosphorylated form of the protein (pp21) (Shih, Stokes, Smythers, Dhar and Oroszlan 1982*c*). The Ha- and Ki- proteins are phosphorylated at amino acid 59, a threonine residue (Shih *et al.* 1979*a*;

Shih, Papageorge, Stokes, Weeks and Scolnick 1980). Phosphorylation of Ha- and Ki-p21 appears to be autocatalytic; the proteins being capable of transferring the γ phosphate of GTP to the threonine residue (Shih *et al.* 1980). Since this threonine is replaced by alanine in the Rasheed *ras* variant, the p29 product is not auto-phosphorylated (Rasheed *et al.* 1983). However, *in vivo* isolated p29 is phosphorylated at a serine residue (Papageorge, Lowy and Scolnick 1982).

Pulse-chase experiments in Ha-*ras* transformed cells using ^{35}S methionine detected a p21 precursor, pro-p21, migrating about 1K Dalton larger than the mature protein (Shih, Weeks, Gruss, Dhar, Oroszlan and Scolnick 1982*b*). By comparing proteolytic digests of pro-p21 and p21, it was concluded that the difference in mobility of the two species was due to processing in the C-terminal portion of the protein. It was speculated that this might involve peptide cleavage of around 10-20 amino acids at the carboxy end, though no direct proof of this has been reported. The pro-21 is synthesized in a non-membrane bound state but the p21 and the pp21 products are associated with a membrane fraction. The two mature forms of the *ras* proteins, i.e. p21 and pp21, both contain tightly bound lipid (Sefton, Trowbridge, Cooper and Scolnick 1982) and around 95 per cent of the *ras* protein is associated with the inner surface of the cytoplasmic membrane in Ha- or Ki-transformed cells (Willingham, Pastan, Shih and Scolnick 1980).

The biochemical properties of p21 *ras* proteins are only poorly understood. p21 appears to have specific binding activity for GTP and GDP and this has been exploited in an assay for the proteins (Furth, Davis, Fleuredelys and Scolnick 1982). The protein will not bind a variety of other nucleotides including GMP or ATP. This is in contrast to several other viral oncogene products typified by pp60 from v-*src*. These products utilize ATP and can phosphorylate tyrosine residues of protein substrates (Collett and Erikson 1978). Interestingly the temperature sensitive variant of the Kirsten *ras* p21 is also thermolabile for GTP binding suggesting that this activity is important for the oncogenic function (Scolnick, Shih, Maryak, Ellis, Chang and Lowy 1980). The overall impression is that the *ras* proteins are GTP-dependant kinases though no substrate for this activity has yet been identified.

A variety of monoclonal antibodies are now available to detect the p21 proteins (Furth *et al.* 1982). These were raised using Ha-MuSV transformed cells injected into rats. Eight rat lymphocyte-myeloma hybrid cell lines were isolated that produced antibodies to v-Ha-*ras* p21 and which reacted with both phosphorylated and non-phosphorylated forms of the protein. All 8 recognized the p21 produced by BALB-MuSV or Ra-SV. Three of the monoclonals reacted strongly with the v-Ki-*ras* protein. The monoclonals have now been used both as an assay for ^{35}S labelled p21 products and to localize the Ha-p21 product to the inner surface of the cytoplasmic membrane using electron microscopic immunocytochemistry (Willingham, Banks-Schlegal and Paston 1983).

Recently the v-Ha-*ras* protein has been fused to the amino terminal portion of the lambda cII gene in an *E. coli* expression vector (Lautenberger, Ulsh, Shih and Papas 1983). Over 10 per cent of *E. coli* protein was a p23 containing 14 vector-derived amino acids and all but four amino acids of the *ras* p21. The protein was immunoprecipitable with a p21 antibody and would bind GTP and autophosphorylate. This confirms that these activities are a property of the p21 protein alone and not an associated activity. The availability of large quantities of p21 proteins through recombinant DNA technology will undoubtedly speed up the physical and biochemical characterization of these proteins.

Mammalian cellular *ras* genes

As we have seen the viral *ras* genes carried by the oncogenic murine sarcoma viruses were derived from cellular sequences present in either the rat (Harvey, Kirsten and Rasheed isolates) or in the mouse (BALB isolate). Cellular *ras* sequences have been found in all vertebrate species so far examined including man (Bishop 1983). Even *Drosophila* and yeast have *ras* related genes. The next section will begin with a description of the Harvey and Kirsten-related *ras* genes that have been identified in the rat genome. Far more information is available on the human *ras* gene family and this will form the bulk of this section.

RAT *ras* GENES

Gene structure

When the viral Harvey *ras* clone, BS-9, (see Fig. 1*b*) was used as a probe on Southern blots of EcoRI digested rat DNA two fragments were observed with sizes of 13 Kb and 20 Kb (Ellis *et al.* 1981). These two fragments have been cloned and each contains a distinct Harvey-related *ras* gene, c-Ha-*ras*1 and c-Ha-*ras*2 (Defeo, Gonda, Young, Chang, Lowy, Scolnick and Ellis 1981). Heteroduplex analysis between the cellular genes and viral Ha-*ras* showed that c-Ha-*ras*1 contains a 900 bp stretch of homology with three intervening sequences. On the other hand c-Ha-*ras*2 annealed to v-Ha-*ras* along 900 bp of uninterrupted sequence. The c-Ha-*ras*1 gene has now been cloned and part of the sequence published (Sukumar, Notario, Zanca and Barbacid 1983). There is only one nucleotide difference between the first exon of this gene and the corresponding region of v-Ha-*ras*, suggesting that the viral gene may have been derived from the rat c-Ha-*ras*1 gene. The c-Ha-*ras*2 gene appears to be intronless, yet it is still capable of being expressed to yield a functional p21 (Defeo *et al.* 1981). This suggests that rat c-Ha-*ras*2 may be a processed gene but unlike human c-Ha-*ras*2 which is a functionless pseudogene (see later), it does not contain any premature termination codons or deletions. No nucleotide sequence analysis has yet been reported. The single nucleotide difference between the first exon of rat c-Ha-*ras*1 and v-Ha-*ras* results in the alteration of a glycine residue at position 12 in the rat p21 to an arginine in v-Ha-*ras*. This alteration has been shown to have dramatic biological consequences for the *ras* protein and this is discussed in more detail later. With a viral Kirsten *ras* probe (Hi-Hi3, Fig. 5.2*b*) several bands were observed in EcoRI digested rat DNA (Ellis *et al.* 1981) but no further work has been reported on the characterization of the Kirsten-related genes in the rat.

Protein products

Rat c-Ha-*ras*1 and c-Ha-*ras*2 are both capable of morphologically trans-forming NIH/3T3 cells in culture, but only if they are first ligated to a strong promoter, for example the LTR of Ha-MuSV (Defeo *et al.* 1981). Transfectants derived from LTR/c-Ha-*ras*1 constructs contained high levels of a specific p21 *ras* product that was immunoprecipable with antisera raised against v-Ha-*ras* transformed cells. The mobility of this single product on SDS/polyacrylamide gels was very similar to the endogenous p21 of normal cells. The LTR/c-Ha-*ras*2 constructs also yielded transfectants with high levels of a p21 product. This was also precipitable with the viral *ras* antiserum, but in this case the protein moved as a doublet. Both the endo-genous p21s have guanine nucleotide binding activity analogous to that of the viral proteins but the c-Ha-*ras*1 product is not autophosphorylated whereas the c-Ha-*ras*2 product is (Ellis, Lowy and Scolnick 1982*a*).

HUMAN *ras* GENES

Four distinct cellular homologues of the viral *ras* genes have been cloned from the human genome; viral Ha-*ras* was used to isolate two Harvey related genes, c-Ha-*ras*1 and c-Ha-*ras*2 and v-Ki-*ras* was used to isolate two Kirsten related genes, c-Ki-*ras*1 and c-Ki-*ras*2 (Chang, Gonda, Ellis, Scolnick and Lowy 1982*a*). Much attention has been focused on this group of genes in the last two years because of results obtained with DNA transfection ex-periments and human tumour DNAs. An introduction to the background and development of the transfection assay will therefore be presented here.

Identification of activated human ras genes by DNA transfection

In 1979 two groups reported making use of the calcium phosphate pre-cipitation technique to introduce DNA, isolated from chemically trans-formed mouse cell lines, into NIH/3T3 cells; NIH/3T3 is an established but non-transformed mouse fibroblast cell line (Shih *et al.* 1979; Cooper, Oken-quist and Silverman 1980). Depending on the source of the DNA they obtained foci of morphologically transformed NIH/3T3 cells. Later they showed that DNA isolated from some human tumours also had transforming activity in this assay (Shih, Padhy, Murray and Weinburg 1981; Krontiris and Cooper 1981). It appeared that genetic information, presumably in the form of an oncogene, was being transferred from the human tumour cell line into NIH/3T3 causing transformation of the mouse recipient. On the other hand DNA isolated from normal human cells, or indeed quite a number of other human tumour cell lines, did not effect this change.

The EJ cell line, derived from a human bladder carcinoma, was the first human tumour line identified with transforming ability (Shih *et al.* 1981; Krontiris and Cooper 1981). In the transfection assay, the 3T3 cells transformed by EJ DNA lost their characteristic properties of contact inhibition and anchorage dependence. The transformants grew either as a focus on a confluent monolayer or as colonies in semi-solid medium. A great deal of work has subsequently been done to characterize the oncogene present in the EJ cell line that is responsible for this transformation of the 3T3 cells. Restriction enzyme digestion of the EJ tumour DNA prior to NIH/3T3 transfection showed that the gene did not contain sites for EcoRI, Bam HI or Hind III but did contain Kpn I and Xba I sites (Perucho, Goldfarb, Shimizo, Lama, Fogh and Wigler 1981). Further detailed analysis made use of the human repetitive ALU sequence (Houck, Rinehart and Schmid 1979) as a probe for human sequences in the mouse transfectants. It has been estimated that about 0.1 per cent of the human genome is transferred into the mouse cells during the transfection process, i.e. about a thousand genes (Perucho, Hanahan and Wigler 1980). If DNA is then made from the transformed cells and used in a second round of transfection on 3T3 cells then about 0.1 per cent of this DNA is expected to be transferred. Assuming the human sequences are unlinked, this represents 0.0001 per cent of the human genome i.e. *ca.* 1 gene. One would expect, in practice, just a handful of human sequences to be present in the secondary focus and one of these would be the oncogene. The human genome contains over 300,000 copies of the ALU family repeat which appears to be randomly distributed throughout the unique sequences (Houck *et al.* 1979). It is clear then that if an ALU sequence is contained within the oncogene it too must be transferred in the transfection assay. Furthermore human ALU sequences can be detected in a mouse genomic background using Southern blot analysis (Murray, Shilo, Shih, Cowing, Hsu and Weinburg 1981; Perucho *et al.* 1981).

By examining DNA from a series of independent secondary foci derived from EJ DNA, it was concluded that the EJ oncogene was located on a 23 Kb EcoRI fragment that also contained an ALU sequence, this fragment being conserved in all the secondary foci looked at (Murray *et al.* 1981). The oncogene has since been cloned by several groups (Shih and Weinberg 1982*a*; Pulciani, Santos, Lauver, Long, Robbins and Barbacid 1982*b*; Goldfarb, Shimizu, Perucho and Wigler 1982). Shih and Weinberg used an ALU sequence probe to isolate the EcoRI fragment from a genomic library that had been constructed using DNA isolated from a secondary transfectant. Goldfarb *et al.* did not find a consistent pattern of ALU containing fragments in secondary foci derived from T24 cells (a human bladder carcinoma cell line which may have in fact been identical to the EJ cell line). It is now known that the single ALU sequence within the 23 Kb EcoRI fragment lies outside of the gene (Shih and Weinberg 1982*a*); whether or not it is maintained depends on the mechanics of the transfection procedure. T24 DNA was digested with Hind III and mixed with an equimolar amount of a Hind III fragment containing an *E. coli* suppressor tRNA gene, SupF. After incubation with T4 DNA ligase this mixture was used to transfect cells. DNA from transformants was found to contain many copies of the SupF gene but after making secondary transformants only a few copies were maintained, one of which it was hoped would be linked to the oncogene. A genomic library was made with DNA from this transfectant in the phage vector λ 1059 Sam[7] which contains an amber mutation in the lysis gene. This phage will not form plaques on a suppressor free (Sup°) *E. coli* host unless the phage contains the SupF gene. Several phage were isolated which grew on a Sup° host and DNA from one of these was found to transform 3T3 cells. It must therefore have contained the intact oncogene.

Immediately the oncogene had been cloned it was tested for homology with any of the known viral oncogenes. It became apparent that this gene was related to v-Ha-*ras* and v-Ki-*ras* (Santos, Tronick, Aaronson, Pulciani and Barbacid 1982; Parada, Tabin, Shih and Weinberg 1982; Der, Krontiris and Cooper 1982). Comparison of the restriction map of this oncogene with the c-Ha-*ras*1 gene (Chang *et al.* 1982*a*) showed that they were identical. The oncogene present in the EJ bladder tumour cell line is therefore an activated form of c-Ha-*ras*1. The exact mechanism of activation will be discussed in detail later. Although activated c-Ha-*ras*1 was the first gene isolated and characterized from a human tumour cell line the most common oncogene detected in human tumours using the NIH/3T3 transfection assay is c-Ki-*ras*2 (Pulciani, Santos, Lauver, Long, Aaronson and Barbacid 1982*a*; Der *et al.* 1982; McCoy, Toole, Cunningham, Chang, Lowy and Weinberg 1983). No examples of activated c-Ha-*ras*2 or c-Ki-*ras*1 have been found.

Not only has the DNA transfection assay led to the detection of altered *ras* genes in human tumours, it has also led to the identification of a new *ras* gene. Characterization in our laboratory of an unknown oncogene present in two human sarcomas and by other groups in a neuroblastoma and a promyelocytic leukemia has shown it to be very related to but distinct from the Harvey and Kirsten *ras* genes (Marshall, Hall and Weiss 1982; Hall, Marshall, Spurr and Weiss 1983; Shimizu, Goldfarb, Perucho and Wigler 1983*a*; Murray, Cunningham, Parada, Doutry, Lebowitz and Weinberg 1983). This gene was not detected by Chang *et al.* when they screened human genomic libraries with the viral *ras* probes (Chang *et al.* 1982*a*). The identification and characterization of this gene, now known as N-*ras*, will be dealt with in more detail later.

The next section is a description of the genetic organization of the five human *ras* genes. This will be followed by an overall description of the expression of these genes, their possible involvement in human cancer and the mechanisms by which these genes can be activated to give oncogenes.

Structure of the ras genes

c-Ha-ras1 and 2. Two phage recombinants were isolated from human genomic libraries using the v-Ha-*ras* BS-9 clone (Fig. 5.1*b*) (Chang *et al.* 1982*a*). Heteroduplex analysis of these clones with v-Ha-*ras* showed that the c-Ha-*ras*1 gene contained at least three introns whereas c-Ha-*ras*2 appeared to contain none, at least in the coding sequence. Superficially this appears similar to the situation in the rat, however, unlike human c-Ha-*ras*1, the human c-Ha-*ras*2 gene hybridizes only weakly to v-Ha-*ras* and not at all to the *ras* sequences present in rat or mouse DNA. The human c-Ha-*ras*2 gene has now been sequenced and found to be a pseudogene (Miyoshi, Kagimoto, Soeda and Sakaki 1984). The gene contains no introns, but has several deletions and insertions and three in frame termination codons. This gene is expected to be biologically silent. This is in contrast to the rat c-Ha-*ras*2 gene which, although apparently a processed gene, can be rendered biologically active by attachment of a promoter (Defeo *et al.* 1981).

The c-Ha-*ras*1 gene has been cloned by many groups on a 6.6 Kb BamHI fragment (see Fig. 5.3*a*) (Capon, Chen, Levinson, Seeburg and Goeddel 1983*a*; Shih and Weinberg 1982*a*; Pulciani *et al.* 1982*b*; Goldfarb *et al.* 1982). All the information required for an intact gene appears to be present within a 2.9 Kb Sst I fragment (Fig. 5.3*b*). Capon *et al.* (1983*a*) have pointed out a potential Goldberg-Hogness RNA polymerase II recognition box, in this case TCTAATT (position 1334, Fig. 5.3*b*), followed 29 base pairs later by TCAGCCC; a common sequence found at RNA cap sites. A so-called 'CAAT' box (Benoist, O'Hare, Breathnach and Chambon 1980), in this case GGTAACCT, is located 83 base pairs upstream of this postulated cap site. However no experimental data are available to verify the position of the 5' end of the human Ha-*ras* mRNA. At the 3' end of the gene is the sequence AGTAAA which may correspond to the consensus sequence AATAAA (Capon *et al.* 1983*a*; Fasano, Taparowsky, Fiddes, Wigler and Goldfarb 1983) found 10–20 bp upstream of eukaryotic polyadenylation sites (Proudfoot and Brownlee 1974). The 3' end of the c-Ha-*ras*1 mRNA is known from sequencing cDNA and is found at position 3751, 17 pb 3' to this putative polyadenylation consensus sequence (Fasano *et al.* 1983).

By comparing genomic sequences with cDNA sequences it has been concluded that there are four protein-coding exons, and one exon coding for most of the 3' untranslated sequence (Fasano *et al.* 1983). If the putative pol

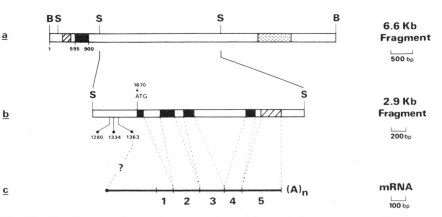

Fig. 5.3. The human c-Ha-*ras*1 gene (*a*) 6.6 Kb BamHI fragment originally cloned from the T24 cell line (Capon *et al.* 1983*a*). Hatched box, upstream sequences with homology to upstream v-Ha-*ras* sequences; black box, possible enhancer sequence (Reddy 1983); speckled box, reiterated 28 bp sequence. (*b*) 2.9 Kb SstI fragment containing four coding exons (black boxes) and 3′ untranslated exon (hatched box). The positions of a putative 'CAAT' box at 1280, TATA box at 1334 and RNA CAP site, 1363 are shown. (*c*) mRNA transcript of 1.2 Kb. The location of the 5′ untranslated sequence (predicted size *ca* 350 bp) on the genomic map is not known. However the distance from the putative CAP site to the first ATG (307 bp) would be consistent with no further introns. B, BamHI; S, SstI.

II promoter is utilised *in vivo* and assuming no further introns between the putative RNA start site and the first coding exon, this would give rise to an mRNA of 1.17 Kb (Fig. 5.3*c*) which is comparable with that observed experimentally on Northern blots (Parada *et al.* 1982; Santos *et al.* 1982; Goldfarb *et al.* 1982). It is likely therefore that the c-Ha-*ras*1 gene contains five exons as shown in Fig. 5.3*b*. However, when Capon *et al.* looked at sequences 5′ of the coding region of v-Ha-*ras* they found extensive homology with sequences located about 1.2 Kb upstream of the c-Ha-*ras*1 initiation codon (Fig. 5.3*a*; Capon *et al.* 1983*a*). They suggest on this basis that the human c-Ha-*ras*1 gene may contain an intron within the 5′ untranslated sequence. If this were the case then the RNA pol II promoter must be outside of the 2.9 Kb Sst I fragment. Analysis of cDNA clones will undoubtedly resolve this issue.

Although the 2.9 Kb Sst I fragment appears to contain all the information required for the whole gene, there is some evidence that an enhancer sequence may be located upstream (Reddy 1983). If the sequence between the two XmaI sites at positions 595 and 900 (Fig. 5.3*a*) is deleted then the transforming activity of the gene isolated from T24 cells is dramatically reduced. An interesting repeated stretch of DNA is located 3′ and outside of the gene. This consists of a 28 bp sequence CACTCCCCCTTCTCTCCAGGGGACGCCA which is repeated 29 times. Using Southern blot analysis, a high level of restriction fragment size polymorphism has been reported in human DNA at the c-Ha-*ras*1 locus and this might be explained by a fluctuation in the copy number of this repeat sequence (Goldfarb *et al.* 1982).

v-Ha-*ras* and human c-Ha-*ras*1 coding sequences show a high (88 per cent) level of homology at the nucleotide level, almost all the differences occurring at the third positions of codons. The amino acid sequence of the cellular Ha-*ras*l p21 is shown later in Fig. 5.5. It can be seen that only three out of 189 amino acids differ from viral Ha p21; two of these, at positions 12 and 59, are particularly interesting. Alanine is located at position 59 in the human c-Ha-*ras*1 p21 whereas threonine is present in viral p21. In the viral protein this is the site of autophosphorylation (Shih *et al.* 1980) and by analaogy with the Rasheed p29 (which also lacks threonine at position 59) it would not be expected that human Harvey p21 is autophosphorylated. The position 12 difference is perhaps the most interesting and will be dealt with in detail later. It appears that this is a critical alteration in the protein. Replacement of glycine at position 12 with a variety of other amino acids has been shown to activate the human c-Ha-*ras*1 oncogene enabling it to transform NIH/3T3 cells. There is some suggestion from sequence comparisons that Ha-*ras* p21 may have structural similarities to mitochondrial ATP-synthase (Gay and Walker 1983) or to the nucleotide binding site of some dinucleotide binding proteins (Wierenga and Hol 1983). This would appear to fit in with the known GTP/GDP binding properties of the p21 proteins. Wierenga and Hol assumed that the sequence surrounding glycine at position 12 constituted this nucleotide binding site though there is no direct evidence for this.

c-Ki-ras*1 and 2.* Using v-Ki-*ras* probes two distinct clones have been isolated from human genomic libraries (Chang *et al.* 1982*a*). One of these c-Ki-*ras*1 contained 900 bp of homology to the viral clone and had a single visible intron in heteroduplex analysis. c-Ki-*ras*2 on the other hand contained only 300 bp of homology and at the time it was speculated that this clone probably represented only one of the exons of a much larger gene.

Since then both c-Ki-*ras*1 and 2 have been sequenced (McGrath, Capon, Smith, Chen, Seeburg, Goeddel and Levinson 1983; Shimizu, Birnbaum, Ruley, Fasano, Suard, Edlund, Taporowsky, Goldfarb and Wigler 1983*b*). The coding region of c-Ki-*ras*1 is closely related to the viral Kirsten sequence but also contains many substitutions, insertions and deletions. It has been concluded that the c-Ki-*ras*1 gene is a pseudogene, there being no open reading frame (McGrath *et al.* 1983). c-Ki-*ras*2 has been found in an activated form in a variety of human tumours including lung, colon and leukemias (Pulciani *et al.* 1982*a*; Der *et al.* 1982; McCoy *et al.* 1983). Southern blot analysis of DNA from second-round transfectants of NIH/3T3 cells showed at least five ALU containing EcoRI bands which were maintained in independent foci. This gave a rough estimate of the size of the gene and suggested it

was probably greater than 35 Kb (Perucho *et al.* 1981). Overlapping recombinant lambda clones have now been obtained that cover the whole of
the c-Ki*ras*2 locus; about 45 Kb (McGrath *et al.* 1983; Shimizu *et al.* 1983*b*).
Four exons, 1, 2, 3 and 4a, were found which had strong sequence homology
with the viral Kirsten *ras* gene. Both groups have also found evidence for a
fifth protein coding exon called 4B. It is located 5.5 Kb downstream of 4A
and contains strong sequence similarities with part of the pseudogene c-Ki-
*ras*1. This exon probably arose through an intragenic duplication event of
exon 4A since they have sequences in common with each other. However
4A and 4B have now significantly diverged in a central region of 60 base
pairs. At least some of the 5′ untranslated sequences of c-Ki-*ras*2 are
encoded in a sixth exon, Ⓓ. The position of the promoter for the Ki-*ras*2
gene is not known.

The major RNA species observed is large, 5.5 Kb, with a minor component of 3.8 Kb also detectable (Capon, Seeburg, McGrath, Hayflick, Edman,
Levinson and Goeddel 1983*b*). Surprisingly the human c-Ki-*ras*2 transcript
observed in several NIH/3T3 transfectants derived from human tumour
DNA is 1.2 Kb and this species has also been observed in a human cell line
(McCoy, M. S., Bargmann, C. I. and Weinberg, R. A. 1984). Analysis of
cDNA libraries generated with a variety of synthetic oligonucleotides
showed that most Ki-*ras*2 mRNA contains exon 3 spliced to 4B yielding a
p21 with its carboxy terminus specified by 4B (Capon *et al.* 1983*b*). About 2
per cent of Ki-*ras*2 cDNAs obtained had both exons 4A and 4B. Since exon
4A ends in a termination codon any p21 translated from this message would
have just 4A coding sequences. Shimizu *et al.* sequenced downstream of the
viral Ki-*ras* coding region indicated in Fig. 5.2c (Shimizu *et al.* 1983*b*).
They found a complete equivalent of the human Ki-*ras* exon 4B, seven base
pairs downstream of the termination codon in v-Ki-*ras*. This suggests that
the rat gene from which v-Ki-*ras* was derived also has two fourth exons.
Again since 4A in the virus is followed by a termination codon only a p21 is
made.

The first three exons of human c-Ki-*ras*2 and v-Ki-*ras* differ in only five
amino acids, two of these being positions 12 and 59 (see Fig. 5.5). Exons 4A
of the two genes also show a high degree of homology. However, as discussed earlier, the majority of human Kirsten p21 uses exon 4B, giving a
protein differing considerably from the viral protein in the carboxy terminus.

N-ras. An oncogene distinct from the Ha- and Ki-*ras* genes was detected
by three groups, including our own, in several different human tumour cell
lines. We identified an oncogene present in two human sarcoma cell lines
HT1080 (a fibrosarcoma) and RD (a rhabdomyosarcoma) (Marshall *et al.*
1982). We showed that the oncogene present in both these cell lines was the
same. The patterns of inactivation of transforming activity by restriction

enzyme digestion were the same and secondary transfectants derived from either cell line all harboured an 8.8 Kb EcoRI fragment that contained a human ALU sequence. Furthermore DNA isolated from transfectants was shown not to contain either the human Ha-*ras*1 and 2 or the Ki-*ras*1 and 2 genes. Two other groups, working with a neuroblastoma cell line (SK-N-SH) and a promyelocytic leukemia line (HL60), also reported non-Ha- or Ki-*ras* genes in their transfectants (Perucho *et al.* 1981; Murray *et al.* 1981) and on the basis of Southern analysis with probes for the human ALU sequence, it was concluded that three different oncogenes were being looked at by the three different groups.

We have cloned the 8.8 Kb EcoRI fragment from a genomic library that was constructed using the phage vector L47 (Loenen and Brammar 1980) and DNA isolated from a secondary transfectant derived from HT1080 (Hall *et al.* 1983). We used nick-translated total human DNA as a probe since around 3 per cent of the human genome is made up of the ALU family repeat (Houck *et al.* 1979). Several positive clones were obtained. One of these contained an 8.8 Kb EcoRI insert (see Fig. 5.4*a*) and this was subcloned into pAT153 yielding a plasmid pAT8.8 (Hall *et al.* 1983). It was already known that EcoRI destroyed transforming activity of the oncogene and it was not expected therefore that pAT8.8 contained an intact gene. Clearly it was necessary to walk along the chromosome in order to clone the remainder. Fortunately we had available two secondary transfectants that no longer possessed an intact 8.8 Kb EcoRI fragment. We therefore analyzed these with a probe derived from the left-hand end (probe D, Fig. 5.4*a*) or from the right-hand end (probe A, Fig. 5.4*a*) of the 8.8 Kb fragment. It was found that neither of these transfectants contained sequences detectable with probe D but they did hybridize to probe A. We concluded that the oncogene must lie to the right of the single Bam HI site within the 8.8 Kb EcoRI fragment.

Using Probe A (Fig. 5.4*a*) it was possible to map a variety of restriction sites in HT1080 located to the right of the cloned segment. In particular we found an Sst I site 5.0 Kb downstream (Fig. 5.4*a*) and a Hind III site 10.0 Kb downstream of the EcoRI site (not shown in Fig. 5.4*a*). Analysis of a number of transfectants with probe A showed several that no longer contained the Sst I site. It was concluded that the oncogene lay within 13 Kb of DNA located between the Bam HI site of pAT8.8 and this Sst I site. We decided therefore that a clone containing an 11.0 Kb Hind III fragment would overlap with the 8.8 Kb fragment and would contain the remainder of the oncogene. This fragment was cloned (Brown, Marshall, Pennie and Hall 1984) and a restriction map of the locus of the oncogene is presented in Fig. 5.4*a*. It can be seen that the oncogene is contained within two EcoRI fragments with sizes 8.8 Kb and 7.0 Kb.

Our first aim after having cloned this oncogene was to look for homology with known viral oncogenes. It was immediately obvious that this gene was

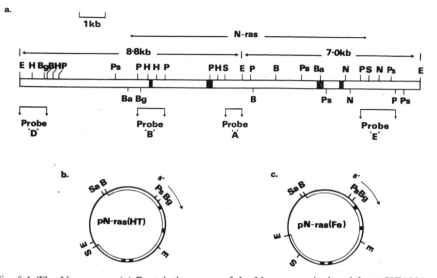

Fig. 5.4. The N-*ras* gene (*a*) Restriction map of the N-*ras* gene isolated from HT1080 (Brown *et al.* 1984). The gene is conveniently split into two by an EcoRI site yielding an 8.8 Kb fragment from the left-hand end and a 7.0 Kb fragment from the right end. The restriction sites are as follows: B, BamHI; Ba, BaII; Bg, BgIII; E, EcoRI; H, HindIII; N, NdeI; P, PvuII; Ps, PstI; S, SstI; Sa, SaII. The restriction map is complete for these enzymes except for PstI, NdeI and BaII in the 8.8 Kb fragment and BaII in the 7.0 Kb fragment. The four coding exons are shown as black boxes. The transcriptional sense of the gene is from left to right as written. The known boundaries of the gene are also indicated. (*b*) Plasmid pN-*ras* (HT) containing a biologically active gene. The single line SstI to BamHI represents vector sequences derived from pHLTR (Chang *et al.* 1982*a*). The approximate positions of the exons are shown within the N-*ras* sequence and the PstI site at the 5′ end of the gene is also shown. (*c*) Plasmid pN-*ras* (Fe) containing a full length N-*ras* gene isolated from foetal liver DNA. The single line BamHI to EcoRI represents vector sequences derived from pAT153.

closely related to the Ha-and Ki-*ras* genes (Hall *et al.* 1983). Comparison of the restriction map with the four maps available for the known *ras* genes (Chang *et al.* 1982*a*) showed that this was a new member of the human *ras* gene family. It has since become clear that the gene detected in the neuro-blastoma cell line (SK-N-SH) (Shimizu *et al.* 1983*a*) and in HL60 (Murray *et al.* 1983) is the same gene despite the discrepancies previously obtained with ALU blots of transfectant DNA. Shimizu *et al.* have called the gene N-*ras* and we have followed their nomenclature. More recently others have detected activated N-*ras* genes in a variety of tumours, in particular leukemias (Eva, Tronick, Gol, Pierce and Aaronson 1983; Gambke, Signer and Moroni 1984).

We have since constructed a plasmid, pN-*ras* (HT) (see Fig. 5.4*b*), containing a full length N-*ras* gene from HT1080, which transforms NIH/3T3 cells and with an efficiency of about 2000 foci/µg. The corresponding full length N-*ras* gene has been isolated from normal human foetal liver DNA (Brown *et al.* 1984). In this case, since we knew that there was only one internal EcoRI site, foetal DNA was partially digested with EcoRI and size-fractionated on 5–20 per cent potassium acetate gradients. Fractions containing both EcoRI fragments were used to construct a phage library using L47.1 as a vector. The library was grown on a P2 lysogen, whereupon only recombinant phage grew, and these were screened using probes derived from pN-*ras* (HT). A plasmid (Fig.5.4c) containing a full length normal N-*ras*, pN-*ras* (Fe), does not transform NIH/3T3 cells.

Using sub-clones of v-Ha-*ras* the transcriptional sense of the gene has been oriented as left to right as written in Fig. 5.4a. We and others have localized four exons of N-*ras*, first using v-Ki-*ras* and v-Ha-*ras* probes and then by sequencing; these are shown in Fig. 5.4 (Brown *et al.* 1984; Taporowsky *et al.*, 1983; Eva *et al.*, 1983). The full protein coding sequence of the N-*ras* gene has been determined by us using MI3 sequencing (see Fig. 5.5) and by others using Maxam-Gilbert (Taporowsky, Shimizo, Goldfarb and Wigler 1983) and the sequence of our foetal clone is presented in Fig. 5.5 The N-*ras* gene codes for a p21 with 189 amino acids (predicted MW 21, 231) which is the same length as Ha-*ras* and Ki-*ras* (exon 4A). As discussed earlier the C-terminus of Kirsten p21 is probably derived from exon 4B resulting in 188 amino acids. No evidence for an alternative fourth exon of N-*ras* has been found within the 7.0 Kb EcoRI fragment (Taporowsky *et al.* 1983).

We have determined the size of the transcript from the N-*ras* gene. Northern blot analysis using probe B (Fig. 5.4a) shows three species of RNA present in HT1080 cells with sizes of 5.2 Kb, 2.2 Kb and 1.2 Kb (Hall *et al.* 1983). Similar analysis of NIH/3T3 cells before transfection with HT1080 DNA showed two major bands of 5.8 Kb and 1.2 Kb. Two Kirsten-related mRNAs (5.2 and 2.0 Kb) and two Harvey-related mRNAs (5.0 and 1.4 Kb) have been reported in mouse cells (Ellis, Defeo, Furth and Scolnick 1982b; Schwab, Alitalo, Varmus, Bishop and George 1983) and it is not clear which if any of these mRNAs is cross-hybridizing with the human N-*ras* probe in our experiments. After transfection of NIH/3T3 a new transcript of 2.2 Kb is observed in all foci and we conclude that this is the N-*ras* transcript. This has been reported by others (Murray *et al.* 1983). Most, though not all, transfectants also contain the 5.2 Kb transcript that is present in HT1080.

Fig. 5.5. Sequence of the p21s. The DNA sequence and the predicted protein sequence from the coding regions of pN-*ras* (Fe) (Brown *et al.* 1984). The amino acid sequences of the normal c-Ha-*ras*1 (Capon *et al.* 1983a) and c-Ki-*ras*2 (exon 4B) (Shimizu *et al.* 1983b) genes, and of v-Ha-*ras* (Dhar *et al.* 1982) and v-Ki-*ras* (Tsuchida *et al.* 1982) are also presented. The position of a dot means identical amino acids at that position. The black triangles within the nucleotide sequence indicate the positions of introns.

```
N-ras       ATG ACT GAG TAC AAA CTG GTG GTG GTT GGA GCA GGT GGT GTT GGG AAA AGC GCA CTG ACA  60
N-ras       met thr glu tyr lys leu val val val gly ala gly gly val gly lys ser ala leu thr  20
c-Ha-ras1    .   .   .   .   .   .   .   .   .   .  gly  .   .   .   .   .   .   .   .   .
c-Ki-ras2    .   .   .   .   .   .   .   .   .   .  gly  .   .   .   .   .   .   .   .   .
v-Ha-ras     .   .   .   .   .   .   .   .   .   .  arg  .   .   .   .   .   .   .   .   .
v-Ki-ras     .   .   .   .   .   .   .   .   .   .  ser  .   .   .   .   .   .   .   .   .

                                                                            ▼
N-ras       ATC CAG CTA ATC CAG AAC CAC TTT GTA GAT GAA TAT GAT CCC ACC ATA GAG GAT TCT TAC  120
N-ras       ile gln leu ile gln asn his phe val asp glu tyr asp pro thr ile glu asp ser tyr  40
c-Ha-ras1    .   .   .   .   .   .   .   .   .   .   .   .   .   .   .   .  glu  .   .   .
c-Ki-ras2    .   .   .   .   .   .   .   .   .   .   .   .   .   .   .   .  glu  .   .   .
v-Ha-ras     .   .   .   .   .   .   .   .   .   .   .   .   .   .   .   .  glu  .   .   .
v-Ki-ras     .   .   .   .   .   .   .   .   .   .   .   .   .   .   .   .  gln  .   .   .

N-ras       AGA AAA CAA GTG GTT ATA GAT GGT GAA ACC TGT TTG TTG GAC ATA CTG GAT ACA GCT GGA  180
N-ras       arg lys gln val val ile asp gly glu thr cys leu leu asp ile leu asp thr ala gly  60
c-Ha-ras1    .   .   .   .   .   .   .   .   .   .   .   .   .   .   .   .   .   .  ala  .
c-Ki-ras2    .   .   .   .   .   .   .   .   .   .   .   .   .   .   .   .   .   .  ala  .
v-Ha-ras     .   .   .   .   .   .   .   .   .   .   .   .   .   .   .   .   .   .  thr  .
v-Ki-ras     .   .   .   .   .   .   .   .   .   .   .   .   .   .   .   .   .   .  thr  .

N-ras       CAA GAA GAG TAC AGT GCC ATG AGA GAC CAA TAC ATG AGG ACA GGC GAA GGC TTC CTC TGT  240
N-ras       gln glu glu tyr ser ala met arg asp gln tyr met arg thr gly glu gly phe leu cys  80
c-Ha-ras1    .   .   .   .   .   .   .   .   .   .   .   .   .   .   .   .   .   .   .   .
c-Ki-ras2    .   .   .   .   .   .   .   .   .   .   .   .   .   .   .   .   .   .   .   .
v-Ha-ras     .   .   .   .   .   .   .   .   .   .   .   .   .   .   .   .   .   .   .   .
v-Ki-ras     .   .   .   .   .   .   .   .   .   .   .   .   .   .   .   .   .   .   .   .

                                                                    ▼
N-ras       GTA TTT GCC ATC AAT AAT AGC AAG TCA TTT GCG GAT ATT AAC CTC TAC AGG GAG CAC ATT  300
N-ras       val phe ala ile asn asn ser lys ser phe ala asp ile asn leu tyr arg glu gln ile  100
c-Ha-ras1    .   .   .   .   .   .  thr  .   .   .  glu  .   .  his gln  .   .   .   .  ile
c-Ki-ras2    .   .   .   .   .   .  thr  .   .   .  glu  .   .  his his  .   .   .   .  ile
v-Ha-ras     .   .   .   .   .   .  thr  .   .   .  glu  .   .  his gln  .   .   .   .  ile
v-Ki-ras     .   .   .   .   .   .  thr  .   .   .  glu  .   .  his his  .   .   .   .  leu

N-ras       AAG CGA GTA AAA GAC TCG GAT GAT GTA CCT ATG GTG CTA GTG GGA AAC AAG TGT GAT TTG  360
N-ras       lys arg val lys asp ser asp asp val pro met val leu val gly asn lys cys asp leu  120
c-Ha-ras1    .   .   .   .   .   .  asp  .   .   .   .   .   .   .   .   .   .   .   .   .
c-Ki-ras2    .   .   .   .   .   .  glu  .   .   .   .   .   .   .   .   .   .   .   .   .
v-Ha-ras     .   .   .   .   .   .  asp  .   .   .   .   .   .   .   .   .   .   .   .   .
v-Ki-ras     .   .   .   .   .   .  glu  .   .   .   .   .   .   .   .   .   .   .   .   .

N-ras       CCA ACA AGG ACA GTT GAT ACA AAA CAA GCC CAC GAA CTG GCC AAG AGT TAC GGG ATT CCA  420
N-ras       pro thr arg thr val asp thr lys gln ala his glu leu ala lys ser tyr gly ile pro  140
c-Ha-ras1   ala ala  .   .   .  glu ser arg  .   .  gln asp  .   .  arg  .   .   .   .   .
c-Ki-ras2   pro ser  .   .   .  asp thr lys  .   .  gln asp  .   .  arg  .   .   .   .   .
v-Ha-ras    ala gly  .   .   .  glu ser arg  .   .  gln asp  .   .  arg  .   .   .   .   .
v-Ki-ras    pro ser  .   .   .  asp thr lys  .   .  gln glu  .   .  arg  .   .   .   .   .

                                                            ▼
N-ras       TTC ATT GAA ACC TCA GCC AAG ACC AGA CAG GGT GTT GAA GAT GCT TTT TAC ACA CTG GTA  480
N-ras       phe ile glu thr ser ala lys thr arg gln gly val glu asp ala phe tyr thr leu val  160
c-Ha-ras1   tyr  .   .   .   .   .   .   .   .   .  gly  .  glu  .   .   .   .   .   .   .
c-Ki-ras2   phe  .   .   .   .   .   .   .   .   .  gly  .  asp  .   .   .   .   .   .   .
v-Ha-ras    tyr  .   .   .   .   .   .   .   .   .  gly  .  glu  .   .   .   .   .   .   .
v-Ki-ras    phe  .   .   .   .   .   .   .   .   .  arg  .  glu  .   .   .   .   .   .   .

N-ras       AGA GAA ATA CGC CAG TAC CGA ATG AAA AAA CTC AAC AGC AGT GAT GAT GGG ACT CAG GGT  540
N-ras       arg glu ile arg gln tyr arg met lys lys leu asn ser ser asp asp gly thr gln gly  180
c-Ha-ras1    .   .   .   .  gln his lys leu arg lys leu asn pro pro asp glu ser gly pro gly
c-Ki-ras2    .   .   .   .  lys his lys glu lys met ser lys asp gly lys lys lys lys lys lys
v-Ha-ras     .   .   .   .  gln his lys leu arg lys leu asn pro pro asp glu ser gly pro gly
v-Ki-ras     .   .   .   .  gln tyr arg leu lys lys ile ser lys glu glu lys thr pro gly cys

N-ras       TGT ATG GGA TTG CCA TGT GTG GTG ATG TAA
N-ras       cys met gly leu pro cys val val met ter  189
c-Ha-ras1   cys met ser cys lys  .  val leu ser ter  189
c-Ki-ras2   ser lys thr     lys  .  val ile met ter  188
v-Ha-ras    cys met ser cys lys  .  val leu ser ter  189
v-Ki-ras    val lys ile lys lys  .  val ile met ter  189
```

We think that there are two transcripts from the N-*ras* gene in human cells. Preliminary cDNA cloning experiments suggest that the larger transcript has an elongated 3′ untranslated region encoded in genomic sequences extending through the EcoRI site at the 3′ end of the 7.0 Kb fragment. We do see a faint band in 3T3 cells of size about 3.0 Kb which could be a mouse N-*ras* transcript. We have found the N-*ras* gene in mouse cells and indeed it has been shown in our laboratory that this gene is activated in the mouse Lewis lung carcinoma cell line (Vousden and Marshall 1984). The mouse N-*ras* gene is also activated in carcinogen-induced mouse thymomas (Guerrero, Calzada, Mayer and Pellicer 1984).

A reported partial cDNA clone of N-*ras* indicates that the 3′ untranslated region of the 2.2 Kb species is about 150 bp long and is mostly encoded within a fifth exon (Taporowsky *et al.* 1983). Since the protein coding exons are 570 bp this leaves about 1.4 Kb of 5′ untranslated sequence. The location of this on the genomic map has not yet been determined. However, it has been reported, and we have confirmed, that only sequences to the right of the Pst I site shown within the 8.8 Kb EcoRI fragment of Fig. 5.4 are required for transformation. This site is about 1.3 Kb upstream of exon one and we would predict therefore no further introns and that the N-*ras* gene like the Ha-*ras* gene probably contains only five exons. No sequence data are available for the putative promoter region of the N-*ras* gene.

Comparison of the human ras genes and their products. The five human *ras* genes have all been localized to different chromosomes, using both somatic cell hybrids studies and *in situ* hybridization. The location of c-Ha-*ras*1 is 11p15 (O'Brien, Nash, Goodwin, Lowy and Chang 1983; de Martinville, Giacalone, Shih, weinberg and Francke 1983*a*; McBride, Swann, Santos, Barbacid, Tronick and Aaronzon 1982). The two Kirsten related genes have been localized to chromosomes 6 (c-Ki-*ras*1) and 12p12 (c-Ki-*ras*2) (O'Brien *et al.* 1983; Sakaguchi, Naylaor, Shows, Toole, the Coy and Weinburg 1983; Jhanawar, Neel, Hayward and Changanti 1983) and we have localized the N-*ras* gene unambiguously to chromosome one (Hall *et al.* 1983) at 1 cen-p21 (Davis, Malcolm, Hall and Marshall 1983). This chromosome localization has been confirmed by others (Ryan, Barker, Shimizu, Wigler and Ruddle 1983; de Martinville *et al.* 1983*b*).

There is no evidence for expression of either the c-Ha-*ras*2 or the c-Ki-*ras*1 genes in any cell. The relative levels of expression of the other three *ras* genes have not been systematically studied. c-Ha-*ras*1 appears to be expressed in most normal cells and tumour cells so far looked at (Eva, Robbins, Andersen, Srinivasan, Tronick, Reddy, Ellmore, Galen, Lautenberger, Papas, Westin, Wong-Staal, Gallo and Aaronson 1982; Goldfarb *et al.* 1982; Shih and Weinberg 1982*a*; Westin, Wong-Staal, Gelman, Dalla-Favera, Papas, Lautenberger, Eva, Reddy, Tronick, Aaronson and Gallo 1982). The levels of RNA are generally relatively low, e.g. 0.01 per cent in the T24 bladder cacinoma line (Goldfarb *et al.* 1982). We have examined adult human fibro-blasts, human foetal brain, liver, heart and skin and found no more than a factor of five difference in RNA levels and no significant difference from the levels found in a number of tumour cell lines (S. Pennie and A. Hall, unpublished results). In agreement with the overall impression obtained in human cells Harvey *ras* RNA has been found at relatively constant levels in total mouse embryos/foetuses and extra-embryonal tissues at all stages of mouse development between days 6 and 18 (Müller, Slamon, Tremblay, Müller, Cline and Verma 1982). Low levels of the mouse c-Ha-*ras* transcript have been found in normal skin epidermis, however these levels are increased about fivefold in experimentally induced papillomas (Balmain, Ramsden, Bowden and Smith 1984). Using antisera raised against the Ha-p21, endogenous p21's have been detected in normal cells from a wide variety of vertebrates (Langbeheim, Shih and Scolnick 1980). In one particular case, a hemopoietic precursor cell line 416B, very high levels of the endogenous p21 were found; around 100 times that in most other cells and five times higher than in Ha-MuSV transformed cells (Scolnick, Weeks, Shih, Ruscetti and Dexter 1981).

Levels of the c-Ki-*ras*2 transcript have been reported to be higher (*ca* 0.05 per cent of total poly A RNA) in cell lines containing an activated Kirsten gene than in tumour cells with activated c-Ha-*ras*1 or in normal cells (Capon *et al.* 1983*b*; Der and Cooper 1983). The mouse Kirsten transcript is present throughout prenatal development, though it appears to decrease during later stages of foetal development (Müller, Verma and Adamson 1983). We have found comparable amounts of the 5.2 Kb and 2.2 Kb N-*ras* transcripts in the human fibrosarcoma line HT1080 (which contains an activated N-*ras* gene), in normal human fibroblasts and in other sarcoma cell lines not containing an activated N-*ras* gene (Hall *et al.* 1983 and unpublished data).

A comparison of the sequences of Ha-, Ki- and N-*ras* shows around 25 per cent differences in the nucleotide sequence of the coding regions. However, the differences in amino acids (see Fig. 5.5) are much more restricted and are concentrated in the C-terminus. Thus, N-*ras* differs from c-Ha-*ras*1 and c-Ki-*ras*2 by a maximum of 14 amino acids (out of 150) in the first three exons, whereas in the fourth exon N-*ras* differs from c-Ha-*ras*1 at 15/39 positions and from c-Ki-*ras*2 (exon 4B) at 22/38 positions. Although the fourth exons of the three human *ras* genes differ considerably from each other, they are very closely related to the corresponding fourth exons of the rat genes. Thus exon four of human c-Ha-*ras*1 is identical to that in the rat Harvey *ras* gene (as deduced from v-Ha-*ras* sequence). It has been suggested, therefore, that this region of the molecule confers different properties on the three different *ras* proteins (Shimizu *et al.* 1983*b*). There is also a region between amino acids 121–128 where Harvey differs from Kirsten in 5/8 positions though N-*ras* resembles Kirsten and differs at only one of these positions (Taporowsky *et al.* 1983). The reason why three highly related gene products are being expressed in all cells so far looked at is not yet clear. It would seem highly likely however that the p21 gene products play a major role in the growth control and/or development of many, if not all, cell types.

Mechanisms of activation of the ras genes

The dramatic increase in interest in the *ras* gene family over the last two years is a consequence of the results obtained with DNA transfection studies. Around 20 per cent of human tumours contain an activated *ras* gene detectable using the NIH/3T3 transfection assay (Pulciani *et al.* 1982*a*) and the mechanism of activation is of major interest. At the time these oncogenes were first detected, it was assumed that activation involved quantitative rather than qualitative changes in the gene product. Indeed ligation of the strong promoter of the Ha-MuSV LTR to the normal human c-Ha-*ras*1 gene resulted in transforming activity in the NIH/3T3 system (Chang, Furth, Scolnick and Lowy 1982*b*). Elevated levels of the normal p21 product could, therefore, result in activation. Consequently cloned activated *ras* genes were used as probes to look for genetic rearrangement or amplification in the tumours from which they were isolated. No changes could be found. Next, levels of RNA were examined. These experiments were difficult to control since a normal progenitor cell for the tumour cells is required for such a comparison. We, for instance, used normal human fibroblasts as a control for levels of N-*ras* mRNA in the fibrosarcoma cell line HT1080 (Hall *et al.* 1983). The conclusion was that if a change in RNA level was the mechanism of activation then it must be a subtle change of less than three fold.

The problem was resolved by constructing chimeric molecules *in vitro*, replacing restriction fragments from the normal gene with corresponding fragments from the active allele. The biological activity of the molecule was then tested in the NIH/3T3 transfection assay. Using these methods it was possible to localize the activating lesion in the c-Ha-*ras*1 genes of the EJ cell line to a small restriction fragment of 350 bp (Reddy, Reynold, Santos and Barbacid 1982; Tabin, Bradley, Bargmann, Weinberg, Pupageorge, Scolnick, Dhar, Lowy and Chang 1982; Taporowsky, Suard, Fasano, Shimizu, Gold-farb and Wigler 1982). This fragment was sequenced and compared to the fragment isolated from the normal gene. The conclusion was that the mechanism of activation involved a single base pair change leading to an alteration in the amino acid sequence. The amino acid at position 12 is changed from a glycine to a valine in the EJ cell line as a consequence of a G to T transversion. This and any other alteration at amino acid 12 can be detected by restriction enzyme analysis since it results in the loss of recognition sites for MspI and NaeI (Reddy *et al.* 1982; Table *et al.* 1982) and this has proved useful for analyzing a large number of normal and tumour DNAs

(Feinberg, Vogelstein, Droller, Baylin and Nelkin 1983). This alteration in the c-Ha-*ras*1 gene has not yet been detected in any other cell type including cells from a variety of known preneoplastic conditions where such a change might have been expected (Needleman, Yuasa, Srivastava and Aaronson 1983). A second activated Ha-*ras* gene has been characterized from the lung carcinoma cell line HS242 and the mechanism of activation again involves the alteration of a single amino acid. In this case a glutamine residue (CAG) at position 61 in the normal gene is altered to a leucine (CTG) (Yuasa, Stivastava, Dunn, Rhim, Reddy and Aaronson 1983). Unfortunately this particular alteration in amino acid 61 is not amenable to restriction analysis even though codon 61 constitutes the middle three nucleotides of a BstNI site (CC_T^AGG). Other changes in this codon would be recognized by loss of the BstNI site.

The c-Ki-*ras*2 gene is activated in a variety of tumours though the mechanism of activation has proved a little more difficult to analyse (Der *et al.* 1982; McCoy *et al.* 1983). Evidence was already available that here too qualitative changes in the protein had taken place. Antisera raised to the p21 protein revealed differences in electrophoretic mobility of the products of activated Ki-*ras* genes (Der and Cooper 1983). Sequence work from two groups has since shown that in two cell lines SW480, a colon carcinoma line, and in Calu-1, a lung carcinoma line, position 12 which is glycine in the normal allele has been altered to valine and cysteine respectively (Shimizu *et al.* 1983*b*; McGrath *et al.* 1983). More recently two activated c-Ki-*ras*2 genes have been cloned from two human lung adenocarcinoma cell lines. In one of these there is an amino acid substitution at position 12 (glycine to cysteine) (Nakano, Yamamoto, Neville, Evans, Mizuno and Perucho 1984*a*) but in the other the lesion is at position 61 (Nakano, Yamamoto, Neville and Perucho 1984*b*).

We have determined the mechanism of activation of the N-*ras* gene in HT1080 (Brown *et al.* 1984). The N-*ras* gene is effectively cut in half by the EcoRI site, exons one and two being in the 8.8 Kb fragment and exons three and four in the 7.0 Kb half (Fig. 5.4*a*). When the 8.8 Kb fragment from HT1080 is ligated to the 7.0 Kb fragment from normal cells the resulting ligation mixture has transforming activity (see Fig. 5.6*c*). However if the 8.8 (Fe) and the 7.0 (HT) fragments are ligated no transforming activity is detectable (Fig. 5.6*d*). The mutation must be located within the 8.8 Kb fragment. We have been able to speed up this assay somewhat by cotransfecting a plasmid containing the 8.8 Kb fragment from HT1080 with a full length normal N-*ras* gene. Neither plasmid alone will transform NIH/3T3 but as a mixture they do. Presumably homologous recombination is taking place *in vivo* yielding some chimeric molecules with identical structure to the *in vitro* produced constructs. This has been observed in other gene transfer experiments (Shapira, Stachelek, Letsou, Soodak and Liskay 1983). A series of chimeric molecules has been tested (see Fig. 5.6) and the smallest fragment

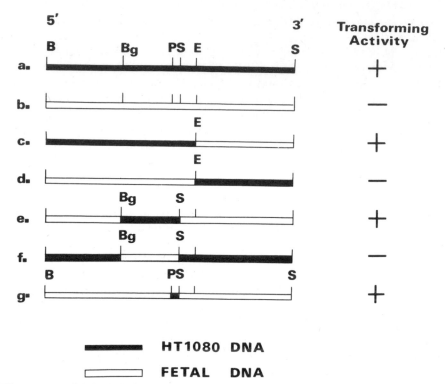

Fig. 5.6. Localization of the HT1080 lesion. Chimeric molecules constructed between the HT1080 and the foetal N-*ras* genes. In *c* and *d*, the BamHI (B) to EcoRI (E) fragment (containing exons one and two) was ligated to the EcoRI (E) to SstI (S) fragment (containing exons three and four) and the mixture added to NIH/3T3 cells in a transfection assay. In *e*, *f* and *g*, a plasmid containing the BamHI to EcoRI chimera was first constructed. The Bam/Eco fragment was removed from this plasmid, ligated to exons three and four (Eco/Sst fragment) and tested in the transfection assay. Bg, Bg1II; P, PvuII.

from HT1080 found to activate the normal allele was a 600 bp Pvu II/Sst I fragment (Fig. 5.6*g*). This contains amino acids 59–97 of the second exon. When this fragment was sequenced and compared to the normal sequence the only difference was a point mutation resulting in an alteration of the glutamine residue (CAA) at position 61 in the normal allele to a lysine (AAA) in HT1080 i.e. a C to A transversion. An identical alteration in the N-*ras* gene has been reported in the neuroblastoma cell line, SK-N-SH (Taporowsky *et al.* (1983). No convenient restriction site is present at this position.

The point mutations observed in human tumour DNAs appear to be somatic, in that DNA isolated from normal tissues of the same individual do not contain the alteration (Gambke *et al.* 1984; Santos, Zanco, Reddy,

Pierotti, Porta and Barbacid 1984; Feig, Bast, Knapp and Cooper 1984), and so far the alterations are all transversions. Both viral Harvey and Kirsten lack glycine at position 12, but in these cases, the alterations involve transitions. Transitions have also been observed in an *in vitro* spontaneously activated human *ras* gene (Santos, Reddy, Pulciani, Feldman and Barbacid 1983) and in nitroso-methylurea (NMU) induced rat mammary carcinomas (Sukumar *et al.* 1983). G → A transitions are exactly the type of mutation expected for a methylating agent such as NMU.

This apparently consistent pattern of activation by amino acid alteration may not be the whole story. As mentioned previously both c-Ha-*ras*1 and 2 from the rat and human c-Ha-*ras*1 can be activated by linking them to strong promoters, e.g. viral LTRs (Chang *et al.* 1982b). It may be that massive overproduction of the p21 product has a similar effect to the point mutations. Attempts to rationalize the dramatic biological effect of amino acid alterations and also explain the activation by strong promoters have been made. An amino acid change at positions 12 or 61 certainly leads to an alteration in the mobility of the p21 product after electrophoresis on SDS-polyacrylamide gels (Tabin *et al.* 1982; Santos *et al.* 1982; Yuasa *et al.* 1983). Computer modelling has also suggested that the loss of glycine at position 12 would have profound effects on the secondary structure of the p21 proteins (Reddy *et al.* 1982). We have carried out a similar analysis for the position 61 alteration in the N-*ras* product, but no major alteration in secondary structure is predicted (Cary and Hall, unpublished results). However, since the two different examples of 61 changes so far reported, glutamine to lysine or to leucine, involve chemically very different amino acid residues, we would still favour the idea of a conformational change as a consequence of the amino acid alteration at this position. It has been proposed that the normal p21 product might exist in two conformations (Pincus, Renswonde, Harford, Chang, Carty and Klausner 1983). One of these, the one which causes the transformed properties, is present in very small equilibrium amounts with normal p21. However the amount of this conformation present in a cell can be increased either by mutations, notably at 12 or 61 which alter the equilibrium constant, or by large increases in the p21 product.

Conclusions

DNA transfection experiments with human tumour DNA have focused a great deal of attention on the human *ras* gene family. First described in laboratory derived acute transforming viruses, the *ras* genes have now become an area of intense research. However, as can be seen in Table 5.1, little is really known about the function of these genes and their products. Three closely related *ras* p21 products appear to be present in most normal and tumour cells so far looked at. It is not clear why three very similar

Table 5.1

	v-Ha-ras	v-Ki-ras	c-Ha-ras1 H	c-Ha-ras1 R	c-Ki-ras2 H	N-ras H	c-Ha-ras2 H	c-Ki-ras1 H
Gene (Kb)	0.6 (coding sequence)	0.6 (coding sequence)	2.9	NK	40	10–15	1	4.2
Chromosomal Location	viral	viral	11p15.1-pter	NK	12p12-pter	1cen-p21	X	6
mRNA (Kb)	—	—	1.2	NK	5.5, 3.8 (1.2)	5.2, 2.2	inactive pseudogene	inactive pseudogene
protein (aa)	189	189	189	p21	189 exon 4A 188 exon 4B	189	—	—
phosphorylated	YES	YES	NK	NO	NK	NK	—	—
amino acid 12	arg	ser	gly	gly	gly	gly	(ser)*	(gly)*
amino acid 59	thr	thr	ala	ala	ala	ala	(ala)*	(thr)*
amino acid 61	gln	gln	gln	gln	gln	gln	(arg)*	(gln)*
GTP/GDP binding	YES	YES	NK	YES	NK	NK	—	—
Cellular location	inner surface plasma membrane		NK	NK	NK	NK	—	—
lipid attached	YES	NK	NK	NK	NK	NK	—	—

Table 5.1. The ras genes and the p21 products. H, human genes; R, rat genes. *These amino acids are those predicted by lining up the DNA sequence; as the pseudogenes contain many substitutions and deletions no protein product could be made. NK, not known.

products are required but this may not be surprising since the function of none of these proteins is understood. Recently three *ras* genes have been identified and cloned from yeast. One of these, YP2, codes for a 206 amino acid product which has around 38 per cent amino acid homology with residues 4-165 of the human p21s (Gallwitz, Donath and Sander 1983). The coding regions of the other two genes *RAS1* (309 amino acids) and *RAS2* (322 amino acids) (Powers, Kataoka, Fasano, Goldfarb, Strathern, Broach and Wigler 1984) or c-*ras*ˢᶜ-1 and c-*ras*ˢᶜ-2 (Defeo-Jones, Scolnick, Koller and Dhar 1983) are much more homologous to the human gene products. These two *ras* proteins are 90 per cent homologous to each other in the first 180 amino acids and are 90 per cent homologous to residues 1–80 of the human p21s and 50 per cent homologous to residues 81–160. It may well be that the delicate genetic manipulations which should be possible with these yeast *ras* genes will lead to a quicker understanding of the role their products play in the cell.

The last two years have seen a great increase in our understanding of the genes themselves. The future lies with understanding the role the gene products play in the normal growth and development of the eukaryotic cell. Through this type of analysis it may become clear why alterations in the *ras* genes can have such dramatic effects on cellular growth control leading to a situation that is one of the most distinctive characteristics of neoplasia.

Note added in proof

Since this chapter was submitted for publication, several reports have been published which have shifted somewhat our ideas concerning the role of *ras* proteins in cells. The normal and activated human c-Ha-*ras*-1 genes have now been cloned into *E. coli* expression vectors and used to generate large quantities of purified p21 protein (McGrath, Capon, Goeddel, and Levinson 1984). This has enabled this group and others to show that the *ras* proteins have a GTPase activity and that this activity is less in the mutant than in the wild-type proteins. Furthermore, it has been found that there is some, albeit limited, sequence homology between p21 and a signal transducing G protein isolated from bovine brain (Hurley, Simon, Teplow, Robishaw, and Gilman 1984). It is a distinct possibilty that the *ras* proteins are G-like proteins, capable of transducing information from a membrane receptor into an intracellular signal leading to cell proliferation. G proteins were originally described as components in the hormone-sensitive adenylate cyclase system (for review see Gilman 1984) and though it seems unlikely that p21 is a component of this classical G protein complex (the molecular weights are different) it is tempting to speculate that it is involved in coupling a receptor to a cellular response by generating some secondary signal, for example, cAMP, cGMP, or phosphatidylinositol breakdown.

The fact that the mutant *ras* proteins have lower GTPase activity than the normal proteins would fit in with the known activity of G proteins where binding of GTP leads to an active conformation resulting in the transduction of a signal. The slower the removal of GTP (via hydrolysis) the longer the G protein will remain in its active configuration. These preliminary findings are already beginning to initiate a large research effort aimed at identifying the effects of *ras* gene products on the levels of known intracellular secondary messengers.

References

Andersen, P. R. and Robbins, K. C. (1976), Rat sequences of the Kirsten and Harvey murine sarcoma virus genomes: Nature, origin and expression in rat tumour RNA. *J. Virol.* **17**, 335–351.

—— Devare, S. G., Tronick, S. R., Ellis, R. W., Aaronson, S. A., and Scolnick, E. M. (1981). Generation of BALB-MuSV and Ha-MuSV by type C virus transduction of homologous transforming genes from different species. *Cell* **26**, 129–134.

Balmain, A., Ramsden, M., Bowden, G. T., and Smith, J. (1984). Activation of the mouse cellular Harvey-*ras* gene in chemically induced benign skin papillomas. *Nature* **307**, 658–660.

Benoist, C., O'Hare, K., Breathnach, R., and Chambon, P. (1980). The ovalbumin gene—sequence of putatitive control regions. *Nucleic Acids Res.* **8**, 127–142.

Bishop, J. M. (1983). Cellular oncogenes and retroviruses. *Ann. Rev. Bioch.* **52**, 301–354.

Brown, R., Marshall, C. J., Pennie, S. G., and Hall, A. (1984). Mechanism of activation of an N-*ras* gene in the human fibrosarcoma cell line HT1080. *The E.M.B.O. Journal* **3**, 913–917.

Capon, D. J., Chen, E. Y., Levinson, A. D., Seeburg, P. H., and Goeddel, D. V. (1983*a*). Complete nucleotide sequences of the T24 human bladder carcinoma oncogene and its normal homologue. *Nature* **302**, 33–37.

—— Seeburg, P. H., McGrath, J. P., Hayflick, J. S., Edman, U., Levinson, A. D., and Goeddel, D. (1983*b*). Activation of Ki-*ras* 2 gene in human colon and lung carcinomas by two different point mutations. *Nature* **304**, 507–512.

Chang, E. H., Ellis, R. W., Scolnick, E. M., and Lowy, D. R. (1980*a*). Transformation by cloned Harvey murine sarcoma virus DNA: Efficiency increased by long terminal repeat DNA. *Science* **210**, 1249–1251.

—— Maryak, J. M., Wei, C.-M., Shih, T. Y., Shober, R., Cheung, H. L., Ellis, R. W., Hager, G. L., Scolnick, E. M., and Lowy, D. R. (1980*b*). Functional organization of the Harvey murine sarcoma virus genome. *J. Virol.* **35**, 76–92.

—— Gonda, M. A., Ellis, R. W., Scolnick, E. M., and Lowy, D. R. (1982*a*). Human genome contains four genes homologous to transforming genes of Harvey and Kirsten murine sarcoma viruses. *Proc. Nat. Acad. Sci. U.S.A.* **79**, 4848–4852.

—— Furth, M. E., Scolnick, E. M., and Lowy, D. R. (1982*b*). Tumorigenic transformation of mammalian cells induced by a normal human gene homologous to the oncogene of Harvey murine sarcoma virus. *Nature* **297**, 479–483.

Chien, Y. H., Lai, M., Shih, T. Y., Verma, I. M., Scolnick, E. M., Ray-Burman, P., and Davidson, N. (1979). Heteroduplex analysis of the sequence relationships between the genomes of Kirsten and Harvey sarcoma virus, their respective parental murine leukemia viruses and the rat endogenous 30S RNA. *J. Virol.* **31**, 752–760.

Collett, M. S. and Erikson, R. L. (1978). Protein kinase activity associated with the avian sarcoma virus *src* product. *Proc. Nat. Acad. Sci. U.S.A.* **75**, 2021–2024.

Cooper, G. M., Okenquist, S., and Silverman, L. (1980). Transforming activity of DNA of chemically transformed and normal cells. *Nature* **284**, 418–421.

Davis, M., Malcolm, S., Hall, A., and Marshall, C. J. (1983). Localization of the human N-*ras* oncogene to chromosome 1 cenp21 by *in situ* hybridization. *The E.M.B.O. Journal* **2**, 2281–2283.

de Martinville, B., Giacalone, J., Shih, C., Weinberg, R. A., and Francke, U. (1983*a*). Oncogene from human EJ bladder carcinoma is located on the short arm of chromosome 11. *Science* **219**, 498–501.

—— Cunningham, J. M., Murray, M. J., and Francke, U. (1983*b*). The N-*ras* oncogene assigned to the short arm of human chromosome 1. *Nucleic Acids Res.* **11**, 5267–5275.

Defeo, D., Gonda, M. A., Young, H. A., Chang, E. H., Lowy, D. R., Scolnick, E. M., and Ellis, R. W. (1981). Analysis of two divergent restriction endonuclease fragments homologous to the p21 coding region of Harvey murine sarcoma virus. *Proc. Nat. Acad. Sci. U.S.A.* **78**, 3326–3332.

Defeo-Jones, D., Scolnick, E. M., Koller, R., and Dhar, R. (1983). *ras*-Related gene sequences identified and isolated from *Saccharomyces cerevisiae*. *Nature* **306**, 707–709.

Der, C. J., Krontiris, T. E., and Cooper, G. M. (1982). Transforming genes of human bladder and lung carcinoma cell lines are homologous to the *ras* genes of Harvey and Kirsten sarcoma viruses. *Proc. Nat. Acad. Sci. U.S.A.* **79**, 3637–3640.

—— and Cooper, G. M. (1983). Altered gene products are associated with activation of cellular *ras* genes in human lung and colon carcinomas. *Cell* **32**, 201–208.

Dhar, R., Ellis, R. W., Shih, T. Y., Oroszlan, S., Shapiro, B., Maizel, J., Lowy, D., and Scolnick, E. M. (1982). Nucleotide sequence of the p21 transforming protein of Harvey Murine Sarcoma Virus. *Science* **217**, 934–936.

Ellis, R. W., Defeo, D., Maryak, J. M., Young, H. A., Shih, T. Y., Chang, E. H., Lowy, D. R., and Scolnick, E. M. (1980). Dual evolutionary origin for the rat genetic sequences of Harvey murine sarcoma virus. *J. Virol.* **36**, 408–420.

—— DeFeo, D., Shih, T. Y., Gonda, M. A., Young, H. A., Tsuchida, N., Lowy, D. R., and Scolnick, E. M. (1981). The p21 *src* genes of Harvey and Kirsten murine sarcoma viruses originate from divergent members of a family of normal vertebrate genes. *Nature* **292**, 506–511.

Ellis, R. W., Lowy, D. R., and Scolnick, E. M. (1982*a*). The viral and cellular p21 (*ras*) gene family. *Advances in Viral Oncology* (ed. G. Klein) Vol. I, pp. 107–126 Raven Press, New York.

—— Defeo, D., Furth, M. E., and Scolnick, E. M. (1982*b*). Mouse cells contain two distinct *ras* gene mRNA species that can be translated into a p21 *onc* protein. *Mol. Cell. Biol.* **2**, 1339–1345.

Eva, A., Robbins, K. C., Andersen, P. R., Srinivasan, A., Tronick, S. R., Reddy, E. P., Ellmore, N. W., Galen, A. T., Lautenberger, J. A., Papas, T. S., Westin, E. H., Wong-Staal, F., Gallo, R. C., and Aaronson, S. A. (1982). Cellular genes analogous to retroviral *onc* genes are transcribed in human tumour cells. *Nature* **295**, 116–119.

——Tronick, S. R., Gol, R. A., Pierce, J. H., and Aaronson, S. (1983). Transforming genes of human hematopoietic tumors: Frequent detection of *ras*-related oncogenes whose activation appears to be independent of tumor phenotype. *Proc. Nat. Acad. Sci. U.S.A.* **80**, 4926–4930.

Fasano, O., Taparowsky, E., Fiddes, J., Wigler, M., and Goldfarb, M. (1983). Sequence and structure of the coding region of the human H-*ras*-1 gene from T24 bladder carcinoma cells. *J. Mol. Appl. Genet.* **2**, 173–180.

Feig, L. A., Bast, R. C., Knapp, R. C., and Cooper, G. M. (1984). Somatic activation of ras^k gene in a human ovarian carcinoma. *Science* **223**, 698–701.

Feinberg, A. P., Vogelstein, M. J., Droller, S. B., Baylin, B. D., and Nelkin, B. D. (1983). Mutation affecting the 12th amino acid of the c-Ha-*ras* oncogene products occurs infrequently in human cancer. *Science* **220**, 1175–1177.

Furth, M. E., Davis, L. J., Fleurdelys, B., and Scolnick, E. M. (1982). Monoclonal antibodies to the p21 products of the transforming gene of Harvey Murine sarcome virus and of the cellular *ras* gene family. *J. Vir.* **43**, 294–304.

Gallwitz, D., Donath, C., and Sander, C. (1983). A yeast gene encoding a protein homologous to the human c-*has*/c-*bas* proto-oncogene product. *Nature* **306**, 704–707.

Gambke, C., Signer, E., and Moroni, C. (1984). Activation of N-*ras* in bone marrow cells from a patient with acute myeloblastic leukemia. *Nature* **307**, 476–478.

Gay, N. J. and Walker, J. E. (1983). Homology between human bladder carcinoma oncogene product and mitochondrial ATP-synthetase. *Nature* **301**, 262–264.

Gelmann, E. P., Wong-Staal, F., Kramer, R. A., and Gallo, R. C. (1981). Molecular cloning and comparative analyses of the genomes of simian sarcoma virus and its associated helper virus. *Proc. Nat. Acad. Sci. U.S.A.* **78**, 3373–3377.

Gilman, A. G. (1984). G proteins and dual control of adenylate cyclase. *Cell* **36**, 577–579.

Goldfarb, M., Shimizu, K., Perucho, M., and Wigler, M. (1982). Isolation and preliminary characterization of a human transforming gene from T24 bladder carcinoma cells. *Nature* **296**, 404–409.

Gonda, M. A., Young, H. A., Elser, J. E., Rasheed, S., Talmadge, C. B., Nagashima, K., Li, C. C., and Gilden, R. V. (1982). Molecular cloning, genomic analysis, and biological properties of Rat Leukemia Virus and the *onc* sequences of Rasheed Rat Sarcoma virus. *J. Virol.* **44**, 520–529.

Graham, F. L. and van der Eb, A. J. (1973). A new technique for the assay of infectivity of human adenovirus 5 DNA. *Virol.* **52**, 456–461.

Gruss, P., Ellis, R. W., Shih, T. Y., Koenig, M., Scolnick, E. M., and Khoury, G. (1981). SV40 recombinant molecules express the gene encoding p21 transforming protein of Harvey Murine Sarcoma virus. *Nature* **293**, 486–488.

Guerrero, I., Calzada, P., Mayer, A., and Pellicer, A. (1984). A molecular approach to leukemogenesis: Mouse lymphomas contain an activated c-*ras* oncogene. *Proc. Natl. Acad. Sci.* **81**, 202–205.

Hager, G. L., Chang, E. H., Chan, H. W., Garon, C. F., Israel, M. A., Martin, M. A., Scolnick, E. M., and Lowy, D. R. (1979). Molecular cloning of the Harvey sarcoma virus closed circular DNA intermediates: Initial structural and biological characterization. *J. Virol.* **31**, 795–809.

Hall, A., Marshall, C. J., Spurr, N., and Weiss, R. A. (1983). Identification of transforming gene in two human sarcoma cell lines as a new member of the *ras* gene family located on chromosome 1. *Nature* **303**, 396–400.

Harvey, J. J. (1964). An unidentified virus which causes the rapid production of tumours in mice. *Nature* **204**, 1104–1105.

Houck, C. M., Rinehart, F. P., and Schmid, C. W. (1979). A ubiquitous family of repeated DNA sequences in the human. *J. Mol. Biol.* **132**, 289–306.

Hurley, J. B., Simon, M. I., Teplow, D. B., Robishaw, J. D., and Gilman, A. G. (1984). Homologies between signal transducing G proteins and *ras* gene products. *Science* **226**, 860–862.

Jhanwar, S. C., Neel, B. G., Hayward, W. S., and Changanti, R. S. K. (1983). Localization of c-*ras* oncogene family on human germ-line chromosomes. *Proc. Nat. Acad. Sci. U.S.A.* **80**, 4794–4797.

Kirsten, W. H. and Mayer, L. A. (1967). Morphological responses to a murine erythroblastosis virus. *J. Nat. Canc. Inst.* **39**, 311335.

Krontiris, T. G. and Cooper, G. M. (1981). Transforming activity of human tumour DNAs. *Proc. Natl. Acad. Sci. U.S.A.* **78**, 1181–1184.

Langbeheim, H., Shih, T. Y., and Scolnick, E. M. (1980). Identification of a normal vertebrate cell protein related to the p21 *src* of Harvey murine sarcoma virus. *Virol.* **106**, 292–300.

Lautenberger, J. A., Ulsh, L., Shih, T. Y., and Papas, T. S. (1983). High-level expression in *Escherichia coli* of enzymatically active Harvey Murine sarcoma virus p21 *ras* protein. *Science* **221**, 858–860.

Levinson, B., Khoury, G., Vande Wonde, G., and Gruss, P. (1982). Activation of SV40 genome by 72 base pair tandem repeats of Moloney sarcoma virus. *Nature* **295**, 568–572.

Loenen, W. A. M. and Brammar, W. J. (1980). A bacteriophage lambda vector for cloning large DNA fragments made with several restriction enzymes. *Gene* **20**, 249–259.

Lowy, D. R., Rands, E., and Scolnick, E. M. (1978). Helper-independent transformation by unintegrated Harvey sarcoma virus DNA. *J. Virol.* **26**, 291–298.

Marshall, C. J., Hall, A., and Weiss, R. A. (1982). A transforming gene present in human sarcoma cell lines. *Nature* **299**, 171–173.

McBride, O. W., Swann, D. C., Santos, E., Barbacid, M., Tronick, S. R., and Aaronson, S. A. (1982). Localization of the normal allele of T24 human bladder carcinoma oncogene to chromosome 11. *Nature* **300**, 773–774.

McCoy, M. S., Toole, J. J., Cunningham, J. M., Chang, E. H., Lowy, D. R., and Weinberg, R. A. (1983). Characterization of a human colon/lung carcinoma oncogene. *Nature* **302**, 79–81.

—— Bargmann, C. I., and Weinberg, R. A. (1984). Human colon carcinoma Ki-*ras*2 oncogene and its corresponding proto-oncogene. *Molecular and Cellular Biology* **4**, 1577–1582.

McGrath, J. P., Capon, D. J., Goeddel, D. V., and Levinson, A. D. (1984). Comparative biochemical properties of normal and activated human *ras* p21 protein. *Nature* **310**, 644–649.

—— Capon, D. J., Smith, D. H., Chen, E. Y., Seeburg, P. H., Goeddel, D. V., and Levinson, A. D. (1983). Structure and organization of the human Ki-*ras* proto-oncogene and a related pseudogene. *Nature* **304**, 501–506.

Miyoshi, J., Kagimoto, M., Soeda, E., and Sakaki, Y. (1984). The human c-Ha-*ras*2 is a processed pseudogene inactivated by numerous base substitutions. *Nucleic Acids Res.* **12**, 1821–1828.

Müller, R., Slamon, D. J., Tremblay, J. M., Müller, D., Cline, M. J., and Verma, I. M. (1982). Differential expression of cellular oncogenes during pre- and postnatal development of the mouse. *Nature* **299**, 640–644.

—— Verma, I. M., and Adamson, E. D. (1983). Expression of c-*onc* genes: c-*fos* transcripts accumulate to high levels during development of mouse placenta, yolk sac, and amnion. *The E.M.B.O. Journal* **2**, 679–684.

Murray, M. J., Shilo, B. Z., Shih, C., Cowing, D., Hsu, H. W., and Weinberg, R. A. (1981). Three different human tumor cell lines contain different oncogenes. *Cell* **25**, 355–361.

—— Cunningham, J. M., Parada, L. F., Dautry, F., Lebowitz, P., and Weinberg, R. A. (1983). The HL-60 transforming sequence: A *ras* oncogene co-existing with altered *myc* genes in hematopoietic tumors. *Cell* **33**, 749–757.

Nakano, H., Yamamoto, F., Neville, C., Evans, D., Mizuno, T., and Perucho, M. (1984a). Isolation of transforming sequences of two human lung carcinomas: structural and functional analysis of the activated c-Ki-*ras* oncogenes. *Proc. Nat. Acad. Sci. U.S.A.* **81**, 71–75.

—— Yamamoto, F., Neville, C., and Perucho, M. (1984b). Isolation of transforming sequences of two human lung adenocarcinomas. *J. Cell. Bioch.* Supplement 8A, 71.

Needleman, S., Yuasa, Y., Srivastava, S., and Aaronson, S. A. (1983). Normal cells of patients with high cancer risk syndromes lack transforming activity in the NIH/3T3 transfection assay. *Science* **222**, 173–175.

O'Brien, S. J., Nash, W. G., Goodwin, J. L., Lowy, D. R., and Chang, E. H. (1983). Dispersion of the *ras* family of transforming genes to four different chromosomes in man. *Nature* **302**, 839–842.

Papageorge, A., Lowy, D. R., and Scolnick, E. M. (1982). Comparative biochemical properties of p21 *ras* molecules coded for by viral and cellular *ras* genes. *J. Virol.* **44**, 509–519.

Parada, L. F., Tabin, C. J., Shih, C., and Weinberg, R. A. (1982). Human EJ bladder carcinoma oncogene is homologue of Harvey sarcoma virus *ras* oncogene. *Nature* **297**, 474–478.

Parks, W. P. and Scolnick, E. M. (1977). *In vitro* translation of Harvey murine sarcome virus RNA. *J. Virol.* **22**, 711–719.

Perucho, M., Hanahan, D., and Wigler, M. (1980). Genetic and physical linkage of exogenous sequences in transformed cells. *Cell* **22**, 309–317.

—— Goldfarb, M., Shimizu, K., Lama, C., Fogh, J., and Wigler, M. (1981). Human tumor-derived cell lines contain common and different transforming genes. *Cell* **27**, 467–476.

Peters, R. L., Rabstein, L. S., Van Vleck, R., Kelloff, G. J., and Huebner, K. J. (1974). Naturally occurring sarcoma virus of the BALB/cCr mouse. *J. Natl. Canc. Instit.* **53**, 1725–1729.

Pincus, M. R., Renswonde, J., Harford, J. B., Chang, E. H., Carty, R. P., and Klausner, R. D. (1983). Prediction of the three dimensional structure of the transforming region of the EJ/T24 human bladder oncogene product and its normal cellular homologue. *Proc. Natl. Acad. Sci. U.S.A.* **80**, 5253–5257.

Powers, S., Kataoka, T., Fasano, O., Goldfarb, M., Srathern, J., Broach, J., and Wigler, M. (1984). Genes in *Sacchamoyces cerevisiae* encoding proteins with domains homologous to the mammalian *ras* proteins. *Cell*, in press.

Proudfoot, N. and Brownlee, G. (1974). Sequence at the 3′ end of globin mRNA shows homology with immunoglobulin light chain. *Nature* **252**, 359–362.

Pulciani, S., Santos, E., Lauver, A. V., Long, L. K., Aaronson, S. A., and Barbacid, M. (1982*a*) Oncogenes in solid human tumours. *Nature* **300**, 539–542.

—— Santos, E., Lauver, A. V., Long, L. K., Robbins, K. C., and Barbacid, M. (1982*b*) Oncogenes in human tumour cell lines: Molecular cloning of a transforming gene from human bladder carcinoma cells. *Proc. Natl. Acad. Sci. U.S.A.* **79**, 2845–2849.

Rasheed, S., Gardner, M. B., and Huebner, R. J. (1978). *In vitro* isolation of stable rat sarcoma viruses. *Proc. Natl. Acad. Sci. U.S.A.* **75**, 2972–2976.

Rasheed, S. (1980). Endogenous virogenes and oncogenes in rat-cell transformation: A new model system. *Cold Spring Harbor Symposium on Quantitative Biology* **54**, 779–786.

—— Norman, G. L., and Heidecker, G. (1983). Nucleotide sequence of the Rasheed Rat Sarcoma Virus oncogene: New mutations. *Science* **221**, 155–157.

Reddy, E. P., Reynold, R. K., Santos, E., and Barbacid, M. (1982). A point mutation is responsible for the acquisition of transforming properties of the T24 human bladder carcinoma oncogene. *Nature* **300**, 149–152.

Reddy, E. P. (1983), Nucleotide sequence analysis of the T24 human bladder carcinoma oncogene. *Science* **220**, 1061–1063.

Rous, P. (1910). A transmissable avian neoplasm: Sarcoma of the common fowl. *J. Exper. Med.* **12**, 696–705.

Ryan, J., Barker, P. E., Shimizu, K., Wigler, M., and Ruddle, F. H. (1983). Chromosomal assignment of a family of human oncogenes. *Proc. Natl. Acad. Sci. U.S.A.* **80**, 4460–4463.

Sakaguchi, A. Y., Naylaor, S. L., Shows, T. R., Toole, J. J., McCoy, M., and Weinberg, R. A. (1983). Human c-Ki-*ras* 2 proto-oncogene on chromosome 12. *Science* **219**, 1081–1083.

Santos, E., Tronick, S. R., Aaronson, S. A., Pulciani, S., and Barbacid, M. (1982). T24 human bladder carcinoma oncogene is an activated form of the normal human homologue of BALB- and Harvey-MSV transforming genes. *Nature* **298**, 343–347.

—— Reddy, E. P., Pulciani, S., Feldman, R. J., and Barbacid, M. (1983). Spontaneous activation of a human proto-oncogene. *Proc. Natl. Acad. Sci. U.S.A.* **80**, 4679–4683.

—— Zanca, D. M., Reddy, E. P., Pierotti, M. A., Porta, G. D., and Barbacid, M. (1984). Malignant activation of K-*ras* oncogene in lung carcinomas but not in normal tissues of same patient. *Science* **223**, 661–664.

Schwab, M., Alitalo, K., Varmus, H. E., Bishop, J. M., and George, D. (1983). A cellular oncogene (c-Ki-*ras*) is amplified, over-expressed and located within karyotypic abnormalities in mouse adrenocortical tumour cells. *Nature* **303**, 497–501.

Scolnick, E. M., Shih, T. Y., Maryak, J., Ellis, R., Chang, E., and Lowy, D. (1980). Guanine nucleotide binding activity of the *src* gene product of rat-derived murine sarcoma viruses. *Annals New York Acad. Sci.* 398–409.

—— Weeks, M. O., Shih, T. Y., Ruscetti, S. K., and Dexter, T. M. (1981) Markedly elevated levels of an endogenous *sarc* protein in a hemopoietic precursor cell line. *Mol. Cell. Biol.* **1**, 66–74.

Sefton, B. M., Trowbridge, I. S., Cooper, J. A., and Scolnick, E. M. (1982). The transforming proteins of Rous Sarcoma Virus, Harvey Sarcoma Virus, and Abelson Virus contain tightly bound lipid. *Cell* **31**, 465–474.

Shapira, G., Stachelek, J. L., Letsou, A., Soodak, L. K., and Liskay, R. M. (1983). Novel use of synthetic oligonucleotide insertion mutants for the study of homologous recombination in mammalian cells. *Proc. Natl. Acad. Sci. U.S.A.* **80**, 4827–4831.

Shih, C., Shilo, B. Z., Goldfarb, M. P., Dannenberg, A., and Weinberg, R. A. (1979). Passage of phenotypes of chemically transformed cells *via* transfection of DNA and chromatin. *Proc. Natl. Acad. Sci.* **76**, 5714–5718.

—— Padhy, L. C., Murray, M., and Weinberg, R. A. (1981) Transforming genes of carcinomas and neuroblastomas introduced into mouse fibroblasts. *Nature* **290**, 261–264.

—— and Weinberg, R. A. (1982*a*) Isolation of a transforming sequence from a human bladder carcinoma cell line. *Cell* **29**, 161–169.

Shih, T. Y., Williams, D. R., Weeks. M. O., Maryak, J. M., Vass, W. C., and Scolnick, E. M. (1978). Comparison of the genomic organization of Kirsten and Harvey sarcoma viruses. *J. Virol.* **27**, 45–55.

—— Weeks, M. O., Young, H. A., and Scolnick, E. M. (1979*a*). Identification of a sarcoma virus coded phosphoprotein in non-producer cells transformed by Kirsten or Harvey murine sarcoma virus. *Virology* **96**, 64–79.

—— Weeks, M. O., Young, H. A., and Scolnick, E. M. (1979*b*). p21 of Kirsten murine sarcoma virus is thermolabile in a viral mutant temperature sensitive for the maintenance of transformation. *J. Virol.* **31**, 546–556.

—— Papageorge, A. G., Stokes P. E., Weeks, M. O., and Scolnick, E. M. (1980). Guanine nucleotide binding and autophosphorylating activities associated with the purified p21 *src* protein of Harvey murine sarcoma virus. *Nature* **287**, 686–691.

—— Weeks, M. O., Gruss, P., Dhar, R., Oroszlan, S., and Scolnick, E. M. (1982*b*). Identification of a precursor in the biosynthesis of the p21 transforming protein of Harvey murine sarcoma virus. *J. Virol.* **42**, 253–261.

—— Stokes, P. E., Smythers, G. W., Dhar, R., and Oroszlan, S. (1982*c*). Characterization of the phosphorylation sites and surrounding amino acid sequences of the p21 transforming proteins coded for by the Harvey and Kirsten strains of Murine Sarcoma Virus. *J. Biol. Chem.* **257**, 11767–11773.

Shimizu, K., Goldfarb, M., Perucho, M., and Wigler, M. (1983*a*). Isolation and preliminary characterization of the transforming gene of a human neuroblastoma cell line. *Proc. Natl. Acad. Sci. U.S.A.* **80**, 383–387.

—— Birnbaum, D., Ruley, M. A., Fasano, O., Suard, Y., Edlund, L., Taporowsky, E., Goldfarb, M., and Wigler, M. (1983*b*). Structure of the Ki-*ras* gene of the human lung carcinoma cell line Calu-1. *Nature* **304**, 497–500.

Sukumar, S., Notario, V., Zanca, D. M., and Barbacid, M. (1983). Induction of mammary carcinomas in rats by nitroso-methylurea involves malignant activation of the H-*ras*-1 locus by single point mutations. *Nature* **306**, 658–661.

Tabin, C. J., Bradley, S. M., Bargmann, C. I., Weinberg, R. A., Papageorge, A. G., Scolnick, E. M., Dhar, R., Lowy, D. R., and Chang, E. H. (1982). Mechanism of activation of a human oncogene. *Nature* **300**, 143–149.

Taparowsky, E., Suard, Y., Fasano, O., Shimizu, K., Goldfarb, M. P., and Wigler, M. P. (1982). Activation of T24 bladder carcinoma transforming gene is linked to a single amino acid change. *Nature* **300**, 762–765.

—— Shimizu, K., Goldfarb, M., and Wigler, M. (1983). Structure and activation of the human N-*ras* gene. *Cell* **34**, 581–586.

Tsuchida, N., Gilden, R., and Hatanaka, M. (1974). Sarcoma-virus related RNA sequences in normal rat cells. *Proc. Natl. Acad. Sci. U.S.A.* **71**, 4503–4507.

—— and Uesugi, S. (1981). Structure and Functions of the Kirsten Murine Sarcoma Virus Genome: Molecular cloning of Biologically active Kirsten Murine Sarcoma Virus DNA. *J. Virol.* **38**, 720–727.

—— Ryder, T., and Ohtsubo, E. (1982). Nucleotide sequence of the oncogene encoding the p21 transforming protein of Kirsten Murine Sarcoma virus. *Science* **217**, 937–938.

Vogt, P. K. (1977). Genetics of RNA tumour viruses. In *Comprehensive Virology, Vol. 9* (ed. H. Fraenkel-Conrat and R. R. Wagner) pp. 341–455. Plenum, New York.

Vousden, K. and Marshall, C. J. (1984). Three different activated *ras* genes in mouse tumours: evidence for oncogene activation during progression of a mouse lymphoma. *The E.M.B.O. Journal*, in press.

Wei, C.-M., Lowy, D., and Scolnick, E. M. (1980). Mapping of transforming region of the Harvey murine sarcome virus genome by using insertion-deletion mutants constructed *in vitro*. *Proc. Natl. Acad. Sci. U.S.A.* **77**, 4674–4678.

Weinberg, R. A. (1983). A molecular basis of cancer. *Sci. Amer.* November, 102–116.

Westin, E. H., Wong-Staal, F., Gelman, E. P., Dalla-Favera, R., Papas, T. S., Lautenberger, J. A., Eva, A., Reddy, E. P., Tronick, S. R., Aaronson, S. A., and Gallo, R. C. (1982). Expression of cellular homologues of retroviral *onc* genes in human haematopoietic cells. *Proc. Natl. Acad. Sci. U.S.A.* **79**, 2490–2494.

Wierenga, R. K. and Hol, W. G. J. (1983). Predicted nucleotide-binding properties of p21 protein and its cancer-associated variant. *Nature* **302**, 842–844.

Willingham, M. C., Pastan, I. S., Shih, T. Y., and Scolnick, E. M. (1980). Localization of the *src* gene product of the Harvey strain of MSV to plasma membrane of transformed cells by electron microscopic immunocytochemistry. *Cell* **19**, 1005–1014.

—— Banks-Schlegel, S. P., and Paston, I. E. (1983) Immunocyto-chemical localization in normal and transformed human cells in tissue culture using a monoclonal antibody to the *src* protein of the Harvey strain of murine sarcoma virus. *Exper. Cell Res.* **149**, 141–149.

Yuasa, Y., Stivastava, S. K., Dunn, C. Y., Rhim, J. S., Reddy, E. P., and Aaronson, S. A. (1983). Acquisition of transforming properties by alternative point mutations within c-*bas*/*has* human proto-oncogene. *Nature* **303**, 775–779.

6 Activation of genes for variant surface glycoproteins in trypanosomes *

PAUL A. M. MICHELS

Trypanosome biology and antigenic variation

African trypanosomes are protozoan parasites that occur in the bloodstream and extracellular fluids of man and domestic animals. These parasites are responsible for serious diseases like sleeping sickness in humans and nagana in cattle. Transmission between the mammalian hosts is mediated by an insect vector, the tsetse fly. When taken up by the fly during a blood meal, the trypanosomes multiply in the insect's midgut before they penetrate the salivary glands. The infective salivarian form of the parasites, the so-called metacyclics, are injected into a new host.

The African trypanosomes can be considered as highly successful parasites, because an infection that is initiated by only a few parasites may persist for months, showing an oscillating parasitaemia with successive waves every 7–10 days. This behaviour can be attributed largely to the parasite's ability to evade the immune response of the host. The trypanosome is able to do this by regularly changing the composition of its surface coat, that is located outside the plasma membrane. In electron micrographs this surface coat appears as a 12–15 nm thick layer (Vickerman 1969; Vickerman and Luckins 1969) and was shown, by biochemical analysis, to be solely composed of one species of protein, the Variant Surface Glycoprotein (VSG) (Cross 1975). The coat completely covers the bloodstream form of the organism, but is absent from the parasite during its stay in the midgut of the insect and in the analogous form that is obtained by *in vitro* culturing (Vickerman 1969). In the bloodstream, the surface coat is therefore the only part of the live parasite that is recognized by the host. The host's immune defence falls short in completely eliminating the parasites, because a few trypanosomes replace their coat by one composed of a different VSG, a process known as antigenic variation. By repeatedly doing so the trypanosomes cause infections that may last for a very long time. It has been observed that from a single trypanosome clone over a hundred different antigenic types can arise (Capbern, Giroud, Baltz and Mattern 1977).

A trypanosome produces the various VSGs one after the other. So far no coat containing different VSGs has been reported, suggesting that a mechanism operates that ensures a mutually exclusive biosynthesis of the proteins. How the switch from the synthesis of one VSG to the next is triggered is as yet unknown. Since switching has also been observed in immuno-

* Abbreviations: AnTat, Antwerp Trypanozoon antigen type; BC, basic copy; ELC, expression-linked extra copy; ILTat, ILRAD Trypanozoon antigen type; Mb, megabase pair(s); MITat, Molteno Institute Trypanozoon antigen type; VAT, variant antigen type; VSG, variant surface glycoprotein.

compromized animals and *in vitro*, it can be assumed that the host's immune system has no inducing role; it only exerts a selective effect on the antigenically heterogeneous population of trypanosomes (Doyle, Hirumi, Hirumi, Lupton and Cross 1979).

Different antigenic types of trypanosomes follow each other during a chronic infection of a mammal in a non-random order (Van Meirvenne, Janssens and Magnus 1975*a*; Van Meirvenne, Janssens, Magnus, Lumsden and Herbert 1975*b*; Capbern *et al.* 1977; Miller and Turner 1981). One can distinguish types that arise early, semi-late and late. After transmission to a new animal, whether *via* the fly or by syringe-passage of blood, in the laboratory, reversion to early types occurs. During fly-transmission the trypanosomes loose at first their coat in the insect's midgut (Vickerman 1969). A new coat is acquired after migration to the salivary gland. The trypanosome population that arises there comprises a special group of early antigenic variants, the metacyclics (Le Ray, Barry and Vickerman 1978; Barry, Hajduk, Vickerman and Le Ray 1979). These metacyclic variants are injected in the mammalian bloodstream and, after relapse, they are succeeded by other variants according to the normal programme; however most often the second wave of the parasitaemia also contains the antigenic types similar to those of the trypanosomes that were ingested by the fly, even if these were late variants (Hajduk and Vickerman 1981). Although the antigenic variants can be grouped into various classes comprising variants that arise at different stages of infection, such a classification cannot be rigid and continuous reprogramming is observed (Van Meirvenne *et al.* 1975*a*, 1975*b*; Miller and Turner 1981; Barry, Crowe and Vickerman 1983).

In nature trypanosomes occur in relatively low number in their mammalian hosts. Nevertheless, biochemical studies on these organisms are made possible by the establishment of laboratory-adapted strains of *Trypanosoma brucei*, which can easily be grown in rats in large numbers (10^9/ml blood). Populations of trypanosomes that are more than 99 per cent homogeneous with respect to the antigenic type of their coat can be obtained for two reasons. Firstly, trypanosomes are sufficiently virulent that a single organism selected under the light-microscope can give rise to an infection in mice or rats (Van Meirvenne *et al.* 1975*a*). Secondly, the rate of antigenic switching of the laboratory-adapted strains is low ($10^{-4} - 10^{-5}$/generation) (Van Meirvenne *et al.* 1975*a*; Doyle *et al.* 1979). Experimental work is further facilitated by the possibility of cryopreservation of trypanosomes, without loss of infectivity (Hill and Hirumi 1983). The parasites can also be grown in culture (Hill and Hirumi 1983). When cultivated above a feeder layer of fibroblasts, the trypanosomes retain the morphology of the bloodstream forms. In this way, however, only low yields are obtained. In contrast, by growth in axenic culture at 27 °C so-called procyclic forms are obtained in large numbers, which are morphologically and metabolically very similar to the coatless trypanosomes found in the insect's midgut.

Nomenclature

Some explanation of the complicated nomenclature that is used to describe the antigenically different variants of trypanosomes, is required. A trypanosome producing a particular VSG is called a variant or Variable Antigen Type (VAT). Different VATs are each denoted by a number, that is also used to indicate the VSG that is produced in that VAT and the corresponding expressed gene. Because different laboratories study different strains (i.e. populations derived from a particular isolate, obtained from an infected animal in nature) and different serodemes (i.e. populations with the same VAT-repertoire), the nomenclature had to be elaborated a little further. A particular VAT is for instance indicated as MITat 1.1, which means: Molteno Institute Trypanozoon antigen type (to the institute where this serodeme has been first studied), serodeme 1, VAT 1. If the same VAT has been isolated more than once within a serodeme, they will be distinguished as 1.1a, 1.1b, etc., because as will be shown later, they can be different at the DNA level, even if the same allele is expressed. Since this nomenclature was only introduced after some VSGs of the lab-strain used in Amsterdam (i.e. *T. brucei* 427) had been well characterized (Cross 1975, 1978), I will partly use the old nomenclature: i.e. VAT 221 instead of MITat 1.2; VAT 117 = MITat 1.4; VAT 118 = MITat 1.5 and VAT 121 = MITat 1.6.

Structure of VSGs and assembly and organization of the surface coat

VSGs are molecules of around 60 kDa (Cross 1975), including the carbohydrate moieties that are attached at the C-terminal amino acid and at some other positions along the C-terminal half (Holder and Cross 1981; McConnell, Gurnett, Cordingley, Walker and Turner 1981). The N-terminal half of the molecule is exposed to the environment, the C-terminus is involved in the attachment to the plasma membrane (Cross 1978; Holder and Cross 1981). This orientation is reflected in the molecular structure: the composition of the N-terminal half, that evokes the immune response, differs largely between various VSGs, while the C-terminal part is much more conserved (Bridgen, Cross and Bridgen 1976; Matthijssens, Michiels, Hamers, Pays and Steinert 1981; Rice-Ficht, Chen and Donelson 1981). Although the carbohydrate chains of different VSGs share cross-reacting determinants, these are not exposed in live trypanosomes and, therefore, do not play a role in the host's immune response (Holder and Cross 1981).

By sequencing of cDNAs and by biosynthesis studies it has been revealed that VSGs are synthesized with both a N- and C-terminal extension that are cleaved off post-translationally (Boothroyd, Cross, Hoeijmakers and Borst 1980; Boothroyd, Paynter, Cross, Bernards and Borst 1981; McConnell *et al.* 1981). The N-terminal sequence consist of 20–40 amino acids, with an overall hydrophobic character. It supposedly mediates the segregation of the VSG molecule into the cisternae of the endoplasmic reticulum. The role of the C-terminal extension is less obvious; it may be involved in routing to the cytoplasmic membrane. This peptide is 17–23 residues long and also largely hydrophobic. Preliminary evidence obtained by pulse-chase experiments indicates that the processing of the C-terminal peptide occurs before its appearance at the plasma-membrane (McConnell, Turner and Rovis 1983). It has to be cleaved off before the carbohydrate chain can be attached. This binding of the carbohydrate is through ethanolamine that is amide-linked to the carboxyl group of the C-terminal aspartyl or serine residue (Holder 1983).

How the VSG is anchored in the plasma membrane is not yet completely clear. Turner and co-workers have demonstrated that VSGs, when bound to the membrane, have a form different from those VSGs that are purified after release from the cell (Cardoso de Almeida and Turner 1983). The membrane-bound form that behaves as a hydrophobic integral membrane protein is transformed into a soluble form by a membrane-bound enzyme, after rupture of the cell. Ferguson and Cross (1984) have shown that this transformation involves the cleavage of a covalently-linked myristic acid-containing moiety. It is likely that this fatty acid constitutes the anchorage of the VSG into the plasma membrane. The precise way by which the myristic acid is attached to the VSG has still to be established.

The remainder of this review will describe our current knowledge and ideas of the structure, organization and activation of VSG genes in trypanosomes. Other reviews on the molecular biology were by Borst and Cross (1982), Englund, Hajduk and Marini (1982), Borst (1983) and Borst, Bernards, Van der Ploeg, Michels, Liu, De Lange and Kooter (1983*b*). For a more extensive discussion of the biology of trypanosomes and the interaction with the host, the reader is referred to Vickerman (1978), Turner and Cordingley (1981) and Vickerman and Barry (1982). The biochemistry of VSGs have been described in detail by Cross (1978) and Turner (1982).

Initial studies on the molecular biology of antigenic variation

The mRNA for VSGs constitute a considerable fraction (approximately 10 per cent) of the total poly(A)$^+$ RNA of the trypanosomes, allowing the cloning of cDNAs without too many problems. Two different approaches have been followed initially to obtain the cDNAs. The first approach, followed by the groups of Williams and Steinert, involved the construction of cDNA libraries with mRNAs, enriched for VSG messengers by immunoprecipitation of polysomes (Williams, Marcu, Young, Rovis and Williams 1978; Lheureux, Lheureux, Vervoort, Van Meirvenne and Steinert 1979). VSG specific clones were identified by hybrid-arrested translation (Williams, Young and Majiwa 1979; Pays, Delronche, Lheureux, Vervoort, Bloch, Gannon and Steinert 1980). Hoeijmakers, Borst, Van den Burg, Weissmann and Cross (1980a) used total poly(A)$^+$RNA to prepare their banks. These were screened for VSG specific clones by differential selection, assuming that different VATs only differ in their mRNAs for VSGs. In later studies, after the sequence of several cDNAs had been compared, the cDNA construction could be largely simplified. At the 3′ end of all VSG mRNAs a conserved block of 14 nucleotides was found (Borst and Cross 1982). Therefore, VSG specific cDNA can be synthesized with a synthetic oligonucleotide that is complementary to this sequence as primer (Michels, Liu, Bernards, Sloof, Van der Bijl, Schinkel, Menke, Borst, Veeneman, Tromp and Van Boom 1983).

The cDNAs, when hybridized to Northern blots, detect homologous mRNA only in the corresponding VAT (Hoeijmakers et al. 1980a; Hoeij- makers, Frasch, Bernards, Borst and Cross 1980b). This indicates that VSG synthesis is controlled at the transcriptional level.

When the cDNAs were used as hybridization probes on Southern blots of trypanosomal DNA the following points were established. (1) Each VSG is encoded in the genome by a separate gene. No reassortment of genomic segments occurs to generate the diversity of VSGs, as is found for im- munoglobulins (Hoeijmakers et al. 1980b). (2) Some genes are part of a multigene family (e.g. VSG gene 117), other genes (e.g. 118) can be easily identified without any interference from other genes (Hoeijmakers et al. 1980b; Pays, Van Meirvenne, Le Ray and Steinert 1981a). The degree of homology between different VSG genes increases from 5′ to 3′, in agreement with the earlier described functions that are attributed to the N- and C- terminal halves of the proteins, respectively (Frasch, Bernards, Van der Ploeg, Hoeijmakers, Van den Burg and Cross 1980). (3) As first observed by Hoeijmakers et al (1980b), activation of some VSG genes is accompanied by a duplication of the basic gene copy. In contrast, other genes, first studied by Williams and co-workers, appear to be activated without any change in copy number (Williams et al. 1979).

Activation of VSG genes by a duplicative transposition

All VSGs are encoded by separate gene copies, the so-called Basic Copies (BC), which are usually not transcribed. Upon activation, an additional gene copy can be detected, that is called the Expression-Linked extra Copy (ELC) (Hoeijmakers et al 1980b). We have observed that the extra gene copies for the VSG genes 117, 118, 121 and 221 are all transposed to an identical or very similar position in the genome that we have called the (dominant) expression site (Van der Ploeg, Bernards, Rijsewijk and Borst 1982a; Michels, Bernards, Van der Ploeg and Borst 1982; Michels *et al* 1983; Bernards, De Lange, Michels, Liu, Huisman and Borst 1984*a*). This is illustrated in Fig. 6.1 by the comparison of the physical maps of the ELCs of the 118 VSG genes in four independently isolated VATs that express this gene. From this comparison several conclusions can be drawn: (1) The basic copy plus 1–2 kb of its 5′ flanking segment are transposed to the expression site. (2) The expression site is located at the end of a chromosome. This was first inferred from the observation that all restriction enzymes tested seem to cut at the same position, some distance downstream of the ELC (Van der Ploeg *et al*. 1982*a*). More substantial evidence for this inference was obtained by the demonstration that the DNA is preferentially shortened from that point by nuclease Bal 31 (De Lange and Borst 1982). (3) The ELC is flanked by regions of DNA that are nearly devoid of recognition sites for restriction enzymes. These so-called barren regions differ in length in different try- panosome clones (Michels *et al*. 1982, 1983). The lack of restriction sites and the length variation of the downstream region is presumably a common feature of all trypanosomal telomeres (see below). The variations of the 5′ region are possibly a result of the gene switch process itself, since this region might be composed of repeats of 70 bp sequences (Campbell, Van Bree and Boothroyd 1984; De Lange, unpublished), which are also present in front of

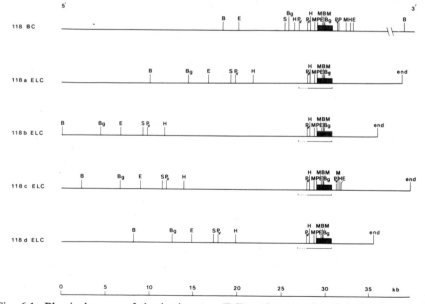

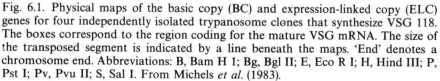

Fig. 6.1. Physical maps of the basic copy (BC) and expression-linked copy (ELC) genes for four independently isolated trypanosome clones that synthesize VSG 118. The boxes correspond to the region coding for the mature VSG mRNA. The size of the transposed segment is indicated by a line beneath the maps. 'End' denotes a chromosome end. Abbreviations: B, Bam H 1; Bg, Bgl II; E, Eco R I; H, Hind III; P, Pst I; Pv, Pvu II; S, Sal I. From Michels *et al*. (1983).

all BC genes (Van der Ploeg, Valerio, De Lange, Bernards, Borst and Gros-veld 1982c; Liu, Van der Ploeg, Rijsewijk and Borst 1983). By variable alignment during the recombination process that leads to the insertion of a new ELC, the variations may arise.

The duplicative activation of VSG genes to a telomeric expression site has also been observed by others (Pays et al. 1981a; Majiwa, Young, Eng-lund, Shapiro and Williams 1982; Longacre, Hibner, Raibaud, Eisen, Baltz, Giroud and Baltz 1983). The expression site in another *T. brucei* strain (EATRO 1125) has been extensively characterized by Steinert and coworkers (Pays et al. 1981a; Pays, Delauw, Van Assel, Laurent, Vervoort, Van Meir-venne and Steinert 1983c). Although it displays a lot of resemblance to the expression site of the 427 strain described above, the physical maps do not seem to be identical.

Experimental support for the assumption that the ELC is indeed the transcribed copy was presented by Pays, Lheureux and Steinert (1981b) who demonstrated the preferential sensitivity of the ELC to DNase I in isolated nuclei. Further proof was obtained by Bernards, Van der Ploeg, Frasch, Borst, Boothroyd, Coleman and Cross (1981) when they showed that the 3′ terminal sequence of the mRNA of VSG 117a was identical to that of the ELC, while it differed from that of the 117 BC. This difference between

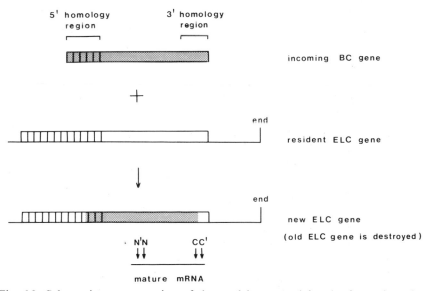

Fig. 6.2. Schematic representation of the model proposed for the formation of an ELC. The incoming gene displaces the resident ELC as result of a recombination mediated by homologous sequences at the edges of the transposed segment. The 70 bp repeats that constitute the 5′ homology region are represented by the series of blocks. The region of the transposed segment that is transcribed is indicated. N, C, N′ and C′ mark the N and C termini of the mature protein and the preprotein that contains N and C-terminal extensions, respectively.

ELC and BC was supposed to be a consequence of the mechanism by which the gene arrived in the expression site.

It was hypothesized that the ELC is inserted into the expression site by an unidirectional gene conversion, mediated by short blocks of homology at the edges of the transposed segment, as depicted in Fig. 6.2 (Bernards *et al.* 1981). Although the switching process can so far not be studied directly due to the low switching rate and the lack of mutants affected in the process, a number of data support this hypothesis. (1) The borders of the transposed segment were found to be located in the repetitive segments: the 3′ trans-position breakpoint of the segment is always found within the last 150 bp of the gene, at a position that is different for each transposition event (Michels *et al.* 1983). This means that it can be anywhere in the approximately 60–70 bp repetitive non-coding trailing sequence, in the sequence coding for the C-terminal extension or even at the end of the coding region of the mature protein. The 5′ edge of the transposed segment is always found in one of the 70 bp imperfect repeats that occur in variable numbers in front of all VSG genes, BCs as well as ELCs (Liu *et al.* 1983; Campbell *et al.* 1984; De Lange, unpublished). Fig. 6.3 shows schematically the transposition unit of the 118 VSG gene, with the features common to all VSG genes (Boothroyd *et al.* 1980; Majumder, Boothroyd and Weber 1981; Matthijssens *et al.* 1981;

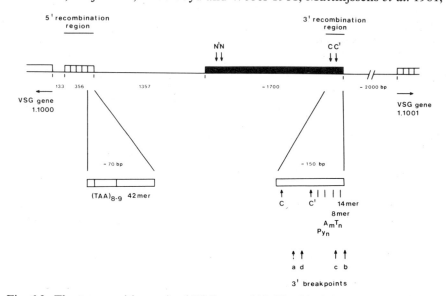

Fig. 6.3. The transposition unit of VSG gene 118. The black bar indicates the 118 VSG gene. Together with the gene an upstream segment of approximately 1.5 kb is co-transposed. The edges of the transposed segment were located in regions that contain characteristic sequence elements, shared by many VSG genes. These common features are indicated. The variable positions of the 3′ breakpoints in the different transposition events (118a–118d) are indicated by the arrows. The 5′ breakpoints have not yet been determined precisely.

Rice-Ficht *et al.* 1981; Liu *et al.* 1983). (2) The finding that the 3′ edge of the transposed segment is within the end of the gene suggests that the newly expressed gene gets an end derived from the preceding ELC (see Fig. 6.2). This is supported by the observation by Liu, Michels, Bernards and Borst (unpublished) that the 3′ end of the VSG mRNA from MITat 1.207 is identical to that of the mRNA from VAT 118b from which MITat 1.207 likely was derived. (3) Expression seemed to be strictly correlated to the presence of an ELC. For the 118 gene we discovered an additional copy every time the gene was activated. After the 118 VATs had switched to the production of a different VSG in the bloodstream of a rabbit, the ELC had disappeared again (Michels *et al.* 1982, 1983).

The existence of an unique expression site to which all VSG genes are transposed would nicely explain the observed mutually exclusive expression of VSG genes in trypanosomes. It suggests that all BC genes are silent because they lack a promoter. By transposition to an unique expression site, a particular VSG gene is activated as a result of the fusion to a putative promoter area.

Telomeric VSG-genes can be activated with and without duplication

Williams *et al.* (1979), working with *T. brucei* strain LUMP 227, first reported the activation of some VSG genes without any change in copy number or detectable genomic rearrangements associated with expression. Subsequently similar observations were made with other strains, e.g. strain 427 studied in Amsterdam, in which among others VSG genes 221 and 1.8 showed such behaviour (Borst, Frasch, Bernards, Van der Ploeg, Hoeijmakers, Arnberg and Cross 1981; Bernards *et al.* 1984*a*; Michels, Van der Ploeg, Liu and Borst 1984). All genes that can be expressed without duplication are invariably found at telomeres, in an environment very similar to the expression site, i.e. the gene is flanked by barren regions, the downstream one being variable in length (Williams, Young and Majiwa 1982; Bernards 1982; Bernards *et al.* 1984*a*).

As observed for the 221 and 1.8 genes, activation can be achieved both without (e.g. in VATs 221a and 1.8c, respectively) and with duplication (in VATs 221b and 1.8b). In VAT 221b the ELC was located at the same site as where the active gene for VSGs 117, 118 and 121 were found (Borst *et al.* 1983*b*; Borst, Bernards, Van der Ploeg, Michels, Liu, De Lange, Sloof, Schwartz and Cantor 1983*c*; Bernards *et al.* 1984*a*). However, analysis of the size of the 221 transposed segment revealed that the duplication process with this telomeric gene has been somewhat different from that involving the chromosome-internal genes. With the 221 genes, the breakpoints were located 2–4 kb 5′ and at least 0.8 kb downstream of the gene; it is even possible that the complete telomere has been duplicated, thereby converting the telomere with the preceding expressed gene copy. A telomere conversion was also observed in MITat 1.3 and 1.8b (Michels *et al.* 1984; Liu, Michels, Bernards and Borst unpublished). However, in these two cases the duplication seems to have involved at least 20 kb of the 5' flanking region of the VSG genes. For lack of probes for the upstream regions the acceptor telomeres could not be identified yet.

As mentioned above, telomeric VSG genes are often activated without duplication; most notably the VSG genes in ILTat 1.2, 1.3 and 1.4, studied by Williams and co-workers (Williams *et al.* 1979, 1982; Young, Donelson, Majiwa, Shapiro and Williams 1982; Young, Shah, Matthijssens and Williams 1983) and the genes in the VATs 221a and 1.8c, studied in Amsterdam. Especially the 221 gene, present as a single copy in VAT 221a, and its flanking regions have been analyzed extensively, in search for its mode of activation (Borst, Bernards, Van der Ploeg, Michels, Liu, De Lange, Sloof, Veeneman, Tromp and Van Boom 1983*a*; Borst *et al.* 1983*c*; Bernards *et al.* 1984*a*). This analysis has been largely guided by the observed mutually exclusive synthesis of VSGs. A mutually exclusive expression of genes would be achieved if only one promoter were available for all VSG genes. To explain the observed data it was anticipated that this could occur in two ways (Borst *et al.* 1983*a*). Firstly, by an unique mobile promotor element that will insert either in telomeres containing a BC VSG gene, or in the telomere that functions as the expression site for chromosome-internal genes. Secondly, the existence of an unique expression site was hypothesized, to which all VSG genes could be transposed in different manners. The chromosome-internal genes would enter this site by a duplicative transposition, the telomeric ones would do so by a reciprocal translocation. These two hypotheses were favoured over others, not involving an unique promoter, by the observation that all VSG mRNAs analyzed carry the same 35 nucleotide sequence at their 5' terminus, whatever the position and mode of activation of their genes (Van der Ploeg, Liu, Michels, De Lange, Borst, Majumder, Weber, Veeneman and Van Boom 1982*b*; Boothroyd and Cross 1982). These 35 nucleotides are not encoded contiguously with the remainder of the RNAs and were therefore supposed to be derived from a mini-exon that is associated with the promoter region. A comparison of the active 221 gene in VAT 221a with the inactive gene in VATs 118 and 118b did not, however, provide support for any of the two alternative hypotheses (Bernards *et al.* 1984*a*). The physical maps of both genes were identical over a distance of more than 55 kb upstream of the gene, rendering the possibility of reciprocal translocation unlikely. A promoter insertion could not be demonstrated either; no sequence coding for the 35 nucleotides was detected within 8.5 kb upstream of the 221 coding region. It should be noted that the 35 nucleotide sequence was also not found in front of the 118 ELCs, either in the transposed segment or in the barren region, implying that it is absent within 28 kb upstream of the 118b ELC (De Lange, Liu, Van der Ploeg,

Borst, Tromp and Van Boom 1983*b*). However, the negative result with the 221 is especially significant because a pseudo-VSG gene is located only 4 kb 5′ of the 221 gene (Bernards, unpublished).

The hypothesis that telomeric genes can be activated by a reciprocal translocation with the expression site telomere predicts that an ELC does not have to be destroyed but can also be rendered silent by disconnecting it from the putative upstream promoter region. Although previous experiments with variants isolated from chronically infected rabbits suggested that an ELC was always lost upon switching, these experiments were not conclusive because in this respect the rabbit is a black box: variants were isolated from successive parasitaemic waves which consisted of large, antigenically heterogeneous populations of trypanosomes (Van Meirvenne *et al.* 1975*a*; Michels *et al.* 1982, 1983). Moreover, to analyze these trypanosomes they had to be amplified in mice, which might introduce additional selection. By a different approach (the single relapse experiments) one can obtain variants that most likely have been derived from a known population that was proven to be homogeneous a few days before the relapse (Miller and Turner 1981). Such experiments nearly always lead to the appearance of known early VATs, producing VSGs that are encoded by telomeric genes (Michels *et al.* 1984; Liu, Michels, Bernards and Borst unpublished). In single relapse experiments started with 118 VATs it was indeed found that activation of telomeric genes was very often not accompanied with the loss of the 118 ELC, but this was retained in silent form (Borst *et al.* 1983*b*, 1983*c*; Michels *et al.* 1984). However, reminiscent of the situation with the 221 gene activation in VAT 221a, no differences were detected between the physical maps of the active and inactivated 118 extra gene copies, neither were activation-associated alterations found in the map of the newly expressed gene, the telomeric 1.8. Therefore these single relapse experiments do not support the reciprocal translocation model, although the lingering of the inactivated ELC is compatible with it. One should realize, however, that the experiments are not conclusive, because the transfer of very large telomeric fragments would remain undetected by conventional Southern blot analysis.

Single relapse experiments have also been performed with VAT 221a (Bernards *et al.* 1984*a*; Liu, Michels, Bernards and Borst unpublished). Again, preferentially telomeric genes were activated (i.e. 1.3 and 1.8). However, in five out of six cases the single 221 gene and at least 8.5 kb of its upstream region were deleted. In one case, involving the activation of VSG gene 1.3, it is possible that the 221 bearing telomere has been converted by the one containing the 1.3 gene, that was shown to be duplicated (see also page 154). Such a conversion, however, remains to be proven. In other cases the 1.8 gene was activated without duplication. Therefore, a direct relation between the 1.8 activation and the disappearance of the 221 gene is not obvious.

Telomeric genes also figured prominently in the extensive studies by Steinert and co-workers with strain EATRO 1125 (Laurent, Pays, Magnus, Van Meirvenne, Matthijssens, Williams and Steinert 1983; Pays, Van Assel, Laurent, Dero, Michels, Kronenberger, Matthijssens, Van Meirvenne, Le Ray and Steinert 1983a; Pays, Van Assel, Laurent, Darville, Vervoort, Van Meirvenne and Steinert 1983b; Pays et al. 1983c). Especially the five members of the AnTat 1.1 gene family have been analyzed in detail. This was done with ten different trypanosome clones, six of them expressing a 1.1 gene. In all six expressions only the two BC genes that were telomerically located were involved. Like the 221 gene in strain 427, these genes could be activated both in a duplicative and a non-duplicative manner. It was also shown independently by these authors that during the antigenic switch the old expressed gene copy is usually lost, but occasionally retained in inactive form (e.g. the 1.16 gene). Furthermore, in two of the trypanosome clones analyzed it was discovered that a partial gene conversion had occurred between different telomeric members of the AnTat 1.1 gene family. The resulting composite genes lead to the production of chimaeric proteins. Partial gene conversions, therefore, can contribute to the antigenic diversity of the trypanosomes.

Is there more than one expression site?

The lack of experimental data supporting the concept of reciprocal translocation has raised the possibility that more than one expression site exists. This was first proposed by Eisen and co-workers when they observed differences in the regions upstream of the ELCs in three different variants of T. equiperdum, expressing the same VSG gene (Longacre et al. 1983). Moreover, they also found that ELCs can be retained in inactive form, seemingly without being transposed to another telomere (Buck, Longacre, Raibaud, Hibner, Giroud, Baltz, Baltz and Eisen 1984).

Direct proof that VSG genes can be activated at telomeres of different chromosomes had to await for the development of techniques that allow hybridization studies on intact trypanosomal chromosomes. Trypanosomes do not show condensed chromosomes in any part of their cell cycle, thus precluding cytological hybridization. Recently an electrophoresis method was developed by Schwartz and Cantor (1984), by which chromosome-sized DNA can be size-fractionated in agarose gels. When this pulsed-field gradient gel electrophoresis was applied to trypanosomes a remarkable genomic organization was revealed (see Fig. 6.4) (Van der Ploeg, Schwartz, Cantor and Borst 1984b). About 60 per cent of the DNA consists of molecules that migrate close to the slot. Three chromosomes of approximately two Megabase (Mb) pairs were observed, at least six molecules of 200–700 kb and about a hundred minichromosomes of 50–150 kb. Hybridization studies with blots of such size-fractionated chromosomes showed that the 118 and 221 BC genes reside in the large DNA. The ELCs of these genes (in VATs

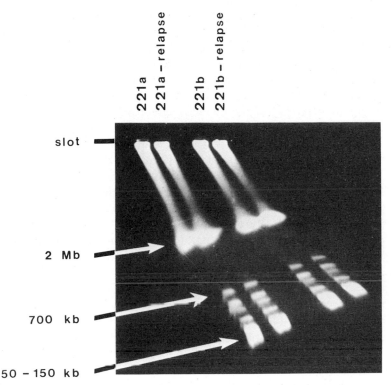

Fig. 6.4. Ethidiumbromide stained gel containing trypanosomal DNA fractionated by pulsed field gradient electrophoresis. Trypanosome samples were lysed and deproteinized in agarose blocks, to avoid shear degradation. The blocks were placed in the slots of a 1 per cent agarose gel and electrophoresed for 18 h at 20 °C, with pulses of 35 sec, as described by Van der Ploeg *et al.* (1984a). As a result, the chromosomes were fractionated parallel to the diagonal of the gel. The four lanes contain DNA of different VATs of *T. brucei* strain 427, as indicated. The size of the chromosomes was determined using yeast chromosomes as markers (not shown on this gel).

118a, 118b, and 221b) were found on a 2 Mb chromosome. However, the single 221 gene that is active in VAT 221a is in the large DNA, possibly at the same chromosome where it was in an inactive state. This demonstrates that at least two telomeres exist where VSG genes can be expressed.

Although this result proves that reciprocal translocation is not indispensable to ensure mutually exclusive expression of VSG genes, recent observations show that ends of chromosomes can be transposed (Van der Ploeg and Cornelissen 1984). Whether such processes play an important role in the activation and inactivation of VSG genes has still to be established.

How many expression sites for VSG genes exist is as yet unknown. The trypanosome has a large number of telomeres at its disposal, provided by the multitude of minichromosomes. Although the majority of the estimated 1000 VSG genes (Van der Ploeg *et al.* 1982*c*) are chromosome-internal, a considerable number has been detected at telomeres. We do not know whether all telomeres can act as expression site, or only a few. The data obtained so far with *T. brucei* 427 indicate that one site is preferentially used.

How the activity of the different sites is controlled remains to be determined. We can not exclude a mobile promoter, although we have not seen detectable alterations upon activation and inactivation of telomeres, indicative for such a promoter module. A speculative explanation is that only one telomere can be active at a time because expression is dependent on the occupation of an unique position in the nuclear matrix (Bernards, Van Harten-Loosbroek and Borst 1984*b*; Van der Ploeg and Cornelissen 1984). Further, a clue for a possible control mechanism is provided by the recent observation by Bernards *et al.* (1984*b*), that an unusual type of DNA modification is invariably found in telomeric VSG genes that are not transcribed.

These models are all based on the assumption that the mutually exclusive production of VSGs observed is due to an obligate intergenic exclusion between VSG genes. It has not been ruled out, however, that several genes can be active simultaneously. Trypanosomes synthesizing a mosaic coat may have little chance of surviving the immune response of the chronically infected host and consequently they may not have been identified yet.

Why different routes to activate VSG genes?

Three different ways have been described by which VSG genes can be activated (summarized in Fig. 6.5). Chromosome-internal genes can enter an expression site by duplicative transposition of the gene and 1–2 kb of its 5′ flanking region, thereby displacing the preceding gene from the expression site. Telomeric genes may use a duplicative mode of activation as well, in which the duplication possibly involves the whole telomere and may start at least 25 kb upstream of the VSG encoding region. In addition, telomeric genes can be activated without alterations in copy number or detectable rearrangements. The rationale for these different options to synthesize a surface coat protein may be found in the biological need for the trypanosome to produce the different VSGs in a loosely defined order. In addition this order has to be subject to regular reprogramming. Analysis of the genes expressed in the VATs appearing in the first relapses and in the different stages of a chronic infection has shown that telomeric genes are preferentially activated early in infection, while the chromosome-internal genes are expressed in later stages (Borst and Cross 1982; Longacre *et al.* 1983; Pays *et al.* 1983*a*; Michels *et al.* 1984). The early expression of telomeric genes can be attributed to the fact that at least some telomeres, harbouring

VSG genes, are potential expression sites with intrinsic properties that give them a high chance of getting activated. The next set of genes that are expressed may be other telomeric genes, the activation of their telomere being accompanied with the inactivation of the first one, or chromosomal internal genes that convert the gene at the active telomere. This conversion of telomeric genes is in line with the instability of genes residing at ends of chromosomes, as for instance described above for the 221 gene in *T. brucei* strain 427 (Frasch, Borst and Van der Ploeg 1982; Borst *et al.* 1983*c*; Bernards *et al.* 1984*a*). An inacceptable homogenization of the VSG gene repertoire by the loss of genes in this manner may be counteracted by the

1   ACTIVATION OF A VSG GENE BY CONVERTING AN OTHER
    GENE AT AN ACTIVE TELOMERE

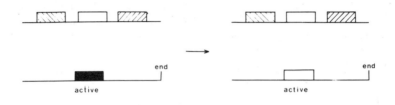

2   ACTIVATION OF A TELOMERIC VSG GENE BY TELOMERE
    CONVERSION

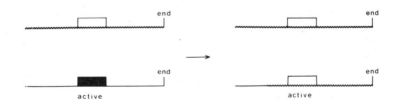

3   ACTIVATION OF A TELOMERIC VSG GENE <u>IN SITU</u>

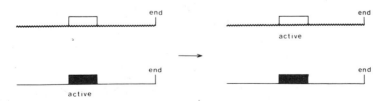

Fig. 6.5. Schematic representation of three ways in which VSG genes could possibly be activated. See text for explanation.

ability of telomeric genes to be duplicated as well. The reason that early VATs are not seen later in infection is most likely not to be sought in an inability of their telomeric genes to be activated any more, but trypanosomes expressing them will be eliminated by the antibodies then present.

The changes in the programme by which VSGs are produced can partly be explained by the changes of the repertoire of telomeric genes. Telomeric genes are occasionally lost due to conversion by other genes (Borst *et al.* 1983*c*; Pays *et al.* 1983*c*; Bernards *et al.* 1984*a*). If chromosome-internal genes can be transposed to silent telomeres, they become typical telomeric genes which may have a high chance of being expressed. In addition, the inactivation of an ELC of a chromosome-internal gene without its loss will have the same result. This latter process has been observed indeed: in the first relapse of variants with a lingering 118 ELC most trypanosomes that grew up produced VSG 118, as a result of the reactivation of the silent telomeric gene copy (Michels *et al.* 1984). The observation made by Miller and Turner (1981) in single relapse experiments that some VATs tend to occur in sequence can possibly also be explained by a reactivation of lingering ELC genes. Equally, one can invoke the reactivation of lingering ELCs to understand the data by Hajduk and Vickerman (1981) about the VATs that constitute the second wave of the parasitaemias started by insect bites. Usually the metacyclic population in the first wave is succeeded by trypanosomes that produce the same coat as the trypanosomes that were ingested by the fly, whether that were early or late VATs.

Currently it is not clear how an order is imposed on the subsequent expression of the approximately thousand chromosome-internal genes during the later stages of an infection. Neither is it known yet what sets the metacyclic repertoire apart. For a discussion of these questions the reader is referred to Borst *et al.* (1983*c*) and Borst, Bernards, Van der Ploeg, Michels, Liu, De Lange and Sloof (1984).

The structure of telomeres

In the mechanism of antigenic variation a prominent role seems to be assigned to telomeres. Accordingly, one may expect that studies on the structure of the telomere may provide clues about the manner in which VSG genes are activated. As discussed, ELC and BC genes that are located at telomeres are flanked by DNA segments that are nearly devoid of recognition sites for restriction enzymes and that vary in length in different VATs. From the first analysis of ELCs it was already inferred that these features of barren regions were due to AT-rich sequences or arrays of short repeats that occasionally undergo duplications and deletions (Van der Ploeg *et al.* 1982*a*; Michels *et al.* 1982). To determine if the size-fluctuations were linked to gene switching, Bernards *et al.* (1983) transferred trypanosomes of VAT 118b serially in mice for 85 days. In this manner the immune selection by the host was prevented and a trypanosome population that remained more than 99 per cent antigenically homogeneous was grown for approximately 350 generations. The 5' barren region remained unaltered during the 350 generations, but the regions downstream of the three VSG genes studied grew continuously at an estimated rate of 7–10 bp per generation. Occasional deletions seemed the mechanism to balance this growth.

The structure of trypanosomal telomeres was recently determined independently by Blackburn & Challoner (1984) and Van der Ploeg et al. (1984b). It is schematically depicted in Fig. 6.6. This result was obtained by direct sequencing of large, uncloned DNA and by analysis of some recombinant clones covering most of some telomeres, but for the very end. From this structure it is obvious that the lack of restriction sites has to be attributed to the unusual sequence: at the end of the chromosome are large stretches of the repeat CCCTAA adjacent to subtelomeric repeats of 29 bp that are derived from the hexamer. In one clone analyzed these 29 bp repeats were found downstream of an AT-rich sequence that previously had been shown to be located next to some VSG genes (De Lange, Kooter, Michels and Borst 1983a).

Hybridization studies with the clones suggests that most, if not all telomeres contain this organization and that, most likely, all telomeres grow by about 6 bp per trypanosome generation, as result of the addition of CCCTAA units. The mechanism for this chromosome lengthening remains to be established. It has been suggested that telomere growth is not unique for trypanosomes, but the result of the replication mechanism of linear DNA molecules common to all eukaryotes (Bernards, Michels, Lincke and Borst 1983).

Raibaud, Gaillard, Longacre, Hibner, Buck, Bernardi and Eisen (1983) have reported that telomeres of T. equiperdum have a very high buoyant density in CsCl resulting from an, as yet unidentified, nucleoside that replaces deoxycytidine. An aberrant buoyant density has not been found for telomeres in T. brucei 427 (Borst et al. 1984). Furthermore, the sequence analysis of T. brucei telomeres shows that an unusual base does not have to be invoked to explain their lack of restriction sites.

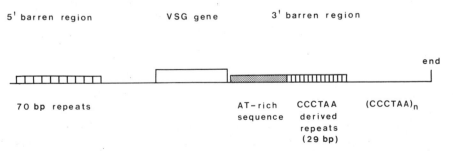

Fig. 6.6. Schematic drawing of the structure of telomeres in T. brucei. See text for explanation.

Part of the barren region 5' of the 117 ELC has recently been sequenced by Campbell *et al.* (1984). They reported the tandem arrangement of many 70 bp repeats and inferred that the complete barren region is composed of such repeats. Similarly, Bernards, Kooter and Borst (unpublished) have shown that the 70 bp repeats constitute the 3.5 kb barren region in front of the telomeric 221 gene. The 70 bp repeats are also present in front of chromosome-internal genes, although in smaller number (Van der Ploeg *et al.* 1982*b*; Liu *et al.* 1983). They presumably guide the gene transpositions, as do the conserved sequences present in the 3' end of all VSG genes.

Transcription of VSG genes

Sequence analysis has revealed that all VSG mRNAs carry the same 35 nucleotides at their 5' end (Van der Ploeg *et al.* 1982*b*; Boothroyd and Cross 1982). This sequence is not encoded contiguously with the remainder of the RNA. The mini-exon that codes for these nucleotides was not detected within the transposed segment of the genes that are activated by duplicative transposition. Therefore, it was assumed that the mini-exon was provided by the expression site (Van der Ploeg *et al.* 1982*b*). However no mini-exon was found nearer to the ELC in the dominant expression site than at least 1.5 kb upstream of the 5' barren region (De Lange *et al.* 1983*b*). No mini-exon was found either in the telomere harbouring the active 221 gene within 8.5 kb of the coding region (Bernards *et al.* 1984*a*). Instead, De Lange *et al.* (1983*b*) showed that about 200 mini-exon copies are present per nucleus, as part of a 1.35 kb repetitive element. These occur as tandem arrays of at least ten repeats. The sequences at the edges of the mini- and main-exon correspond to the consensus splice site sequences for eukaryotes (Mount 1982). These data lead to the proposal that a tandem arrangement of 1.35 kb elements is present upstream of the expressed gene in the expression site. This would lead to a concentration of polymerase molecules, so that a high rate of transcription is ensured. The resulting long precursor molecules would be spliced to yield the mature VSG mRNAs. As expected from this speculative model, mini-exon arrays were found both on the 2 Mb chromosome with the dominant expression site and in the large DNA where the active 221 gene was located (Van der Ploeg *et al.* 1984*b*). However, two fundamental predictions of this model could not be verified: the physical linkage between the expressed VSG gene and a mini-exon repeat, and the synthesis of long primary transcripts.

Further analysis revealed that the 35 nucleotide sequence is not restricted to VSG mRNAs. Many, if not all polyadenylated transcripts contain this sequence at their 5' end (De Lange, Michels, Veerman, Cornelissen and Borst 1984). Thus, the mini-exon is not a special device for transcriptional control of VSG genes, but it seems to play a role in the transcription of many genes. Alternatively it may be involved in translation or in rendering stability to the mRNA molecules. The importance of the mini-exon is underlined by the finding that the sequence is conserved among diverse members of the *Trypanosomatidae* family (De Lange, Berkvens, Veerman, Frasch, Barry and Borst unpublished).

On the one hand, many mRNAs carry the 35 nucleotide sequence; on the other hand, this sequence is encoded by only about 200 copies per nucleus, which are highly clustered. Taken together those observations suggest that the trypanosomes employ an extraordinary mechanism for transcription. Two models have been proposed to accommodate these observations (De Lange *et al.* 1984; Campbell *et al.* 1984). Firstly, the main-exons of many genes could be organized in an operon-like manner, downstream of a mini-exon array. A lot of differential splicing and/or termination will be required to yield the different mature mRNAs from a single transcription unit. Secondly, transcription may be discontinuous: after the polymerase has transcribed the mini-exon, it changes its template to continue at the main-exon. In an alternative form of discontinuous transcription, the mini- and main-exon are transcribed independently, to be joined subsequently by bi-molecular splicing. To distinguish between these models it will be important to determine the transcription units and to look for specific regulatory signals. One can envisage that, in discontinuous transcription a specific sequence is required in front of the active gene, for instance to enable a jumping polymerase to select the proper gene. Such a regulatory signal might be provided by a mobile element. Alternatively, a control element common to all VSG genes could be unmasked at a specific telomere by an as yet unidentified mechanism.

Conclusion

The trypanosomes seem to have developed an unusual genomic organization and control mechanism for the expression of their genes to meet the problems that face mammalian bloodstream parasites. The study of the antigenic variation in trypanosomes has been, therefore, a fascinating area of the molecular biology of eukaryotes. Much more research will be required, however, before the activation of the VSG genes is understood in detail.

Acknowledgements

I am grateful to my colleagues in Amsterdam for allowing me to quote their unpublished results; to Titia de Lange, André Bernards, Lex van der Ploeg, David Hart and Piet Borst for their critical reading of the manuscript; to Françoise Van de Calseyde-Mylle for her help in the preparation of the manuscript. The experimental work in Amsterdam, on which this review is largely based, was supported by a grant to P. Borst from the UNDP/World Bank/WHO Special Programme for Research and Training in Tropical Diseases (T16/181/T7/34).

References

Barry, J. D., Crowe, J. S., and Vickerman, K. (1983). Instability of the *Trypanosoma brucei rhodesiense* metacyclic variable antigen repertoire. *Nature* **306**, 699–701.

—— Hajduk, S. L., Vickerman, K., and Le Ray, D. (1979). Detection of multiple variable antigen types in metacyclic populations of *Trypanosoma brucei*. *Trans. Roy. Soc. Trop. Med. Hyg.* **73**, 205–208.

Bernards, A., Van der Ploeg, L. H. T., Frasch, A. C. C., Borst, P., Boothroyd, J. C., Coleman, S., and Cross, G. A. M. (1981). Activation of trypanosome surface glycoprotein genes involves a duplication-transposition leading to an altered 3'-end. *Cell* **27**, 497–505.

—— (1982). Transposable genes for surface glycoproteins in trypanosomes. *Trends biochem. sci.* **7**, 253–255.

—— Michels, P. A. M., Lincke, C. R., and Borst, P. (1983). Growth of chromosome ends in multiplying trypanosomes. *Nature* **303**, 592–597.

—— De Lange, T., Michels, P. A. M., Liu, A. Y. C., Huisman, M. J., and Borst, P. (1984a). Two modes of activation of a single surface antigen gene of *Trypanosoma brucei*. *Cell* **36**, 163–170.

—— Van Harten-Loosbroek, N., and Borst, P. (1984b). Modification of telomeric DNA in *Trypanosoma brucei*; a role in antigenic variation? *Nucleic Acids Res.* **12**, 4153–4169.

Blackburn, E. H. and Challoner, P. B. (1984). Identification of a telomeric DNA sequence in *Trypanosoma brucei*. *Cell* **36**, 447–457.

Boothroyd, J. C., Cross, G. A. M., Hoeijmakers, J. H. J., and Borst, P. (1980). A variant surface glycoprotein of *Trypanosoma brucei* is synthesized with a hydrophobic carboxy-terminal extension absent from purified glycoprotein. *Nature* **288**, 624–626.

—— and Cross, G. A. M. (1982). Transcripts coding for variant surface glycoproteins of *Trypanosoma brucei* have a short, identical exon at their 5'-end. *Gene* **20**, 281–289.

—— Paynter, C. A., Cross, G. A. M., Bernards, A., and Borst, P. (1981). Variant surface glycoproteins are synthesized with cleavable hydrophobic sequences at the carboxy and amino termini. *Nucleic Acids Res.* **9**, 4735–4743.

Borst, P. (1983). Antigenic variation in trypanosomes. In *Mobile Genetic Elements* (ed. J. A. Shapiro) pp. 621–659. Academic Press, New York.

—— and Cross, G. A. M. (1982). The molecular basis for trypanosome antigenic variation. *Cell.* **29**, 291–303.

—— Frasch, A. C. C., Bernards, A., Van der Ploeg, L. H. T., Hoeijmakers, J. H. J., Arnberg, A. C., and Cross, G. A. M. (1981). DNA rearrangements involving the genes for variant antigens in *Trypanosoma brucei*. *Cold Spr. Harb. Symp. Quant. Biol.* **45**, 935–943.

—— Bernards, A., Van der Ploeg, L. H. T., Michels, P. A. M., Liu, A. Y. C., De Lange, T., Sloof, P., Veeneman, G. H., Tromp, M. C., and Van Boom, J. H. (1983a). DNA rearrangements controlling the expression of genes for variant surface antigens in trypanosomes. In *Genetic Rearrangement* (ed. K. F. Chater, C. A. Cullis, D. A. Hopwood, A. A. W. B. Johnston, and H. W. Woolhouse) pp. 207–233. Croom Helm, London.

—— Bernards, A., Van der Ploeg, L. H. T., Michels, P. A. M., Liu, A. Y. C., De Lange, T., and Kooter, J. M. (1983b). The control of variant surface antigen synthesis in trypanosomes. *Europ. J. Biochem.* **137**, 383–389.

—— Bernards, A., Van der Ploeg, L. H. T., Michels, P. A. M., Liu, A. Y. C., De Lange, T., Sloof, P., Schwartz, D. C., and Cantor, C. R. (1983c). The role of minichromosomes and gene translocation in the expression and evolution of VSG genes. In *Gene Expression* (ed. D. Hamer and M. J. Rosenberg) pp. 413–435. Liss, New York.

—— Bernards, A., Van der Ploeg, L. H. T., Michels, P. A. M., Liu, A. Y. C., De Lange, T., and Sloof, P. (1984). Gene rearrangements controlling the expression of surface antigen genes in trypanosomes. In *Molecular Biology of Host-Parasite Interactions* (ed. N. Agabian and H. Eisen) in press, Liss, New York.

Bridgen, P. J., Cross, G. A. M., and Bridgen, J. (1976). N-terminal amino acid sequences of variant-specific surface antigens from *Trypanosoma brucei*. *Nature* **263**, 613–614.

Buck, G. A., Longacre, S., Raibaud, A., Hibner, U., Giroud, C., Baltz, T., Baltz, D., and Eisen, H. (1984). Stability of expression-linked surface antigen gene in *Trypanosoma equiperdum*. *Nature* **307**, 563–566.

Campbell, D. A., Van Bree, M. P., and Boothroyd, J. C. (1984). The 5′-limit of transposition and upstream barren region of a trypanosome VSG gene: tandem 76 base-pair repeats flanking $(TAA)_{90}$. *Nucleic Acids Res.* **12**, 2759–2774.

Capbern, A., Giroud, C., Baltz, T., and Mattern, P. (1977). *Trypanosoma equiperdum*: Etude des variations antigéniques au cours de la trypanosome expérimentale du lapin. *Exper. Parasit.* **42**, 6–13.

Cardoso de Almeida, M. L. and Turner, M. J. (1983). The membrane form of variant surface glycoproteins of *Trypanosoma brucei*. *Nature*, **302**, 349–352.

Cross, G. A. M. (1975). Identification, purification and properties of clone-specific glycoprotein antigens constituting the surface coat of *Trypanosoma brucei*. *Parasit.* **71**, 393–417.

—— (1978). Antigenic variation in trypanosomes. *Proc. Roy. Soc. London. Series B* **202**, 55–72.

De Lange, T. and Borst, P. (1982). Genomic environment of the expression-linked extra copies of genes for surface antigens of *Trypanosoma brucei* resembles the end of a chromosome. *Nature* **299**, 451–453.

—— Kooter, J. M., Michels, P. A. M., and Borst, P. (1983a). Telomere conversion in trypanosomes. *Nucleic Acids Res.* **11**, 8149–8165.

—— Liu, A. Y. C., Van der Ploeg, L. H. T., Borst, P., Tromp, M. C., and Van Boom, J. H. (1983b). Tandem repetition of the 5′ mini-exon of variant surface glycoprotein genes: A multiple promoter for VSG gene transcription? *Cell* **34**, 891–900.

—— Michels, P. A. M., Veerman, H. J. G., Cornelissen, A. W. C. A., and Borst, P. (1984). Many trypanosome mRNAs share a common 5′ terminal sequence. *Nucleic Acids Res.* **12**, 3777–3790.

Doyle, J. J., Hirumi, H., Hirumi, K., Lupton, E. N., and Cross, G. A. M. (1979). Antigenic variation in clones of animal-infective *Trypanosoma brucei* derived and maintained *in vitro*. *Parasitology* **80**, 359–369.

Englund, P. T., Hajduk, S. L., and Marini, J. C. (1982). The molecular biology of trypanosomes. *Ann. Rev. Biochem.* **51**, 695–726.

Ferguson, M. A. J. and Cross, G. A. M. (1984). Myristylation of the membrane form of a *Trypanosomona brucei* variant surface glycoprotein. *J. Biol. Chem.* **259**, 3011–3015.

Frasch, A. C. C., Bernards, A., Van der Ploeg, L. H. T., Borst, P., Hoeijmakers, J. H. J., Van den Burg, J., and Cross, G. A. M. (1980). The genes for the variable surface glycoproteins of *Trypanosoma brucei*. In *The Biochemistry of Parasites and Host-Parasite Relationships: The Host-Invader Interplay* (ed. H. Van den Bosche) pp. 235–239. North-Holland, Amsterdam.

—— Borst, P., and Van den Burg, J. (1982). Rapid evolution of genes coding for variant surface glycoproteins in trypanosomes. *Gene* **17**, 197–211.

Hajduk, S. L. and Vickerman, K. (1981). Antigenic variation in cyclically transmitted *Trypanosoma brucei*. *Parasitology* **83**, 609–621.

Hill, G. C. and Hirumi, H. (1983). African trypanosomes. In In Vitro *Cultivation of Protozoan Parasites* (ed. J. B. Jensen) pp. 193–219. CRC Press, Inc, Boca Raton, Florida.

Hoeijmakers, J. H. J., Borst, P., Van den Burg, J., Weissmann, C., and Cross, G. A. M. (1980*a*). The isolation of plasmids containing DNA complementary to messenger RNA for variant surface glycoproteins of *Trypanosoma brucei. Gene* **8**, 391–417.

—— Frasch, A. C. C., Bernards, A., Borst, P., and Cross, G. A. M. (1980*b*). Novel expression-linked copies of the genes for variant surface antigens in trypanosomes. *Nature* **284**, 78–80.

Holder, A. A. and Cross, G. A. M. (1981). Glycopeptides from variant surface glycoproteins of *Trypanosoma brucei.* C-terminal location of antigenically cross-reacting carbohydrate moieties. *Mol. Biochem. Parasit.* **2**, 135–150.

—— (1983). Carbohydrate is linked through ethanolamine to the C-terminal amino acid of *Trypanosoma brucei* variant surface glycoprotein. *Biochem. J.* **209**, 261–262.

Laurent, M., Pays, E., Magnus, E., Van Meirvenne, N., Matthijssens, G., Williams, R. O., and Steinert, M. (1983). DNA rearrangements linked to expression of a predominant surface antigen gene of trypanosomes. *Nature* **302**, 263–266.

Le Ray, D., Barry, J. D., and Vickerman, K. (1978). Antigenic heterogeneity of metacyclic forms of *Trypanosoma brucei. Nature* **273**, 300–302.

Lheureux, M., Lheureux, M., Vervoort, T., Van Meirvenne, N., and Steinert, M. (1979). Immunological purification and partial characterization of variant-specific surface antigen messenger RNA of *Trypanosoma brucei brucei. Nucleic Acids Res.* **7**, 595–609.

Liu, A. Y. C., Van der Ploeg, L. H. T., Rijsewijk, F. A. M., and Borst, P. (1983). The transposition unit of variant surface glycoprotein gene 118 of *Trypanosoma brucei. J. Mol. Biol.* **167**, 57–75.

Longacre, S., Hibner, U., Raibaud, A., Eisen, H., Baltz, T., Giroud, C., and Baltz, D. (1983). DNA rearrangements and antigenic variation in *Trypanosoma equiperdum*: multiple expression linked sites in independent isolates of trypanosomes expressing the same antigen. *Mol. Cell. Biol.* **3**, 399–409.

Majiwa, P. A. O., Young, J. R., Englund, P. T., Shapiro, S. Z., and Williams, R. O. (1982). Two distinct forms of surface antigen gene rearrangement in *Trypanosoma brucei. Nature* **297**, 514–516.

Majumder, H. K., Boothroyd, J. C., and Weber, H. (1981). Homologous 3′-terminal regions of mRNAs for surface antigens of different antigenic variants of *Trypanosoma brucei. Nucleic Acids Res.* **9**, 4745–4753.

Matthijssens, G., Michiels, F., Hamers, R., Pays, E., and Steinert, M. (1981). Two variant surface glycoproteins of *Trypanosoma brucei* have a conserved C-terminus. *Nature* **293**, 230–233.

McConnell, J., Gurnett, A. M., Cordingley, J. S., Walker, J. E., and Turner, M. J. (1981). Biosynthesis of *Trypanosoma brucei* variant surface glycoprotein. 1. Synthesis, size and processing of an N-terminal signal peptide. *Mol. Bioch. Parasit.* **4**, 226–242.

—— Turner, M. J., and Rovis, L. (1983). Biosynthesis of *Trypanosoma brucei* variant surface glycoproteins – analysis of carbohydrate heterogeneity and timing of post-translational modifications. *Mol. Bioch. Parasit.* **8**, 119–135.

Michels, P. A. M., Bernards, A., Van der Ploeg, L. H. T., and Borst, P. (1982). Characterization of the expression-linked gene copies of variant surface glycoprotein 118 in two independently isolated clones of *Trypanosoma brucei. Nucleic Acids Res.* **10**, 2353–2366.

—— Liu, A. Y. C., Bernards, A., Sloof, P., Van der Bijl, M. M. W., Schinkel, A. H., Menke, H. H., Borst, P., Veeneman, G. H., Tromp, M. C., and Van Boom, J. H.

(1983). Activation of the genes for variant surface glycoproteins 117 and 118 in *Trypanosoma brucei. J. Mol. Biol.* **166**, 537–556.

—— Van der Ploeg, L. H. T., Liu, A. Y. C., and Borst, P. (1984). The inactivation and reactivation of an expression-linked gene copy for a variant surface glycoprotein in *Trypanosoma brucei. E.M.B.O. J.*, **3**, 1345–1351.

Miller, E. N. and Turner, M. J. (1981). Analysis of antigenic types appearing in first relapse populations of clones of *Trypanosoma brucei. Parasitology* **82**, 63–80.

Mount, S. M. (1982). A catalogue of splice junction sequences. *Nucleic Acids Res.* **10**, 459–472.

Pays, E., Delronche, M., Lheureux, M., Vervoort, T., Bloch, J., Gannon, F., and Steinert, M. (1980). Cloning and characterization of DNA sequences complementary to messenger ribonucleic acids coding for the synthesis of two surface antigens of *Trypanosoma brucei. Nucleic Acids Res.* **8**, 5965–5981.

—— Van Meirvenne, N., Le Ray, D., and Steinert, M. (1981a). Gene duplication and transposition linked to antigenic variation in *Trypanosoma brucei. Proc. Natl. Acad. Sci. U.S.A.*, **78**, 2673–2677.

—— Lheureux, M., and Steinert, M. (1981b). The expression-linked copy of surface antigen gene in *Trypanosoma* is probably the one transcribed. *Nature* **292**, 265–267.

—— Van Assel, S., Laurent, M., Dero, B., Michiels, F., Kronenberger, P., Matthijssens, G., Van Meirvenne, N., Le Ray, D., and Steinert, M. (1983a). At least two transposed sequences are associated in the expression site of a surface antigen gene in different trypanosome clones. *Cell* **34**, 259–369.

—— Van Assel, S., Laurent, M., Darville, M., Vervoort, T., Van Meirvenne, N., and Steinert, M. (1983b). Gene conversion as a mechanism for antigenic variation in trypanosomes. *Cell* **34**, 371–381.

—— Delauw, M. F., Van Assel, S., Laurent, M., Vervoort, T., Van Meirvenne, N., and Steinert, M. (1983c). Modifications of a *Trypanosoma b. brucei* antigen repertoire by different DNA recombinational mechanisms. *Cell* **35**, 721–731.

Raibaud, A., Gaillard, C., Longacre, S., Hibner, U., Buck, G., Bernardi, G., and Eisen, H. (1983). Genomic environment of variant surface antigen genes of *Trypanosoma equiperdum. Proc. Natl. Acad. Sci. U.S.A.* **80**, 4306–4310.

Rice-Ficht, A. C., Chen, K. K., and Donelson, J. E. (1981). Sequence homologies near the C-termini of the variable surface glycoproteins of *Trypanosoma brucei. Nature* **294**, 53–57.

Schwartz, D. C. and Cantor, R. C. (1984). Separation of yeast chromosome-sized DNAs by pulsed field gradient gel electrophoresis. *Cell* **37**, 67–75.

Turner, M. J. (1982). Biochemistry of variant surface glycoproteins of salivarian trypanosomes. *Adv. Parasit.* **21**, 69–153.

Turner, M. J. and Cordingley, J. S. (1981). Evolution of antigenic variation in the salivarian trypanosomes. In *Molecular and Cellular Aspects of Microbial Evolution* (ed. M. J. Carlile, J. F. Collins, and B. E. B. Moseley) pp. 313–347. Cambridge University Press, Cambridge.

Van der Ploeg, L. H. T., Bernards, A., Rijsewijk, F. A. M., and Borst, P. (1982a). Characterization of the DNA duplication-transposition that controls the expression of two genes for variant surface glycoproteins in *Trypanosoma brucei. Nucleic Acids Res.* **10**, 593–609.

—— Liu, A. Y. C., Michels, P. A. M., De Lange, T., Borst, P., Majumder, H. K., Weber, H., Veeneman, G. H., and Van Boom, J. (1982b). RNA splicing is required to make the messenger RNA for a variant surface antigen in trypanosomes. *Nucleic Acids Res.* **10**, 3591–3604.

—— Valerio, D., De Lange, T., Bernards, A., Borst, P., and Grosveld, F. G. (1982c). An analysis of cosmid clones of nuclear DNA from *Trypanosoma brucei* shows that the genes for variant surface glycoproteins are clustered in the genome. *Nucleic Acids Res.* **10**, 5905–5923.

—— and Cornelissen, A. W. C. A. (1984). The contribution of chromosomal translocations to antigenic variation in *Trypanosoma brucei. Proc. Roy. Soc. Lond. Series B*, in press.

—— Liu, A. Y. C., and Borst, P. (1984*a*). The structure of the growing telomeres of trypanosomes. *Cell.* **36**, 459–468.

—— Schwartz, D. C., Cantor, C. R., and Borst, P. (1984*b*). Antigenic variation in *Trypanosoma brucei* analysed by electrophoretic separation of chromosome-sized DNA molecules. *Cell* **37**, 77–84.

Van Meirvenne, N., Janssens, P. G., and Magnus, E. (1975*a*). Antigenic variation in syringe passaged populations of *Trypanosoma* (*Trypanozoon*) *brucei.* I. Rationalization of the experimental approach. *Ann. Soc. Belge Médic. Tropic.* **55**, 1–23.

—— Janssens, P. G., Magnus, E., Lumsden, W. H. R., and Herbert, W. J. (1975*b*). Antigenic variation in syringe passaged populations of *Trypanosoma* (*Trypanozoon*) *brucei.* II. Comparative studies on the antigenic-type collections. *Ann. Soc. Belge Médec. Tropic.* **55**, 25–30.

Vickerman, K. and Luckins, A. G. (1969). Localization of variable antigens in the surface coat of *Trypanosoma brucei* using ferritin conjugated antibody. *Nature* **224**, 1125–1126.

—— (1969). On the surface coat and flagellar adhesion in trypanosomes. *J. Cell Sci.* **5**, 163–193.

—— (1978). Antigenic variation in trypanosomes. *Nature* **273**, 613–617.

—— and Barry, J. D. (1982). *African Trypanosomiasis.* In *Immunology of Parasite Infections* (ed. S. Cohen and K. S. Warren) pp. 204–260. Blackwell, Oxford.

Williams, R. O., Marcu, K. B., Young, J. R., Rovis, L. and Williams, S. C. (1978). A characterization of mRNA activities and their sequence complexities in *Trypanosoma brucei*: partial purification and properties of the VSSA mRNA. *Nucleic Acids Res.* **5**, 3171–3182.

—— Young, J. R., and Majiwa, P. A. O. (1979). Genomic rearrangements correlated with antigenic variation in *Trypanosoma brucei. Nature* **282**, 847–849.

—— Young, J. R., and Majiwa, P. A. O. (1982). Genomic environment of *T. brucei* VSG genes: presence of a minichromosome. *Nature* **299**, 417–421.

Young, J. R., Donelson, J. E., Majiwa, P. A. O., Shapiro, S. Z., and Williams, R. O. (1982). Analysis of genomic rearrangements associated with two variable antigen genes of *Trypanosoma brucei. Nucleic Acids Res.* **10**, 803–819.

—— Shah, J. S., Matthijssens, G., and Williams, R. O. (1983). Relationship between multiple copies of a *T. brucei* variable surface glycoprotein gene whose expression is not controlled by duplication. *Cell* **32**, 1149–1159.

7 Regulation of immunoglobulin transcription*
CARY QUEEN

Background

The immunoglobulin genes have been among the most intensively studied of all gene families (Wall and Keuhl 1983; Tonegawa 1983). The wide interest in immunoglobulin genes can be attributed both to the importance of their protein products in higher organisms, and to the variety and complexity of their biological regulation. The use of recombinant DNA technology during the last several years has led to a good, if not complete, understanding of the structure of the immunoglobulin gene family at the DNA level. More recently, cloned immunoglobulin genes have been introduced into cultured cells and their expression studied. These experiments have let us begin to understand, at the level of RNA transcription, how the expression of immunoglobulin genes is regulated during cellular development. After reviewing the structural background, I will discuss the recent experiments from the perspective of two important questions: (1) Why are immunoglobulin genes expressed only in cells of B-lymphoid type, and not in other types of cells, (2) Why does each B-cell generally express only two immunoglobulin genes, out of hundreds of genes in the immunoglobulin family?

STRUCTURE OF THE IMMUNOGLOBULIN GENE FAMILY

The polypeptide encoded by a single immunoglobulin gene is generally referred to as an immunoglobulin chain. There are two kinds of immunoglobulin chains—light and heavy. A light chain consists of two structurally homologous protein domains, each having about 110 amino acids, while a heavy chain consists of four or five such domains. A complete immunoglobulin molecule, or an antibody molecule in its monomeric form, contains two identical light chains and two identical heavy chains, covalently linked by disulphide bonds. There are two classes of light chains, designated κ and λ, which were originally distinguished by serologic criteria. Similarly, there are five classes of heavy chains, designated μ, δ, γ, α, and ε. In mice and humans, there are four subclasses of the γ class, denoted in the mouse by γ, γ_{2a}, γ_{2b} and γ_3. Protein sequencing data shows that, within a class of immunoglobulin chains, the amino terminal domain varies significantly from molecule to molecule (Hilschmann and Craig 1965). This part of an immunoglobulin chain is therefore called the variable or V region. However, the other domains are essentially invariant within a class or subclass in a given species (except for occasional allelic differences called allotypes). These domains are therefore said to constitute the constant or C region of an immunoglobulin chain. The V regions of immunoglobulin chains confer antigen specificity on antibody molecules, while the C regions mediate interactions with other components of the immune system.

The division of immunoglobulin chains into two regions, one of which varies between chains of a class and one of which does not, requires a special organization of the immunoglobulin gene family, which was first elucidated by Tonegawa and colleagues (Brack, Hirama, Lenhard-Schuller and Tonegawa 1978). We will begin by reviewing the structure of the genes that encode the κ light chains (Fig. 7.1), as determined by Seidman and Leder 1978. There is a unique gene segment in the mouse or human haploid genome, denoted C_κ, which encodes the constant region (the carboxy domain) of all κ light chains. There are also 100 or more different gene segments, generically denoted V_κ, that encode the variable regions of various κ chains. Each V_κ segment is preceded by an L_κ or leader segment, which encodes a signal peptide that is cleaved off when the immunoglobulin chain is secreted. The V_κ segments are dispersed over a long region on the same chromosome as the C_κ segment. In germline DNA, there is a very large but unknown separation between the C_κ segment and any of the V_κ segments. During the development of a stem cell into a B-lymphocyte, an actual rearrangement takes place at the DNA level (Fig. 7.1) that brings one of the V_κ segments into proximity with the unique C_κ segment. More precisely, the V_κ segment is joined to one of five short J_κ segments located 2.5–3.8 kilobase (kb) upstream of the C_κ region (Max, Maizel and Leder 1981). The J_κ segment

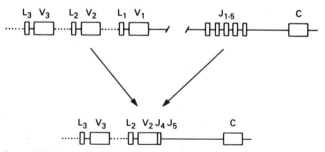

Fig. 7.1. Schematic diagram of κ immunoglobulin gene family. The upper line shows the organization of the family in germline DNA. Broken and dotted lines represent large and indeterminate distances. The C_κ, J_κ, and three of the many V_κ segments are shown. The lower line shows one representative gene after the DNA rearrangement has taken place. In this example, the variable segment denoted V_2 has joined to the J_4 segment; many other combinations are possible.

encodes the last section of the immunoglobulin V region as defined by protein sequencing.

A complete, rearranged κ gene (Fig. 7.2a) thus consists of three exons (coding segments) and two introns (intervening sequences). The L_κ segment is the most 5' exon, followed by a short intron, and then an exon consisting of the fused V_κ and J_κ segments. There is then a long intron, which includes any J_κ segments that were 3' of the one fused, and finally the C_κ segment. RNA transcripts initiate about 30 bp before the L_κ segment (Kelley, Cole-clough and Perry 1983) and proceed through the entire gene, with the two introns spliced out to form mRNA. The large number of V_κ regions contribute to antibody diversity, with additional diversity provided by somatic mutations in the V_κ regions during cellular development. The organization of the λ light chain family follows the same principle of split genes as the κ family, but the details are somewhat different and need not be described here. Successful rearrangement of a κ light chain gene on one chromosome appears to prevent rearrangements on the sister chromosome (Perry, Kelly, Coleclough, Seidman, Leder, Tonegawa, Matthyssons and Weigert 1980)— a phenomenon called allelic exclusion—as well as preventing λ light chain rearrangement. Hence, a given B-cell only produces one type of functional light chain.

The organization of the heavy chain gene family is analogous to that of the κ gene family, but is more complex. There are eight heavy chain constant gene segments in the mouse, one for each of the heavy chain classes and subclasses. These form a linked family on one chromosome, extending over about 200 kb in the 5' to 3' order C_μ, C_δ, $C_{\gamma3}$, $C_{\gamma1}$, $C_{\gamma2b}$, $C_{\gamma2a}$, C_ε, C_α (Shimizu, Takahashi, Yaoita and Honjo 1982). Thus the subclasses have the same genetic status as classes, but their sequences are more homologous. Each constant segment itself consists of several coding regions separated by

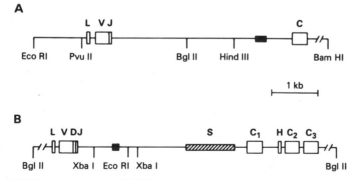

Fig. 7.2. (a) Diagram of the MOPC41 κ light chain gene (Seidman and Leder 1978). The enhancer element discussed in the text is denoted by a filled-in box. (b) Diagram of a γ_{2b} heavy chain gene (Gillies *et al.* 1983). The enhancer element discussed in the text is denoted by a filled-in box. S = switch region, H = hinge exon, C_{1-3} = constant segment exons.

introns, corresponding to the structural domains of heavy chain immunoglobulin constant regions. The most 5' heavy chain constant segment (C_μ) is preceded at a distance of several kb by four J_H segments. In analogy to the κ chain family, there are several hundred V_H segments on another part of the chromosome, which code for heavy chain variable regions. Each V_H segment is preceded at a short distance by an L_H segment. On still another part of the chromosome, presumably between the V_H and C_H segments, is a family of at least 12 short D or diversity segments. At an early stage in the development of a B-lymphocyte, a DNA rearrangement takes place that joins together a V_H, D, and J_H segment to form a V-D-J exon that encodes a heavy chain variable region (Sakano, Maki, Kurosawa, Roeder and Tonegawa 1980; Early, Huang, Davis, Calame and Hood 1980). This segment is preceded by an L_H segment and followed by a C_H segment to form a complete heavy chain immunoglobulin gene, as in Fig. 7.2b.

Because C_μ is the most 5' heavy chain constant segment, the heavy chain gene formed directly by the V-D-J rearrangement is always a μ class gene. This corresponds to the observed fact that IgM, the class of complete immunoglobulin molecule containing two μ chains and two light chains, appears first among the five classes during the development of a B-cell. The genes for the other heavy chain classes are formed by additional DNA rearrangements that may take place during the development of a particular B-cell. In fact, each heavy chain constant segment is preceded by a region of repetitive DNA about 1–2 kb long, known as a switch region (Fig. 7.2b). After the V-D-J rearrangement, a second recombinational event may join the C_μ switch region to the switch region preceding another constant segment, deleting the DNA between the two regions. The effect of this recombination is to replace the C_μ constant segment with another constant segment, and thus to change the class of the immunoglobulin chain synthesized, while retaining the V region. Allelic exclusion applies to heavy chains as well as light chains. This brief description of the DNA structure of immunoglobulin genes is adequate for what follows; a more detailed review is provided by Tonegawa 1983.

TRANSFECTION OF CLONED GENES

The introduction, or transfection, of cloned genes into cultured cells has become a powerful method for studying gene expression (Kessel and Khoury 1983). The earlier experiments of this type established that the transfected gene can be transcribed and translated, and is sometimes subject to the same regulation as when in its normal chromosomal environment. In more recent experiments, recombinant DNA methods have been used to make *in vitro* modifications to the cloned gene before transfecting it into cells. By studying the effect of the modifications on expression of the gene after transfection, regulatory elements in the DNA sequence can be located. Most recently, this technique has been fruitfully employed to study the regulation of immunoglobulin genes, by modifying the cloned genes and transfecting them into antibody-producing cells.

Two different experimental strategies have been used after transfecting cloned genes into cells. In transient expression experiments, the cells are assayed for expression of the transfected gene after a brief period of time, typically 48 h. By analogy with viral infection, it is presumed that in this case most or all RNA transcripts of the transfected gene are transcribed from DNA that is not integrated into the cellular genome. Transient expression experiments have the advantage that results may be obtained quickly and readily, so this protocol is especially useful when many modifications of a gene must be tested. However, a sensitive assay for expression must be employed because only a small proportion of the transfected cell population actually takes up the gene, so that total expression is relatively low. My laboratory has used the transient expression method extensively in conjunction with an S1 nuclease assay for RNA, as detailed below.

An alternative strategy in transfection experiments is permanent transformation of the cells. In this method, the gene under study is transfected together with a second gene that, under appropriate conditions, is required for cell survival. For example, the gene may be cloned into the plasmid vectors pSV2-gpt or pSV2-neo, which contain genes that in suitable media confer resistance respectively to mycophenolic acid and the antibiotic G-418 (Mulligan and Berg 1980; Southern and Berg 1982). Cells that have taken up the plasmid can thus be selected and cloned, and are often found to express the gene of interest. In the transformation protocol, the gene generally becomes integrated into the cellular DNA, so that in each clone of cells it is transcribed from a particular chromosomal location. The transformation method has the advantage that a cell population can be obtained in which each cell expresses the transfected gene, yielding higher level expression than in transient expression experiments. However, transformation experiments require more time and effort than transient experiments. Moreover, the particular location where the gene has integrated may affect regulation of its expression. The latter problem has recently been ameliorated to some extent by studying pools of cloned cells, thus obtaining average values for expression.

Three different techniques have been commonly used to actually transfect DNA into mammalian cells, and all have been successfully applied with lymphoid cells. In one method, purified DNA is dissolved in a solution of DEAE-dextran in culture medium and applied for a period of time to the cells (McCutchan and Pagano 1968; Sompayrac and Dana 1981). The DEAE-dextran binds the DNA and is taken up by the cells much more readily than DNA alone. In a similar but more delicate method, the DNA is mixed with a fine calcium phosphate suspension before application to the cells (Graham and Van der Eb 1973; Chu and Sharp 1980). Most recently, plasmid DNA has been introduced into cells by removing the cell walls from plasmid-containing *E. coli*, and fusing the cells with the protoplasts obtained (Schaffner 1980). The preferred method depends on the cell line being used and, surprisingly, on whether transient expression or permanent transformation is desired. For example, in my laboratory the DEAE-dextran method gives about 5-fold higher transient expression than the calcium phosphate method in MPC11 myeloma cells, but we have been successful only with the calcium phosphate method in transforming the same cells (unpublished data). Analogous results have been obtained in the laboratory of D. Baltimore (personal communication). Clearly the method of transfection affects the state of the DNA upon entering the cells and its ultimate fate.

Cell-type specific expression of immunoglobulin genes

EXPRESSION OF TRANSFECTED IMMUNOGLOBULIN GENES

Rice and Baltimore 1982, first reported expression of a transfected immunoglobulin gene. They inserted a κ light chain gene (Fig. 7.2a), which had been cloned from the mouse myeloma MOPC41 (Seidman and Leder 1978), into the plasmid vector pSV2-gpt (Mulligan and Berg 1980). Using the calcium phosphate technique, this plasmid construct was transfected into a B-lymphoid line of cells that had previously been immortalized by Abelson murine leukemia virus (A-MuLV). The cell line used does not synthesize any κ chain, and in fact has lost its own C_κ segments. Cells that integrated the plasmid were selected and cloned. The selected cells were shown by immunoprecipitation to synthesize κ chain, necessarily from the transfected κ gene. The κ chain was assembled into IgG-like molecules with the endogenous heavy chain. Rice and Baltimore also showed by Northern blotting that the cells synthesized an RNA transcript of the expected size from the transfected gene. Moreover, the amount of transcript increased when the cells were stimulated with lipopolysaccharide (LPS). Hence, the transfected κ gene retained a regulatory mechanism observed for the endogenous immunoglobulin genes of many A-MuLV-transformed cell lines.

Similar results have also been reported by other researchers. Oi, Morrison, Herzenberg and Berg 1983, inserted another κ light chain gene into pSV2-gpt and transfected the construct into several lymphoid cell lines, using both the calcium phosphate and protoplast fusion techniques. In general, the protoplast fusion method yielded a higher transformation efficiency than the calcium phosphate method. The plasmid integrated stably into mouse myeloma and hybridoma cells. The transformed cells synthesized κ chain from the integrated gene, as shown by immunoprecipitation and protein gel analysis. The amount of protein synthesized from the introduced gene varied considerably in different cloned transformants, and in some cases equalled the amount of endogenous light chain. Moreover, the new κ chain was assembled into antibody-like molecules with the endogenous heavy chain in the hybridoma cells and was secreted. Ochi, Hawley, Hawley, Shulman, Traunecker, Kohler and Hozumi 1983, have used pSV2-neo as a vector to introduce both a heavy chain and light chain gene into a non-producing myeloma line by protoplast fusion. The proteins synthesized from the integrated genes were assembled into hapten-specific, functional antibody molecules.

The first report of transient expression of a complete immunoglobulin gene after transfection into lymphoid cells was by Queen and Baltimore 1983. We transfected a plasmid containing the MOPC41 κ light chain gene (Fig. 7.2a) into mouse MPC11 cells by the DEAE-dextran technique. After 48 h, total RNA was extracted from the transfected cells. An S1 nuclease method, described in detail below, was used to assay for transcripts of the transfected κ gene. (Control experiments showed that the S1 probe, which was made from the MOPC41 κ gene, did not detect RNA from the endogenous MPC11 κ genes.) We found that the MPC11 cells actively transcribed the transfected κ gene. Moreover, the transcripts initiated in the promoter region about 25 bp before the first ATG codon of the gene, as expected. Transient expression of heavy chain immunoglobulin genes after transfection into myeloma cells has been reported by Neuberger 1983, and by Deans, Denis, Taylor and Wall 1984. In Neuberger's experiments, the genes were transfected by the DEAE-dextran technique, and the transcripts assayed by the S1 method or indirectly by immunofluorescence of the protein product. The immunofluorescence assay showed that 0.8 per cent of the cells in the transfected population took up the DNA and expressed the heavy chain gene.

CELL-TYPE SPECIFICITY OF TRANSFECTED GENES

While expression of immunoglobulin genes was readily detected after transfection into B-lymphoid cells, in either transient or transformation assays, there were early indications that immunoglobulin genes might not be transcribed well after introduction into other cell types. Thus Falkner and Zachau 1982, were unable to detect any transcription from the promoter of a κ gene transfected into monkey CV1 cells. Picard and Schaffner 1983, were able to detect normal transcription from a λ light chain gene transfected into HeLa cells only when a viral enhancer element was inserted close to the λ promoter. Oi et al. 1983, did not detect any protein made from a κ gene after integration into thymoma cells, and Queen and Baltimore 1983, found that a κ gene was transcribed transiently from an aberrant startsite when transfected into monkey COS cells. However, the multiplicity of genes, species, and assay methods employed in these experiments, as well as the absence of internal controls, made it difficult to draw any firm conclusions.

More definite evidence that a transfected immunoglobulin gene is expressed in a cell-type specific manner was provided by Stafford and Queen 1983. For this purpose, we constructed a plasmid pLX31 (Fig. 7.3) which had four important elements: (1) the pBR322 Amp gene and origin of replication, (2) the MOPC41 κ light chain gene, (3) the SV40 early promoter attached to the bacterial neo gene, (4) the polyma T-antigen gene and origin of replication. The MOPC41 gene (Fig. 7.2a) was the same κ gene that had been employed in previous transfection experiments. The SV40 recombinant gene played the essential role of an internal standard—a gene that is expressed at comparable levels in all the cell lines used. The function of the polyoma replicon was to allow the plasmid to replicate in mouse cells, thus increasing the amount of RNA synthesized transiently by increasing the amount of DNA template. This idea was originated by R. Deans and R. Wall (personal communication and Deans *et al.* 1984) and had been used previously by Queen and Baltimore 1983.

After transfecting pLX31 into various cell types, RNA was extracted and assayed with separate probes for the presence of neo and κ gene transcripts. The S1 assay employed is illustrated in Fig. 7.4 for the κ gene probe. Specifically, a double-stranded DNA fragment was labelled at one end with ^{32}P, denatured, and hybridized with the extracted RNA under conditions which favor RNA–DNA annealing. The hybrids were digested with S1 nuclease, which is specific for single-stranded nucleic acids and therefore eliminates any DNA not protected by hybridization to an RNA transcript. The hybrids were denatured and resolved on a polyacrylamide-urea gel, and the labelled DNA detected by autoradiography. The length of a protected fragment of

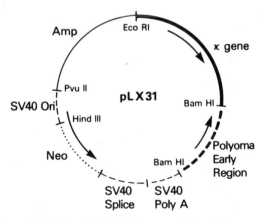

Fig. 7.3. Diagram of the plasmid pLX31. Arrows indicate the approximate initiation sites and directions of transcription for the SV40 early promoter, the polyoma early promoter and the κ promoter. The figure is not drawn to scale.

probe reflects the startpoint of the RNA transcript. The quantity of protected fragment is proportional to the amount of transcript, because the
hybridization reaction is done with an excess of probe. The S1 assay for neo
transcripts was similar, using a probe labelled at a site within the neo gene
and extending upstream of the SV40 promoter.

We transfected the plasmid pLX31 into two non-lymphoid lines of mouse
cells, 3T3 and L, and one lymphoid line of mouse cells, MPC11. After 48 h,
RNA was extracted from each line, and aliquots of each RNA sample were
assayed by the S1 nuclease method with κ- and neo-specific probes, as
described above. RNA extracted from the three cell lines after transfection
with pLX31 (Fig. 7.5a–c) protected a long fragment of the neo-specific probe
that was not protected by RNA from cells that were not transfected with
DNA (Fig. 7.5d,e). The size of the protected fragment, by comparison with
markers, indicated the presence of a transcript initiating from the SV40
promoter on pLX31. Hence, the plasmid DNA was able to penetrate all
three cell lines in a transcribable state and direct comparable amounts of
RNA synthesis from the SV40 promoter. (The protection of the full-length
neo probe by RNA from the transfected cells is due to some transcription
originating upstream of the probe in pBR322 sequences.)

RNA extracted from MPC11 cells after transfection with pLX31 strongly
protected a fragment of the κ-specific probe (Fig. 7.5f) that was not protected
by RNA from cells that were not transfected with DNA. Hence, as shown
before (Queen and Baltimore 1983), the transfected κ gene is actively transcribed in the MPC11 line of lymphoid cells. In contrast, no transcripts of

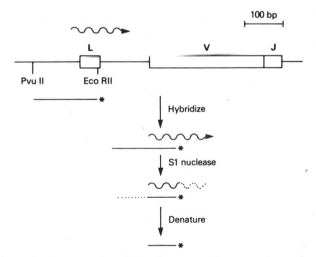

Fig. 7.4. Schematic diagram of an S1 nuclease experiment to detect transcripts initiating at the κ promoter. The 5′ region of the MOPC41 κ light chain gene is shown.
The DNA probe is indicated as a straight line, with the ^{32}P-labelled end denoted by
an asterisk, and the RNA transcript is indicated as a wavy line.

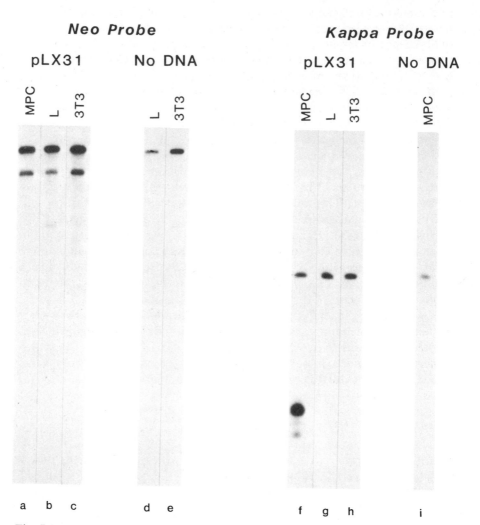

Fig. 7.5. S1 nuclease assay of RNA from transfected cells. The probes, DNA and cell lines used are indicated. The S1 treated samples were analyzed on a polyacrylamide-urea gel; 12-h photographic exposure of the gel is shown here. The topmost band in each lane ran at the position of undigested probe.

the κ gene were detected by the S1 assay in 3T3 or L cells transfected with pLX31 (Fig. 7.5g,h), with transcripts from the SV40 promoter on pLX31 serving as an internal control for the state of the DNA template. This result must therefore be due either to the specific inability of the transfected κ gene to initiate RNA synthesis or to instability of κ transcripts in non-lymphoid cells. However, substantial evidence exists that, once synthesized, immunoglobulin transcripts are in fact stable in non-lymphoid cells (Stafford and Queen 1983). Hence, the current results show that the non-lymphoid cells tested cannot initiate transcription of the transfected κ gene. This cell-type specificity of κ transcription appears to be nearly absolute: the transient level of κ transcripts after transfection of pLX31 into MPC11 cells is at least 1000 times greater than in 3T3 or L cells.

Brinster, Ritchie, Hammer, O'Brien, Arp and Storb 1983, adopted another approach in their study of the cell-type specific expression of a complete κ light chain gene. Instead of transfecting the κ gene, they microinjected it into fertilized mouse embryos, which were then implanted into foster mothers and allowed to develop. Many of the resulting mice were found to have integrated multiple copies of the injected κ gene into their DNA. Two tissues from offspring of these mice were analyzed for expression of the κ gene: spleen tissue, which contains immunoglobulin-producing B-lymphocytes, and liver as a representative non-lymphoid tissue. RNA from the injected κ gene was found to be transcribed at a high level in the spleen tissue, but at a very low or undetectable level in the liver tissue. While analysis of other tissues and determination of the κ RNA startsite would be desirable, these results clearly represent a counterpart at the organism level of our results in tissue culture cells.

Additional evidence for the cell type specific expression of transfected immunoglobulin genes has been obtained by Gillies and Tonegawa 1983. A λ light chain gene was transfected into the mouse myeloma line X63Ag8 and mouse L cells, and stable transformants selected. As measured by an S1 nuclease assay, the level of transcripts from the transfected gene was 125 to 250-fold higher in the myeloma cells than in the L cells. Moreover, the transcripts in the L cells initiated aberrantly about 200 bp before the normal startsite, so that no transcripts from the usual λ promoter were detected. Similar results were obtained for a κ light chain. A γ_{2b} heavy chain gene did exhibit some correct transcription when transfected into L cells, but the level of stable transcripts was at least two orders of magnitude less than in the original myeloma line from which the gene was cloned. Unfortunately, the γ chain was not transfected into other lymphoid lines, which would give a fairer comparison with the L cell results. Deans *et al.* 1984, also showed that a heavy chain gene is not expressed as well in non-lymphoid cells as in lymphoid cells, but that some expression is detectable in the non-lymphoid cells. It seems possible that the cell-type specificity of transfected heavy chains is not as complete as for light chains.

INTERPRETATION OF CELL-TYPE SPECIFICITY

The cell-type specific expression of transfected immunoglobulin genes stands in some contrast to results obtained with other gene systems. Indeed, many other specialized genes are transcribed after transfection into a variety of heterologous cell types (Kurtz 1981; Robins, Paek, Seeburg and Axel 1982).

A notable example is the high-level transcription of the β-globin gene, normally expressed only in erythroid cells, after transfection into HeLa cells (Banerji, Rusconi and Schaffner 1981). The apparent difference in specificity of immunoglobulin genes and other genes may to some extent be due to variations in experimental design and to the emphasis placed when interpreting results. For example, β-globin genes are expressed at a high level in HeLa cells only when stimulated by a viral enhancer element; the β-globin gene itself is transcribed in these cells very weakly. Until recently, researchers had been unsuccessful in transfecting specialized genes back into the corresponding cell type. This made it impossible to compare the levels of transcription after transfection into heterologous and homologous cells, and perhaps led to an undue emphasis on the fact of transcription in heterologous cells, rather than on the frequently low level or artificial nature of that transcription.

However, it is clear that after accounting for variations in experimental design and interpretation, there are still authentic differences between the specificity of immunoglobulin genes and many other genes. One possible explanation is that the cloned immunoglobulin genes contain all their regulatory elements, but other genes are regulated by distant sequence elements that are lost when they are cloned. If this explanation is correct, the missing regulatory elements must indeed be at a considerable distance from the genes, because many of the cloned genes include substantial flanking sequences. The study of other genes that display cell-type specific expression after transfection, of which insulin and chymotryposin are the best established cases (Walker, Edlund, Boulet and Rutter 1983), may help to resolve this problem.

Two conclusions about the developmental regulation of immunoglobulin genes may be inferred from the cell-type specificity of their expression after transfection. First, since the DNA template is introduced into the cells as an unintegrated plasmid, regulation of transcription does not depend on the original chromosomal location of the genes. Second, since the immunoglobulin genes are transfected into terminally differentiated cells, activation or inactivation of the genes does not depend on DNA modifications made during cell development. Rather, the already differentiated cells contain all the information needed to appropriately regulate the expression of immunoglobulin genes. It seems likely that these conclusions apply to some, but not all, other genes.

Immunoglobulin gene enhancers

As described above, DNA rearrangements take place in a developing B-lymphocyte that form complete immunoglobulin genes from the separately encoded V and C segments (Fig. 7.1). After the rearrangements take place, RNA transcripts of the complete genes can be detected. As the B-lymphocyte enters the terminally differentiated, antibody-secreting plasma cell stage, the rate of transcription of the rearranged genes increases, so that transcripts of a single immunoglobulin gene may represent 10 per cent of the total mRNA population (Schibler, Marcu and Perry 1978). However, no transcription of the remaining unrearranged V segments can be detected (Mather and Perry 1981). The question therefore arises of how the cell activates the rearranged V segments for transcription, while leaving the unrearranged V segments completely inactive. Any explanation must be consistent with the fact that rearrangement does not alter the DNA sequences 5′ to the V region, where signals for transcription initiation would normally be expected to occur (Clarke, Berenson, Goverman, Boyer, Crews, Siv and Calame 1982).

A clue to answering this question was provided by the existence of enhancer elements in certain viral genomes. Enhancers are DNA sequences that strongly stimulate transcription from many eukaryotic promoters; they can act from either an upstream or downstream position on promoters that are thousands of base pairs away (Banerji, Olson and Schaffner 1981; Moreau, Hen, Wasylyk, Everett, Gaub and Chambon 1981; Fromm and Berg 1982). It seemed possible that there are enhancer-like activating elements near the C segments of immunoglobulin genes. Such an element would act from a downstream location to activate the V region promoter brought into range by the rearrangement that forms a complete immunoglobulin gene. This hypothesis has recently been verified for both κ light chain genes (Queen and Baltimore 1983; Queen and Stafford 1984) and heavy chain genes (Gillies, Morrison, Oi and Tonegawa 1983; Neuberger 1983; Banerji, Olson and Schaffner 1983). I will discuss the experiments that led to this conclusion first for light chain and then for heavy chain genes.

THE κ LIGHT CHAIN ENHANCER

Our strategy for defining an activating element in the mouse κ gene was based on the vector pLX1 (Fig. 7.6). This vector was constructed starting from pML1, a pBR322 derivative from which sequences that inhibit replication in eukaryotic cells have been deleted (Lusky and Botchan 1981). To provide a site for inserting an immunoglobulin gene segment, a region of the plasmid pSV2-dhfr (Subramani, Mulligan and Berg 1981) was placed between the Eco R1 and Bam H1 sites of pML1. The region of pSV2-dhfr used contains a bacterial gene that may be readily excised, followed by an SV40 splice site and polyadenylation signal. The entire early region of polyoma virus was also inserted. As described above, the purpose of the polyoma replicon was to allow the plasmid to replicate in mouse cells, thus increasing the amount of RNA synthesized transiently by increasing the amount of DNA template.

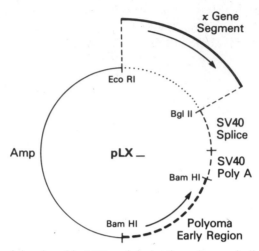

Fig. 7.6. Diagram of the plasmid pLX1 and derivatives. Arrows indicate the approximate initiation sites and directions of transcription for the SV40 early promoter and the κ promoter. The figure is not drawn to scale.

Our experimental strategy was to make various deletions in the 3′ end of the cloned MOPC41 κ gene. The deleted genes were inserted in pLX1 so that the SV40 polyadenylation signal replaced the deleted 3′ region (Fig. 7.6), allowing transcripts of the genes to be processed into stable mRNA. In the first deletion studied (Queen and Baltimore 1983), all of the gene 3′ of the Hind III site in the intron (Fig. 7.2a) was deleted before insertion into pLX1. This deleted construction was transfected into MPC11 cells, as was a similar pLX1 construct that contained the entire κ gene. RNA was extracted after 48 h and assayed for κ transcripts with the S1 nuclease assay described above. Whereas a large amount of RNA was transcribed from the promoter of the complete κ gene, no transcripts of the deleted gene were detected. This resulted indicated that an element required to activate κ transcription is located in the deleted region.

To locate the activating element more precisely, we constructed a series of deletions that successively removed more of the 3′ part of the κ gene (Queen and Stafford 1984). A region of the intron that is well conserved in sequence among the mouse, human, and rabbit genes (Emorine, Kuehl, Weir, Leder and Max 1983) provided a good candidate for the activator, so most of the deletions were chosen to extend into this area. After insertion into pLX1, the deleted genes were transfected in parallel into MPC11 cells. Total RNA was extracted from the cells and analyzed by the S1 nuclease assay to determine the quantity of transcripts initiating from the κ promoter. After determining the largest 3′ deletion that did not reduce κ promoter activity, and therefore by definition did not extend into the κ gene activator, a new series of deletions were made in this gene segment from the 5′ side. These deleted genes were also tested in parallel in MPC11 cells for their ability to initiate transcription from the κ promoter.

The extent of the various gene segments used and the amount of RNA

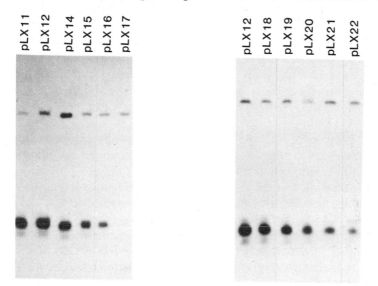

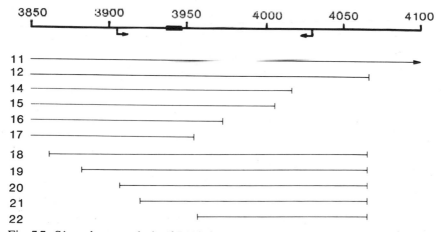

Fig. 7.7. S1 nuclease analysis of RNA from cells transfected with deletion plasmids. The parts of the κ gene remaining in each plasmid are indicated by lines beneath a numbered line that represents part of the $V_κ$–$C_κ$ intron (Fig. 7.2a). The nucleotide numbers are from Max, Maizel and Leder 1981. The region between the arrows is conserved among the mouse, rabbit and human genes; the region conserved in mouse and human extends about another 40 bp 3′. The heavy line near nucleotide 3950 represents a perfect 11-bp homology with the SV40 enhancer. The numbers at the left of the lines refer to the plasmid numbers above the gel lanes.

transcribed from each in a typical experiment are shown in Fig. 7.7 (Queen and Stafford 1984). The plasmid pLX11 contains the entire MOPC41 κ gene cloned into pLX1. This plasmid was transfected into MPC11 cells and RNA extracted for S1 analysis with a κ-specific probe (Fig. 7.4). The analysis showed 2 major bands (Fig. 7.7). The upper band ran in the position of undigested probe and is due to some reannealing of the probe during hybridization. The lower band, which was not present in the analysis of RNA from cells mock-transfected without DNA, is the band characteristic of transcripts initiating from the κ promoter about 25 bp before the initial codon of the gene (Queen and Baltimore 1983, and Fig. 7.5). Hence, as shown before, the κ promoter is active when the entire gene is transfected into MPC11 cells.

In the plasmid pLX12, the deletion extended up to the beginning of the sequence conserved between the mouse and human genes (Emorine *et al.* 1983). This plasmid synthesized no less κ RNA than the undeleted plasmid pLX11, indicating that the κ activating region remained intact. In the plasmid pLX14, the deletion extended into the conserved region and resulted in a two-fold reduction in RNA synthesis. The plasmid pLX15, with an additional 11 bp deleted from pLX14, showed another drop of about 3-fold. The plasmid pLX16, which has lost about half the conserved sequences, showed 3 per cent the transcriptional activity of pLX11; and pLX17, missing 18 more base pairs, displayed essentially no activation of κ transcription. Considering now the 5' deletions, the plasmid pLX18, in which the deletion extended up to 40 bp 5' of the conserved region, showed no decline in transcription from pLX12. However pLX19, in which the deletion extended up to 20 bp 5' of the conserved region, showed an approximately two-fold decline in κ transcription. The plasmid pLX20, missing the first few base pairs of the conserved sequence, showed another two-fold drop; and pLX21, with another 13 bp removed, showed an additional reduction of about two-fold. The deletion in pLX22 removed another 37 bp including a perfect 11-bp homology with the SV40 enhancer sequence. This plasmid transcribed three-fold less κ RNA than pLX21, or about 20-fold less than the original plasmid pLX12, but κ transcription was still detectable. We did not determine how much more 5' sequence must be removed to completely eliminate κ activation, but it is clear that the activating region coincides remarkably well with the conserved sequence (Fig. 7.7).

Enhancer elements can function from a variety of locations and orientations with respect to a promoter (Banerji, Rusconi and Schaffner 1981). To determine whether the κ activator defined by the deletion experiments has this property, Queen and Stafford 1984, began with a deletion plasmid in which the entire activating element had been removed from the κ gene. Of course, no κ transcription was observed when this plasmid was transfected into MPC11 cells. When a 205-bp fragment containing the activator was then inserted upstream of the deleted κ gene in either orientation, transcription was restored to the same level as when the κ activator is in the usual downstream position. This experiment also showed that the reduced κ transcription observed in the deletion experiments is not due to instability of the mRNA, because transcription can be completely recovered by inserting the activator at an upstream site where it cannot affect the structure of the RNA transcript. Picard and Schaffner 1984, and our unpublished results show that the κ activator can also stimulate transcription from promoters other than the κ promoter, so the activator has all the properties of an enhancer element.

THE HEAVY CHAIN ENHANCER

Simultaneously with the discovery of the κ gene enhancer, several groups found an enhancer associated with the mouse heavy chain constant segments (Gillies *et al.* 1983; Neuberger 1983; Banerji, Olson and Schaffner 1983). Gillies *et al.* cloned a complete γ_{2b} heavy chain gene (Fig. 7.2b) into the plasmid vector pSV2-gpt (Mulligan and Berg 1980) and transfected the construct into J558L mouse myeloma cells. Stable transformants were selected, and these cells expressed the γ_{2b} gene at a high level. However, when a 1kb Xba 1 fragment (Fig. 7.2b) that occurs in all heavy chain genes was deleted from the gene before transfection, expression of the γ_{2b} protein in transformed cells was drastically reduced. Expression was restored from plasmids in which the Xba 1 fragment was reinserted upstream of the gene, in either orientation. Hybridization experiments suggested that the deletion acted by reducing RNA synthesis from the γ_{2b} gene, so the Xba 1 fragment must contain a transcriptional activator. Additional experiments with smaller deletions of the gene indicated that the heavy chain activator is contained in a 140 bp region slightly 5' of the Eco R1 site (Fig. 7.2b).

Neuberger 1983, adopted an analogous approach, using a μ heavy chain gene. When the intact gene was transfected into myeloma cells, RNA transcripts could be readily detected transiently with an S1 nuclease assay. However, when a large deletion was made in the intron, transcription was entirely eliminated. Reinsertion of the deleted fragment upstream of the promoter restored transcription. Banerji, Olson and Schaffner 1983, analyzed the effect of the heavy chain activator on other promoters, rather than its own V_H promoter. Using immunofluorescence and S1 nuclease assays for transient expression, they found that the 1 kb Xba 1 fragment (Fig. 7.2b) strongly stimulates transcription from the SV40 early and β-globin promoters. Deletion studies localized the activator to 300 bp extending 5' of the Eco RI site. This fragment encompasses the 140 bp fragment found by Gillies *et al.* 1983, to contain the activating potential; the slight discrepancy in observed length of the activator may be due to the indirect assays for transcription employed.

Taken together, these experiments show that a region of DNA situated upstream of the heavy chain constant segments serves to activate heavy chain transcription, and this region has all the properties of an enhancer. Because the enhancer is located between the J_H segments and the switch region, it is preserved during the recombinations that change the class of a heavy chain gene. An enhancer analogous to the mouse heavy chain enhancer has recently been identified in the human heavy chain locus (Rabbitts, Foster, Baer and Hamlyn 1983; Hayday, Gillies, Saito, Wood, Wiman, Hayward and Tonegawa 1984); it occupies a similar location and is homologous in sequence to the mouse enhancer.

There is no overall homology among the sequences of the mouse κ gene enhancer, mouse heavy chain enhancer, and various viral enhancers such as that of polyoma. Short homologous segments have been noted among the various enhancers (Gillies *et al.* 1983; Banerji, Olson and Schaffner 1983; Emorine *et al.* 1983), but the homologies do not seem statistically convincing, and their importance has not yet been substantiated by mutation studies. Indeed, removal of a perfect 11-bp homology with the SV40 enhancer from the κ enhancer is accompanied by only a three-fold drop in activating ability, as noted above, while deletion of other, non-homologous segments has at least as great an effect. Moreover, it appears that the activating ability of the immunoglobulin enhancers is distributed over 100–200 base pairs and not confined to a small segment. Enhancers presumably interact with specific protein factors in order to effectuate their function and may serve as an entry point onto the chromosome for some component of the transcriptional machinery. The paucity of homology among the various enhancers thus suggests the possibility that different enhancers may interact with different protein factors. And the large size of the immunoglobulin enhancers relative to usual protein binding sites suggests that enhancers may to some extent act by modifying chromatin structure directly.

Explanation of cell-type specificity

THE DNA LEVEL

Two important conclusions follow from the work described above: (1) Immunoglobulin genes are transcribed at a high level when transfected into antibody-secreting cells, but at a much lower or undetectable level in non-lymphoid cells, (2) Immunoglobulin genes require two separate regions for transcription initiation—a promoter and an enhancer. Thus, a natural question is whether the cell-type specificity resides in the promoter or the enhancer. The surprising answer is, apparently, both: the functions of the promoter and enhancer are independently specific for lymphoid cells. However, while the cell-type specificity of immunoglobulin enhancers has been established in several published studies, the specificity of immunoglobulin promoters is just becoming known.

Banerji, Olson and Schaffner 1983, showed that the heavy chain enhancer is cell-type specific at the same time that it was discovered. In transient expression assays, they found that the enhancer strongly stimulates transcription from SV40 early and β-globin promoters transfected into myeloma cells. However, no stimulation was observed after transfection into non-lymphoid cells. Gillies *et al.* 1983, also found that the heavy chain enhancer stimulates the SV40 promoter only in lymphoid cells, using transformation frequency as an indirect assay for transcription. Because the SV40 early and β-globin promoters can be stimulated by other enhancers in non-lymphoid cells, this result implies that the heavy chain enhancer itself is cell-type specific. Similar experiments (Picard and Schaffner 1984) show that the κ enhancer functions specifically in lymphoid cells, thus providing one explanation for the cell-type specificity of the κ gene detailed above.

Although the cell-type specificity of immunoglobulin enhancers would be sufficient to account for the specificity of the complete genes, it is in principle possible that immunoglobulin promoters are also cell-type specific. My laboratory has recently begun experiments to examine this possibility (J. Foster, J. Stafford, and C. Queen, unpublished data). We started with a derivative of the plasmid pLX31 (Fig. 7.3) from which part of the κ gene including the enhancer was deleted. According to an SI nuclease assay, no κ RNA was transcribed from this plasmid when transfected into either lymphoid or non-lymphoid cells, as expected. When the enhancer of polyoma virus was inserted at the Eco RI site, transcription from the κ promoter was restored after transfection into myeloma cells, but κ RNA could still not be detected after transfection into mouse L cells. Transcription from the SV40 promoter served as a positive control for the integrity of the plasmid in both cell lines. Since the polyoma enhancer functions in both lymphoid and non-lymphoid cells, this experiment indicates that the κ promoter can only function in lymphoid cells. Analogous results have also been obtained in the laboratory of D. Baltimore (personal communication), who suggests that the specificity of immunoglobulin enhancers and promoters may play physiological roles at different stages of B-cell differentiation.

THE PROTEIN LEVEL

What is the molecular mechanism of the cell-type specificity of immunoglobulin genes? It seems likely that lymphoid cells contain specific protein factors which interact with immunoglobulin promoters and enhancers and which are not present in non-lymphoid cells. Isolating such a factor would be a significant advance in the study of gene expression and cellular development, because very few activating factors for genes in eukaryotes have been isolated thus far. The strong cell-type specificity of the transient transfection systems developed for immunoglobulin genes (Fig. 7.5) makes this goal feasible, but formidable problems remain. A major difficulty is that eukaryotic *in vitro* transcription systems (Manley, Fire, Cano, Sharp and Gefter 1980) in general respond poorly to regulatory factors.

To circumvent the need for *in vitro* regulation, our laboratory is collaborating with the laboratory of Laurence Korn to use frog oocytes as an assay system for factors involved in the transcription of immunoglobulin genes. It has been shown that after injection into oocytes, an immunoglobulin gene is accurately transcribed from its promoter (Bentley, Farrell and Rabbitts 1982). However, examination of the data presented shows that the transcription is at a very low level, so that one might hope to stimulate transcription from the injected immunoglobulin genes by co-injecting extracts of myeloma cells. When we injected plasmid DNA containing the MOPC41 κ gene (Fig. 7.2a) into oocytes and later extracted RNA, no transcription from the κ promoter was detected by our usual S1 nuclease assay (Fig. 7.8a). However, when intact myeloma nuclei prepared by lysolecithin treatment of myeloma cells were co-injected with the DNA, strong immunoglobulin transcription was observed (Fig. 7.8c). The major protected probe fragment comigrated with the probe fragment protected by RNA from myeloma cells transfected with the κ gene (Fig. 7.8h), indicating that nuclei-stimulated κ transcription initiates accurately in oocytes.

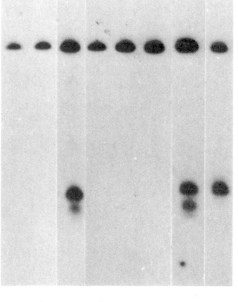

a b c d e f g h

Fig. 7.8. SI nuclease analysis of RNA from injected oocytes. The oocytes were injected with (a) κ gene DNA alone, (b) intact myeloma nuclei alone, (c) κ gene DNA plus myeloma nuclei; and κ gene DNA plus myeloma nuclear extracts that had been prepared by (d) osmotic shock, (e) triton X-100 treatment, (f) dounce homogenization and (g) sonication. Lane h is an S1 analysis of RNA from myeloma cells transfected with κ gene DNA.

To proceed further, the myeloma nuclei were broken open in a variety of ways before being co-injected into oocytes with the κ gene (L. Korn and C. Queen, unpublished data). When the nuclei were broken by osmotic shock (Fig. 7.8d), triton X-100 treatment (Fig. 7.8e) or dounce homogenization (Fig. 7.8f), the nuclear extracts failed to stimulate κ transcription after injection into oocytes. However, extracts prepared by sonication of the myeloma nuclei strongly stimulated κ transcription in oocytes (Fig. 7.8g). While most of the transcripts initiated accurately, a lower band of protected probe (Fig. 7.8g) indicates that some transcripts initiated from an aberrant startsite, which is also utilized when the κ gene is transfected into monkey COS 7 cells (Queen and Baltimore 1983). Although these initial experiments were encouraging, recent experiments have been more ambiguous. We have found that the myeloma nuclear extracts also stimulate transcription from injected genes other than immunoglobulin genes, and conversely, that nuclear extracts from non-lymphoid cells also stimulate immunoglobulin transcription. Hence, at the present time, it seems that the stimulation of immunoglobulin transcription we observed (Fig. 7.8c, i) may be due to general transcription factors in the myeloma nuclei rather than factors specific for immunoglobulin genes. Experiments are in progress with L. Korn to attempt to increase the specificity of the oocyte assay. Certainly the isolation of the protein factors that regulate transcription of immunoglobulin genes, by this or another method, is an important goal.

References

Banerji, J., Rusconi, J., Rusconi, S., and Schaffner, W. (1981). Expression of a β-globin gene is enhanced by remote SV40 DNA sequences. *Cell* **27**, 299–308.

——— Olson, L., and Schaffner, W. (1983). A lymphocyte-specific cellular enhancer is located downstream of the joining region in immunoglobulin heavy chain genes. *Cell* **33**, 729–740.

Bently, D. L., Farrell, P. J., and Rabbitts, T. (1982). Unrearranged immunoglobulin variable region genes have a functional promoter. *Nucleic Acids Res.* **10**, 1841–1856.

Brack, C., Hirama, M., Lenhard-Schuller, R., and Tonegawa, S. (1978). A complete immunoglobulin gene is created by somatic recombination. *Cell* **15**, 1–14.

Brinster, R. L., Ritchie, K. A., Hammer, R. E., O'Brien, R. L., Arp, B., and Storb, U. (1983). Expression of a microinjected immunoglobulin gene in the spleen of transgenic mice. *Nature* **306**, 332–336.

Chu, G. and Sharp, P. (1980). SV40 DNA transfection of cells in suspension: analysis of the efficiency of transcription and translation of T-antigen. *Gene* **13**, 197–201.

Clarke, C., Berenson, J., Goverman, J., Boyer, P. D., Crews, S., Siv, G., and Calame, K. (1982). An immunoglobulin promoter region is unaltered by DNA rearrangement and somatic mutation during B-cell development. *Nucleic Acids Res.* **10**, 7731–7749.

Deans, R., Denis, K. A., Taylor, A., and Wall, R. (1984). Expression of an immunoglobulin heavy chain gene transfected into lymphocytes. *Proc. Nat. Acad. Sci. U.S.A.* **81**, 1292–1296.

Early, P., Huang, H., Davis, M., Calame, K., and Hood, L. (1980). An immunoglobulin heavy chain variable region gene is generated from three segments of DNA: V_H, D and J. *Cell* **19**, 981–992.

Emorine, L., Kuehl, M., Weir, L., Leder, P., and Max, E. E. (1983). A conserved sequence in the immunoglobulin J_κ—C_κ intron: possible enhancer element. *Nature* **304**, 447– 449.

Falkner, F. and Zachau, H. (1982). Expression of mouse immunoglobulin genes in monkey cells. *Nature* **298**, 286–288.

Fromm, M. and Berg, P. (1982). Deletion mapping of DNA regions required for SV40 early region promoter function *in vivo*. *J. Mol. Appl. Genet.* **1**, 457–481.

Gillies, S. and Tonegawa, S. (1983). Expression of cloned immunoglobulin genes introduced into mouse L cells. *Nucleic Acids Res.* **11**, 7981–7997.

Gillies, S. D., Morrison, S. L., Oi, V. T., and Tonegawa, S. (1983). A tissue-specific transcription enhancer element is located in the major intron of a rearranged immunoglobulin heavy chain gene. *Cell* **33**, 717–728.

Graham, F. L. and Van der Eb, A. J. (1973). A new technique for the assay for infectivity of human adenovirus 5 DNA. *Virology* **52**, 456–467.

Hayday, A., Gillies, S. D., Saito, H., Wood, C., Wiman, K., Hayward, W. S., and Tonegawa, S. (1984). Activation of a translocated human c-myc gene by an enhancer in the immunoglobulin heavy-chain locus. *Nature* **307**, 334–340.

Hilschmann, N. and Craig, L. C. (1965). Amino acid sequence studies with Bence Jones proteins. *Proc. Nat. Acad. Sci. U.S.A.* **53**, 1403–1409.

Kelley, D. E., Coleclough, C., and Perry, R. P. (1982). Functional significance and evolutionary development of the 5'-terminal regions of immunoglobulin variable-region genes. *Cell* **29**, 681–689.

Kessel, M. and Khoury, G. (1983). Induction of cloned genes after transfer into eukaryotic cells. In *Gene Amplification and Analysis*, 3 (Papas, T. S., Rosenberg, M., and Chirikjinn, J. G., eds.) New York: Elsevier North Holland, pp. 234-260.

Kurtz, D. T. (1981). Hormonal inducibility of α_{2u} globulin genes in transfected mouse cells. *Nature* **291**, 629–631.

Lusky, M. and Botchan, M. (1981). Inhibition of SV40 replication in simian cells. *Nature* **293**, 79–81.

Manley, J. L., Fire, A., Cano, A., Sharp, P., and Gefter, M. (1980). DNA-dependent transcription of adenovirus genes in a soluble whole-cell extract. *Proc. Nat. Acad. Sci. U.S.A.* **77**, 3855–3859.

Mather, E. L. and Perry, R. P. (1981). Transcriptional regulation of immunoglobulin V regions. *Nucleic Acids Res.* **9**, 6855–6867.

Max, E. E., Maizel, J. V., and Leder, P. (1981). The nucleotide sequence of a 5.5 kilobase DNA segment containing the mouse κ immunoglobulin J and C region genes. *J. Biol. Chem.* **256**, 5116–5120.

McCutchan, J. H. and Pagano, J. S. (1968). Enhancement of the infectivity of simian virus 40 deoxyribonucleic acid with diethylamino-ethyl dextran. *J. Nat. Cancer Inst.* **41**, 351–356.

Moreau, P., Hen, R., Wasylyk, B., Everett, R., Gaub, M. D., and Chambon, P. (1981). The SV40 72 base repeat has a striking effect on gene expression both in SV40 and other chimeric recombinants. *Nucleic Acids Res.* **9**, 6047–6068.

Mulligan, R. C. and Berg, P. (1980). Selection for animal cells that express the Escherichia coli gene coding for xanthine-guanine phosoribosyltransferase. *Proc. Nat. Acad. Sci. U.S.A.* **78**, 2072–2076.

Neuberger, M. (1983). Expression and regulation of immunoglobulin heavy chain gene transfected into lymphoid cells. *EMBO J.* **2**, 1373–1379.

Ochi, A., Hawley, R. G., Hawley, T., Shulman, M. J., Traunecker, A., Kohler, G., and Hozumi, N. (1983). Functional immunoglobulin M production after transfection of cloned immunoglobulin heavy and light chain genes into lymphoid cells. *Proc. Nat. Acad. Sci. U.S.A.* **80**, 6351–6355.

Oi, V. T., Morrison, S. L., Herzenberg, L. A., and Berg, P. (1983). Immunoglobulin gene expression in transformed lymphoid cells. *Proc. Nat. Acad. Sci. U.S.A.* **80**, 825–829.

Perry, R. B., Kelly, D. E., Coleclough, C., Seidman, J. G., Leder, P., Tonegawa, S., Matthyssons, G., and Weigert, M. (1980). Transcription of mouse κ chain genes: implications for allelic exclusion. *Proc. Nat. Acad. Sci. U.S.A.* **77**, 1937–1941.

Picard, D. and Schaffner, W. (1983). Correct transcription of a cloned mouse immunoglobulin gene in vivo. *Proc. Nat. Acad. Sci. U.S.A.* **80**, 417–421.

—— and Shaffner, W. (1984). A lymphocyte-specific enhancer in the mouse immunoglobulin κ gene. *Nature* **307**, 80–83.

Queen, C. and Baltimore, D. (1983). Immunoglobulin gene transcription is activated by downstream sequence elements. *Cell* **33**, 741–748.

—— and Stafford, J. (1984). Fine mapping of an immunoglobulin gene activator. *Mol. Cell. Biol.*, **4**, 1042–1049.

Rabbitts, T. H., Foster, A., Baer, R., and Hamlyn, P. H. (1983). Transcription enhancer identified near the human C_μ gene is unavailable to the translocated c-myc gene in a Burkitt lymphoma. *Nature* **306**, 806–809.

Rice, D. and Baltimore, D. (1982). Regulated expression of an immunoglobulin κ gene introduced into a mouse lymphoid cell line. *Proc. Nat. Acad. Sci. U.S.A.* **79**, 7862–7865.

Robins, D. M., Paek, L., Seeburg, P. H., and Axel, R. (1982). Regulated expression of human growth hormone genes in mouse cells. *Cell* **29**, 623–631.

Sakano, H., Maki, R., Kurosawa, Y., Roeder, W., and Tonegawa, S. (1980). Two types of somatic recombination are necessary for the generation of complete immunoglobulin heavy-chain genes. *Nature* **286**, 676–683.

Schaffner, W. (1980). Direct transfer of cloned genes from bacteria to mammalian cells. *Proc. Nat. Acad. Sci. U.S.A.* **77**, 2163–2167.

Schibler, U., Marcu, K. B., and Perry, R. P. (1978). The synthesis and processing of the messenger RNAs specifying heavy and light chain immunoglobulins in MPC 11 cells. *Cell* **15**, 1495–1509.

Seidman, J. G. and Leder, P. (1978). The arrangement and rearrangement of antibody genes. *Nature* **276**, 790–795.

Shimizu, A., Takahashi, N., Yaoita, Y., and Honjo, T. (1982). Organization of the constant-region gene family of the mouse immunoglobulin heavy chain. *Cell* **28**, 499–506.

Sompayrac, L. M. and Dana, K. (1981). Efficient infection of monkey cells with DNA of simian virus 40. *Proc. Nat. Acad. Sci. U.S.A.* **78**, 7575–7578.

Southern, P. J. and Berg, P. (1982). Transformation of mammalian cells to antibiotic resistance with a bacterial gene under control of the SV40 early region promoter. *J. Mol. App. Genet.* **1**, 327–341.

Stafford, J. and Queen, C. (1983). Cell-type specific expression of a transfected immunoglobulin gene. *Nature* **306**, 77–79.

Subramani, S., Mulligan, R., and Berg, P. (1981). Expression of the mouse dihydrofolate reductase complementary deoxyribonucleic acid in simian virus 40 vectors. *Mol. Cell. Biol.* **1**, 854–864.

Tonegawa, S. (1983). Somatic generation of antibody diversity. *Nature* **302**, 575–581.

Walker, M. D., Edlund, T., Boulet, A. M., and Rutter, W. J. (1983). Cell-specific expression controlled by the 5′-flanking region of insulin and chymotrypsin genes. *Nature* **306**, 557–561.

Wall, R. and Kuehl, M. (1983). Biosynthesis and Regulation of Immunoglobulins. *Ann. Rev. Immunol.* **1**, 393–422.

8 The uteroglobin gene, structure and interaction with the progesterone-receptor

J. F. SAVOURET, A. GUIOCHON-MANTEL AND E. MILGROM

The protein

Initial studies on mammalian uterine fluids have shown important variations in protein contents under the action of steroid hormones in physiological conditions (Beato 1980). One of the most extensively studied models has been the rabbit endometrium where a single protein, uteroglobin (formerly called blastokinin) (Krishnan and Daniel 1967; Beier 1968) represents 40 to 60 per cent of the total proteins in the uterine fluid at its peak on the fifth day after mating. Uteroglobin then decreases to complete disappearance on day 12 after mating, despite continuously elevating hormonal concentrations.

STRUCTURE AND STEROID-BINDING PROPERTIES

Uteroglobin has been purified to homogeneity from uterine washings of pregnant rabbits or progesterone-treated animals (Fridlansky and Milgrom 1976). It is composed of two identical subunits of 70 amino acids (MW $\approx$ 8,000). The amino acid sequence has been established and it has been shown that the subunits are held together by two disulphide bridges and other noncovalent bonds. (Ponstingl, Nieto and Beato 1978).

Uteroglobin binds progesterone with a dissociation constant of $4 \times 10^{-7}M$, and one of its metabolites with an even higher affinity: 5-α pregnane-3,20-dione ($\kappa_d = 1.3 \times 10^{-7}M$) (Arthur, Cowan and Daniel 1972; Fridlansky and Milgrom 1976). Although the affinity is relatively low, this binding is probably biologically relevant due to the abundance of the protein. Uteroglobin may exist in two states, either with oxidized or reduced disulphide bridges. Only in the reduced state does it bind steroids (Fridlansky and Milgrom 1976; Beato and Beier 1975; Tancredi, Temussi and Beato 1982). No progesterone-metabolizing activity could be linked to uteroglobin.

Uteroglobin has been crystallized in various forms (Mornon, Fridlansky, Bailly and Millgrom 1979; Mornon et al. 1980) and X-ray diffraction studies have been performed (Fig. 8.1). The structure of one of the crystalline forms has been established at a resolution of 2.2 Å. Preliminary characterization of the structure of the steroid-binding site has been performed. An oblong hydrophobic pocket with the characteristic features of a progesterone-binding site has been found at the centre of the molecule.

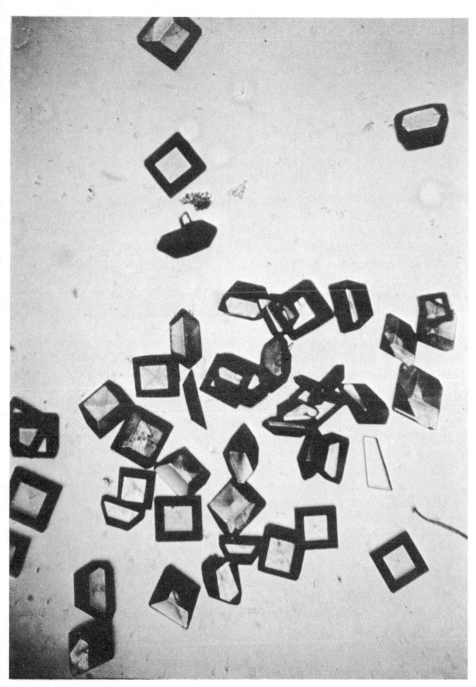

Fig. 8.1. Crystals of uteroglobin.

Spectrometric studies showed that a tyrosyl radical may be involved in the interaction with Progesterone (Beato, Arnemann and Voss 1977).

Unlike the progesterone receptor, uteroglobin binds synthetic progestins poorly. Other steroid hormones, such as cortisol, testosterone and oestrogen, show practically no affinity for uteroglobin. Uteroglobin binds diethylstilbestrol slightly better than synthetic progestins (Fridlansky and Milgrom 1976).

Some substituted diphenyl-ketones have been shown to inhibit the binding of progesterone to uteroglobin, and one showed a higher affinity for uteroglobin than progesterone itself (Saxena, Seth, Bhaduri and Sahib 1983).

DISTRIBUTION

Uteroglobin was first believed to be uterine-specific and only progesterone-dependant (Beir 1966). However, further studies have shown specific effects of oestradioll on synthesis of uteroglobin and its mRNA (Loosfelt, Fridlansky, Savouret, Atger and Milgrom 1981a), and the presence of an identical protein has been reported in several rabbit tissues including oviduct (Goswami and Feigelson 1975; Kirchner 1976), blastocyst (Beier 1968), and lung (Noske and Feigelson 1976; Beier, Kirchner and Mootz 1978; Savouret, Loosfelt, Atger and Milgrom 1980), where it is expressed constitutively.

Uteroglobin has not been found in other mammals, except in members of the order *Lagomorpha*, which includes the Hare and Pika as well as the rabbit (Nieto and Lombardero 1982). Similar research in the human species has shown a protein bearing electrophoresis and immunological similaries with uteroglobin, but clear identification is not yet demonstrated (Beier 1982; Lambadarios 1982; Daniel 1973). Uteroglobin has also been found in the rabbit seminal fluid demonstrating that it is not restricted to the female genital tract (Noske and Feigelson 1976; Beier, Bohn and Muller 1975). Recently the presence of uteroglobin in the paraprostatic glands of male rabbits was reported. Immunofluorescence data showed the intracellular distribution of fluorescence grana in those glands to be similar to the endometrial situation, suggesting the mode of secretion in both sexes as identical, though controlled by different steroid hormones (Müller 1983).

Moreover, using a computer programme designed to compare amino-acid-sequences, Baker (1983) has reported some analogies between uteroglobin and rat prostatic steroid binding protein, suggesting they may belong to a family of related proteins present in the genital tract and under endocrine control. Apparently, the function of uteroglobin has a broader scope than the early phase of pregnancy.

PHYSIOLOGICAL ROLE

Some authors have proposed that uteroglobin exerts a stimulatory effect on the blastocyst (hence the other name of blastokinin), together with retarding egg implantation (Beier 1968; Krishnan 1971; El Banna and Daniel 1972). These experiments have however been criticized and the effect of uteroglobin considered as non-specific.

The ability to bind its own regulator has prompted some investigators to consider that its mode of action might be to modulate progesterone activity and transport within the blastocyst (Beato 1977). High concentrations of progesterone in the uterus are necessary to maintain pregnancy; however, these amounts of hormone may be detrimental to the blastocyst, and hence uteroglobin might sequester a fraction of endo-uterine progesterone. Totally different functions have also been proposed for uteroglobin.

Since the initial studies of Beier (1968, 1970) on proteinase inhibitor activity in uterine fluids, several authors have proposed that uteroglobin may be responsible for that activity, but Hackenberg and Beier (1982) demonstrated that it was actually due to a comigrating proteinase inhibitor in the uteroglobin fraction. They also showed that its activity parallels the secretion of uteroglobin in the uterus.

Recently Mukherjee, Ulane and Agrawal (1982) reported that uteroglobin or prostatic fluid suppressed antigenicity of epididymal sperm as well as early embryonic antigenicity. They proposed that uteroglobin supresses the antigenicity of developing embryos during implantation by crosslinking to transplantation antigens containing β_2 microglobulin. These authors also reported that the crosslinking of uteroglobin may be catalyzed by transglutaminase, which could explain the potentiating effect of this enzyme on antigenicity suppression by uteroglobin.

EXPRESSION AND REGULATION

Endometrium

Studies conducted in our laboratory involved immature rabbits to approximate the conditions of the classic Clauberg test as closely as possible (Clauberg 1933). Initial experiments attempted to define the hormonal conditions which provoke a maximal induction of uteroglobin. In other well-studied systems such as the induction of egg white proteins or vitellogenin by oestrogens, a primary stimulation by the hormone elicits a minimal response in specific proteins, whereas further stimulations generate strong responses. To explain this priming effect, it was proposed that the first stimulation induces cellular differentiation and the second stimulation acts on newly developed cells which are able to respond by synthesizing specific proteins. [This explanation was however recently criticized in the case of egg white proteins in the chick oviduct (Moen and Palmiter 1980).] Initially, a similar situation was suggested for uteroglobin in the endometrium. A first injection of progesterone, alone or after oestrogen priming, increased less uteroglobin and its mRNA per uterus than a second injection. However, this was primarily due to an increase in the number of cells in the endometrium provoked by the injection of progesterone. If the DNA content of the endometrium is taken into account, primary and secondary stimulation by progesterone (with or without oestrogen priming) elicit similar responses in terms of protein and mRNA. These experiments show that cellular differentiation is not necessary, and that it is possible to study the action of progesterone on endometria of prepubertal rabbits without hormonal pretreatment (Atger and Milgrom 1977; Atger, Mornon, Savouret, Loosfelt, Fridlansky and Milgrom 1980a).

The messenger of uteroglobin. The messenger RNA (mRNA) for uteroglobin has been prepared from the endometrium of 5-day pregnant rabbits (Atger and Milgrom 1977). The poly(A)$^+$ fraction of endometrical RNA has been translated in different systems, and the newly synthetized peptides immunoprecipitated by anti-uteroglobin serum prepared in goats. Polyacrylamide gel electrophoresis in denaturing conditions showed the presence of a single amino-acid chain (MW $\approx$ 10,000), larger than the mature subunit of uteroglobin. This peptide was identified as preuteroglobin (Atger and Milgrom 1977; Atger, Mercier, Haze, Friedlansky and Milgrom 1979; Beato and Rungger 1975; Beato and Nieto 1976) and shown to contain a 21-amino acid N-terminal extension. The amino acid sequence of this signal peptide was established and displayed the usual characteristics, i.e. high content of hydrophobic amino acids, methionine as the initial amino acid, and an alanine-glycine transition from the signal peptide to the secreted protein.

Purified uteroglobin mRNA has a sedimentation constant of 8.5S in sucrose gradients and its molecular weight is about 200,000 daltons, as determined by polyacrylamide gel electrophoresis in 99 per cent formamide. Thus, this mRNA is composed of about 600 nucleotides, only 273 of which are necessary to code for the 91 amino acids of uteroglobin.

A DNA complementary to uteroglobin mRNA was synthesized and characterized (Atger, Savouret and Milgrom 1980b; Arnemann, Heins and Beato 1979). It hybridizes to pure mRNA with an $R_0t_{\frac{1}{2}}$ of 6×10^{-4} and has been used for regulation studies.

The transcription of the gene has been studied by Northern blot analysis which reveals four RNA species, corresponding to the full transcript after polyadenylation (3.2 kb), partially spliced precursors (2.9 kb and 1 kb), and the mature message (0.6 kb) which contains 465 transcribed nucleotides plus the poly(A) tail (Snead, Day, Chandra, Mace, Bullock and Woo 1981). The 5' non coding sequence of the mRNA exhibits complementarity with the 18S ribosomal RNA (Menne, Suske, Arnemann, Wenz, Cato and Beato 1982).

Hormonal regulation. Following early data on uteroglobin secretions in various hormonal situations, (see Table 8.1) the obtention of labelled specific probes enabled us to ascertain the direct effect of oestradiol and progesterone on the transcriptional activity of the gene.

Table 8.1

Uteroglobin in the lung and endometrium: Developmental and hormonal regulation (from Loosfelt et al. 1981; Savouret et al. 1980; Torkkeli et al. 1978)

Hormonal treatment	Lung		Endometrium	
	µg uteroglobin /mg DNA	µg uteroglobin /mg protein	µg uteroglobin /mg DAN	µg uteroglobin /mg protein
Controls (prepuberal)	13.8 ± 1.2	1.65 ± 0.25	0.26 ± 0.09	0.06 ± 0.02
Progesterone	8.1 ± 1.3	1.55 ± 0.25	130 ± 15	36.3 ± 4.4
Oestradiol + Progesterone	9.2 ± 2.0	1.60 ± 0.35	176 ± 20	40.6 ± 4.2
Oestradiol	9.0 ± 1.7	1.50 ± 0.30	8.30 ± 0.85	1.40 ± 0.20
Cortisol	9.8 + 0.8	1.45 ± 0.20	1.21 ± 0.20	0.30 ± 0.07
Dexamethasone	31 ± 3.3	3.10 ± 0.25	13.3 ± 6.4	2.84 ± 1.65
Untreated newborn	ND	0.6 + 0.1	ND	ND
Untreated adults	ND	3 ± 1.09	ND	0.41 ± 0.33
5 days pregnants	ND	ND	329 ± 100	70 ± 10

It has been proposed that steroid hormone action on mRNAs synthesis could either be a primary effect of the steroid-receptor complex on the genome or be secondary to the synthesis of regulatory proteins, which in turn would act at the genomic level to promote transcription of specific genes. The latter mechanism would imply some delay in hormone response. This problem was studied by measuring uteroglobin mRNA concentrations at short times after progesterone injection. Two h after hormone administration, uteroglobin mRNA had increased by 70 per cent and after 4 h by 500 per cent (Loosfelt *et al* 1981a). Cycloheximide (100 mg) coupled to progesterone (5 mg) and injected 4 h before lowered the response to progesterone, but the effect of the steroid was not abolished. A postranscriptional effect of progesterone could be shown by the dissociated effect observed on concentrations of uteroglobin and its mRNA in the endometrium. The mRNA level was increased by 6 days of hormonal treatment, but protein levels rose threefold more than could be accounted for by the increased mRNA. Oestradiol alone did not duplicate this effect and high doses of oestradiol coupled to progesterone inhibited the posttranscriptional amplification. The level at which that stimulation takes place is unknown (Loosfelt, Fridlansky, Atger and Milgrom 1981b). Oestradiol alone stimulated uteroglobin mRNA synthesis, but increased the concentration of uteroglobin much less (Loosfelt *et al.* 1981a). Other authors have reported an inhibitory effect of elevated doses of oestradiol on the progesterone stimulation of uteroglobin mRNA production in the endometrium of mature animals. This discrepancy with results from our group can be explained by differences in experimental procedures such as the use of mature animals instead of prepubertal animals, and the noncorrelation of data to cell number in biological samples by the measure of DNA content (Loosfelt *et al.* Hemminki, Torkkeli and Janne 1979; Isomaa, Isotalo, Orave, Torkkeli and Janne 1979). Using purified endometrial nuclei in RNA polymerase 'run-off' experiments Kumar, Chandra, Woo and Bullock (1982) reported that uteroglobin gene transcription increased from day 0 to day 4 and then decreased after day 6 after mating, despite continuously rising hormonal levels, showing that increase in the steady-state level of mRNA is the major factor in regulating the production of the protein. No differences in RNA degradation or preferential degradation of uteroglobin transcripts could be found during early pregnancy (Kumar *et al.* 1982).

As seen by Northern blot analysis of endometrial poly A[+] RNA, hormonal stimulations did not modify the steady-state of splicing events, as the ratio of precursors to mRNA remained constant when measured by scanning of the autoradiographs (Rauch, unpublished observations).

Nonhormonal factors. The effect of nonhormonal factors on uteroglobin and total protein content of uterine fluids has also been studied. Light deprivation seemed to amplify protein production, dietary protein deficiency lowered it and ageing showed no significant effect (Daniel 1980).

Lung

While uteroglobin in the digestive tract has not received much attention, there is a wealth of information about its physiology in the lung (Noske and Feigelson 1976; Beier, Kirchner and Mootz 1978; Savouret, Loosfelt, Atger and Milgrom 1980; Torkkeli, Kontula and Janne 1977; Torkkeli, Krusius and Janne 1978). Lung uteroglobin is a secretory protein destined to the tracheo-bronchial fluid in a manner very similar to the uterine situation. The identity of lung and uterine uteroglobin has been confirmed by a variety of physio-chemical and immunological techniques including amino acid sequencing of preuteroglobin synthesized *in vitro* from endometrium and lung mRNAs (see above references). Sucrose gradient analysis of lung uteroglobin mRNA as well as hybridation kinetics and thermal stability of hybrids of uterine uteroglobin cDNA and the uteroglobin mRNA found in the lung show both messengers are indistinguishable in size and sequence (Savouret *et al.* 1980). This was later confirmed by SI nuclease-mapping analysis which indicated the same transcription start for both molecules in lung and endometrium (Fig. 8.5) (Bailly, Atger, Atger, Cerbon, Alizon, Vu Hai, Logeat and Milgrom 1983). Data from Table 8.1 show that the basal concentration of uteroglobin in the lung varies during the rabbit's life; there is a twofold increase after puberty. Lombardero and Nieto (1981), also report a developmental variation of uteroglobin in the lung and suggest that glucocorticoid control of lung maturation is responsible for it. The production of uteroglobin in the lung by bronchial epithelial cells is constant and insensitive to oestradiol or progesterone. Dexamethasone seems to have a posttranscriptional effect since it enhances the level of the protein threefold in prepuberal rabbits but does not modify the level of mRNA. Cortisol has a similar but much weaker effect (Savouret et al. 1980). Somewhat different results have been reported wherein dexamethasone stimulates uteroglobin mRNA in parallel with the protein, but this may be due to experimental differences (Lombardero and Nieto 1981). These authors used sexually mature animals instead of prepuberal animals, and the strategy for hormonal stimulation is quite different from ours. Although lung metabolizes progesterone and contains progesterone receptors (Savouret et al. 1980; Loosfelt et al. 1981b), the function of lung uteroglobin is unknown. Insensitivities to stimulation by progesterone can either be explained by the presence of uteroglobin and progesterone-receptor in different cell types or by differences at the chromatin level.

Other tissues

Steroid regulation in the oviduct is moderate and limited to oestradiol, whereas progesterone shows no effect on uteroglobin concentration in the fluid. Ovariectomy suppressed uteroglobin in oviductal fluid as in uterine fluids (Goswami and Feigelson 1975).

The gene

SEQUENCE

The molecular study of the gene has been carried out in several groups (Atger et al. 1980b; Atger, Perricaudet, Tiollais and Milgrom 1980c; Atger, Atger, Tiollais and Milgrom 1981; Arnemann, Heins and Beato 1979; Snead et al. 1981; Menne et al. 1982; Bailly et al. 1983; Suske, Wenz, Cato and Beato 1983). The nucleotide sequence (Fig. 8.2) and restriction map (Fig. 8.3) are taken from those references. Nucleotides are numbered from the first of the sequence determined in our laboratory (Bailly et al. 1983). The main site for initiation of transcription is nucleotide 598, which is numbered as 1 on Fig. 8.4 which shows the intron/exon structure and gene/protein relation as determined by Bailly et al. (1983). Discrepancies in the published sequences can be seen in Fig. 8.2. There is one copy of the gene per haploid genome. It is 3 kb long and contains two intervening sequences and three exons. Exon I contains the 5′ untranslated region and most of the signal peptide (18 out of 21 aminoacids). Exon 2 contains the coding sequence up to threonine 60 and Exon 3 codes for the last ten amino acids (up to methionine 70) and the 3′ end of the messenger RNA. The amino acids preceding threonine 60 constitute the main part of the protein, including the putative steroid binding site, while the following ones are involved in subunits interactions.

```
M      1 GGGCAGGGCA TTGGCTCGGC TAGGTATGGG GTTTGGGTCT TTGGTGGGTG TTCTGCGGAA

M     61 GTCCTTTTTC TGTCCACGTG TTCAGGCCAG GGTCTCCTCC AGGCAATGCT CACAGCAATG

M    121 CTCTGAACCC AGTGACCTTC ACGGCTCAAC GTCCAGCCAC CTTCCTCGGA GGGGGGGAAGC

M    181 AGAGGAGCCC AGTGCAGCCA CAGGATCCTG GGTGCTCCTA TCCTGTCACA GCCACTTGGG
B    181                     GATCCTG GGTGCTCCTA TCCTGTCACA GCCACTTGGG

M    241 CCTCAGCTTC TCCTGGGGTG ACAGGAGACA CACTTGCTTC TGTTGGTCTG GGCTGCCCAA
B    241 CCTCAGCTTC TCCTGGGGTG ACAGGAGACA CACTTGCTTC TGTTGGTCTG GGCTGCCCAA

M    301 ATGCCCTGGT TCAAAGAGAA GACGCAGGTG GCCAGGTCAC CATGCCCTCG GGGGCAGGCA
B    301 ATGCCTTGGT TCAAAGAGAA GACGCAGGTG GCTAGGTCAC CATGCCCTCG GGGGCAGGCA

M    361 CCCCTTGCCA CACCCCTGCA CAAGACTCCG GGCTCTCCCT CCCCCCGAGG GACCCATTGT
B    361 CCCCTTACCA CACCCCCGCA CAAGACTCCG GGCTCTCCCT CCCCCCGAGG GACCCATTGT

M    421 GTGAGTTCAG TTTCAATAGG GATGGAAACT GGATTGAGAA AAGGGAATAT TTACTTATCC
B    421 GTGAGTTCAG TTTCAATAGG GATGGAAACT GGATTGAGAA AAGGGAATAT TTACTTATCC

M    481 CACCAAGTCA ATGCCCAAGT AAATAATGCA GTCAAGTAAG TGGAGCCCAG GCCCTGCCCT
B    481 CACCAAGTCA ATGCCCAAGT AAATAATGCA GTCAAGTAAG TGGAGCCCAG GCCCTGCCCT

M    541 CTTCTATCTG GGCACTGCCC GGAGAATACA AAAAGGCACC TGACGGCCGT CCCCCTCAAG
B    541 CTTCTATCTG GGCACTGCCC GGAGAATACA AAAAGGCACC TGACGGCCGT CCCCCTCAAG

M    601 ATCACCGGAT CCAGAGCCAG CCCAGAGCCT TCCCATTCTG CCACCATGAA GCTCGCCATC
B    601 ATCACCGGAT CCAGAGCCAG CCCAGAGCCT TCCCATTCTG CCACCATGAA GCTCGCCATC

M    661 ACCCTCGCCC TGGTCACCCT GGCTCTCCTC TGCAGCCCTG GTGAGTGCCC AGCGTCCCTT
B    661 ACCCTCGCCC TGGTCACCCT GGCTCTCCTC TGCAGCCCTG GTGAGTGCCC AGCGTCCCTT

M    721 TCCCCCAGGC AACCCTCTCC GCCACCCACT TCTGCTCAGA GGGAGAGGTG AGCTGCCTGT
B    721 TCCCCCAGGC AACCCTCTCC GCCACCCACT TCTGCTCAGA GGGAGAGGTG AGCTGCCTGT

M    781 GCCCTCCCTG CAGCTGCTGG CAGGGCCTGA GAACGTG
B    781 GCCCTCCCTG CAGCTGCTGG CAGGGCCTGA GAACGTGGAC TTTCGGAAAA TGGGGTCTGG

B    841 TGAGCGACCC CACGTTGAGA ACCTGGGGAG GGCCCTGCGG CTGTTAGGAA ACTAGGAAGG

B    901 ATGTCCTCTT CCACATCCAA CAACCTCCGC GTTCCGGGGG ACAGGACAGG CTAGAGGGAG

B    961 GGAGGAGGCC CCTGCGGGTG AACAGTGCAA CAGCAAGTGG GAGAGGAATA CAGTCTCCCA

B   1021 AAGCCCAGAC TTGTGTAGAC CCCAAGATGC CCAAGGACCA CTGGGGCCTC CGCCCGACTC

B   1081 TGGCAGCCAC AGGGCCTGAA AGGGGAGCTG CAGAGACGGA CATCCCCGAA AGAAACCCAA

B   1141 GCCAAGGCAC AGCTTCCGGG TCTGGGCCTA AAGGACAAGT CCAGAAAAAG GATCTTCCCT

B   1201 TTGGGACAAC GCCAGCCCAG AGTGCCGTTT TCTAAACAAT TCTGTTCTCT GCAAAAAGGG

B   1261 CTACAAGTCT CCAAGTGGCT GCTGCTGTTG CTAGGAGGAA AGGAATGGGA AAGGAGAAAG

B   1321 CGGGGAGGAA GGGAGGGGAG AAGAGGGGAG GGCTCACATC TCCCTCCGAG CGCCCTGCCA
```

```
B 1381  TTTGGGAAGG AGGTTACCTA ACTCGGCTTT TCACCCTGCA TCAGCCTCTT CCACTCCCAT
B 1441  CTGAAAATGC TGTTGCTGTT GTTATTGTTG TTGTTTTCAT CAGCAAACCC CAACGGAAAG
B 1501  TTTCACACAA CTCCTAGATG TGAGTTTGAC GACCTTGGGG GATTGGAAAA ACCAAACCGA
B 1561  GAGGGAGTGG GAACAACTGT TTGGCAGAGA GTGTTACTTG TTTCTCCGGT GGGAAATGAC
B 1621  ATCATTTGGG GCTGAAATGT ATGAATTAGA AGATCTGGGT ACTGAGTATA GAGGTGGTGA
B 1681  CTCAGGAGGA CAGGACTGAA CCACCCCCCG CCTCTTTTTT AAAAAACAGA TTGTATTTAT
B 1741  TTGAGAGGTA GAGTTACAGA GAGAGGGAGA GAGAGAGAGA ATCTTCCATC CACTGGTTCA
B 1801  CTCCCCAGTT GGCCACAGTG GCAGAGCTGG GCCGATCCAA AGCCAGGAGC TTTTTCTGGG
B 1861  TTTCCCATGC AGGTATAGGG GCCCAAACAC TTGGGCCGTT TTCCACTGCT TTCCTAGGCC
B 1921  AAAAGCAGAG AGCTGGATCG GAAGAGGAGC TGCCGGACAT GAGCTGACAT CCATATGGGA
B 1981  TGCTGGTGCT GCAGGTGGAG GCTTAGCCTA CAATGCCACA GCACCAGCCC TAGACTGAAA
B 2041  CCCTTTAAGG GGTGGATCAG GGACACAACA CCCATTCATA TACTTTTGTG TGCACACGTG
B 2101  TAATAATGTC TGCTCTTAAC CCTTTGACAT ACACCTCTTT TCTTTCTTAC AACCTCATGA
B 2161  GGAGGGGACA TTGTACCCAT TTTACAGATG ATAAAAACTG AGCTATTAGC ACTTTGTAAG
B 2221  ATCAAGTAAC TCCTGAGGGC ATAGTAAGTT GCAAGGTGGG GATCTGHGCT CTGGAGAGGG
B 2281  TGTGGTTTGG AATGGCCACC CTGAGTAGGG CCTCCAGTCT GAGAGCAGAC ATTGAGTTGG
B 2341  CACATGAAGC AGAGAATTCA AGGACAGGGA TTTGAGACTT CATGGGAAGA TGGAGGCAAA
B 2401  TAGAGGTGGG GCGTGGTGAG TCCCCCCCAC AACCTGGGGG CAGGGGCCTG AGAAACAGTT
B 2461  ATAGGGACAG TGGCACAAGT GGTTGGTCTG TGTTGAGCTG AGCAAACCAC AAAGCCCACC
B 2521  ACTCACATGT GCACGCCTGT CCCGTGCCAG GTGGGGAGCC CCATGCTGGG CTGGTACCAG
B 2581  CCTCAGCCTG GCTTTGCCAC ATCCCCTCAG TGACACGTGG CTCCAACCAC CATGGACCAC
B 2641  AGAAGACAGG CAAGGTCCTG GTAGGAACCA AAGCTCTCAG TGGCCTCTTC CCAGCCCCAC
B 2701  CCTGCATTAA AAATCAGCCC AGCAGCTTCT ATTATCAATA CTCCACCCAG AACATGAGCA
B 2761  TAAAAACAA ATGGCACCCT GGCCCACGCC AGCCCAGGAA GTCCAGGGAA GGCTCAGGCC
M 2821                                GAATTCACC CAGCGCTTAG AGCACCAGCA
B 2821  AACCACAAAA ACACCAGCTG TAACCTAGAG AGAATTCACC CAGCGCTTAG AGCACCAGCA
M 2881  GAGCTGATTT CCCCTCCCCG TCCATGAAAA GCTGTCTAGT CTCAAACTGA CTGACGAGCC
B 2881  GAGCTGATTT CCCCTCCCCG TCCATGAAAA GCTGTCTAGT CTCAAACTGA CTGACGAGCT
M 2941  TGGCTGTGTG CCCCTGGTTC CTGGGCTTCT CCTGCTCTGT TCTCAGCATC TGCAGGCATC
B 2941  TGGCTGTGTG CCCCTGGTTC TTGGGCTTCT CCTGCTCTGT TCTCAGCATC TGCAGGCATC
```

```
M 3001 TGCCCGAGAT TTGCCCACGT CATTGAAAAC CTCCTCCTGG GCACGCCCTC CAGTTACGAG
B 3001 TGCCCGAGAT TTGCCCACGT CATTGAAAAC CTCCTCCTGG CCACGCCCTC CAGTTACGAG

M 3061 ACATCCCTGA AGGAATTTGA ACCTGATGAC ACCATGAAAG ATGCAGGGAT GCAGATGAAG
B 3061 ACATCCTTGA AGGAATTTGA ACCTGATGAC ACCATGAAAG ATGCAGGGAT GCAGATGAAG

M 3121 AAGGTGTTGG ACTCCCTGCC CCAGACGACC AGAGAGAACA TCATGAAGCT CACGGTAACC
B 3121 AAGGTCTTGG ACTCCCTGCC CCAGACGACC AGAGAGAACA TCATGAAGCT CACGCTAACC

M 3181 AGCGCCTATT GCCCACGCCA CCTATAAGTG GCTTCCGGAG CCCCTCAGCT GTGGTCTCAT
                           ••
B 3181 AGTGCCTATT GCCCACGCC    TATAAGTG GCTTCCGGAG CCCCTCAGCT GTGGTCTCAT

M 3241 CCCATGCTAA GACCCTTTCC TAACCCAGAG AAAAGACTTG CAATACCAAC ATCCCCGTAG
B 3241 CCCATGCTAA GACCCTTTCC TAACCCAGAG AAAAGACTTG CAATACCAAC ATCCCCGTAG

M 3301 TACCCATGTC CTCACGGGCA CAGCCACCTC TCCAGGCATT TCCCCTTACC CATTTCTAAA
                            •
B 3301 TACCCATGTC CTCACGGGCA  AGCCACCTC TCTAGGCATT TCCCCTTACC CATTTCTAAA

M 3361 ATGGCTTTTT GAGAAGGAAA AAAAATGCCC TTACAACCAT CATTCCTCCC AGAGTTTACT
                                          •          •               ••
B 3361 ATGGCTTTTT GAGAAGGAAA AAAAATGTCC TTATAATCAT CATTCTTCCC AGAGTTTCTT

M 3421 GGACATCTCC ACTGACATTG ATGTTTGTGT CTCCGCATCT CTGCCTCACC TGCAGCCTCA
                              •                       •            •••••
B 3421 GGACATCTCC ACTGACATTG ACGTTTGTGT CTCCGCATCT CTGCCTCAC  TGCAGAGGTC

M 3481 CGGGGGCTTT TGTTTCTCTT TTTCAGGAAA AAATAGTGAA GAGCCCACTG TGTATGTAGG
       ••
B 3481 ACGGGGCTTT TGTTTCTCTT TTTCAGGAAA AAATAGTGAA GAGCCCACTG TGTATGTAGG

M 3541 ATGGAGGAAT CCGAGGTCCT GCGGACTTGA GAAGCCGAAG ATTTCCACCT GCTGAAGCCC
B 3541 ATGGAGGAAT CCGAGGTCCT GCGGACT GA GAAGCCGAAG ATTTCCACCT GCTGAAGCCC

M 3601 CTGCTGCTGC CCCTGGCCCC TTGGGTCCCC CACCCACCCA ACCCAGCCAG CCTTTGCTTT
B 3601 CTGCTGCTGC CCCTGGCCCC TTGGGTCCCC CACCCACCCA ACCCAGCCAG CCTTTGCTTT

M 3661 CAATAAACTG CAAGCAGATC ACATCCGTCG TCCTGAGCTC TTATTTACCT GCTTGAGGGA
B 3661 CAATAAACTG CAAGCAGATC ACATCCGTCG TCCTGAGCTC TTATTTACCT GCTTGAGGGA

M 3721 GAGAGGCGTG CACCTGCCAG GGAAGGGTAG CCAGGACTCC CAGGAAGGCG GCGGAGCCTG
                               •
B 3721 GAGAGGCGTG CACCTGCCAG G AAGGGTAG CCAGGACTCC CAGGAAGGCG GCGGAGCCTG

M 3781 CCCTTGGACC CCACGAGGAA ACTCTGACGC CTTCCAAAGT CCTTTCCTCT AGGTTTCTGC
B 3781 CCCTTGGACC CCACGAGGAA ACTCTGACGC CTTCCAAAGT CCTTTCCTCT AGGTTTCTGC

M 3841 CATTGGCCAC CCAAAAAGCT GAGCCCTCTC CCCTTACATT CTACCACCTA CGTCTCAAAC
B 3841 CATTGGCCAC CCAAAAAGCT GAGCCCTCTC CCCTTACATT CTACCACCTA CGTCTCAAAC

M 3901 TCCACCTGTG GGAGAGAA
                   ••
B 3901 TCCACCTGTG GGA   GAATT C
```

Fig. 8.2. The complete nucleotide sequence of the uteroglobin gene as determined by Suske *et al.* (1983) 'B' and Bailly *et al.* (1983) 'M'. Dots show discrepancies. The asterisk show the main initiation site for transcription. Peculiar sequences discussed in the text are underlined.

Introns separate functional donnains of the protein, as in many other cases. However threonine 60 is one of the few hydrophilic residues that are buried inside the molecule (Mornon *et al.* 1980) and thus this intron/exon boundary does not follow Craik's rule which states that splice functions map at the surface of proteins (Craik, Sprang, Fletherick and Rutter 1982).

Intron boundaries follow the GT/AG rule and present complementarities with the 5′ end of U_1 snRNA (according to the generally accepted model for messenger RNA splicing Rogers and Wall 1980; Lerner, Boyle, Mount, Wolin and Steitz 1980). The gene contains a canonical polyadenylation signal AATAAA (3662–3667), but the 'TATA' box is quite unusual, since a sequence 'AATACAAAAA' is found between position −33 to −24 (565 to 574). Other AT rich stretches can be found around position −95 (500–507) and −130 (468–473), respectively TAAATAAT and TATTTA. S1 mapping experiments showed the former to be part of a minor transcription start site. The main site for initiation of transcription is a very frequent one, at an A (position +1) preceded by one or more of pyrimidines, usually Cs (Corden, Wasylk, Buchwalder, Sassone-Corsi, Kedinger and Chambon 1980). The discrepancy with the actual result of S1 mapping experiment (Fig. 8.5) where the main initiation site maps at position −4 can be explained by the protection of additional nucleotides by the cap structure of the mes-

Enzyme	N	Site	Positions									
AatII	2	GACGT/C										
AccI	2	GT/(A-C)(G-T)AC	1037									
AhaIII	3	TTT/AAA	1721									
AluI	16	AG/CT	247	652	773	794	1108	1153	1827	1850	1933	1950
			1964	2203	2269	2498	2674	2726	2838	2884	2912	3169
			3229	3698	3859							
ApaI	0	GGGCC/C	875	1884								
AvaI	1	C/PyCGPuG	348	485	3004							
AvaII	8	G/G(A-T)CC	411	1056	2635	2655	3556	3625	3787			
BalI	1	TGG/CCA	332	1813	2296	3847						
BamHI	1	G/GATCC	204	608								
BbvI	21	GCAGC8/12	207	705	803	1096	2735	3485	280	760	781	1095
			1266	1269	1937	1976	3591	3594				
BclI	0	T/GATCA										
BglI	3	GCCN4/NGGC	238	1819								
BglII	0	A/GATCT	1652									
BssHII	0	G/CGCGC										
BstEII	0	G/GTNACC	336	673	1393	3175						
BstNI	6	CC/(A-T)GG	89	101	209	254	307	334	529	671	680	699
			727	864	1845	2435	2549	2589	2659	2780	2796	2805
			2941	2955	2962	3038	3334	3614	3739	3753	3762	
BstXI	0	CCHN5/NTGG	1891									
BvuI	2	GPuGCPy/C	190	395	528	875	1355	1884	2271	2561	3223	3526
			3700	3866								
ClaI	1	AT/CGAT										
DdeI	8	C/TNAG	243	756	808	1663	1682	2003	2199	2234	2265	2302
			2320	2449	2499	2583	2607	2677	2814	2867	2983	3225
			3248	3694	3860							
EcoRI	1	G/AATTC	2355	2853								
EcoRV	1	GATHI/C										
Fnu4HI	42	GC/NGC	196	294	694	774	792	795	879	1085	1109	1280
			1283	1951	1990	2724	3474	3605	3608	3770		
FnuDII	23	CG/CG	930									
FokI	12	GGATGN9/13	454	913	1992	3121	3553	901	1108	1774	1955	2587
			3049	3225	3277	3669						
HaeII	11	PuGCGC/Py	1374	2867	3186							
HaeIII	22	GG/CC	87	241	332	532	587	806	873	969	1067	1095
			1167	1813	1832	1882	1896	1919	2296	2311	2447	2515
			2684	2783	2819	3617	3847					
HgaI	11	GACGCN5/10	331	3816	782							
HgiAI	8	G(A-T)GC(A-T)/C	217	2095	2271	2534	2875	3700	3733			
HgiCI	9	CCPuPyGG/G	2635									
HgiDI	6	GPu/CGPyC	3808									
HhaI	31	GCG/C	1373	2866	3185							
HincII	2	GTPy/PuAC										
HindIII	1	A/AGCTT										
HinfI	10	G/ANTC	385	1077	1680	1780	2419	3131	3548	3756		
HpaI	0	GTT/AAC										
HpaII	26	C/CGG	389	560	606	935	1157	1607	1954	3216		
HphI	12	GGTGAN8/7	270	713	780	852	990	1689	2428	330	595	652
			667	1404	2849	3459						
KpnI	0	GGTAC/C	2578									
MboI	22	/GATC	204	600	608	1191	1652	1834	1936	2055	2220	2261
			3677									
MboII	11	GAAGAN8/7	331	1353	1662	1954	2399	2655	3130	3531	3590	533
			900	1186	1420	1775	2679					
MluI	0	A/CGCGT										

Enzyme	N	Sequence	Sites
MnlI	26	CCTCN7/7	107 175 252 357 409 549 605 674 698 745 794 916 935 1078 1374 1436 1722 2145 2164 2322 2592 2616 2695 2904 3041 3044 3058 3234 3321 3338 3416 3475 3487 3837 3876 162 175 400 752 758 861 947 951 955 958 996 1288 1318 1326 1336 1341
MspI	26	C/CGG	389 560 606 935 1157 1607 1954 3216
MstI	4	TGC/GCA	
MstII	0	CC/TNAGG	2234
NaeI	4	GCC/GGC	
NarI	4	GG/CGCC	
NciI	10	CC/(G-C)GG	390 560 936 1158
NcoI	0	C/CATGG	2631
NdeI	1	CA/TATG	1974
NruI	1	TCG/CGA	
PaeR7I	0	C/TCGAG	
PstI	1	CTGCA/G	695 793 1113 1994 2995 3475
PvuI	1	CGAT/CG	
PvuII	1	CAG/CTG	794 2838 3229
RsaI	3	GT/AC	1661 2175 2576 3302
SacI	0	GAGCT/C	2271 3700
SacII	0	CCGC/GG	
SalI	1	G/TCGAC	
Sau3A	22	/GATC	204 600 608 1191 1652 1834 1936 2055 2220 2261 3677
Sau96I	15	G/GNCC	239 411 531 804 871 872 968 1056 1065 1093 1165 1830 1880 1881 1894 2309 2445 2514 2635 2655 2782 3556 3616 3625 3787
ScrFI	16	CC/NGG	89 101 209 254 307 334 390 529 560 671 680 699 727 864 936 1158 1845 2435 2549 2589 2659 2780 2796 2805 2941 2955 2962 3038 3334 3614 3739 3753 3762
SfaNI	22	GCATCN5/9	1428 2996 3006 3465 1037 1970 3091 3099
SmaI	0	CCC/GGG	
SphI	1	GCATG/C	
StuI	0	AGG/CCT	
TaqI	7	T/CGA	
Tth111I	1	GACN/NNGTC	
XbaI	0	T/CTAGA	
XhoI	0	C/TCGAG	
XmaI	0	C/CCGGG	
XmaIII	1	C/GGCCG	585
XmnI	2	GAANN/NNTTC	

Fig. 8.3. Computer restriction map of the uteroglobin gene. The number of restriction sites in pBR 322 for each enzyme is indicated before the recognition sequence.

senger RNA (Lai, Roop, Tsai, Woo and O'Malley 1982).

The minor band at -71 can be attributed to an A which fits the initiation consensus described by Corden *et al.* (1980), at position -69. This start would then be related to the 'TATA box' around position -95.

The consensus (known as CAT box) described in the -80 region of several genes by Benoist, O'Hare, Breathnach and Chambon (1980) and Benoist and Chambon (1981) is poorly represented in the uteroglobin gene, showing AGTCAAGTA instead of the canonical $GG\frac{C}{T}CAATCT$ (see Fig. 8.2, nucleotides 510 to 518).

However, it is difficult to ascertain the role of divergent canonical sequences since mutations and deletions on these sequences yielded quite contradictory results during *in vivo* or *in vitro* transcription experiments. Derbyshire, Guy, Molko, Roget, Teoule and Chambon 1980; Corden *et al.* 1980; Benoist and Chambon 1981; Grosveld, De Boer, Shenmaker and Flavell 1982).

1 [598]   50
AAGATCACCGGATCCAGAGCCAGCCCAGAGCCTTCCCATTCTGCCACCATGAAGCTCGCCAT
                                            Met Lys Leu Ala Ile

                      100
CACCCTCGCCCTGGTCACCCTGGCTCTCCTCTGCAGCCCTGgtgagtgcccagcgtcccttt
Thr Leu Ala Leu Val Thr Leu Ala Leu Leu Cys Ser Pro
                      150
cccccaggcaaccctctccgccacccacttctgctcagagggagaggtgagctgcctgtgcc

             200
ctccctgcagctgctggcagggcctgagaacgtg--------------------------

-------------------------------gaattcacccagcgcttagagcaccagc

             2300
agagctgatttcccctccccgtccatgaaaagctgtctagtctcaaactgactgacgagcct

          2350   2400
ggctgtgtgcccctggttcctgggcttctcctgctctgttctcagCATCTGCAGGCATCTGC
                                           Ala Ser Ala Gly Ile Cys
                                     2450
CCGAGATTTGCCCACGTCATTGAAAACCTCCTCCTGGGCACGCCCTCCAGTTACGAGACATC
Pro Arg Phe Ala His Val Ile Glu Asn Leu Leu Leu Gly Thr Pro Ser Ser Thy Glu Thr Ser
                                   2500
CCTGAAGGAATTTGAACCTGATGACACCATGAAAGATGCAGGGATGCAGATGAAGAAGGTGT
Leu Lys Glu Phe Glu Pro Asp Asp Thr Met Lys Asp Ala Gly Met Gln Met Lys Lys Val Leu
                                   2550
TGGACTCCCTGCCCCAGACGACCAGAGAGAACATCATGAAGCTCACGgtaaccagcgcctat
Asp Ser Leu Pro Gln Thr Thr Arg Glu Asn Ile Met Lys Leu Thr
          2600   2650
tgcccacgccacctataagtggcttccggagcccctcagctgtggtctcatcccatgctaag

                             2700
accctttcctaacccagagaaaagacttgcaataccaacatccccgtagtacccatgtcctc

                             2750
acgggcacagccacctctccaggcatttcccccttacccatttctaaaatggctttttgagaa

                            2800
ggaaaaaaaatgcccttacaaccatcattcctcccagagtttactggacatctccactgaca

          2850   2900
ttgatgtttgtgtctccgcatctctgcctcacctgcagcctcacgggggcttttgtttctct

                             2950
ttttcagGAAAAAATAGTGAAGAGCCCACTGTGTATGTAGGATGGAGGAATCCGAGGTCCTG
       Glu Lys Ile Val Lys Ser Pro Leu Cys Met
                             3000
CGGACTTGAGAAGCCGAAGATTTCCACCTGCTGAAGCCCCTGCTGCTGCCCCTGGCCCCTTG

          3050   3082 [3680]
GGTCCCCCACCCACCCAACCCAGCCAGCCTTTGCTTTCAATAAACTGCAAGCAGATC

Fig. 8.4. The intron/exon pattern of the uteroglobin gene. Nucleotides are numbered from the start of the messenger RNA.

REPEATED ELEMENTS

Repeated sequences are found throughout the eukaryotic genome and they have been found in the uteroglobin gene as well (Suske *et al.* 1983; A. Guiochon-Mantel, unpublished observations). Two signals have been detected

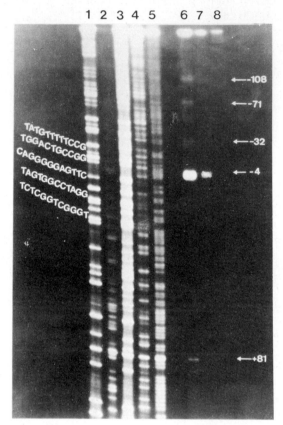

Fig. 8.5. S1 mapping of the 5′ end of the uteroglobin premessenger RNA. The labelled DNA probe was hybridized to endometrial (lane 6), lung (lane 7) and control (*E. coli* transfer) (lane 8) RNAs. Lanes 1–5, Maxam and Gilbert sequence reactions of the labelled probe (lane 1 = C; lane 2 = G; lane 3 = T + C; lane 4 = A > C; lane 5 = G + A). Electrophoresis was on a 6 per cent polyacrylamide denaturing gel (Bailly *et al.* 1983).

when a Southern blot of uteroglobin gene restriction fragments was hybridized with nick translated total rabbit genomic DNA. The stronger signal lies within the Bg12-PstI fragment of Intron I where a long cluster of purines can be found (Suske *et al.* 1983) while the weakest one is found between PstI and EcoRI sites. The nature of the latter is yet unknown, but further sequence analysis in our group has brought information on the former. Besides the main genomic clone λ Ug1I, another clone (λ Ug12) has been analyzed in our laboratory (Atger *et al.* 1981). Southern blots of EcoRI digests of this clone showed hybridation of several fragments (4,4; 2,2 and 1,3 kb) with a probe encompassing the Bg12-PstI fragment of intron I. The 1,3 kb fragment was partially sequenced, which showed an 205 bp strech bearing 82 per cent homology with a portion of the Bg12-PstI fragment in intron I (Guiochon-Mantel, unpublished results). Hybridization of Southern blots of restriction digests of the uteroglobin gene with Alu-family probes was negative, although a sequence 5'-CCAGCCCTAG-3' (2024–2033) homologous to conserved sequences in the Alu repeats could be found (Jelinek, Toomey, Leiwand, Duncan, Biro, Chouday, Weissman, Robin, Houck, Derninger and Schmid 1980; Schmid and Jelinek 1982). No regulatory activity could be linked to those sequences which role, if any, remains unknown.

An interesting hypothesis was recently made, based on a commun repeated 82 bp intronic sequence transcribed from the growth hormone gene and other genes in neural cells (as part of a 160 bp RNA), but not in liver nor kidney. Sutcliffe, Milner, Bloom and Lerner (1982) have coined the name 'identifier sequences' for such species, that would be carried within introns and prescribe tissue-specific expression of the gene they are contained in. This line of work may elicit answers to the existence and function of such intragenic short repeats. So far, no RNA species could be linked to the specific transcription of repeated elements within the uteroglobin gene.

Finally, the PstI-EcoRI fragment of intron I contains a purine-riche sequence (TGTGGTTTG, 2281–2289) identical to the 'core sequence' of enhancers described by Gillies, Morrisson, Oi and Tonegawa (1983) in the large intron of several immunoglobulin genes. These authors report the strong homology of immunoglobulin enhancers with the corresponding viral elements, and their ability to stimulate proximal promoters for polymerase II *in vivo*, as viral enhancers do.

PROGESTERONE-RECEPTOR INTERACTION WITH THE GENE

Direct evidence of specific chromosomal binding sites for a steroid (presumably bound to its receptor) was first obtained in the study of *Drosophila* polytene chromosomes interaction with Ecdysone (Gronemeyer and Pongs 1980). Payvar, Wrange, Carlstedt-Duke, Okret, Gustafsson and Yamamoto (1981) have reported the selective binding of glucocorticoid receptor complexes *in vitro* to several parts of the MMTV genome, including the region immediately upstream the main promoter for RNA transcription, which is regulated *in vivo* by glucocorticoids. Other sites were also found within and adjacent to that transcriptional unit. The exact role of each site is yet unknown, but one can conceive that some may be non functional while the promoter proximal sites would be responsible for regulation as was shown in prokaryotic genes (Reznikoff, Winter and Hurley 1974). With the purification of progesterone receptor (Logeat, Vu Hai and Milgrom 1981) filtre binding studies have been adapted to the uteroglobin gene. Fragments of the gene have been subcloned to obtain the promoter (this term refers to the 404 bp BamH/BamHI fragment from nucleotides 204 to 608, or −394 to +10 when the initiation site of transcription (598) is taken as nucleotide I)

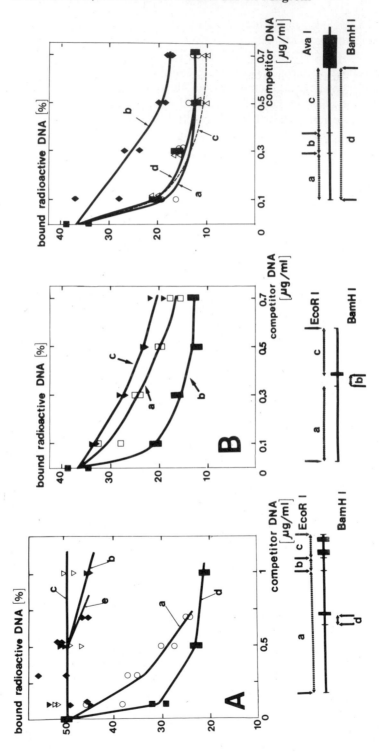

as an isolated fragment separated from upstream foreign sequences and subsequent coding sequences. This fragment has been further digested by AvaI to yield 3 sub-fragments. Filter binding studies of the uteroglobin sequences led to the discovery of a situation similar to MMTV's (Bailly *et al.* 1983): while the highest affinity for progesterone-receptor complex was located in the promoter zone (BamHI/BamHI fragment), the 2800 bp fragment immediately upstream (up to an EcoRI site) and the 1757 bp fragment downstream (which includes exon I and intron I) also exhibited some affinity for the receptor (Fig. 8.6a). AvaI-generated subfragments of the promoter: 144 bp: − 394 to − 251; 57 bp: − 250 to − 194 and 203 bp: − 193 to + 10) were also tested: the larger fragments behaved similarly to the complete promoter while the smaller (57 bp) one showed a markedly lower affinity (Fig. 6b). Thus it seems to exist at least two distinct sites in that portion of the gene. The 'progesterone-receptor complex binding sequence' described by Mulvihill, Lepennec and Chambon (1982): $\text{ATC}^{CC}_{TT}\text{ATT}^{A}_{T}\text{TCTG}^{G}_{T}\text{TTGTA}$ could not be found in the uteroglobin gene. These authors presented quite similar results showing the dispersion of progesterone receptor complex binding sites throughout the chicken ovalbumin gene. The common feature in the 3 models described above, of a main binding site nearby the promoter and several others dispersed along the gene sustains the hypothesis that multiple binding may be necessary for a gene-wide structural modification of chromatin preliminary to transcriptional activity regulation (Yamamoto and Alberts 1976).

Fig. 8.6a. Affinity of various parts of the uteroglobin gene for the progesterone receptor. Labelled 404-base pair BamHI fragment (1600–2500 cpm in the various experiments) was incubated with progesterone receptor (2.6 µg/ml) in the presence of various concentrations of nonlabelled competing DNA. Bound radioactivity was measured. The DNA fragments which were used are shown at the bottom of the figure. Also represented is the structure of the uteroglobin gene (■, exons). A, a, b, and c are EcoRI fragments of about 5, 0.49, and 1 kilobases, respectively, encompassing the uteroglobin gene; d is the 404-base pair BamHI fragment (nucleotides − 394 to + 10). e is BamHI-digested calf thymus DNA. Experimental conditions are as in Fig. 2. B, a, b, and c are fragments of ∼ 2,800 base pairs, 404 base pairs, and ∼ 1,800 base pairs, respectively, obtained by BamHI digestion of the 5-kilobase EcoRI fragment (Bailly *et al.* 1983).

Fig. 8.6b. Presence of several affinity sites for progesterone receptor in the 'promoter region of the uteroglobin gene. Labelled 404-base pair BamHI 'promoter' fragment was incubated with progesterone receptor (5 µg/ml) in presence of various concentrations of unlabelled competing DNA. Bound radioactivity was measured. The DNA fragments which were used are shown at the bottom of the figure a, fragment extending from nucleotide − 394 to nucleotide − 251; b, fragment extending from nucleotide − 193 to nucleotide + 10; d, fragment extending from nucleotide − 394 to nucleotide + 10 (Bailly *et al.* 1983).

Conclusion

Several lines of interest can be drawn from the model of the uteroglobin gene. As a steroid-hormone induced gene, it allows the study of hormonal regulation of the genome at large and may give insight on the eventual role of repeated DNA in this regulation. It is also quite interesting to observe completely different hormonal regulations of the same gene between its endometrial and pulmonary expression.

As a progesterone-inducible gene in the genital tract, it allows the physiological and pharmacological study of progesterone and progestins. It may also be a source of information on the mechanism of blastocyst implantation, development, and protection against maternal hormones and immune systems.

Finally, the only steroid-binding protein to have been analyzed by X-ray diffraction crystallography so far, it is a model for the study of atomic interactions between binding proteins and steroid hormones that will certainly facilitate the comprehension of the physiology and evolution of receptor proteins for steroidal physiological compounds.

References

Arnemann, J. F., Heins, B., and Beato, M. (1979). Synthesis and characterization of a DNA complementary to preuteroglobin mRNA. *Europ. J. Biochem.* **99**, 361–367.

Arthur, A. T., Cowan, B. D., and Daniel, J. C., Jr. (1972). Steroid binding to blastokinin. *Fert. Ster.* **23**, 85–92.

Atger, M. and Milgrom, E. (1977). Progesterone induced messenger RNA. Translation, purification and preliminary characterization of uteroglobin mRNA. *J. Biol. Chem.* **252**, 5412–5418.

—— Mercier, J. C., Haze, G., Fridlansky, F., and Milgrom, E. (1979). N-terminal sequence of uteroglobin and its precursor. *Biochem. J.* **177**, 985–988.

—— Mornon, J. P., Savouret, J. F., Loosfelt, H., Fridlansky, F., and Milgrom, E. (1980a). Uteroglobin: A model for the study of the mechanism of action of steroid hormones. In: *Steroid Induced Proteins* (ed. M. Beato) pp. 341–350. Elsevier/North-Holland, Biochemical Press, Amsterdam.

—— Savouret, J. F., and Milgrom, E. (1980b). Synthesis, purification and characterization of a DNA complementary to uteroglobin messenger RNA. *J. Ster. Biochem.* **13**, 1157–1162.

—— Perricaudet, M., Tiollais, P., and Milgrom, E. (1980c). Bacterial cloning of the rabbit uteroglobin structural gene. *Biochem. Biophys. Res. Comm.* **93**, 1082–1088.

—— Atger, P., Tiollais, P., and Milgrom, E. (1981). Cloning of rabbit genomic fragments containing the uteroglobin gene. *J. Biol. Chem.* **256**, 5970–5972.

Bailly, A., Atger, M., Atger, P., Cerbon, M. A., Alizon, M., Vu Hai, M. T., Logeat, F., and Milgrom, E. (1983). The rabbit uteroglobin gene. Structure and interaction with the progesterone receptor. *J. Biol. Chem.* **258**, 10384–10389.

Baker, M. E. (1983). Amino acid sequence homology between rat prostatic steroid binding protein and rabbit uteroglobin. *Biochem. Biophys Res. Comm.* **114**, 325–330.

Beato, M. (1980). *Steroid induced proteins.* North-Holland, Amsterdam.

—— Arnemann, J. F., and Voss, H. J. (1977). Spectrophotometric study of progesterone binding to uteroglobin. *J. Ster. Biochem.* **8**, 725–730.

—— and Beier, H. M. (1975). Binding of progesterone to the proteins of the uterine luminal fluid. Identification of uteroglobin as the binding protein. *Biochim. Biophys. Acta* **392**, 346–356.

—— and Rungger, D. (1975). Translation of the messenger RNA for rabbit uteroglobin in Xenopus oocytes. *FEBS Letters* **59**, 305–309.

—— and Nieto, A. (1976). Translation of the mRNA for rabbit uteroglobin in cell-free systems. Evidence for a precursor protein. *Europ. J. Biochem.* **64**, 15–25.

Beier, H. M. (1966). Das protein in serum, uterus and blastocysten des Kaninchens vor der nidation. In: *Biochemie der Morphogenese* (ed. W. Beermann) pp. 1–10. Deutsche Forschung Sgenrinschagt, Konstanz.

—— (1968). Uteroglobin: A hormone-sensitive endometrial protein involved in blastocyst development. *Biochim. Biophys. Acta* **160**, 289–291.

—— (1970). Hormonal stimulations of Protease inhibition activity in endometrial secretion during early pregnancy. *Acta Endo.* (Copenhague) **63**, 141–149.

—— Bohn, M., and Muller, W. (1975). Uteroglobin-like antigen in male genital tract secretions. *Cell Tis. Res.* **165**, 1–11.

—— Kirchner, C., and Mootz, U. (1978). Uteroglobin-like antigen in the pulmonary epithelium and secretion of the lung. *Cell Tis. Res.* **190**, 15–25.

—— (1982). Uteroglobin and other endometrial proteins: Biochemistry and biological significance in beginning pregnancy. In: *Proteins and Steroids in Early Pregnancy* (ed. H. M. Beier and P. Karlson) pp. 38–71. Springer-Verlag, Berlin.

Benoist, C. and Chambon, P. (1981). The SV40 early promoter region: Sequence requirements *in vivo*. *Nature* **290**, 304–310.

—— O'Hare, K., Breathnach, R., and Chambon, P. (1980). The ovalbumin gene. Sequence of putative control regions. *Nucleic Acids Res.* **8**, 127–142.

Corden, J., Wasylyk, B., Buchwalder, A., Sassone-Corsi, P., Kedinger, L., and Chambon, P. (1980). Promoter Sequences of Eukaryotic Protein-Coding genes. *Science* **209**, 1406–1414.

Clauberg, C. (1933). *Die weiblichen sexual hormone* (ed. J. Springer) pp. 88–100. Springer-Verlag, Berlin.

Craik, C. S., Sprang, S., Fletterick, R., and Rutter, W. J. (1982). Intron-Exon splice functions map at protein surfaces. *Nature* **299**, 180–182.

Daniel, J. C., Jr. (1973). A blastokinin-like component from the human uterus. *Fert. Ster.* **24**, 326–358.

—— Jr. (1980). Factors influencing uteroglobin synthesis. In: *Steroid-Induced Proteins* (ed. M. Beato) Elsevier/North-Holland, Amsterdam.

Dunbar, B. S. and Daniel, J. C., Jr. (1979). High molecular weight components of rabbit uterine fluids. *Biol. Repro.* **21**, 723–733.

El Banna, A. A. and Daniel, J. C., Jr. (1972). Stimulation of rabbit blastocyst in vitro by progesterone and uterine proteins in combination. *Fert. Ster.* **23**, 101–104.

Fridlansky, F. and Milgrom, E. (1976). Interaction of uteroglobin with progesterone 5-alpha pregnane 3,20 dione and estrogens. *Endocrin.* **99**, 1244–1251.

Gillies, S. D., Morrisson, S. L., Oi, V. T., and Tonegawa, S. (1983). A tissue specific transcription enhancer element is located in the major intron of a rearranged immunoglobulin heavy chain gene. *Cell* **33**, 717–728.

Goswami, A. and Feigelson, M. (1975). Differential regulation of a low molecular weight protein in oviductal and uterine fluids by various hormones. *Endocrin.* **95**, 669–675.

Gronemeyer, H. and Pongs, O. (1980). Localization of Ecdysterone on Polytene chromosomes of Drosophila melanogaster. *Proc. Nat. Acad. Sci. U.S.A.* **77**, 2108–2112.

Grosveld, G. C., De Boer, E., Shenmaker, C. K., and Flavell, R. A. (1982). DNA sequences necessary for transcription of the rabbit β globin gene *in vivo*. *Nature* **295**, 120–126.

Hackenberg, R. and Beier, H. M. (1982). Proteinase inhibitor identification in the uteroglobin fraction of rabbit uterine secretion. *Arch. Gyn.* **231**, 189–297.

Isomaa, V., Isotalo, H., Orave, M., Torkkeli, T. K., and Janne, O. A. (1979). Changes in cytosol and nuclear progesterone receptor concentrations in the rabbit uterus and their relation to induction of progesterone-regulated uteroglobin. *Biochem. Biophys. Res. Commun.* **88**, 1237–1243.

Jelinek, W. R., Toomey, T. P., Leiwand, L., Duncan, C. H., Biro, P. A., Chouday, P. V., Weissman, S. M., Robin, C. M., Houck, L. M., Derninger, P. L., and Schmid, C. W. (1980). Ubiquitous, interspersed repeated sequences in mammalian genomes. *Proc. Nat. Acad. Sci. U.S.A.* **77**, 1398–1402.

Kirchner, C. (1976). Uteroglobin in the rabbit. *Cell Tis. Res.* **170**, 415–424.

—— (1980). Non-uteroglobin proteins in the rabbit. In: *Steroid-Induced Proteins*. (ed. M. Beato) North-Holland, Amsterdam.

Kopu, H. T., Hemminki, S. M., Torkkeli, J. K., and Janne, O. A. (1979). Hormonal control of uteroglobin secretion in rabbit uterus. *Biochem. J.* **180**, 491–500.

Krishnan, R. S. and Daniel, J. C., Jr. (1967). 'Blastokinin' inducer and regulator of blastocyst development in the rabbit uterus. *Science* **158**, 490–492.

—— (1971). Effect of passive administration of antiblastokinin on blastocyst development and maintenance of pregnancy in rabbits. *Experientia* **27**, 955–965.

Kumar, N. M., Chandra, T., Woo, S. L. C., and Bullock, D. W. (1982). Transcriptional activity of the uteroglobin gene in rabbit endometrial nuclei during early pregnancy. *Endocrin.* **3**, 1115–1120.

Lai, E. C., Roop, D. R., Tsai, M. J., Woo, S. L. C., and O'Malley, B. W. (1982). Heterogeneous initiation regions for transcription of the chicken ovomucoïd gene. *Nucleic Acids Res.* **10**, 5553–5567.

Lambadarios, C. (1982). Evidence for the existence of human uteroglobin. In: *Protein and Steroids in early pregnancy* (ed. H. M. Beier and P. Karlson) pp. 99–115. Springer-Verlag, Berlin.

Lerner, M. R., Boyle, J. A., Mount, S. M., Wolin, S. L., and Steitz, J. A. (1980). Are snRNPs involved in splicing? *Nature* **283**, 220–224.

Logeat, F., Vu Hai, M. T., and Milgrom, E. (1981). Antibodies to rabbit progesterone receptor: Cross-reaction with human receptor. *Proc. Nat. Acad. Sci. U.S.A.* **78**, 1426–1430.

Lombardero, M. and Nieto, A. (1981). Glucocorticoid and developmental regulation of uteroglobin synthesis in rabbit lung. *Biochem. J.* **200**, 487–494.

Loosfelt, H., Fridlansky, F., Savouret, J. F., Atger, M., and Milgrom E. (1981a). Mechanism of action of progesterone in the rabbit endometrium. Induction of uteroglobin and its messenger RNA. *J. Biol. Chem.* **56**, 3456–3470.

—— Fridlansky, F., Atger, M., and Milgrom, E. (1981b). A possible non-transcriptional effect of progesterone. *J. Ster. Bioch.* **15**, 107–110.

Menne, C., Suske, G., Arnemenn, J., Wenz, M., Cato, A. C. B., and Beato, M. (1982). Isolation and structure of the gene for the progesterone-inducible protein uteroglobin. *Proc. Nat. Acad. Sci. U.S.A.* **79**, 4853–4857.

Moen, R. C. and Palmiter, R. D. (1980). Changes in hormone responsiveness of chick oviduct during primary stimulation with estrogen. *Develop. Biol.* **78**, 450–463.

Mornon, J. P., Fridlansky, F., Bailly, A., and Milgrom, E. (1979). Characterization of two new crystal forms of uteroglobin. *J. Mol. Biol.* **127**, 237–239.

——— Fridlansky, F., Bailly, A., and Milgrom, E. (1980). X-Ray crystallographic analysis of a progesterone binding protein. The C222, crystal form of oxidized uteroglobin at 2.2 A resolution. *J. Mol. Biol.* **137**, 415–429.

Mukherjee, A. B., Ulane, R. E., and Agrawal, A. K. (1982). Role of uteroglobin and transglutaminase in masking the antigenicity of implanting rabbit embryos. *Amer. J. Repro Imm.* **2**, 135–141.

Müller, B. (1983). Genital tract proteins in the male rabbit. I. Localization of uteroglobin. *Andrologia* **15**, 380–384.

Mulvihill, E. R., Lepennec, J. P., and Chambon, P. (1982). Chicken oviduct progesterone receptor: Localization of specific regions of high affinity binding incloned DNA fragments of hormone responsive genes. *Cell* **24**, 621–632.

Nieto, A. and Lombardero, M. (1982). Uteroglobin-like antigen in species of lagomorpha. *Comp. Biochem. Phys.* **71b**, 511–514.

Noske, I. G. and Feigelson, M. (1976). Immunological evidence of uteroglobin (blastokinin) in the male reproductive tract and in non-reproductive ductal tissues and their secretion. *Biol. Repro.* **15**, 704–713.

Payvar, F., Wrange, O., Carlstedt-Duke, J., Okret, S., Gustafsson, J. A., and Yamamoto, K. R. (1981). Purified glucocorticoid receptors bind selectively in vitro to a clone DNA fragment whose transcription is regulated by glucocorticoids *in vitro. Proc. Nat. Acad. Sci. U.S.A.* **78**, 6628–6632.

Ponstingl, H., Nieto, A., and Beato, M. (1978). Amino acid sequence of progesterone-induced rabbit uteroglobin. *Biochem.* **17**, 3908–3912.

Rogers, J. and Wall, R. (1980) A mechanism for RNA splicing. *Proc. Nat. Acad. Sci. U.S.A.* **77**, 1877–1879.

Reznikoff, W. S., Winter, R. B., and Hurley, C. K. (1974). The localization of the repressor binding sites in the *lac* Operon. *Proc. Nat. Acad. Sci. U.S.A.* **11**, 2314–2318.

Savouret, J. F., Loosfelt, H., Atger, M., and Milgrom, E. (1980). Differential hormonal control of a messenger RNA in two tissues; uteroglobin in RNA in the lung and the endometrium. *J. Biol. Chem.* **255**, 4131–4136.

Saxena, S. K., Seth, M., Bhaduri, A. P., and Sahib, M. K. (1983). Specific interactions of some non-steroidal compounds with the progesterone binding uteroglobin. *J. Ster. Biochem.* **18**, 303–308.

Schmid, W. and Jelinek, W. R. (1982). The Alu family of dispersed repetitive sequences. *Science* **216**, 1065–1070.

Snead, R., Day, L., Chandra, T., Mace, M. R., Jr., Bullock, D. W., and Woo, S. L. C. (1981). Mosaic structure and mRNA precursors of uteroglobin a hormone-regulated mammalian gene. *J. Biol. Chem.* **256**, 11911–11916.

Suske, G., Wenz, M., Cato, A. C. B., and Beato, M. (1983). The uteroglobin gene region: hormonal regulation, repetitive elements and complete nucleotide sequence of the gene. *Nucleic Acids Res.* **11**, 2257–2271.

Sutcliffe, J. G., Milner, R. J., Bloom, F. E., and Lerner, R. A. (1982). Commun 82 nucleotide sequence unique to brain RNA. *Proc. Nat. Acad. Sci. U.S.A.* **79**, 4942–4946.

Tancredi, T., Temussi, P. A., and Beato, M. (1982). Interaction of oxidized and reduced uteroglobin with progesterone. *Europ. J. Biochem.* **122**, 101–104.

Torkkeli, T. K., Kontula, K. K., and Janne, O. A. (1977). Hormonal regulation of uterine blastokinin like antigens in non uterine tissues. *Mol. Cell. Endocr.* **9**, 107–118.

——— Krusius, T., and Janne, O. A. (1978). Uterine and lung uteroglobins in the rabbit. Two similar proteins with differential hormonal regulations. *Biochim. Biophys. Acta* **544**, 578–592.

Wasylyk, B., Derbyshire, R., Guy, A., Molko, D., Roget, A., Teoule, R., and Chambon, P. (1980). Specific *in vitro* transcription of conalbumine gene is drastically decreased by single point imitation in TATA box homology sequence. *Proc. Nat. Acad. Sci. U.S.A.* **77**, 7024–7028.

Yamamoto, K. R. and Alberts, B. M. (1976). Steroid receptors: Elements for modulation of eucaryotic transcription. *Ann. Rev. Biochem.* **45**, 421–746.

Index